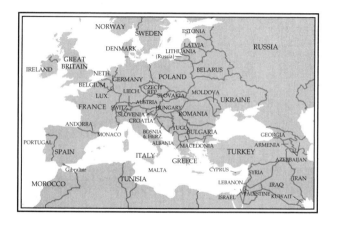

EXCURSIONS IN WORLD MUSIC

Fourth Edition

EXCURSIONS IN WORLD MUSIC

Fourth Edition

Bruno Nettl
Charles Capwell
Isabel K.F. Wong
Thomas Turino

University of Illinois
Urbana-Champaign

Philip V. Bohlman

University of Chicago

PEARSON
Prentice
Hall

Upper Saddle River, New Jersey 07458

Library of Congress Cataloging-in-Publication Data

Excursions in world music / Bruno Nettl . . . [et al.].—4th ed.
    p. cm.
  Includes discographies, bibliographical references, and index.
  ISBN 0-13-140305-2
  1. World music—Analysis, appreciation. I. Nettl, Bruno, 1930-

  MT90.E95 2004
  780'.9—dc21   2003048683

VP, Editorial Director: Charlyce Jones-Owen
Senior Acquisitions Editor: Christopher T. Johnson
Managing Editor: Joanne Riker
Editorial Assistant: Evette Dickerson
Marketing Manager: Chris Ruel
Marketing Assistant: Kimberly Daum
Production Editor: Laura A. Lawrie
Manufacturing and Prepress Buyer: Benjamin D. Smith
Cover Illustration/Photo: Fukuhara, Inc./CORBIS. Musician playing the Japanese Koto.
Composition: This book was set in 10.5/12.5 Caledonia by Stratford Publishing Services
Printer/Binder: Interior printed by RRD Harrisonburg. The cover was printed by Phoenix Color Corp.

Credits and acknowledgments borrowed from other sources and reproduced, with permission, in this textbook appear on appropriate page within text.

Copyright © 2004, 2001, 1997, 1992 by Pearson Education, Inc., Upper Saddle River, New Jersey, 07458.
Pearson Prentice Hall. All rights reserved. Printed in the United States of America. This publication is protected by Copyright and permission should be obtained from the publisher prior to any prohibited reproduction, storage in a retrieval system, or transmission in any form or by any means, electronic, mechanical, photocopying, recording, or likewise. For information regarding permission(s), write to: Rights and Permissions Department.

Pearson Prentice Hall™ is a trademark of Pearson Education, Inc.
Pearson® is a registered trademark of Pearson plc
Prentice Hall® is a registered trademark of Pearson Education, Inc.

Pearson Education LTD.
Pearson Education Singapore, Pte. Ltd
Pearson Education, Canada, Ltd
Pearson Education—Japan

Pearson Education Australia PTY, Limited
Pearson Education North Asia Ltd
Pearson Educación de Mexico, S.A. de C.V.
Pearson Education Malaysia, Pte. Ltd

10 9 8 7 6 5 4
0-13-140305-2

Contents

List of Recordings

Preface

The fourth revised edition of *Excursions in World Music* incorporates many of our responses to the rapidly changing conditions and repertories of world music since the beginning of the twenty-first century: globalization, the explosion of new technologies, the often dramatically shifting landscapes of a postcolonial and neonationalist world. World music responds to these changes and offers students a considerable range of perspectives for understanding the contemporary world of which they are increasingly a part. The authors take the opportunity of this new edition to include essential material about the most recent world music phenomena, especially popular music and emerging repertories that help us sort out the dizzying processes of hybridization and exchange that affect almost all world musics in some way. In particular, the chapters on music in sub-Saharan Africa (7), Europe (8), and Ethnic North America (10) have included substantial new perspectives on global popular music. Chapter bibliographies and discographies, too, have been updated and revised to included the most recent writings on and recordings of world music.

The authors of *Excursions in World Music*, however, remain committed in this edition to the approach, structure, and content with which they have always conceived the textbook. It remains a set of chapters, by scholars writing with conviction and a sense of devotion, about cultures in which they have had substantial field experience, providing information and in-depth syntheses of the musical cultures of the world. We remain committed to a belief that knowledge of world music not only opens many doors to a better understanding of today's most pressing problems but also engenders respect for those who make and experience music throughout the world.

ACKNOWLEDGMENTS

Many thanks to Damon Sink (University of Dayton) for preparing a new study guide for the fourth edition and to Robert Swanson for composing the index for this edition. We also wish to express our gratitude for the numerous helpful suggestions provided by our students, anonymous readers, and all loyal users of the book alike.

Bruno Nettl, Charles Capwell, Isabel K. F. Wong,
Thomas Turino, Philip V. Bohlman

About the Authors

Bruno Nettl studied at Indiana University, has taught at the University of Illinois since 1964 and has done fieldwork in Iran (where he studied the Persian setar), among the Blackfoot people of Montana, and in South India, and is the author of *The Study of Ethnomusicology, Blackfoot Musical Thought: Comparative Perspectives*, and *Heartland Excursions: Ethnomusicological Reflections on Schools of Music*.

Charles Capwell, a Harvard Ph.D., did field research among the Bauls of Bengal, India, and in Calcutta (where he also studied sarod), and he has studied Muslim popular music in Indonesia. He is the author of *Music of the Bauls of Bengal* and of numerous articles on aspects of South Asian musical culture, and has been on the faculty of the University of Illinois since 1976, where he also supervises the gamelan program.

Isabel Wong studied at Brown University and teaches Chinese and other East Asian musics at the University of Illinois. She has done research on a large variety of music of her native China, including music drama, urban popular music, politics and music, and the history of musical scholarship in Chinese culture. More recently she has devoted herself also to the study of Chinese-American musical culture.

Thomas Turino studied at the University of Texas and has taught at the University of Illinois since 1987. He is the author of *Moving Away from Silence* and *Nationalists, Cosmopolitans, and Popular Music in Zimbabwe*. In 1992–93 he lived for a year in Zimbabwe, where he did research on village music and musical nationalism. He is an expert performer on the African Mbira and founder of the Peruvian panpipe ensemble at Illinois.

Philip Bohlman studied at the University of Illnois and has been, since 1987, at the University of Chicago. He has done fieldwork in ethnic communities in Wisconsin, Chicago, and Pittsburgh, as well as Israel, Germany, and Austria, He is the author of *The Land Where Two Streams Flow, The Study of Folk Music in the Modern World*, and *World Music: A Very Short Introduction*. He is the Artistic Director of The New Budapest Orpheum Society, a Jewish cabaret ensemble at the University of Chicago.

1

Introduction: Studying Musics of the World's Cultures

Bruno Nettl

OUR PURPOSE: PRESENTING THE WORLD OF MUSIC

The purpose of this book is to introduce the reader to the world of music, the music of the world's cultures, emphasizing their diversity and the uniqueness of each. Directing ourselves to students—particularly those without a technical background in music—and to general readers, we want to give our readers a sense of the character of music and musical life of all of the world's peoples. There are thousands of peoples, each with its own music, and so, clearly, we can do this only by sampling and by judicious synthesis. But rather than simply providing an introduction to non-Western music or "ethnic" music, we include also the musical culture of Europe, its academic or art music along with its folk and popular traditions, among the musics of the world. We have divided the world into ten major culture areas or blocks, devoting a chapter to each, mindful of course that within each of them there is a great deal of cultural and musical variation. In each region and for that matter in the whole world, we have tried to provide a representative sample. Even so, there are large areas that we have had to leave untouched.

In order to provide a degree of depth as well as breadth, we have had to be selective. We can do no more than provide excursions that, taken together, will, we hope, provide the reader a picture of the way the world's peoples make music, think about it, use it in their lives, and also what all this music sounds like and how it is structured. The world's musical diversity is reflected to some degree in the diversity of the organization of our chapters; but there are some things on which all chapters touch. Thus, in each chapter we first focus upon detailed description of a musical event that may be considered broadly representative of its culture area. Ordinarily, this is followed by an introduction to the cultures and societies of the area, and then a more synthetic treatment of musical life and ideas about music, of musical style (described in terms comprehensible by nonspecialists), music history, and musical instruments, a brief description of a few additional musical genres or contexts, and, finally, a consideration of recent developments and popular music. We describe musical cultures as they exist in the twentieth century, but wherever possible we provide some information about their history. We do this in some measure in order to dispel the notion that Western academic or art music lives in a sense through its history, while the musics of other societies have no history at all, or at best a very different sort of history.

There is one thing we should make clear right now, and also in every chapter: Every musical system, that is, the music and musical life of each society, from the multifarious society of New York City, say, to a native Amazonian tribe of two hundred persons, is a very complex phenomenon that may be analyzed and comprehended from many perspectives. We certainly would not be able to provide the amount of detail necessary to illustrate this point for all of the cultures and musics with which we deal. We therefore introduce the world's musical complexity selectively, each chapter featuring one or a few concepts. Thus, in addition to providing a set of general and essentially parallel introductions to the musics of ten world areas, this book may also be read as an introduction to the topics within world music study. For example, in Chapter 4, on China, the reader will find a detailed examination of the role of music in the political development of a modernizing nation as an illustration of the kinds of things that also happened elsewhere in the world. Chapter 2, on India, gives special attention to the relationship of music and dance, something that might have but could not be stressed in all of the chapters. Chapter 7, on Sub-Saharan Africa, provides special insight into the world of popular music in non-Western urban societies. Chapter 3, on the Middle East, concentrates on different conceptions of music in the world's cultures, and on ways musicians learn to improvise. Chapter 8, on Europe, shows the close relationships among folk, art, and popular musics in the contemporary world, and also, along with Chapter 9 (on Latin America) looks at the relationship of musical and social values. Chapter 6, on Indonesia, examines the place of Indonesian music in the Western world, and of the role of Western artists and tourists in Indonesian musical culture. Chapter 5, on Japan, shows the discovery, by very modernized society, of its older traditions. Chapter 10, on Native Americans, provides information on the study of history and pre-history of musical cultures without written records. And Chapter 11, on North America, provides insight into the interaction of traditional, rural folk music, and modern urbanized though multiethnic culture.

For each area of the world covered by a chapter, we have tried to provide an overview; thus, Chapter 2 speaks at least briefly to many of the kinds of music found in India; Chapter 7 tells of the differences between East, Central, and West Africa, between rural and urban musics; Chapter 10 gives an overview of the musics of the hundreds of Native North American tribes. But, while we believe that our accounts achieve this kind of breadth, we also wish to show the reader the depth of musical culture, the many things that go into the composing, performance, and understanding of even a simple song or ritual, its history and the effects it has, how it is perceived and judged by the people who render it and who hear it. This we have tried to accomplish by concentrating, in each chapter, on a limited number of representative cultures, communities, events, and even instruments within the broad geographical area that it covers. Thus, in Chapter 3, the author concentrates on Iran, where he had done original research, to impart a sense of the many things to be noted, even though space limitations prevent giving the same attention to the Arabic peninsula or Turkey. Chapter 8 presents the scope of European music, with all its variety, through the prism of the city of Vienna.

One of our purposes is to explain music as a cultural phenomenon. We do hope to persuade the readers to listen to music of at least some of the world's many societies, and to find it enjoyable. But the idea that music is principally to be "enjoyed" is a notion characteristic of Western culture, not necessarily shared by other societies. Indeed, much of the music we will be discussing has purposes far beyond enjoyment. The significance of much of the world's music is in the realm of religion and society—in the way humans interact with the supernatural, and with each other. In some societies, music identifies clans and social classes, confirms political status, expresses communication from the supernatural, and cures the sick. Thus, while readers will want to know how the musical pieces of the world's cultures are put together and what general principles of composition may dominate in a given society, it is perhaps even more important for them to understand each culture's ideas of what music is, what its powers are, how it relates to other aspects of life, and how it reflects important things about its people and their view of the world. For this reason, while we wish to explain the nature of musical sound, we also have tried to present a holistic picture of musical life and musical culture.

NOTES ON THE "MARRIAGE OF FIGARO"

Our purpose, then, is to present the varieties of the world's musics, and to present several ways of looking at music, all of them necessary for understanding a particular work of music as it interacts with its culture in many ways. The world's music includes the music of Western culture, and so let me illustrate our approach first by commenting on a work familiar to many readers, Mozart's opera, *The Marriage of Figaro* (originally named *Le Nozze di Figaro*). Its structure is an alternation of recitatives, in which the action is carried forward through quick dialogue barely sung, with arias and vocal ensembles such as trios and quartets, in which characters make lyrical and contemplative statements, or react on what has just happened. Knowing this tells us something about the aesthetics and, if you will, the attention span of the patrons. But it also tells us about the relationship of opera to spoken drama, about the way Mozart and other composers of his time, and their audience, perceived the relationship of music and language.

The fact that this is an opera with Italian words, composed by a German-speaking Austrian for a German-speaking audience in Vienna, speaks to this relationship as well. The well-educated audience of patrons for whom *Figaro* was composed presumably understood Italian and felt that this knowledge set them off from the general population, which would have wished for operas in German, and so we see this work as directed towards an elite segment of society. But this elite society also comes in for criticism in the content of the opera, because the plot actually depicts a mild social revolution. Figaro, the lowly but clever barber, wants to protect his fiancée from having to spend the night before their honeymoon with his boss, the count—this was at the time part of the contract between landowners and their employees. Figaro succeeds, of course, without violence and through his wit, and everyone lives happily ever after, but when this opera was first presented it definitely raised the eyebrows of the Austrian aristocracy.

Mozart was not widely regarded as a great genius in his own day, but now he holds that status more than any other. In his lifetime (1756–1791), the concept of "great master" of music had not really been developed, and when they were writing music, composers did not expect it to become great art for all times. Today, *Figaro* is considered one of the great musical works of all times, but in its day it was seen, at best, to be fine entertainment. In Mozart's time, the difference in musical style between academic music and music for popular entertainment wasn't all that great; the two sounded rather alike. Around 1800 this began to change, and today we expect academic music, what we call "classical" or "art" music, to sound quite different from popular music.

By now Mozart has become a deity among composers, and much is said and written about the greatness of *Figaro* and the reasons for it. In today's American society, the concepts of genius and talent, innate ability that sets an artist apart, are important to musical culture. It is very important to us to know that Mozart already composed acceptable music at the age of seven; and to assert the myth that he composed masterworks with enormous speed, as if they sprang ready-made from his brain. We have developed, it seems, a kind of athletic view of music: We are impressed when something takes many hours to accomplish, or when someone can carry out significant work quickly, or when a composer or performer can accomplish an extremely difficult task of memory or dexterity. A quick look at *The Marriage of Figaro* tells us certain essential things about the culture of Mozart's time, but, more significantly, because this opera is an important component of musical life today, also about our own musical culture as North Americans, our musical values and attitudes.

But now to stress another point. The attitudes that make us extol Mozart and *Figaro* may not be the attitudes of other societies. Doing something difficult musically may not be a criterion for judging a song in Native American societies, and the concept of the musical masterwork, which may not be altered and must always be performed as the composer intended it, is not relevant to understanding the music of India. But it would be a mistake to see the musical world as bifurcated, the Western masterworks such as *Figaro* on one side, and the rest of the world's music on the other. *Figaro* fits well into the world's musical picture. Many societies have drama rather like opera, in which the characters sing; many have forms of communication that, like Italian recitative, fall between ordinary speech and song; in many societies, music is used to express criticism of society. Social elites have musical ways of symbolizing their superiority—artistic resources such as the orchestra, linguistic techniques such as having opera in a foreign language. And we will need to remember that just as the European view of Mozart has changed since his death, all societies change in their views of music as well as in their musical styles. And, further, that Western academic musical culture requires constant innovation and rapid change as a hallmark of its series of masterworks, while other societies may restrict and inhibit change as detrimental to the function of music.

Ideas about music, and contexts of creation and performance, help us to understand the music itself, which in turn provides insight into the values that led to it and the culture of which it is a part. And a look at a single work or performance gives us insight into the entire musical system.

CERTAIN BASIC ASSUMPTIONS

This book, in presenting the world's musical cultures, employs certain basic assumptions, the most important of which should be understood by the reader at the outset.

A Relativistic View

If *The Marriage of Figaro* is a great work of music, this must be because to its consumers—Europeans and Americans who listen to operas—it satisfies certain criteria: It is a work of great complexity; its structure has internal logic; it has harmony and counterpoint, whereby several simultaneous melodies are both independent and united; the composer shows ability to write music particularly suited to voices, instruments, and orchestra, and facility in relating words and music; the work carries a particular social and spiritual message; and so on. Using these criteria to judge the musics of other cultures would quickly lead us to conclude that Western music is the best and greatest. But from the viewpoint of an Indian musician whose task is improvising within a framework of melodic and rhythmic rules, the performers of *Figaro* might not come off so well, since they must reproduce an existing work precisely and rely on notation to keep them from deviating, thus finding little opportunity to be creative. A Native American who considers a song to be a way for spirits to communicate with humans might marvel at the counterpoint of Bach, but he might also feel that this whole notion of what is "good" or "better" (or "lousy") music makes no sense. Performers in a West African percussion ensemble might find the melodic and harmonic structure of Figaro interesting but its rhythms simpleminded.

As students of world music, we cannot reconcile these divergent viewpoints. We are better off taking a relativistic attitude. We—the authors—believe that each society has a musical system that suits its culture, and while we may compare them with each other in terms of their structure and function, we avoid making these comparisons the basis of qualitative judgments. Instead, we recognize that each society evaluates its own works of music by its own criteria. In American society, we take it for granted that music should be an enjoyable auditory experience; elsewhere, the musical ideal may be quite different. We want to understand each music as an aspect of its own culture, and we recognize that each human community creates the kind of music it needs for its particular rituals and cultural events, to support its social system, and thus, to reflect its principal values.

World Music is a Group of Musics

We see the world of music as consisting of a group of *musics*. It makes sense to think of *a* music somewhat as if it were a language. Each society has its own principal music, and the members of a society know and respond to their music with a kind of common understanding, in the way they communicate through their language. But just as languages borrow words from each other, musics also influence each other. Indeed, as mass media and the Internet along with radio, TV, and CDs facilitate worldwide communication, most people of the world have access to the same body of popular music that they add to their native music (and maybe most people know at least a bit of English, making them part of their language). And just as a society sometimes replaces one language with another (the Anglo-Saxons learned Middle English after the Norman invasion in 1066, and native peoples of South America took up Spanish after the arrival of Columbus), a community of people may cease using their tradition of music and replace it with another. Some individuals and some entire communities are bilingual; this is true of many North American Native American peoples today. Similarly, many Native American communities are "bimusical," using traditional Native American music and Western music equally but for different purposes, considering both to be, now, their cultural property.

We think of each music as a system, in the sense that changes in one of its components cause changes in the rest. Thus, if an Asian society begins using the Western piano to perform its traditional musical repertory, this music may change in its melodic and harmonic aspects because of the kinds of things (e.g., playing chords) that cannot be easily done on the older instruments but are normal for the piano.

Bringing in the piano might also cause performance contexts to change. Consider, for example, a kind of music performed by itinerant street musicians. If this music were taken up by the piano it would no longer be itinerant, and if the piano were located in a concert hall, the idea of what this music should be and do would also change radically. Or, bringing notated music into a culture in which all music was transmitted orally, through hearing, for the teaching of exercises, such as etudes, whose purpose has been teaching improvisation (as happened in Iran) might gradually make musicians want to increase their respect for the performance of complex composed pieces that are best transmitted through notation, and decrease their interest in improvising.

The Three-Part Model

This leads us to the third basic assumption. Using a model suggested by Alan P. Merriam, we look at music as a phenomenon that has three sides to it: sound, behavior, and conception or ideas. These three are closely interrelated, as each plays a role in determining the nature of the others. Let me illustrate. At a concert we sit to hear musicians make sounds, and that to us is music. But if it's a classical piano recital, the performer usually plays as if she were alone and acknowledges the audience only when bowing before and after the numbers. If it's a folk concert, the singer always addresses the audience, makes jokes about himself, and sings "at" the audience. If it's an orchestra concert, the audience sits quietly; if a rock concert, members of the audience may make all sorts of sounds or get up and dance. These different kinds of behavior are really just as important to the music as a social and aesthetic event as are the sounds. But now imagine a church service. The congregation sings a hymn, but the minister doesn't think to himself, "My, they sang that hymn badly today; last week it was much better." The idea behind this music is that the congregation communicates with God, and musical virtuosity isn't an issue. But at the same service, the organist improvises on a theme by Bach during the offertory, and she does this so well that each of the members of the music committee, listening in the congregation, determines to renew her contract and give her a raise. But imagine now a Native American medicine man who, having experienced a vision in which he was visited by his guardian spirit, Muskrat, who sang a song for him; the man does not say to himself, "This was a particularly beautiful song I learned," but rather perhaps, "This song has a lot of power," and he would be sure to remember it precisely and not forget a note of it. But Mozart, suddenly inspired with one of his grand themes, may have said to himself, "This tune that came to me is really fine, I had better change it, fix it, work it out so it will be just right." To be properly understood, music should be studied as a group of sounds, as behavior that leads to these sounds, and as a group of ideas or concepts that govern the sound and the behavior.

And so, in considering the music of the world's societies, the following chapters will concentrate on music as sound, or "the music itself," one might say; but just as much on the kinds of activities music accompanies, that go into music-making and into the consumption of music by audiences and communities; and also, on the ideas about music that a society has. It is actually this third area that seems to me to be paramount, because it is the basic ideas about music—what it does for human society and how it relates to other components of culture such as religion, economic life, class structure, relationship of genders—that determine in the end the quality of a society's musical life. The ideas about music determine what the contexts for music will be and how the music will sound. If, for example, innovation is an important component of the system of ideas about music, the music will change frequently. If the notion of masterworks is present in the culture, great technical complexity and stylistic uniqueness may characterize its pieces. If the idea of conformity is important, well-disciplined orchestral performances may result. If individualism is important, then solo performances or improvised jam sessions may be the musical counterpart. If a society has complex music, then the notion of virtuosity in the realm of ideas may be reinforced, and social contexts for performances by virtuosi may be established.

UNIVERSALS OF MUSIC

Throughout the following chapters, the reader will be struck by the great differences among musics. Each society has a unique musical system related to the character of its culture. The most important thing that the reader should take away from this book is the enormous diversity in the world's music in sound, behavior, and ideas. But are there not some things about music that all, or virtually all, societies share? There surely are, and we use, for them, the term "universals."

The most obvious universal is music itself: All societies, to our knowledge, at least have something that sounds to us like music. Not many societies have a concept of music for which they have one word, like our "music." In the Persian language (spoken in Iran), there is one word for instrumental music and another for vocal. The Blackfoot language has a word for song, but it includes dancing and ritual as well as music-making. Certain African languages have no term for music but a separate term for each of many genres of song. But all societies do have music in the sense that all have some kind of vocal production (to us it may sound like song, or chant, or ceremonial speech), which they themselves distinguish from ordinary speech. So, we are justified in identifying music, and especially vocal music, as a cultural universal. But the matter is complicated. For us Americans, music is a broad concept—it may be vocal or instrumental, sacred or secular, solo or ensemble—and it has its metaphoric extensions, such as the notion that a "pleasant" sound is said to be "musical," that birds sing and elephants trumpet. But actually not all societies share our idea that all of these sounds—singing and instruments, ritual and entertainment, human and animal—can be brought together under one conceptual umbrella.

The first musical universal, then, is singing. All peoples sing. Virtually all peoples also have instruments, though in some instances they are very rudimentary.

And in the realm of instruments, virtually all peoples have percussion instruments. The most widespread are rattles and notched sticks that are rubbed, with drums actually not quite so universal. Virtually all peoples, even the most isolated tribal societies, have some kind of flutes, usually blown at the end rather than the side—like our orchestral flute. And everywhere one finds singing that is accompanied by percussion.

There are universals in the way music functions in societies—the "behavior" and "ideas" part of our three-part model. In all societies, music is found in religious ritual—it is almost everywhere a mainstay of sacred ceremonies—leading some scholars to suggest that perhaps music was actually invented for humans to have a special way of communicating with the supernatural. And, too, it seems that, in all cultures, music is used in some sense for transforming ordinary experience—such as producing anything from trance in a ritual to edification in a concert. Everywhere, dance is accompanied by musical sound. And everywhere, too, an important function of music is helping society to reinforce boundaries between social groups, who can then view their music as an emblem of identity. Music is used to integrate society and to provide a way of showing its distinctiveness.

Most societies share some important genres of music, which include: ritual and religious music; ritual calendric music (music appropriate to certain times in the year's cycle, such as winter solstice, spring, harvest songs; and music appropriate to rituals in the course of life, such as songs for adolescent ceremonies, wedding music, and funeral music); children's game songs; songs somehow involving love and romance; narrative music (everything from folk ballads to music for dramas and operas); music for entertainment (evening family sings, or concerts); music to accompany labor (work songs, or factory background music).

Returning to universals in musical sound, music everywhere is presented in units that can be identified as "songs" or "pieces," with some kind of identity, a name, an opus number, a ritual designation, an owner. Nowhere do people "just" sing; they always sing *something*, and in this respect music contrasts with some other art forms such as dance. And everywhere, people can recognize and identify a tune or a rhythmic pattern, tell whether it is performed high or low, sung by a man or a woman. There aren't too many things to which we can point as universals when it comes to the details of musical sound. The principal melodic interval in most of the world's musics is approximately a major second, the distance in pitch between two white keys on the piano if they are separated by a black key. But we can't go much further.

There is then the question of innate musicality of humans. We know that all normal humans inherit the ability to learn language—it is somehow "hard-wired" in the human brain—but whether all humans can learn to sing at least minimally is not clear, in part because cultures differ so much in their conception of "singing." Yet it seems likely that (with the occasional exception of individual handicaps) all humans can learn to sing minimally, to beat rhythms accurately, to recognize simple pieces. Not all can attain professional proficiency; but then, while all humans can learn to speak, not all can learn to become great orators. The world's societies differ in the degree to which they encourage individuals to participate in music. In some folk societies, most people are considered about equally good at singing, and everyone participates in music-making at public events. In many urban societies, musical participation is largely listening to live music—but even more to recordings—while performance is left to highly trained professionals.

The world's societies also differ greatly in the participation of men and women in music. In devout Muslim nations of the Middle East, public performance by women is discouraged, and in some Native American societies, women were traditionally thought to lack musical ability. By contrast, in many traditional European societies, women were the main transmitters of music and the prime participants in folkloric activities. In virtually all of the world's societies, the late twentieth century has seen a significant trend to equalization of participation by gender, and roles that were once reserved for men are now filled by women as well.

But if music is a cultural universal, it is not a universal language. Language is a human attribute, but humans speak many mutually unintelligible languages. Music is found in all cultures, but the world of music consists of musics that are not mutually compatible.

MUSICAL CHANGE, TRANSMISSION, AND HISTORY

It is tempting to think of Western music as dynamic and all other musics as static. We often hear about the "Stone Age" music of tribal peoples and that the music of China and India is very ancient. But all musics have a history and all music changes, has always been changing, though at various rates and not always in the same direction. It would be a great mistake to assume that the music of India, because it is largely melodic and without harmony, somehow represents an earlier stage through which Western music has already passed; or that Europeans, in the days when they lived in tribes, had music similar to that of Native Americans. Musics do not uniformly change from simple to complex. Each music has its own unique history. If there are patterns, they have to do with the relationships of cultures to one another. Thus, in the twentieth century, as Western culture has affected most others, most non-Western musics now show some influence of Western music. But the results of this influence vary.

For example, when the violin was introduced into the music of South India, it was incorporated into the Indian soundscape and began to be used in imitation of the Indian singing style. The same instrument, when introduced to Iran, brought with it the Western sound of violin playing, thus effecting changes in the Iranian notion of how music should sound. Brought to Amerindian peoples in the southwestern United States, it motivated the Navajo and Apache to develop the single-string "Apache fiddle," combining aspects of the violin and the traditional hunting bowlike musical bow.

One of the things that determines the course of history in a musical culture is the method of transmission. In most societies, music lives in oral (or better, "aural") tradition; that is, it is passed on by word of mouth and learned by hearing live performance. It is often assumed that such a form of transmission inevitably causes songs to change, as each person who learns one develops his or her own variant, lacking the control of notation. Societies differ, however, in their attitude toward musical stability; to some it is important that a song remain stable and unchanged, while in others individual singers are encouraged to have their personal versions. In aural traditions, music cannot perhaps go beyond a certain degree of complexity, as limits of memory and coordination of simultaneous performers or components must function in the end as inhibitions.

Western academic music is traditionally notated, and there are also notation systems for some Asian musics, although these are usually not as detailed as the Western and are not normally used by performers while they play or sing. Notated traditions also may be divided into written and printed. Musical notation appeared in Europe long before the development of music printing in the late fifteenth century, but the number of handmade copies of one piece was inevitably small, and they could differ. The change from written to printed music surely led to a different set of ideas about the nature and stability of a musical work. The development of sound recording has affected both aural and written traditions, as a recording allows someone learning a piece to hear it repeatedly in identical form, incorporating those aspects of music often inadequately represented in Western notation such as tone, color, ornaments, and phrasing. The nature of a musical tradition is affected greatly by the way it is transmitted and by the way its content is taught and learned.

If music has always been changing, it has surely changed more, and more rapidly, in the late nineteenth century, but especially in the period since 1950, than ever before. Among the reasons are (1) the colonization of most of the world by Western nations and, after 1945, the increased political and economic integration of nations that were formerly colonies into a global system: (2) the incredible advances in communication by mass media, airlines, computer networks: and (3) the dissemination of Western and Middle Eastern cultural values through the diffusion of Christianity and Islam through much of the world. The musical world in the late twentieth century is much more homogeneous than it was some three hundred years ago. Musical styles everywhere have begun to partake of the sounds of Western (and often also Middle Eastern) music. Western-style harmony, synthesizers, instrumental ensembles have come to pervade much of the world's music, as have Islamic singing styles and African-derived percussion rhythms. Much of this is a layer of music added to the older traditional, and so the diversity of musics available within each society has increased. One may argue that the musics of the world are becoming more alike, and that a cultural gray-out is developing; but we also need to recognize that because of the globalization of communication, the variety of music available to each individual has increased enormously. Each society maintains, and correctly, that it has a music with at least a certain degree of uniqueness.

For most of human history, the world's musics lived in relative isolation from each other. True, as pointed out here, Christianity and Islam spread Western and Middle Eastern musical sounds throughout the world, African musical sounds were spread through the Americas as a result of the slave system, and, in the twentieth century, composers of art and popular music made increasing use of inspirations from the world's musics. Instruments have always traveled from country to country, continent to continent. But these kinds of exchange are modest compared to the ways music from everywhere has become available throughout the world as a result of the ubiquity of CDs, and through computer technology and the Internet, and also through the increase in international diasporic migration and large-scale tourism. It would seem that virtually all kinds of music are available to peoples everywhere, at least in urban societies, and thus that the musical distinction between peoples is receding to a point at which all cultures begin to be musically almost alike. At the same time, the diversity of musical experience of each person has increased enormously, as all of us can hear recordings (and often live performances) of all musics. Musical diversity is moving from the experience of peoples to that of the individual.

MUSICAL INSTRUMENTS

Virtually all cultures have instruments. In one sense, there is an infinite variety of instruments, but there is also a good deal of similarity among instruments across cultures. Bowed, stringed instruments held vertically, like the cello, appear throughout Asia, Europe, and parts of Africa. As we have just seen in the case of the Apache fiddle, they probably developed in the native cultures of the Americas as a result of culture contact with Europeans. Xylophone-like instruments were highly developed in Indonesia, Africa, and Central America. Flutes, drums, and rattles are found throughout the world. Yet each culture has its own version of an instrument type, its own set of ideas about it, and its own terminology. Thus, the African instrument sometimes known as "thumb-piano" or "finger-xylophone"—its metal or reed keys are actually attached to a bridge and plucked, and therefore it is neither a piano nor a xylophone—is known in African languages as mbira, sansa, kalimba, likembe, kasai, and many other names.

What to call such an instrument in scholarly literature or even in this book? Whenever possible, we use the native designation—sitar instead of "North Indian lute," erhu instead of "Chinese spike fiddle." In some cases of terminological variety, one term has come to be widely used; for the thumb-piano, for example, mbira is now the most common term. But for more general groupings, it is useful to draw on a classification of instruments. Musicians in Western culture use a four-fold grouping—strings, woodwinds, brass, and percussion—that is actually derived not from the nature of the instruments themselves but from their roles in the eighteenth-century orchestra of Mozart and Haydn, as each group fulfilled certain functions in the music. This is a European kind of classification that one needs to know in order to understand European ideas about music, and most of the world's cultures have their own ways of classifying instruments.

In order to talk about instruments of different cultures comparatively, however, students of world music commonly use a classification system that divides instruments into four main groups on the basis of the way in which the sound is produced. Developed by two prominent German scholars of the early twentieth century. Erich M. von Hornbostel and Curt Sachs, it is based on the way a Belgian museum curator, Victor Mahillon, arranged a large and varied instrument collection in Brussels in the nineteenth century, and ultimately on a way of grouping instruments in philosophical treatises of India.

One of the four classes consists of aerophones, basically wind instruments, subdivided into flutelike, trumpetlike, and reed instruments, among others. A second is chordophones, or stringed instruments. These are divided principally into zithers, which consist of sets of strings stretched in parallel fashion along a board, and lutes, on which strings are stretched along a fingerboard and its attached resonator. Most of the stringed instruments of Western culture—violins, double basses, guitars, mandolins—are lutes that are bowed or plucked. A third group is idiophones, instruments whose bodies themselves vibrate. Among these are rattles, xylophones, bells, gongs, and many other instruments that are struck or rubbed. This is actually the largest group of instruments by far, and there are societies that have representatives of this class only and of no other. Fourth, there are membranophones, instruments in which a membrane vibrates—basically drums.

Each of these classes is elaborately subdivided, so that the system provides a space for each of the world's instruments and perhaps even for instruments not yet discovered. A fifth category, developed long after Hornbostel and Sachs published their scheme, has been suggested: electrophones, instruments that depend on electric power for producing and synthesizing sounds and for amplification. These would include modern synthesizers and computers and also electric guitars and electric organs, and also older inventions such as the Theremin, invented in 1920, whose performer moves his hands above the instrument without touching it.

WHY DIFFERENT CULTURES HAVE DIFFERENT KINDS OF MUSIC

If the following chapters succeed in making it clear that each culture has a unique musical system, it is natural that the reader should ask why there are these differences and what it is that determines the particular music that a culture has. Why indeed did Western music develop its pervasive system of harmony, and why do Native Americans of the North American plains sing in a harsh and tense manner, and why do Sub-Saharan African peoples stress rhythmic complexity and the concept of improvised variation? Though these are the questions that we may wish ultimately to answer in this book, we will not be able to do so definitively.

But we can suggest some answers. There are some factors that we should eliminate from serious consideration at the outset. One is the genetic. There is no evidence that the musical style of a society is determined by heredity. It is true, for example, that black societies in Africa and the New World share certain musical traits; these are not, however, the result of the same factors that determine their physical similarity, but come rather from their common African cultural roots. After all, it has been amply demonstrated by such artists as Zubin Mehta, Yo-Yo Ma, and Seiji Ozawa that members of non-Western societies can become leading musicians in the sphere of Western music; and despite the problems occasioned by exposure delayed until adult life, there are Americans and Europeans who have become accepted as excellent performers of African and Indian music. As is the case with language, anyone can learn any music; but to become as much at ease and as proficient as a native, to speak musically without accent, requires exposure early in life or special talent and effort.

We should also eliminate the notion that all musics pass through a set of stages, and that we can explain the variety of world musics by suggesting that we are observing each of them at a different stage of the same development. It is possibly true that musics evolve in a sense similar to that of biological species. But just as it was not inevitable that "lower" species would eventually lead to humans, it is not inevitable (or even likely) that a non-Western music would gradually change to become like Western music. Rather, the concept of evolution suggests that musical systems change in accordance with the needs of the social environment to be able to survive.

Take, for example, the role of music in human migration. In the late nineteenth century, many European peasants moved to North America in search of jobs and a higher standard of living, settling in cities and becoming factory workers. They brought with them their rural folk songs from Poland, Italy, Rumania, or Greece to Cleveland, Detroit, and Chicago. But in these cities they no longer needed ritual songs to accompany agricultural festivals, social songs to sing on the village square while courting, or narrative ballads to entertain on evenings, because instead they worked in factories, went to high school dances, and watched television. They did need music, however, to help remind them of their European heritage and of their special origins. Therefore, folk songs passed down in aural tradition became national songs learned from songbooks and taught in classes on Saturday mornings and sung at special Polish or Hungarian concerts. In the course of these kinds of performances, they changed from melodies sung unaccompanied to choral settings with harmony, and from songs that existed in many variants to standardized versions. In this way the music changed in order to satisfy a new social need.

This suggests that a society develops its music in accordance with the character of its social system. While such a statement surely does not account for all the aspects of a music or all the differences among musics, it may come closest to answering the general question previously raised. A typical ensemble in South Indian classical music has a clear hierarchy, somewhat along the lines of the Hindu caste system. The solo vocalist is highest and most prestigious, socially and musically; the accompanying drummer is next, followed by the accompanying violinist, the second percussionist, and finally the player of the drone instrument. Among the Mambuti Pygmies of Zaire, an egalitarian society with no formal leadership, musical ensembles also have no formal leaders, and the singers in choruses blend their voices.

The Western symphony orchestra began to develop seriously about the time of the industrial revolution. It is in effect a factory for producing music, in which group precision plays a great role, as does specialization. Each section has its boss, the concertmaster is a kind of factory foreman, and the conductor, who is symbolically different, making no sounds but standing on a pedestal and getting his or her name on the recording package, represents management. In those societies in which the social roles of men and women are extremely different, the genders have separate repertoires and different ways of using the voice. It has been suggested that those societies in which there is good cooperation and relative equality create large ensembles in which this cooperation is reflected, while others in which a part of the population is dominated by an elite develop soloistic music.

One should not carry the argument too far. Surely music is created in part to support and symbolize important aspects of culture, but it also has other functions, for example, to counteract rather than support the dominant cultural characteristics. There are, after all, societies in which one may say in music what one may not express in words and in which music and musicians represent deviation from societal norms. And yet, if we wish to identify what it is that determines the nature of a music, we should look first to the general character of its culture and particularly the types of relationships among people within its society, and to the way the society relates to other societies.

THE FIELD OF ETHNOMUSICOLOGY

The subject of this book properly belongs to the field of ethnomusicology, which includes both the comparative study of the musics of the world and the study of music as an aspect of culture. Ethnomusicologists customarily regard themselves as either members of the discipline of musicology (the scholarly study of music from historical and social viewpoints) or of sociocultural anthropology (the study of humans with emphasis on culture). Some have, therefore, defined ethnomusicology as the anthropological study of music. But most ethnomusicologists, even the ones who consider themselves to be anthropologists first, are musicians of some sort; that is, they have studied music formally or informally, and have some background as performers of classical or popular music.

Ethnomusicologists typically enter their field because they came into contact with the music of some "other" culture, and fell in love with it and determined to learn how to perform it, study the society from which it came, and figure out, if we can put it that way, how it functions in its society and how it is created and transmitted. Most ethnomusicologists are specialists in one culture, but many eventually study a second culture, in part for comparative perspective. Virtually all who pursue graduate study specializing in ethnomusicology take about equal amounts of work in music departments and in departments providing training in the study of culture, history, and the analysis of musical life from the viewpoint of social sciences such as anthropology and area studies, and it is important for them, as well, to attain proficiency in the languages of the cultures in which they will do research. Fieldwork is the most characteristic aspect of ethnomusicological research, but much energy is also devoted to transcribing music from recordings to notation, analyzing interviews, and explicating musical life in the context of theories derived from anthropology and other social sciences.

Fieldwork is a very personal activity, but all fieldwork depends on close interaction with members of a society—musicians and others—who become one's teachers and informants. The quality of the interaction depends on the type of project and on the fieldworker's personality, whether it is shy or outgoing, the person's gender and age, ethnic background, family status, and much more. But there is no doubt that ethnomusicological research as a whole owes an enormous debt to the musicians of the world who have undertaken to teach their musical system to outsiders, hoping that their students will "get it right" and represent them properly. Field projects vary enormously. Many students of Indian music spend most of their time with one teacher, becoming disciples, and learning the musical system through one musician's perspective. Others survey by making large numbers of sound or video recordings. Others spend most of their time interviewing intensively or—more rarely—administering questionnaires widely. Detailed description of events such as rituals or concerts may be the focus. Most typically, a fieldworker does all of this. These activities must be carried out at the convenience of the teachers, who have their own lives to lead. At the same time, the fieldworker must cope with practical problems of keeping house, dealing with medical, bureaucratic, and equipment problems, while striving to learn the nuances of a foreign language. Gathering the kinds of information provided in this book required much hard work on the part of many. Yet direct experience in the field provides a depth of understanding unavailable through secondary sources.

In the most recent two or three decades, a few important developments have caused fieldwork to change. Most nations and ethnic groups now produce—commercially—recordings of their own music, and this has changed the role of field recording to one for accommodating special projects (see the project for Persian improvisation described in Chapter 3). Increasingly, ethnomusicological research is also carried out by scholars who come from the cultures they study, and there are now many Japanese, Chinese, Indian, Indonesian, and African ethnomusicologists.

Before c. 1970, most ethnomusicologists concentrated on traditional music of non-Western and folk cultures, which had been unaffected by Western music and musical practices. They avoided the many kinds of music in which style elements from various cultural sources were combined; for example, they would avoid Middle Eastern music performed on the piano or African music using European choral harmony; and as a result, they avoided the study of popular musics in the world's cultures. Realizing that most of the world's music is in fact the result of cultural mixes, ethnomusicology today is perhaps more concerned with popular musics of the Western and non-Western world than any other music. And finally, North American and European ethnomusicologists have begun to look at their own musical culture, trying to see what they would learn if they addressed to their own institutions and organizations the questions that they had asked in foreign cultures.

Courses in ethnomusicology in the United States and Canada are most commonly offered in music departments (but in a few cases, in anthropology), and most ethnomusicologists who are university teachers serve in departments or schools of music. Since about 1980, ethnomusicologists have begun to participate in recent developments of academic work such as gender studies, critical and interpretive theory, the study of popular culture; and they have begun, increasingly, to examine their own cultures and to look analytically at the relationship between themselves as scholars and the culture they are observing, realizing that the identity and position of observers are major factors in the resulting interpretation. And while direct analysis of music, beginning with the transcription of recordings into notation and the study of performance in the field continue to be important, the mainstream of ethnomusicological thought has moved increasingly to the understanding of music in its relationship to the rest of human culture.

With their variety of backgrounds and interests, ethnomusicologists comprise an extremely diverse population of academics. They do have this in common: They try to combine their own detached observations as cultural outsiders with the views of a society about its own musical culture. The following chapters attempt to maintain this combination of viewpoints.

INTRODUCTION BIBLIOGRAPHY

The Field of Ethnomusicology   Alan P. Merriam, *The Anthropology of Music* (Evanston, Ill.: Northwestern University Press, 1964); Mantle Hood, *The Ethnomusicologist* (New York: McGraw-Hill, 1971); John Blacking, *How Musical Is Man?* (Seattle: University of Washington Press, 1973); Bruno Nettl, *The Study of Ethnomusicology* (Urbana: University of Illinois Press, 1983); Bruno Nettl and Philip Bohlman, eds., *Comparative Musicology and Anthropology of Music: Essays in the History of Ethnomusicology* (Chicago: University of Chicago Press, 1991); Helen Myers, ed., *Ethnomusicology: An Introduction* (New York: Norton, 1992); Charles Seeger, *Essays on Musicology 1935–1975* (Berkeley: University of California Press,

1977); Ann Briegleb Schuursma, *Ethnomusicology Research: A Select Annotated Bibliography* (New York: Garland, 1992); Gregory F. Barz and Timothy J. Cooley, *Shadows in the Field: New Perspectives for Fieldwork in Ethnomusicology* (New York: Oxford University Press, 1997).

Surveys of World Music and Musical Cultures   William P. Malm, *Music Cultures of the Pacific, the Near East, and Asia*, 3rd ed. (Englewood Cliffs, N.J.: Prentice Hall, 1996); Bruno Nettl, *Folk and Traditional Music of the Western Continents*, 3rd ed. (Englewood Cliffs, N.J.: Prentice Hall, 1990); Elizabeth May, ed., *Musics of Many Cultures* (Berkeley: University of California Press, 1980); David Reck, *Music of the Whole Earth* (New York: Scribner's, 1977); Jeff Titon and others, *Worlds of Music*, 3rd ed. (New York: Schirmer Books, 1992); Patricia Shehan Campbell, *Lessons from the World: A Cross-Cultural Guide to Music Teaching and Learning* (New York: Schirmer Books, 1991); John E. Kaemmer, *Music in Human Life* (Austin: University of Texas Press, 1993); Bruno Nettl with Melinda Russell, ed., *In the Course of Performance: Studies in the World of Musical Improvisation* (Chicago: University of Chicago Press, 1998); Kip Lornell and Anne Ramussen, eds., *Musics of Multicultural America* (New York: Schirmer Books, 1997); Ellen Koskoff, ed., *Women and Music in Cross-Cultural Perspective* (Urbana: University of Illinois Press, 1989); Lawrence Sullivan, ed., *Enchanting Powers: Music in the World's Religions* (Cambridge, Mass.: Harvard University Press, 1997); *The Garland Encyclopedia of World Music*, ten vols. (New York: Garland, 1997–2001); Philip V. Bohlman, *World Music: A Very Short Introduction* (Oxford: Oxford University Press, 2002); Peter Fletcher, *World Musics in Context* (Oxford: Oxford University Press, 2002).

Musical Change   Bruno Nettl, ed., *Eight Urban Musical Cultures: Tradition and Change* (Urbana: University of Illinois Press, 1978); Bruno Nettl, *The Western Impact on World Music* (New York: Schirmer Books, 1985); Gerard Béhague, ed., *Performance Practice: Ethnomusicological Perspectives* (Westport, Conn.: Greenwood, 1984); Stephen Blum and others, eds., *Ethnomusicology and Modern Music History* (Urbana: University of Illinois Press, 1991); Charles Keil and Steven Feld, *Music Grooves* (Chicago: University of Chicago Press, 1994).

Instruments   Curt Sachs, *The History of Musical Instruments* (New York: Norton, 1940); Sibyl Marcuse, *Musical Instruments: A Comprehensive Dictionary* (Garden City, N.Y.: Doubleday, 1964); *The New Grove Dictionary of Musical Instruments* (New York: Macmillan, 1984).

Determinants of Music   Curt Sachs, *The Wellsprings of Music* (The Hague: Martinus Nijhoff, 1961); Alan Lomax and others, *Folk Song Style and Culture* (Washington, D.C.: American Association for the Advancement of Science, 1968); John Blacking, *Music, Culture, and Experience* (Chicago: University of Chicago Press, 1994).

Views of Western Music   Henry Kingsbury, *Music, Talent, and Performance: A Conservatory Cultural System* (Philadelphia: Temple University Press, 1988); Bruno Nettl, *Heartland Excursions: Ethnomusicological Reflections on Schools of Music* (Urbana: University of Illinois Press, 1995); Kurt Blaukopf, *Musical Life in a Changing Society* (Portland, Ore.: Amadeus Press, 1992); Christopher Small, *Musicking* (Hanover, N.H.: Wesleyan University Press, 1998).

Periodicals   These provide articles as well as book and recordings reviews. *Ethnomusicology: Journal of the Society for Ethnomusiocology; Asian Music; The World of Music; Yearbook for Traditional Music; British Journal of Ethnomusicology; Popular Music.*

2

The Music of India

Charles Capwell

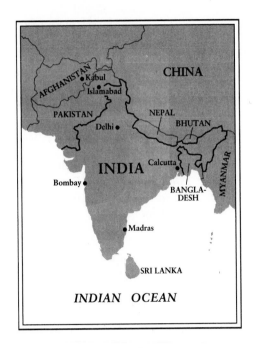

ATTENDING A MUSIC CONFERENCE IN CALCUTTA

Getting There

As the sun disappeared from the late afternoon sky of a January day, a mild temperature inversion progressively trapped more and more visible pollutants in the thickening air hovering above the streets and buildings of Calcutta. Ignoring my smarting eyes and abandoning the search for a taxi, I settled on taking a more economical bus ride downtown. The first bus to arrive at the stop, however, was full to overflowing and was besieged by a group far hardier than I, some of whom managed to buffet their way onto the stair landing or grab on to the rear of the bus for a free but perilous ride. The situation didn't improve much with the arrival of the second bus, so when the third one showed up, I joined the siege and succeeded in intimidating enough of my rivals with a judicious use of elbows and feet to get a purchase on the first stair. Pressure from those descending the bus threatened to wrest this foothold from me until the impatience of those boarding behind me propelled me upward into the aisle. Having gotten inside, all of us who viewed one another as opponents to be overcome outside suddenly felt a comradely warmth towards our neighbors, and a flurry of apologies and wry comments accompanied the liberties we were compelled to take with one another's bodies, though a moment earlier these would have been deliberate and unexcused.

As the bus lurched into traffic, I necessarily struck up an acquaintance with the young man against whom I fell and on whose toes I trampled as I tried to steady myself. My excessive clumsiness tested his fading spirit of camaraderie, but when he learned that we were both headed towards the same "music conference"—series of recitals, that is—he overlooked my assaults and began to chat enthusiastically about the musicians we were going to hear.

When we reached the southeast corner of the Maidan, Calcutta's enormous equivalent of Central Park, Swarup—that was my new acquaintance's name—and I extricated ourselves from the bus and walked the short distance to the entrance of Rabindra Sadan, the modern concert hall named for Rabindranath Tagore.[1]

Preliminaries

Although we had arrived just on time at 6 P.M., the hall was sparsely populated because the conference was to extend over several days, and the lesser-known artists appear earliest in the series as well as at the beginning of each evening. Swarup had come early because the first performer was to be a young dancer who was his class-mate at the University of Calcutta, where they both studied physics, Many young dancers these days come from the middle class and are well educated, he told me, although traditionally professional performers in music and dance had little educa-tion outside their art and held relatively low social positions. His friend Premlata was just about to complete her M.A. and was torn between continuing her studies in physics and trying to establish a reputation as a professional dancer. If she chose the latter, he said, she would face fierce competition and relatively small rewards.

As people milled about in the audience greeting one another and chatting, a few people began to appear on stage adjusting microphones and vases of flowers. At last, a couple of musicians came out, removed their sandals at the edge of the stage, and placed a few instruments on the carpet at the right. Swarup named them for me: There was a harmonium, a small box with a bellows and a keyboard; a sitar, remotely related to a guitar with a very long, wide neck; a tambura, similar to the sitar but with no frets, since its strings were simply plucked to provide a drone; a pair of small drums called tabla; and another drum, barrel-shaped and having two heads, called pakhavaj (See Figs. 2–1 and 2–2). Since no one paid any attention to the musicians and they left once again, I started to wonder if something were amiss, but as no one else seemed to be concerned, I relaxed. Soon all the musicians came out, sat on the carpet, and started tuning their instruments. I was a little startled when the tabla player picked up a hammer and started striking his instrument with it; after a few taps at the edge of the skin, however, he would tap the head with his fingers, and I realized he was simply tuning.

---

[1]Rabindranath Tagore (1861–1941), winner of the Nobel Prize for poetry in 1913, was one of India's greatest artists. Besides being a poet, he was also a novelist, dramatist, composer, painter, and educator.

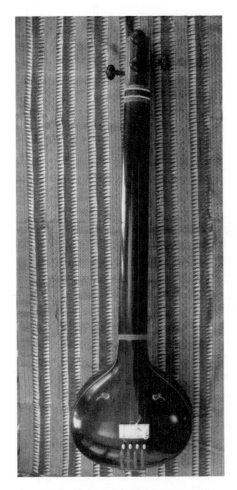

Figure 2-1   North Indian tambura.

The audience still did not seem very interested in the musicians, and even after they started playing many people continued their conversations while others began to settle down. Not until the dancer made her entrance and gracefully made obeisance to the musicians, the instruments, and the audience in the Indian way by bringing her palms together in front of her face did most of the audience direct their attention to the stage.

Kathak Dance—Nritta (Abstract Dance)

Since everything had struck me as being rather casual so far, I was totally unprepared for what happened next. Premlata suddenly leapt into action, flailing her arms, flicking her wrists in circles, snapping her head from side-to-side, twitching her brows, and madly pirouetting about, all the while jingling her ankle bells in crisp rhythms

Figure 2–2   A tabla maker lacing a new head to the dahina or right drum of the pair.

that mimicked the drum, which she punctuated by sharply slapping the soles of her bare feet against the floor of the stage. Then in an instant all this dizzying activity was coordinated into one brilliant movement, bringing everything to a complete and astonishing halt, and the dancer froze—one arm straight out and the other arched above her head, fingers twitching and eyebrows quivering as though to express the uncontainable kinetic vitality the rhythms inspired in her.

Watching her repeat these waves of activity and repose, I began to understand why this music conference had begun with a dancer. It was as though she were simply a physical realization of the musical rhythms the drummer played, all of which seemed to be magically transmitted to Premlata's feet, while the rest of her body exquisitely ornamented these rhythms. Sometimes the drummer and Premlata would speak to one another in a string of special rhythmic syllables called bols, whose rhythms they would then reproduce on the drum and with the feet.

Kathak Dance—Abhinaya (Mimed Dance)

There was more to it than just this, I soon discovered. As the harmonium player started to sing, Premlata's physical abstractions of rhythm gave way to mime, and she began to act out the words of his song with gestures and facial expressions but no props. Swarup interpreted for me the words to the beautiful melody, which the sitar and harmonium duplicated, as is customary, without adding any harmony.

It is a very familiar story to many Indians, in large part because it has been retold for many generations in many different media such as kathak, the kind of dance we were enjoying. The Hindu god Krishna is said to have been inordinately fond of butter as a child. As the story begins, Krishna's foster mother, Yashoda, is churning butter. When she has finished her tiring household chore, she puts the butter into a clay pot and hangs it from a rafter in her simple cottage—otherwise, it would be too easy for Krishna to help himself to the butter. (This made me think of the cookie jar naughty American children are always said to be stealing from.) Then Yashoda leaves the cottage to do some other chore. As the dancer depicts Yashoda's departure, she suddenly twirls about and transforms herself into an impish child to show us the mischievous Krishna intent on retrieving the butter. Frustrated by its being out of reach, he pouts and frets until he thinks of hurling a stone at the pot. At last he succeeds in breaking it and is covered with a torrent of butter, which he greedily licks from hands and arms. Satisfied and very pleased with himself, Krishna quickly realizes he is in trouble, for he sees the look on Yashoda's face when she returns home and discovers his mischief. Now Premlata shifts quickly from one character to the other; she shows Yashoda, beside herself with fury, dragging Krishna about by the ear as she scolds him, then the terrified child cowering in expectation of a beating. Just as Yashoda is indeed raising her hand to give Krishna a solid box on the ear, she sees the terror in the little boy's face and comes to her senses; rather than lashing out at the frightened child, she is overwhelmed with motherly protectiveness. Subject to the irresistible charm of childish innocence that Krishna embodies, she scoops him up in a fond embrace and cuddles and fondles him in delight.

Although the audience was small and was a little inattentive at the start, there were many appreciative cries of "Bah, bah!" (Bravo!) and "Bahut accha!" (Very good!) for her skill both in abstract dance and in mime. Swarup seemed pleased with the response, which he had done his best to encourage as a less than impartial critic.

During the brief interval before the next item on the program we stepped outside for a cup of tea, and I mentioned to him my initial surprise at having a dancer in a music concert.

"Not surprising at all," he replied. "After all, the name of the sponsoring association is 'Kolkata Sangita Mela.'"

"That's the Calcutta Music Festival, right?" I asked.

"Yes, but sangita, which we generally translate as 'music,' means not just the melody and rhythm of instrument and voice, but also the embodiment of rhythm in dance and the dramatic expression of story and mood through dance and song as well."

Vocal and Instrumental Performance: Khyal and Gat-Tora

Two days later, Swarup and I had tea together again during a break in the last evening's group of performances, which were continuing throughout the night. As it was four in the morning, I desperately needed the stimulant and wished that I had taken the opportunity for a catnap during one of the earlier performances, as some of my neighbors had surprised me by doing. I certainly did not want to fall asleep during the next performance, since the artist was considered among the foremost musicians in India and had been given the position of honor as the final performer. We had just heard a singer, however, who was also considered one of the great musicians performing today, and I wanted Swarup's opinion about his performance. I confessed that I had difficulty keeping awake at the start because the pace seemed so slow.

"Well, that's to be expected, since you don't know what to listen for," Swarup told me rather baldly, I thought. But of course he was right, I admitted to myself, that's why I wanted his opinion. "A full-scale performance of khyal, the kind of piece we just heard, begins in vilambit lay, slow tempo, and concludes—maybe thirty or forty minutes later—in drut lay, or fast tempo. You probably found the faster part more enjoyable, right?"

"That's right!" I readily agreed. "I could hardly believe my ears when he sang those rapid passages, the virtuosity was so astonishing."

"Yes, his tans are exceptionally clean and precise, but his alap is even more satisfying to the connoisseur."

"That's the slow part?"

"Right. In the beginning the singer's task is to show subtlety rather than virtuosity in the artistry he employs to reveal the raga, the particular set of pitches, that he has chosen to sing."

"He must have been very successful, then," I suggested, "because I noticed many people in the audience shaking their heads and making other gestures and comments of approval."

"Oh, yes, he was in particularly good form tonight—but then, artists are often inspired to do their best in Calcutta because they know the audience is especially sophisticated and demanding here."

We decided to finish our tea quickly and return to the hall in order not to miss the beginning of the final performance. I noticed a palpable air of excitement in the hall as people roused themselves for the arrival of the last star performer just as the dawn was breaking outside. Appreciative applause greeted the famous sitarist's presence on stage, and a murmur of excitement went round the audience as he announced the raga he would play—one that he himself had created, Swarup said.

The sitarist, too, began with an alap that started slowly with a careful, step-by-step revelation of the raga; he began in a low range and slowly worked higher, setting each pitch in its particular melodic relationship to the others. Unlike the singer's alap, however, this one had no drum accompaniment, and the melody seemed to float freely with no awareness of time. Eventually, as Swarup had prepared me to expect, this insinuating melody mysteriously acquired a pulse to which I realized I was lightly tapping my finger—this was the jor section. Not long after, though, the pace became so furious I could only listen in amazement as the artist concluded with the jhala section. Only after this, did the sitarist begin the gat-tora, joined at last by the tabla player.

I had mentioned to Swarup that in the slow khyal I had been distracted by the drone pitches that were constantly played on the tamburas, but as he had assured me I would do, I was beginning to learn to focus on the melody and to be aware of the drone only subliminally. During the alap, with no other harmony to distract me, I could appreciate the individual pitches of the melody as they stood out against the tonal backdrop of the droning tamburas and began to understand why others would occasionally shake their heads or murmur in approval of something the artist did. Rather than feeling drowsy, I was entranced by the contemplation of these beautiful sounds (Fig. 2–3).

Figure 2–3   Nikhil Banerjee playing sitar at a 1971 concert in the former princely state of Maihar on the occasion of a birthday celebration for his teacher "Baba" Alauddin Khan, who was once the court musician there. Alauddin Khan was also the teacher of his son, the sarod player Ali Akbar Khan, and of the sitariya Ravi Shankar.

This contemplative mood changed, of course, to a more active one, especially with the added interest of tabla accompaniment and tala—that is, meter.[2] At the climax, the tabla player, too, displayed an amazing skill that rivaled the soloist's, whereas in the fast khyal, the tabla had only occasionally drawn my attention. At the end, the two performers engaged in a kind of duel in which the intricate rhythms the soloist initiated on the sitar were reproduced by the tabla player as a sort of answer—jawab—to a challenging rhythmic question—sawal. After a while the patterns of the sawal-jawab became shorter and shorter, until the sitar and tabla merged for a hair-raising finish that brought the house down.

Leaving the hall thinking we had certainly gotten our money's worth during the previous night, Swarup and I decided to walk home and take advantage of the brisk morning air to refresh ourselves for the long day ahead. Having patiently answered many of my questions during the last few days, Swarup now proceeded to interrogate me about how I perceived the differences between his classical music tradition and my own.

"The most striking difference," I began, "is certainly that every performance we've seen in the last few days has focused on solo performance, vocal or instrumental or dance, with the accompaniment of a drum and the support of a drone. At home, I've attended concerts ranging from true solo recitals to performances by a couple of hundred instrumentalists and singers."

"That's the very thing I like about Western music," Swarup agreed enthusiastically. "There's such a wide range of groups. But you know, when I visited my uncle in London last year and he took me to a performance of Handel's *Messiah*, he complained afterwards about its all sounding the same to him though he's been in London twenty years now! He said, I remember, 'It's all the same raga'."

Laughing, I nonetheless had to agree with Swarup's uncle, "Yes, I guess he's right. We have a variety of combinations of voices and instruments but are limited in much classical music to major or minor, whereas you use an enormous variety of ragas. How do you remember them all, anyway? We must have heard at least a dozen different ones in these recitals, and yet you seemed acquainted with them all. For us it doesn't matter whether a piece is in E-flat or C-sharp; it's still the same old scale just placed a little higher or lower. And for the great majority of music lovers, knowing the difference between one chord and another doesn't enter into it."

"Well, most of the audience here doesn't recognize more than a few common ragas either, but those who've studied music seriously, as I have, eventually come to recognize dozens, while any good performer has to be able to keep a couple of dozen or so active in his performing repertory."

---

[2]CD 1, #1 is a very abbreviated representation of the elements described in this live performance which might take ten times as long as the recorded example. The sitarist's alap is extremely brief and he soon proceeds to the gat-tora section in medium tempo (madhya laya) tintal having 16 beats at a tempo of about 132 beats per minute. About halfway through, he switches to a fast tempo of about 200 and ends with a brisk jhala using many strokes on the drone strings of the sitar.

"Without the use of notation, either," I added in admiration.

"Not for performance, no, but students often do write down a short composition they're learning in order to record a kind of capsule summary of the way a raga should go."

"That can't be too much help," I objected, "since a performance is almost entirely improvised. As you pointed out to me, the composition is simply used as a kind of cadence, an occasional resting place for the soloist to plan what's coming next and to let the tabla player do more than simply keep time."

"Speaking of the tabla," Swarup interrupted, "you've not said anything about tala so far."

"You mean how I feel it is different from Western meter?"

"Yes. You see, I'm afraid that as regards meter I feel somewhat similarly about Western music to the way my uncle felt about keys or major and minor. Although something like the waltz is very catchy, it's all pretty limited, don't you think?"

Again I laughed and agreed. "Our meters are basically simple and repetitive until the twentieth century, anyway, when all sorts of possibilities have arisen to replace the idea of key as well as regular meter."

By this time we had arrived in front of Swarup's home, and we decided to continue our discussion sometime in the future—when we would, we hoped, be a little less sleepy. As we parted, we thought of the old saw, "Music is a universal language." Perhaps, we agreed, it had started out as something closer to "Music, like language, is universal," since we both felt that, though music might be everywhere, to understand someone else's music was like learning to understand someone else's language.

ROOTS

The Vedas

Music in India is a lively phenomenon of contemporary life, but of course it has a history and is founded on the continuity of tradition. As the record of India's civilizations and learning stretch back for millennia, it is not surprising to find music as one of the elements figuring in that record. A charming statuette of a dancing girl, for example, is found among the archeological remains of one of the world's oldest civilizations, the Harappan, located in Pakistan and northwestern India, which had connections with the early agricultural theocracies of Mesopotamia in the second millennium B.C.E. During this period new people were arriving in the area from further north and west who, though they apparently had a more primitive culture than that of the people in Harappan urban centers, nevertheless managed through a combination of circumstance and force to supplant the culture of their predecessors.

One of the attributes of the Harappan civilization was a writing system, but the newcomers were nonliterate, and for them the power of sound embodied in speech was an aspect of the divine. Speakers of an Aryan language related to most of those spoken in Europe today, the newcomers extolled the power and beauty of their gods in a body of poems they had brought with them which they preserved through oral transmission. Eventually, these poems of the Rig-Veda came to be the special responsibility of the top ranking of the four divisions or varnas of society, whose many ramifications we call "castes." The Brahmins (also spelled Brahmans), as the members of the top varna were called, were entrusted with supernatural and intellectual matters and were given a long and intensive education from childhood, the purpose of which was to ensure the correct transmission and the correct pronunciation of the Vedic hymns. Particular care had to be taken to preserve these because their very sounds were considered to be the necessary means for coercing the gods to provide for the needs of the people, and after many generations in a new land the people feared that the archaic language and pronunciation of the Vedas would be lost. In order to preserve the accent patterns of ancient Vedic, for example, the Brahmins adopted the practice of associating the three types of spoken accent with a relative pitch level; this gives the recitation of Rigvedic texts the quality of chant, a chant whose melodic contour depends precisely upon the succession of accent in the sung syllables. A further musical component is evident in the durations of the pitches. These too depend on the syllables, since Vedic, like classical Latin or Greek, based its prosody on the relative length of syllables rather than on a pattern of feet as English verse does. So important was the sound of the text that, long after the enormously elaborate ritual sacrifices of Vedic religion had died out, the Vedas continued to be preserved in oral transmission; the habit of writing them down is relatively recent. Even today some Brahmin boys are trained to memorize the Vedas in chant, although contemporary Hinduism, while venerating the Vedas, has little connection with the ancient ritualistic religion founded upon them.

The Antiquity of Theory

A further musical element entered into the preservation of the Rigvedic texts when these were rearranged for use as hymn texts in the Sama-Veda and were sung to a collection of special tunes called Samagana. It is these religiously based traditions of chant and song to which the early Sanskrit writers on musical theory and practice refer as the source for the secular art music with which they are concerned. Being intellectuals themselves, the theoretical and prescriptive writers on music naturally looked to the intellectual tradition that preserved the Vedas as a means to provide their own tradition with prestige and dignity; therefore, in the dramaturgical treatise Natyasastra, written sometime before the fifth century c.e., the performing arts are considered a "new" Veda, more suited for the enlightenment of humankind in a degenerate age than its predecessors.

Music, as one of the performing arts, is treated at some length in the Natyasastra, since it is considered an adjunct of drama, or natya. The purpose of drama according to Bharata, the eponymous author of this work, is to create an experience of aesthetic pleasure, or rasa, in the spectator. To effect this the dramatist must use a panoply of particular devices in certain ways, and these are carefully codified in the Natyasastra. Among them, for example, are special types of scales and patterns derived from them and distinct types of songs, all of which have prescribed uses for certain types of scenes or situations.

Continuity and Divergence of Theory and Practice

While the technical matter of the musical discussion in the Natyasastra is not entirely clear today and it is certain that much has changed over the centuries, it is nevertheless evident that some aspects of musical practice today are related to some of those mentioned in the treatise. To cite one aspect, the matter of prescribing a variety of scales and their characteristic patterns (that is, the defining of modes, or ragas, as they were later to be called in India) continues to be one of the main theoretical concerns of classical music in India. In the Natyasastra, the scale that completely filled in an octave was said to contain twenty-two steps, and this continues to influence the way many musicians and theorists think about the octave today, even though for all practical purposes only twelve steps are now used, as in the Western scale. (Play, for example, twelve successive keys on the piano, white and black, and the thirteenth will sound much like the pitch you began with, only higher or lower.) Such is the prestige of ancient theory that, though it may contradict current practice, it is nevertheless accommodated.

But how is it possible to say that twelve and twenty-two are the same? On an instrument like the piano, this is indeed difficult to conceive, but the distinct and precise pitches of the piano can, when sung or played on a violin, be made to slide from one to another, the space between them being imperceptibly filled. Such flexibility is used to great advantage in Indian melody, which is expressively ornamented to a much greater degree than in the West. The ornamentation is, therefore, integral to Indian melody and not incidental, and in these ornaments, a musician may say, lie the ancient twenty-two divisions of the scale, which have given their names—sruti—to the modern subtleties of intonation and ornamentation of the twelve-pitch modern scale. Herein, too, lies the Western misconception that Indian music uses scales constructed on pitches quite different from those of the Western chromatic scale of twelve pitches. While a musician of Tehran who uses the piano to play a dastgah may, in fact, have to tune it differently from "normal," harmonium players in India find that a single set of twelve pitches suffices to play any raga.

North and South: The Hindustani and Karnatak Systems

The concept of raga has been used in the previous paragraphs to suggest the continuity of musical thought over many centuries in India, but it may also help us to understand the current dichotomy in Indian classical music, which today exists in two related systems, the Hindustani system of North India and the Karnatak (Carnatic) system of South India. Along the lines laid down over the centuries by theorists, both the Hindustani and Karnatak systems represent ragas as more than just a collection of pitches in a scale. For example, specifying certain pitches for particular emphasis, or forbidding some pitch or pitches from being used in ascending or descending the scale, or requiring that the scale double back on itself before continuing in the original direction, or stating what form a note is to take (sharped, flatted, or natural) in ascent or descent—all these are common features of raga in both systems. Although a raga in the Hindustani system may be essentially the same as its Karnatak counterpart according to such rules and may be recognizably similar in performance, the styles of performance are nevertheless sufficiently different to make it difficult for someone acquainted with one style to appreciate the other. This is a difficulty encountered more, perhaps, by the Hindustani music lover listening to Karnatak music than vice versa; the smoother, more sensuous quality of North Indian performance often seems more melodious, and therefore, more accessible than the intricately ornamented and demanding melodies of the South, which require longer familiarity and attention to appreciate—even for North Indians.

This distinction in style has developed over the last seven centuries, according to the documentation of theory, which has, since the thirteenth-century treatise Sangitaratnakara, tended to reflect a divergence in musical culture that nevertheless remains founded on a common heritage. One may now find ragas of the North and South that have a common name—bhairavi, to name a popular example—although their different evolutions have resulted in their having quite different musical features, even different scales.

Hindu/Muslim Attitudes toward Music and its Transmission

In part, this divergence in musical culture is attributable to the fact that North India came under the increasing political and cultural influence of a new group of people who entered from the northwest in the manner of the ancient invaders who brought the Vedas with them. Millennia ago, the Aryan-speaking invaders settled in the North and had the profoundest influence there, and the Dravidian speakers of the South—although they adopted Vedic practices, the Sanskrit language of learning, and many elements of social culture such as caste—retained their own regional languages and many other aspects of their regional heritage. From the thirteenth century on, the influence of Persian and Turkish culture and of the Islamic religion, which had been sporadically encountered during the previous five centuries, became of singular importance for North India when the foreigners established political control over the area from the city of Delhi.

As the importance of Persian culture and language grew, the significance of Sanskrit learning waned, and expertise in music came largely to mean knowledge of a repertory and style of performance learned through oral transmission in certain families of professional musicians, mostly Muslim. By the time the British had made the last Mughal Emperor a puppet in the early nineteenth century, the lineages, or gharanas, established by these families and their students jealously guarded their various musical heritages as trade secrets to be shared only with talented sons or especially dedicated and loyal men from outside the family. To become the shagird (pupil) of an ustad (master) was to become an apprentice in a closed guild. While this apprentice system still obtains to a degree in India, and many people feel it is the only proper way to be trained as a professional musician, it is also felt that the remnants of exclusivity and jealousy of the old system of training have hampered the development of Hindustani music.

In Karnatak music the attitude toward musical preservation and transmission has been somewhat different from that of the North. The gharanas of the North ultimately derive their legitimacy from the famous sixteenth-century musician Tansen, who was brought to the imperial court near Delhi by Akbar at the high point of the Mughal reign (Fig. 2–4). In the South the name to conjure with is that of Tyagaraja, who is remembered not simply as a great musician but also as a remarkable saint.

Figure 2–4   A pavilion surrounded by water in the imperial city Fatehpur Sikri where Tansen is said to have performed for the Mughal Emperor Akbar in the sixteenth century.

Unlike Tansen, who during his lifetime accepted positions at various courts, Tyagaraja steadfastly refused an appointment to the southern court of Tanjore, where Karnatak musical culture was flourishing at the end of the eighteenth century. Instead he composed his songs exclusively for his chosen deity Rama, and not being a professional musician he was not concerned about keeping these songs as the inheritance of his family tradition alone. Over the last couple of centuries, as the songs of Tyagaraja and his contemporaries came to form the core of Karnatak music and were passed from guru (teacher) to shishya (disciple), different traditions of repertory and style inevitably arose, but these did not acquire the same sense of familial exclusivity and professional secrecy as did the northern gharanas.

In the stories of the careers of Tansen and Tyagaraja, we note some distinctions between Hindu and Muslim attitudes toward music as well. Tansen, himself a Hindu, established himself and his Muslim descendants essentially as professional entertainers, with the association of relatively low status. His legendary predecessor Gopal Nayak, like Tyagaraja, remained primarily a Hindu religious devotee, and the Hindu view that music is a worthy religious offering and a means to spiritual enlightenment continues to ensure him, as it does Tyagaraja, great respect and high status. The orthodox Muslim fear of music as a sensual enticement that may lead to debauchery rather than to spiritual advancement has tainted the practice of music, particularly in the North, and musicians have carefully tried to maintain a distinction between music as high art and music as mere sensual gratification. Musicians who were members of Hindustani gharanas, for example, fought to keep exclusive control of their heritage, in part to guarantee them higher status than that accorded to their accompanists, who often accompanied women dancers and served as their teachers.

A similar distinction prevailed in dance. The dance we encountered in the Calcutta concert, kathak, began as an elaborate form of storytelling employing music and gesture for the recounting of religious tales. In the nineteenth century, it reached its apogee as an art form preserved by Brahmin men at the Shi'a Muslim court of Lucknow, where the dance was so admired that even the Shi'a king Wajid Ali Shah was a student of the dance—by all accounts quite a competent one, too! Being based in the Hindu religion and performed by Brahmin men, kathak had as much respectability as a performing art could have which is to say, not a great deal. Other types of dance—or nautch, as it was known during the British period—were performed by professional female dancers for the enjoyment of male audiences, who sometimes paid for sexual entertainment as well; naturally these were less respectable.

In the South, trained dancers were required at temples and courts for various rituals and ceremonies. The devadasis, or "servants of the gods," were dedicated as children to the service of the temple and received an intensive training in the art of dance. Being "married" to the temple deity, they were not allowed to marry in the usual sense and were therefore not constrained to the limited world of the respectable housewife. Living outside the normal social role for women, they did not have the housewife's "respectability"; but being married to a deity, they could never become widows, who were believed to bring misfortune to all, including themselves. In fact, because of their good fortune in this regard, devadasis were also known as "ever auspicious," and their presence at rites and ceremonies was believed to ensure the welfare of all involved.

While not permitted to marry, the devadasis often became the concubines of prominent men, and the children they had by them often became dancers, if girls, or musicians and dance teachers, if boys. These families, having a hereditary association with music and dance, had a lesser status than did Brahmin musicians like Tyagaraja. Thus in South India there was a difference in status among musicians similar to that found in the North between gharana members and the men who accompanied them as well as accompanying dancing girls.

In the late nineteenth and early twentieth centuries, some prominent intellectuals sought to remove the stigma associated with the performing arts and to rehabilitate them, so that the growing middle class could take over their patronage and development as the importance of the aristocracy and religious institutions waned in this regard. The change they effected just before independence from Britain in 1949 was perhaps most noticeable in the dance, where, as we have seen in the description of the concert in Calcutta, women of the middle class may now take up a career in dancing without necessarily losing their status. In the South, too, there are probably more middle-class women dancing Bharata Natyam, the classical style of Karnatak dance, than women from the traditional families of performers. The traditional distinction between the high caste of Brahmins and the low castes associated with musical professions has created a social tension in the musical life of South India, as the latter naturally feel they have been the repository for real musical competence, while the former feel they have made it possible to continue the heritage of Karnatak music in the new venue of the public concert hall.

THE KARNATAK RECITAL AND TYPES OF PIECES

In our discussion of a concert series in Calcutta we briefly mentioned some aspects of the performance of dance, instrumental music, and vocal music. Now let us consider the components of a music recital and a dance recital in South India as we might encounter them in the major South Indian city of Madras. In doing so, we can make a comparison with what we have learned about Hindustani performance and elaborate upon it as well.

Vocal music has a special importance in South India because it also provides the repertory for instrumental music. In other words, instrumentalists play the tunes of vocal music, and in doing so they generally try to maintain the articulation of the tune as determined by the pronunciation of the words in the original text. Where a syllable of text would be enunciated in a song, for example, a vina player (following section, *Instruments*) will pluck a string. Vocal music is important in Hindustani music, too, but instrumentalists rarely reproduce it, and then only as an item of light classical music at the end of a recital.

A Karnatak recital normally starts with a piece called varnam, whose purpose is to allow the performer to warm up with a familiar item. Often compared to a Western "etude"—a technical "study," as the name indicates—this is a kind of musical exercise that prepares the musician for the demands of the rest of his or her program.

The major portion of the program normally consists of pieces called kritis, which consist of three sections: pallavi, anupallavi, and caranam. The first portion of the pallavi serves as a refrain, recurring at the end of the pallavi as well as at the end of the anupallavi and of the caranam. The kritis of Tyagaraja and of his contemporaries Syama Sastri and Muttuswami Dikshitar, all stemming from the late eighteenth and early nineteenth centuries, form a significant part of the repertory of most performers; though these pieces were not written down by their composers, they are "compositions" in the sense of being fixed songs preserved through oral transmission. They have, in fact, been notated in recent times as an alternative to preservation through performance.

In the performance of a kriti, the singer or instrumentalist has several options despite the "fixed" aspect of the composition. First, he or she may decide to precede the composition itself with an improvised exposition of the ragam (as raga is named in the South) in which the kriti is composed. This performance, which is itself also called ragam or, alternatively, alapanam, allows the artist to demonstrate accomplishment in depicting the specific musical characteristics of the ragam in which the kriti has been composed. The audience thereby either learns the nature of the ragam, if it is unfamiliar, or, if it is well known, can judge the skill and expertise of the artist in his or her rendition.

The alapanam is in free rhythm; that is, it is without a regular pulse. It is also, therefore, unaccompanied by percussion; only the tambura provides a drone. Eventually the alapanam progresses to tanam when the artist introduces a regular pulsation into the improvisation. Although there is now a pulse, there is no regularity in its arrangement that would produce a meter, or talam (the Karnatak version of tala), and the percussion is still absent. The equivalent procedures in Hindustani instrumental music like the sitar performance discussed earlier are called alap-jor; jor is often followed again, as in the sitar recital with a flashy section of rhythmic drone strumming called jhala, but this lacks an equivalent in Karnatak music.

Melodic accompaniment of the Karnatak soloist is generally provided by a violinist who tries to imitate the soloist, immediately reproducing every turn of phrase. The violinist also alternates with the soloist in providing his or her own rendition of ragam and tanam, but during these periods the soloist is silent.

After the ragam-tanam has been concluded, the soloist begins the kriti, which, being in a regularized meter, or talam, is accompanied by percussion. If the artist has preceded the kriti with an improvised ragam-tanam, then he or she will likely insert appropriate kinds of improvisation into the composition as well. These are of two types: niraval and svarakalpana. In the former, the articulation of the melody—derived from the text—is maintained while the pitch content is varied within the prescriptions of the ragam. In the latter, the names of the pitches—sa, re, ga, ma, pa, dha, ni—are sung instead of the text or, if played instrumentally, each pitch is articulated separately. This practice is somewhat similar to Western solfège or solfeggio, a kind of vocal exercise that uses do, re, mi, and so on, in place of words.

The beginner who wants to determine when improvisation is being used in the kriti should try to notice when the violinist and soloist no longer perform in unison. During the unison, of course, they both have the composition in mind, but when the soloist improvises, the accompanist must follow as in the alapanam. And there will normally be an alternation between soloist and accompanist as well, so that the accompanist temporarily becomes a soloist, too, again as in the improvised alapanam.

After the kriti, if the soloist is particularly good at improvisation, ragam-tanam-pallavi may be performed. In this case the pallavi that follows the ragam-tanam may be the first section of a kriti or may be newly composed by the soloist, but it is merely a composed fragment that is not followed by the remainder of a full-scale composition. Instead the artist immediately begins to perform niraval and svarakalpana on a more extensive scale than would be usual in a kriti. Yet a third kind of improvisation may be used; this is trikala, in which the artist will alter the relation of the pallavi to the talam by, for example, doubling, then tripling, then quadrupling the duration of its notes, and then perhaps reversing the process to return to the original note values. The purpose of this type of improvisation is to demonstrate virtuosic control over the time component of performance, since the most important feat in any type of improvisation is never to lose one's place in the talam and to be able to conclude precisely at its first beat, samam, or at the beginning of the pallavi.

Ragam-tanam-pallavi is considered the ultimate test of a musician, since it requires exceptional training, great confidence, and spontaneous creative ability. Although composed songs play a very great role in Karnatak music, improvisation nevertheless has special prominence. In Hindustani music, serious vocal and instrumental styles are both almost entirely improvised and in this regard are more like pallavi in Karnatak music. Relatively fixed songs are used only in so-called light classical music, the repertory for which derives from regional folk styles, religious devotional music, and lyric songs of an erotic nature associated with dance.

After a performance of ragam-tanam-pallavi, the mood of a Karnatak recital generally changes to something less profound and demanding, and as in Hindustani recitals, pieces of a lyrical, erotic mood may be sung. Padams and javalis constitute this repertory; these are pieces associated with the lighter side of the bharata natyam dance style, in which emphasis is placed on mime and gesture for the interpretation of the songs' lyrics. Similar in construction to kritis, padams and javalis also have pallavi, anupallavi, and caranam sections. In performing these, the artist is expected to display a sensitively expressive style rather than the technical virtuosity of the earlier part of the recital.

In a Hindustani recital the pieces comparable to padam and javali would be, for example, thumri, associated with the female dancers of Lucknow and Benares, or dhun, a folk tune from a particular region of India. A Hindu vocalist may also conclude with a devotional bhajan, particularly if he or she wants to avoid any stigma of impropriety.

The Karnatak recitalist may likewise conclude with songs of a devotional nature. While the bulk of Karnatak performance is of fixed compositions, improvisation is of great importance. In Hindustani music it is fair to say that it is all important, since the "fixed" composition is often no more than a tag of recognizable melody. Such a tag—the eduppu in Karnatak music, the mukhra in Hindustani—is important, however, because it plays a role similar to that of the first beat of the tala, called the sam. It is a reference point which the performer must skillfully pick up at the end of an improvisatory passage to demonstrate that he or she has maintained an awareness of the meter during the improvisation.

To illustrate this, let us consider the kriti "Banturiti" by Tyagaraja, a brief but complete performance of which is heard in CD 1, #2. After the briefest of alapanams, the singer begins the kriti which is in the commonest talam, called adi. Having eight beats, it is indicated by a clap on samam and two other claps on beats 5 and 7; the three beats following samam are indicated by tapping the fingers of the right hand, starting with the little finger, on the palm of the left, and "waving" the right hand, that is, turning it palm upwards on the palm of the left hand, for beats 6 and 8. The eduppu, or beginning, of this song is midway between beats 2 and 3—that is, after a clap and a tap of the little finger—and the performer must return to this point accurately whenever finishing a passage of niraval or svarakalpana. (To find this point, listen for the return of the first word "Banturiti.") Alternatively, the performer may choose to conclude at samam.

In the recorded example, the singer is accompanied by violin and mridangam; note that these instruments are briefly heard alone after the conclusion of the pallavi and anupallavi. When these instruments are next heard alone, about midway through the caranam, the singer is alternating niraval improvisation with the violinist; then the performance quickly proceeds to svarakalpana as she improvises by singing the note names—sa, ri, ga, ma, pa, dha, ni—before coming to a conclusion by returning to the pallavi theme.

In a sitar performance that uses the similarly common Hindustani tala called tintal, a gat melody in slow tempo would normally begin on beat 12 of this sixteen-beat tala (as does the medium tempo gat recorded in CD 1, #1), which is kept by clapping on beats 1, 5, and 13 and waving the hand on beat 9. The portion of the gat between beats 12 and 1 is the mukhra, which the performer will pick up precisely at the right place in concluding a passage of improvisation. Again, alternatively, the performer may conclude on sam.

INSTRUMENTS

Our discussion of Hindustani music has often mentioned the sitar and tabla for the reason—as many of you may have guessed—that these are the most familiar instruments to foreigners. Ever since George Harrison of the Beatles became the temporary disciple of Pandit Ravi Shankar in the midsixties, these instruments have occasionally cropped up in Euro-American pop music, and their sounds have become relatively familiar to our ears if not always immediately identifiable. Many other instruments are used in India, of course; the list below is limited to some of the most important.

Sitar   As a group, plucked stringed instruments are the most important in Indian music. A plucked stringed instrument with a long neck, the sitar has frets that allow for shortening a string to produce a change in pitch as on a guitar. The frets do not cover all pitches, however, and are therefore adjustable according to the needs of a particular raga. Many pitches may be played from the same fret by pulling the string sideways and increasing the tension; the neck is particularly wide, to accommodate this technique. The pitches played in this way are, of course, joined seamlessly to one another rather than discretely separated. The strings are of three categories— those used for melody, those used for a drone, and those which are not usually plucked but vibrate in sympathy with the vibrations of the other strings. These "sympathetic" strings and the peculiar construction of the bridge that transmits the sound of the melody and drone strings to the soundboard help to produce the typical buzzing tone color of the sitar. A wire plectrum or pick is worn on the index finger of the right hand to pluck the strings (Fig. 2–3).

Vina   Somewhat similar to the sitar but without sympathetic strings, this instrument has fixed rather than moveable frets. It is the most important Karnatak instrument. The Hindustani vina (also called bin) is much less common and is associated with an old style of vocal music called dhrupad and may have fixed or moveable frets.

Violin   This Western instrument has become so totally assimilated into Indian music over the last two hundred years that it is sometimes difficult for Indians to think of it as nonnative. The performer plays the violin, like other Indian instruments, while seated cross-legged on the floor. This position allows the instrument to be propped between the chest and the ankle, thus freeing the fingering hand to slide up and down the fingerboard with ease to join pitches smoothly to one another. Much more common in the South than in the North, it is frequently used for accompaniment there, as well as for solo performance; the Hindustani violin is normally a solo instrument.

Harmonium   Introduced by Christian missionaries in the midnineteenth century, the harmonium quickly became established in the homes of wealthy Indians of Calcutta, who used it for their own musical entertainment. Now modified to portable size, its bellows are pumped with one hand while the melody is played on the keyboard by the other. Despite being considered a foreign adulteration of Indian music by the British who founded All-India Radio, it has nevertheless managed to become a universal favorite among Indians, who find it eminently useful for accompanying all kinds of vocal music.

Tabla   The common drums for Hindustani music, tabla are paired drums that have individual heads and are played with the hands. The treble drum is called dahina, meaning "right," although it may be played with the left hand by a left-hander; the baya, or "left," drum is the bass. The dahina can be tuned, in part, by means of a spot of black, hardened paste in the center of its head; it is normally tuned to sa, or do. The baya also has a spot, but it is not precisely tuneable and merely aims at a clear bass resonance.

Mridangam   The common drum for Karnatak music, the mridangam is a single, barrel-shaped drum having two heads, a treble one normally at the right and a bass one at the left. Like the dahina of the tabla, the right head of the mridangam is normally tuned to sa, while the left is not tuned to a pitch. Unlike the baya, however, the left head of the mridangam has no permanent spot of dried paste; instead the player applies a small spot of a porridgelike substance during performance to attain the desired resonance from this head. From time to time, as it dries out, this will be removed and reapplied. A similar drum of Hindustani music is the pakhavaj, mentioned in the discussion of kathak dance; this drum is also used to accompany the Hindustani vina.

Shehnai   A kind of oboe, the Hindustani shehnai has a Karnatak equivalent in the nagasvaram. Both have traditionally been associated with temple rituals, court ceremonies, wedding festivities, and other public music. Now brought into the concert ball to play the concert repertory, they still maintain strong associations with their traditional roles.

The drums used for these oboes are different from the usual tabla of the North and mridangam of the South: louder drums than these were needed for large outdoor ceremonies. The shehnai is accompanied by a small pair of kettledrums called khurdak, although the tabla are often used today, too. A single-barrel drum with two heads, the tavil, is used to accompany nagasvaram. To increase the sound from this drum, the player uses a stick for one head and wears hard thimbles of a plasterlike substance on the fingers of the other hand.

Sarod   Next to the sitar, the sarod is the most popular Hindustani instrument (Fig. 2–5). It too is a plucked stringed instrument, but it has no frets. To produce a smooth transition from one pitch to another, the player often slides a finger along the string rather than pulling it to the side as is done on fretted instruments. To facilitate this, the fingerboard is covered with a chrome-plated sheet of metal, and the fingernail rather than the pad of the fingertip is used to stop the string. A plectrum, or pick, of coconut shell is used to pluck the strings. Deriving from a popular Afghani instrument, the sarod has been indigenized for about the last two hundred years. It has undergone greater change than the violin during that period and has become just as firmly established in its importance for Indian music.

Figure 2–5   Sarod.

Bansuri   The Indian flute known as the bansuri has a special significance since it is the instrument played by the Hindu god Krishna, who is said to bewitch his devotees with its seductive music. The Karnatak version is called venu or kuzhal. Both Hindustani and Karnatak flutes are among the simplest instruments, being made from a tube of bamboo with the necessary holes bored into it. Despite the simplicity of their technology, Indian flutes are capable of producing the most sophisticated and technically demanding music in the hands of a skilled performer. Particularly in the South, flutes are connected with dance and temple music and are also used in folk music, but like oboes they have also become "naturalized" into the concert hall.

Less common instruments than those discussed also play a role in India's music. Just a few of these are mentioned.

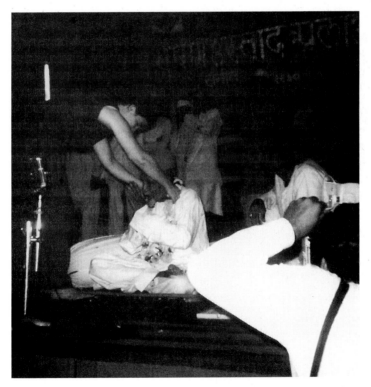

Figure 2–6   Alauddin Kahn being garlanded by a visiting American student at the concert honoring him in Maihar (see Figure 2–3).

Guitar   Played in slide-guitar fashion, this Western instrument has been adopted for Hindustani music quite successfully. Perhaps the existence of a type of vina, also played in slide fashion, helped to prepare entry of the instrument into Indian music. The Hindustani slide vina (vichitra vina) is now rarely heard, but its Karnatak counterpart, the gottuvadyam, is more common.

Santur   Counterparts of this instrument, all related to the Persian santur, are found throughout the world, from the hammered dulcimer of American folk music to the cimbalom of Hungarian Roma (Gypsies) and the yang qin of China. The santur's recent entry into Hindustani music came via the northwestern state of Kashmir, where it has traditionally been used in music accompanying ceremonies of the Sufi sect of Islam.

Saxophone   Another instrument borrowed from the West, this instrument, like its relative the clarinet, has become a substitute for the nagasvaram in Karnatak music, and like the latter it is accompanied by tavil (see shehnai).

Jalatarang   This instrument is a collection of small porcelain bowls whose pitch is regulated by filling them with different amounts of water. The bowls are sounded by being struck with a stick.

THE REALM OF INDIAN MUSIC

In considering the instruments of Indian music, we necessarily had to mention that influence from outside has made a significant contribution to this aspect of Indian culture. India itself, however, has had a profound influence on music outside its borders as well. First of all, we should remember that borders are political entities brought about through circumstances that do not always reflect "natural" linguistic and ethnic groupings. The India that came into existence as an independent state in 1947 when British rule ended, for example, was not the same as "British India." The latter included the present-day countries of Pakistan and Bangladesh but not, technically speaking, the independent princedoms of the Indian subcontinent, which were compelled to join the Indian union only on the dissolution of British India. Not surprisingly, Hindustani music is an important part of the musical life of Bangladesh and Pakistan. In Afghanistan, too, Hindustani music is viewed as having great prestige. Because in the past the court at Kabul favored Hindustani music, musicians from other areas of Afghanistan as well have come to accept its performance and its theory as a standard of excellence. In this Muslim country, the technical and theoretical apparatus associated with Hindustani music helps to distance it from the stigma of sensual indulgence and thereby to raise the status of musicians. Regional styles still persist, of course, and are generally more favored by the masses of people than the Hindustani. Hindustani music performed for the guests at a wedding may lend prestige to the affair, but the familiar chaharbeiti songs and atan, the national dance, are what will get the audience most involved.

The island country of Sri Lanka (formerly Ceylon) has longstanding cultural links with India, and both Hindustani and Karnatak music are to be heard there. The indigenous Sinhalese population, speaking an Aryan tongue, and the Tamil-speaking immigrant community from South India naturally tend to view the difference in musical styles as yet another of the differences that separate their unfortunately antagonistic ethnic groups.

While India's musical links with nearby countries might be expected, we should not overlook the fact that many Indians—and Pakistanis and Bangladeshis—now live abroad and have brought elements of their musical culture with them. In Europe and America many communities of immigrants from the subcontinent have formed societies for sponsoring musical events that serve as potent reminders to those recently settled abroad of their cultural heritage. They also serve to introduce traditional cultural values to the younger generation born abroad.

Of course, the younger generation, whether born in India or abroad, is often more interested in something less highfalutin than classical music, and there is no doubt that the most widely supported type of Indian music is that associated with the film industry. An Indian film without musical numbers is almost unheard of, and India makes more films than any other country; it stands to reason, therefore, that films are the greatest source of popular music. A filmigit ("film song") hit is virtually impossible to escape even if one does not attend the movies or listen to the radio in India, because it is sure to be broadcast over the public address systems used by neighborhood organizations to help celebrate numerous festivals that occur throughout the year. Many kinds of music serve to provide filmigit with material—from folk songs and classically based melodies to rock and jazz—and a variety of instruments and studio recording techniques all help to make it a diverse music with something for nearly every taste. Because the early filmmaking practice of dubbing musical numbers has been continued to the present, actors lip-synch to the recordings of famous singers. Dozens of actresses, for example, have appeared on the screen all singing with the voice of the enormously popular Lata Mangeshkar! Lata's voice alone could offer the hope of rescue to a film that might otherwise have been a flop. The well educated and musically sophisticated often denigrate this enormous quantity of mass-produced music. In so doing, however, they often miss out on a good deal of musical pleasure.

New experiments fusing Western popular music and jazz with Indian music are taking place both in India and abroad, with the impetus coming from Western as well as Indian musicians. For example, Ananda Shankar, son of the dancer Uday Shankar and nephew of the sitarist Pandit Ravi Shankar, has developed a sophisticated stage show of music and dance that is an original amalgam of Western and Indian ideas—not surprising in a man whose father and uncle were already entertaining Europeans with original music and dance in the thirties. Abroad, the Karnatak violinist L. Shankar (not related) and the tabla player Zakir Hussain have had great success playing a remarkably Indianized jazz with artists like the American guitarist John McLaughlin.

Perhaps one of the most interesting and successful blends of Indian and Western music is taking place in a type of song with roots in Islamic culture but with a broad appeal to all who appreciate the tradition of romantic Urdu poetry. The ghazal is a well-loved poetic form that consists of a chain of related couplets—each of which, however, expresses a self-contained idea—often culminating in a kind of "punchline" couplet that will bring exclamations of appreciation from a group attending a traditional poetry-reading session called a mushaira. Ghazals are also sung and may be performed by singers with considerable classical training as in CD 1, #3. This ghazal is sung to the traditional accompaniment of tabla, harmonium, and tambura in the raga Pahari, considered appropriate for light classical music, and the tala kaharwa which has eight beats and is also appropriate for this type of music. In the past, singing ghazals was often one of the accomplishments of courtesans. While these types of ghazal recitation and singing are at the sophisticated and elegant end of the spectrum, more popular types of ghazal are to be found, for example, among filmigit, in which the form has an important place.

Popular ghazal has reached a new level of sophistication and refinement in its own right in a blend of Western jazz harmony and synthesized instrumentation with more traditional features of ghazal performance produced in modern multitrack recording studios. The flexibility of ghazal has made it an excellent medium for experimentation and is sure to guarantee it continued vitality in the musical life of Indian communities throughout the world.

The kind of blend we find in the new ghazal raises the possibility of cross-over from the Indian community to its host environment. There has not been much evidence of this so far, but a type of Indo-British pop music combining aspects of hip-hop, trance, and re-mix techniques with a folk music and dance style from the state of Punjab called bhangra has made some slight inroads in this direction and may point to possibilities for the future. This amalgam of styles has special appeal for urban teenagers of Indian parentage. It allows them to identify themselves ethnically and at the same time to participate in social dancing at clubs, which lets them distance themselves from their parents' heritage and participate in a style of life more similar to that of other young people. In Toronto, where bhangra has also recently become popular, it has been a focus for violent action by conservative elements among the Punjabi Sikh community who feel it has a deleterious effect on youth, young women in particular. Bhangra has become more than simply a phenomenon of "world beat" here where a new immigrant culture is trying to emerge from old roots in a new environment.

PROSPECTS

While Indian music has had an influence on international pop styles, it is perhaps overshadowed today by the phenomenal spread of Afro-pop, which is now becoming well known in Europe and America. But since the advent of groups like the Beatles,

Oregon, and Shakti, Western pop and jazz have acquired new possibilities through an awareness of Indian music.

This is not to say that Western classical music has remained uninfluenced, however. Western composers have always had an interest in "exotic" music such as that of the Janissaries, the Turkish military guards. (Listen to Mozart's opera *The Abduction from the Seraglio* or to the finale of Beethoven's Ninth Symphony, for example, and you will hear the bass drum, triangle, and cymbals used to conjure up the Janissary band.) In the twentieth century, composers like the Frenchman Olivier Messiaen and the American John Cage have found inspiration in the abstract theoretical components of Indian music. The former, for example, found in the theoretical descriptions of ancient talas material that helped him construct his *Turangalila Symphony*, while the latter, in his piano sonatas, attempted to write pieces that would reflect his understanding of the theory of rasa, which we encountered in our discussion of the Natyasastra.

During the last twenty to thirty years, recordings of Indian music have become widely available, making the sounds as easy to refer to on LPs, cassettes, and CDs as the theory is in books, and ease of travel has allowed Indian artists to appear abroad. The result has been a more readily apparent influence of the sounds and performance practice of Indian music in the works of composers like Terry Riley, Steve Reich, and Philip Glass, many of whom have taken the time to study with musicians from India and other countries (as have, for that matter, a number of pop musicians).

The vitality of Indian music does not depend, however, solely on its vicarious existence in transformation; the latter merely confirms that Indian music is becoming a significant component of world music. The musical traditions of India continue to have a vital role in the cultural life of Indians at home, and despite the influential role of Western music, classical and pop, around the world, it does not yet seem to coexist on an equal footing with, much less be supplanting, filmigit or kriti or khyal in India. Compared with the importance of East Asians in the world of Western classical music, too, the lesser role played by Indians would seem indirectly to imply the strength of Indian musical traditions. Those traditions are undergoing considerable change in the modern world, but their ability to adapt and respond to new circumstances is also an indication of their vitality.

INDIA BIBLIOGRAPHY

Indian Music as a Whole Bonnie C. Wade, *Music in India: The Classical Traditions* (Englewood Cliffs, N.J.: Prentice Hall, 1979); Bonnie C. Wade, ed., *Performing Arts in India: Essays on Music, Dance, and Drama*, Monograph Series No. 21 (Berkeley: University of California Press, 1983); Peggy Holroyde, *The Music of India* (New York: Praeger, 1972); M. R. Gautam, *The Musical Heritage of India* (New Delhi: Abhinav, 1980); Peter Manuel, *Popular Musics of the Non-Western World* (New York: Oxford University Press, 1988); Lewis Eugene Rowell, *Music and*

Musical Thought in Early India (Chicago: University of Chicago Press, 1992); Gerry Farrell, *Indian Music and the West* (Oxford: Oxford University Press, 1997); Alison Arnold, ed., *South Asia: The Indian Subcontinent, The Garland Encyclopedia of World Music,* vol. 5 (New York and London: Garland Publishing, 2000).

North Indian Music   Nazir Jairazbhoy, *The Rags of Northern Indian Music: Their Structure and Evolution* (Middletown, Conn.: Wesleyan University Press, 1971); Daniel Neuman, *The Life of Music in North India: The Organization of an Artistic Tradition* (Chicago: University of Chicago Press, 1990); Bonnie C. Wade, *Khyal: Creativity within North Indian Classical Music Tradition* (Cambridge: Cambridge University Press, 1984); James Kippen, *The Tabla of Lucknow* (Cambridge: Cambridge University Press, 1988); Regula Qureshi, *Sufi Music of India and Pakistan* (Chicago: University of Chicago Press, 1995); Charles Capwell, *The Music of the Bauls of Bengal* (Kent, Oh.: Kent State University Press, 1986); Stephen Slawek, *Sitar Technique in Nibaddh Forms* (Delhi: Motilal Banarsidas, 1987); Walter Kaufmann, *The Ragas of North India* (Bloomington: Indiana University Press, 1968); Edward O. Henry, *Chant the Names of God: Musical Culture in Bhojpuri-speaking India* (San Diego: San Diego State University Press, 1988); Peter Manuel, *Cassette Culture: Popular Music and Technology in North India* (Chicago: University of Chicago Press, 1993); Ravi Shankar, *My Music, My Life* (New York: Simon and Schuster, 1968); Ravi Shankar, *Raga Mala: The Autobiography of Ravi Shankar* (New York: Welcome Rain Publications, 1999); Allyn Miner, *Sitar and Sarod in the 18th and 19th Centuries* (Wilhelmshaven: F. Noetzel, 1993); Sunil Kothari, *Kathak, Indian Classical Dance Art* (New Delhi: Abhinav Publications, 1989); Martin Clayton, *Time in Indian Music: Rhythm, Metre, and Form in North Indian Rag Performance* (Oxford: Oxford University Press, 2000).

South Indian Music   Walter Kaufmann, *The Ragas of South India: A Catalog of Scalar Materials* (Bloomington: Indiana University Press, 1976); P. Sambamoorthy, *South Indian Music,* 5 vols. (Madras: Indian Music Publishing House, n.d.); R. Rangaramanuja Ayyangar, *History of South Indian (Carnatic) Music from Vedic Times to the Present* (Madras: privately published, 1972); Mrinalini Sarabhai, *Understanding Bharata Natyam* (Ahmedabad: Darpana, 1981); Matthew Allen, "Rewriting the Script for South Indian Dance," *The Drama Review,* 41/3:63–100.

INDIA DISCOGRAPHY

Anthologies   *A Musical Anthology of the Orient,* Vols. 6,7,18 (Bärenreiter 30L 2006, 2007, 2018); *Classical Indian Music* (Odeon MOAE 147-9); *Anthology of Indian Classical Music: A Tribute to Alain Daniélou* (Auvldis/Unesco, D8270).

North India   *Parveen Sultana* (khyal) (Gramophone Co. of India ECSD 2785); *Ram Chatur Mallick* (dhrupad and dhamar), *Musiques de l'Asie Traditionelle,* Vol. 9

(Inde du Nord); *Ravi Shankar* (sitar) (Gramophone Co. of India EASD 1307); *Ananda Shankar and His Music* (modern instrumental pop) (Gramophone Co. of India ESCD 2528); *Begum Akhtar Sings Ghalib* (ghazal) (Gramophone Co. of India ECSD 2399); *Film Hits from Hit Films*, Vol. 2 (Gramophone Co. of India ECLP 5470); Joep Bor, ed., *The Raga Guide: A Survey of 74 Hindustani Ragas* (Nimbus Records, NI 5536/9).

South India   *Kaccheri* (vocal) (Nonesuch H-72040); *Vidwan* (vocal) (Nonesuch H-72023); *Dhyanam/Meditation* (vocal) (Nonesuch H-72018); *Musik für Vina* (Telarc MC8); *S. Balachander: Veena Maestro of South India* (Odeon MOCE 1026); *Pallavi* (flute) (Nonesuch H-72052).

3

Music of the Middle East

Bruno Nettl

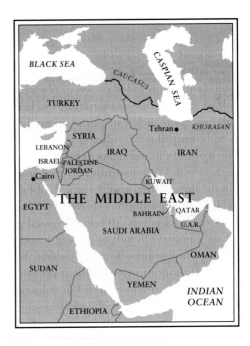

THE MIDDLE EAST

CONCERTS IN TEHRAN

In the Great Concert Hall

We are in Tehran, the capital of Iran, a rather modern city of about four million people, close to the last years of the reign of the shah—that is, about 1970. We are in a modern concert hall, have paid about $3.00 for each ticket, and sit in the seventh row; there are some twelve hundred seats, only half occupied. The audience is well dressed, in modern Western clothes; we see ladies in very fine dresses of Paris fashion and we recognize academics, professional people, and a fairly large number of foreigners. We have been shown to our seats by ushers and given printed programs, and we feel as if we were in a concert hall in an American city ready to hear a string-quartet concert. On the stage are a few chairs and some music stands.

The program tells us that we will hear several pieces, that there will be an intermission, and that there will be some ensemble music at the beginning and end, with several solo or duet numbers in between. The labeling of the numbers gives us, in a couple of cases, the composers of the music, and in all cases, an unfamiliar designation that turns out to be the name of the mode—or, in Persian, *dastgah*—of each piece.

Fifteen minutes after the official beginning time, six male musicians appear on the stage with instruments and sit down on the chairs. They are dressed in costumes approximating the clothes one sees on seventeenth- and eighteenth-century Persian miniatures. They are greeted with applause and begin tuning. The instruments are quite different from each other. There is a heavy-looking lute with long neck and frets, the tar (Fig. 3–1), which turns out to be played with a pick; also a kamancheh (Figs. 3–5, 3–6), a spiked fiddle with a small round body and four strings, which will be held upright on a peg like a miniature cello and bowed with the palm upward, like an early European viol player rather than a modern cellist. There is a trapezoidal zither or dulcimer, the santour (Fig. 3–2), with seventy-two strings (tuned to twenty-seven different pitches), which sits on a stand and will be played with two small balsa-wood mallets. A fourth player brings an ordinary Western violin, and a fifth, a cane flute, the ney, which he will play by blowing across the end (rather than across a hole in the side, as on the standard Western flute). Finally there is a drummer, who brings out a goblet-shaped drum with one skin, called dombak or zarb. These are most of the principal instruments of Persian classical music (Figs. 3–1 to 3–6).

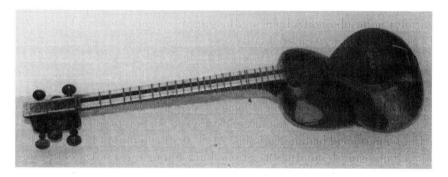

Figure 3–1   Iranian tar. *Photo: Wanda Nettl.*

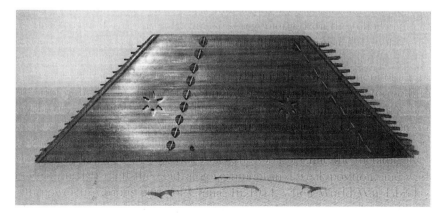

Figure 3–2   The santour, used in Iran and neighboring countries. *Photo: Wanda Nettl.*

The program says that the first section of the concert will be in the dastgah of Shur. I ask my neighbor what that means and am told that there are twelve dastgahs in Persian music, which provide the basic material for all music making in the Persian classical system. Each has a scale or collection of pitches from which composers or improvisors make selections, and each has a unique configuration of intervals. But each dastgah also has a basic musical motif, a tune consisting of some five or six tones which characterizes it. My neighbor softly sings the main musical motif of Shur into my ear and says, "This is the heart of the dastgah of Shur; when you play Shur, you must always keep coming back to it, otherwise your audience will say you don't really know our music." An example of music in the dastgah of Shur may be heard in CD 1, #6.

In the first piece all of the musicians sitting behind music stands play together. (I strain to see whether they actually have music, and conclude that they either don't or are just barely looking at it.) They are playing a type of piece called pishdaramad, which means "before the introduction," and it is by Darvish Khan, who I'm told was a great musician early in the century. They play in unison, but hardly perfect unison, and it is easy to pick out the flute's ornamented tune, the nasal voice of the kamancheh, the heavy plucked sounds of the tar, and the brilliant runs of the santour. The drummer keeps meter and tempo, and the piece is obviously in slow three-quarter time. As I make out the form, I discover that it consists of a line of music that is repeated with a final ending. This pair of lines keeps reappearing, alternating with other pairs, so that the piece could be represented by letters like this: A^1A^2, B^1B^2, C^1C^2, A^1A^2, D^1D^2, B^1B^2, A^1A^2, C^1C^2. In form it is a bit like an eighteenth-century European rondo, but also like the dances of the European Middle Ages, and for that matter some European instrumental folk music.

The audience applauds. In the front are a few young men, music students from a conservatory, who wag their heads sideways and cry out gently, "Bah, bah!" For the next section all the musicians remain onstage, but it is performed by only two of the group, the santour player and the drummer. The santour plays a very rapid piece in which a rhythmic pattern keeps being repeated as the basis of a short bit of melody, which is itself repeated many times with variations, alternates with other tunes, and eventually returns. All this is done with enormous emphasis on virtuosity. The santour player throws his arms around to show his expertise; halfway through, he takes out a cloth and places it over the strings to show that he can play correctly even without seeing the instrument. It is a great show. In all of this he is accompanied by the drummer, who takes a modest stance musically and physically. At those points when the audience hears something particularly difficult, it bursts into brief applause while the musicians go on uninterrupted. The name of this kind of piece is chahar mezrab, which means "four picks" or "four hammers," possibly because it is so fast that it sounds as if there were four hands flying over the instrument. An example of a chahar mezrab, performed on santour, may be heard in CD 1, #5.

For the third section, the group is joined by a female singer who comes onstage to enthusiastic applause. Dressed in modern evening dress, flamboyant and colorful, she sings, accompanied by the tar, music whose words, as my neighbor tells me, are a poem from the fourteenth century by Hafez, "our greatest poet." This section of the performance is called Avaz, and it is the part everyone has perhaps been waiting for. She sings short phrases and I hear the motif of Shur (still sounding a bit out of tune to me, with its intervals that don't quite fit into the scale of our piano) at the beginning, and again at various times moving gradually from the low part of her range to the higher. She doesn't sound at all like an American opera singer, or someone with a rock group, or for that matter a country-and-western singer. She has a strong, husky chest-voice, free of vibrato, but she uses lots of ornaments, and as she moves to the higher part of her range the lines get longer and she dwells for two, three, then fifteen or twenty notes on one syllable. Eventually, she sings lines without using words at all, long passages simply on "Aaah," with a tone that sounds like a combination of yodeling and sobbing, and the audience breaks into applause. Finally, after some fifteen minutes of singing, the performer allows her song to draw to a close, moving to lower pitches and softer sounds. Meanwhile, the tar player has been accompanying in an interesting style, following the singer but lagging a note or two behind, and at the end of a phrase quickly repeating what she has just sung, precisely or approximately.

We have heard what is clearly the high point of the performance. Now we hear another number sung by the same female singer, this time accompanied by the entire ensemble, and with a meter—a rather vigorous three-quarter time—set by the drum. This is a song in stanzas, roughly the length of stanzas in American folk music or in hymns, and the ensemble plays interludes between them as well as short introductory and closing sections. The instruments play in approximate unison with the singer except for an occasional flourish or quick passage between stanzas. The printed program tells me that this is a type of song called tasnif, and that both the music and the words are by 'Aref Qazvini, the most noted composer of tasnifs, who lived in the first half of our century. The words are those of a love song, but my helpful neighbor tells me that many tasnifs are about social and political matters and criticize the social system.

There follows another number played by the ensemble, but without the singer. In the same dastgah, it has a rollicking rhythm and sounds a bit as if its composer had been hearing old English folk songs. In the program it is called a reng, which is a kind of dance, but of course, no one comes on stage to dance. At the end of the performance there is applause. Fifty minutes have gone by and the audience is ready for the intermission, which has the flavor of intermissions at concerts and operas in London, New York, or Vienna. What we have just heard is a full-blown performance of one mode, or dastgah, that of Shur. If done properly it has five parts, always in the order given here, but one or several of the movements may be omitted. I am told that this was really a "very classical" performance, and that things will be lighter in the second half.

To be sure, they are. There is first another tasnif, sung by a male singer this time. Then the performer on the goblet-shaped zarb (Fig. 3–3) comes out alone and

Figure 3–3   Left: Darbucca, the most widely used drum type in the Middle East. **Right**: Iranian zarb or dombak. *Photo Wanda Netti.*

puts on a display of pyrotechnics, showing many rhythms and imitating on his drum various sounds from nature as well as the sound of a moving steam engine. A new group of performers—a singer in peasant costume, a player of a long-necked two-string lute called dotar (Fig. 3-8), and a drummer with a kind of tambourine—appears and performs three short folk songs, but they are greeted and dismissed with little applause. Five ladies in costume join them for a few folk dances, and then our original ensemble, with its classical instruments, comes out to play a couple of pieces rather like the first piece of the evening, stately and metric. But while the program gives names and composers, it does not indicate that they are cast in some traditional type. The audience applauds with modest enthusiasm, there are no encores, and everyone leaves in search of buses and taxis.

The Majles   As the audience breaks up, I tell my neighbor that it has been fun but that I was a bit puzzled. I had been told that Middle Eastern classical music is largely improvised, but here out of some ten movements, only one was clearly in that category. And I had thought that the music would be contemplative, but it struck me as more of a variety show. "Yes," my neighbor agreed, "but that's the modern way of performing Iranian classical music. But perhaps I can invite you to a place where they perform the same music in a much more traditional way."

I took him up on it, but the invitation was long in coming. Finally, after two months, I was asked to come at dinner time on a particular evening to an address in the wealthier section of northern Tehran. It was made clear that I should not (as would most Americans) bring along wife, daughter, or date, but that I should come alone, and that being invited to this gathering was a rather special thing. Those who attend this kind of event don't usually accept outsiders into their midst.

A bit apprehensive, I showed up. It was a modern home, but in the living room there were no chairs, and six men were sitting in a circle leaning against large pillows. Three of them were wearing loose, pajamalike garments. I recognized two of them, one a physicist and the other a doctor, and it was clear that they were all old friends, although they spoke to each other in rather formal terms. Women's voices were heard—there must have been half a dozen—from the kitchen, but no women were to be seen that evening. Some of the men smoked (a bit of opium in one case), a servant brought some wine and brandy, eventually we were served a traditional meal, and as soon as we had finished eating one of the men present opened an instrument case and began tuning his setar (Fig. 3–4). This was a small lute, like a mandolin but with a much longer neck. It had not been used in the formal concert but now I was told that it was really the truest, most characteristic instrument of Persian traditional music. It had four strings and frets, and was strummed with the forefinger's long nail, melody and drone together. The tone is usually very soft but sometimes it can be loud and vigorous.

The setar player followed the same plan as the ensemble in the first half of the formal concert, but the introductory pishdaramad was very short, while the chahar mezrab, obviously improvised this time, went on at length. The musician made a great deal of the nonmetric avaz, in which he moved from low pitches very gradually up the scale over a good half hour, clearly watching the reactions of his audience and obviously stimulated by it to move gradually into excited and emotional musical utterances. There followed a brief tasnif, but there was no fifth section. In contrast to the public concert, the nonmetric and improvised sections were clearly featured here. During the performance there was a bit of conversation, but usually in the way of comments on the music, such things as "He always does this very well," and "I heard so-and-so play hesar [the section being performed] quite differently last week." At the end there was a bit of conversation about music, local politics, and the weather, and the guests left, this time bidden farewell at the door by the host's wife. My friend accompanied me to my taxi. "Don't tell people you were here," he said. "A lot of people don't approve of sessions like this."

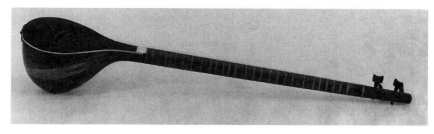

Figure 3–4 Iranian setar. *Photo: Wanda Nettl.*

MUSICAL AND CULTURAL VALUES

Attributes of Music

These are two contexts in which one could hear Persian classical music around 1970, and these experiences tell us some important things about Middle Eastern music: certain forms of music, the interaction between improvisation and composition, the role of modernization in musical life, some of the instruments, and most important, the attitude of society toward music. It is the last of these that may be most significant in explaining the peculiarities of Middle Eastern musical culture.

Let's begin by asking a basic question, but maybe a strange one: Is music a "good" thing? Does one even need to ask the question? In American society we think of music unequivocally as a good thing. All of it may not be good, but music improves an action or context, adding dignity or formality, marking its subdivisions, or providing an entertaining component. If a person is singing or whistling, he or she is assumed to be happy. Sounds we like are "music to our ears." A beautiful sound such as a beautiful speaking voice, is said to be "musical." On the other hand, music is not thought to be seriously significant; it does not seriously affect the essence of life.

It may be a surprise to some that not all societies have this view. But in many cultures, music is a principal form of mediation between humans and the supernatural. Many Native American peoples believe that their songs are taught to them by supernatural figures. Tibetan Buddhists have loudly playing orchestras to attract the attention of deities. In these instances, music is surely regarded as extremely important; but the notion that one should "like" it in the American sense and even decide which of its pieces one should prefer might be strange to those peoples. Similarly, in Middle Eastern Muslim societies, music is simultaneously feared and loved, enjoyed but viewed with suspicion; it is subject to a kind of ambivalence.

This sort of attitude is actually widespread in the world. In earlier periods of European and American culture, music was regarded as acceptable only when it was religious. Musicians have been viewed with suspicion in many parts of the world. But in the Middle East, the character of the entire musical culture is in certain respects related to this ambivalence.

Just why music should be held in low esteem is not quite clear, as the Koran does not direct this attitude, although it cautions believers to avoid the kinds of music that lead to frivolous and lewd behavior. But whatever the roots, in Islamic society in the Middle East music must be kept far from the centers of religion; devout Muslims should avoid it; instruments in particular are to be viewed with suspicion; dancing, even more. But these undesirable aspects of music are mitigated by the fact that in Islamic societies there is great respect for scholarly activity and for poetry, there is a place for non-Muslims, and there is a tradition of intellectual argumentation that can justify exceptions to rules.

On the one hand, we find that musicians are held in low esteem. On Islamic holidays, they dare not appear in the streets with their instruments. There is no tradition of instrumental religious music, and there are no concerts in the mosques. There is also no tradition in Arabic or Persian rhetoric of using metaphorical extensions of the concept of music to symbolize the good and beautiful. And while Iranians and Turks take their traditions of poetry and visual art, their miniatures and their carpets, very seriously, they usually cannot imagine that music deserves the same dignified treatment.

On the other hand, Middle Eastern societies have a lot of what we consider to be music, and they are very good at it. They have found ways to reconcile their religion's ambivalence toward music and their own desire to have music, some of which should be briefly mentioned.

A great deal of musical activity has been turned over to members of non-Muslim minorities, particularly Jews and to a smaller extent Christians. While there have certainly been many Muslim musicians, there has always been a disproportionate number of Jewish musicians. Instrument making and selling, as well, has been in the hands of non-Muslims; in Tehran around 1970, most instrument makers were Armenian Christians.

If music making was dangerous, the intellectual study of music was not, and thus there developed in Islamic society a tradition of scholarship in music theory that resulted in the writing, between 900 and 1900, of almost two thousand treatises in Arabic, Persian, and Turkish. Among the philosophical and scientific branches of learning, music played a major part.

In visual art, architecture, literature, even in political and social structures, the heartland of Islam has always showed an interest in and an aptitude for grand designs. Large structures with complicated interrelationships such as Persian carpets and long, complex works of literature such as the Shahnameh of Ferdowsi, the national epic of Iran, are illustrative. Music was sometimes treated in such a grand manner, but only in treatises. In practice it was composed of small units with tenuous relationships. Only in the late nineteenth century, under the influence of Western musicianship with its own grand designs, did Persian musicians organize a comparable work, the radif (described later), a large repertory of music that is memorized and becomes the basis for improvisation and composition. It seems significant that

Figure 3–5   Older and highly decorated kamancheh. *Photo: Wanda Nettl.*

the radif came into existence precisely at the time when the more positive Western approach to music became known in Iran. The previous Middle Eastern system of music could be considered quite analogous to that of India, except that there was simply much less in the way of content and structural sophistication.

Defining Music

The definition of music was narrower. In Persian, for example, there are two terms to denote music—musiqi, derived from Greek and meaning "music," and khandan, meaning "to sing, to recite, to read." A particular sound or context of music may be considered one or the other, or in some respect both. Thus, we may say that certain sounds have more "musicness" about them than others. The kinds of music (in our sense) that are least objectionable are those that are khandan. Most important, they include the reading of the Koran, which in formal situations is always sung (but in a way that emphasizes the words, always in Arabic), always by a man, is nonmetric, has no instrumental accompaniment, and, in accordance with certain rules, is improvised. Singing the Koran is illustrated in a short excerpt in CD 1, #4. The more a performance of music is like that of the Koran in sound, structure, and social context, the more socially acceptable it is, and actually the less likely to be labeled as "music."

Slightly more "musical" is the music of the Zurkhaneh, a kind of traditional gymnasium where men exercise to the chanting of a specialized singer, or morshed, who accompanies himself on drum and bells, using the latter also to direct the participants to change exercises. Chanting secular literature such as the Iranian national epic, he is somewhat more metric in his improvisation and does use some instruments; but even secular music has a dignified function and is not just for entertainment.

Going further, a rather more "musical" type of sound (which might actually be called musiqi) is the vocal performance of avaz, the improvised nonmetric section of a classical performance. It would be considered a bit more dangerous because it is

Figure 3–6   Kamancheh used by students and folk musicians. *Photo: Wanda Nettl.*

often accompanied, is performed for entertainment (if indeed of a high order), emphasizes some vocal pyrotechnics, and is frequently performed by women, as can be heard in CD 1, #6. Instrumental avaz, the same kind of music but using one of the dangerous things most symbolic in music, would be next—and definitely called musiqi. The excerpts in CD 1, #8, which we will discuss later, illustrate instrumental avaz.

A similar degree of "musicness" might be enjoyed by vocal tasnifs, which are songs in a more Western sense, as they are metric and usually sung with instrumental accompaniment, but not improvised, less associated in their sound with spoken language, and also often sung by women. Quite close to the extreme of musicness would be metric instrumental pieces such as the introductory pishdaramad in a classical performance, followed by virtuosic instrumental pieces such as the chahar mezrab (again, see CD 1, #5), in which rhythmic predictability is greatest on account of the use of repeated rhythmic patterns as well as steady meter.

The classical genres described are nevertheless not totally unacceptable. Classical music is entertainment, but it has intellectual components, being associated with music theory and musical scholarship. To traditionalists, the most "undesirable" kind of music is the popular, and at the extreme end would be music explicitly for dancing such as the ensemble music that accompanies belly dance.

Music in the Middle East, then, is a phenomenon about which people have ideas quite different from those held in North America or India. How do the two performances in Tehran that we described fit into this set of attitudes? They were performances of the same kind of music, but they were surely different. The second one was part of a tradition called dowreh, a word denoting a small group of men who meet periodically for a special purpose such as reading the Koran to each other, or reading poetry, or hearing music. Such a group is often based on an extended family, and certainly its members belong to the same social class and perhaps even occupation. They feel very close to each other and depend on the ambience provided by this sense of belonging and of privacy. In earlier times, music was often heard in such venues, and the notion of music as dangerous accompanies the concept of keeping it within a closed social circle. But the familiarity of the dowreh also goes with the concept of freedom that is essential in an improvised music. In any event, while the improvised sections of a program were very much controlled in the public concert and were relatively short compared to the composed materials, improvisation played a much greater role in a small private performance.

The Musician

In many parts of the world, musicians are looked down on or are regarded as a peculiar group of people. In Europe, throughout history, musicians were of low status. One expected foreigners to take the roles of musicians, and there is folklore in which the musician is somehow associated with the supernatural, in league with the devil.

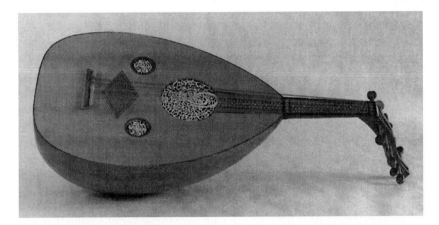

Figure 3–7   The oud, the most famous of the Arabic lutes. *Photo: Wanda Nettl.*

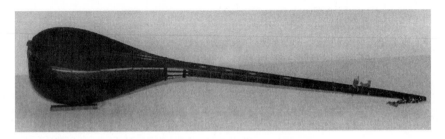

Figure 3–8   The dotar, a long-necked two-string lute. *Photo: Wanda Nettl.*

His ability to be creative and virtuosic was ascribed to the supernaturally tinged concept of talent. He was permitted and even expected to engage in unconventional social, sexual, and even religious behavior.

In the Middle East, although being a musician was not generally a good thing, there were a number of different types of musician. In the classical-music scene of Tehran, one might be a professional musician or an amateur, as is the case here; but contrary to Western practice, technical competence aside, the well trained and artistic amateur has higher status than the professional. It has to do with the status of music, but also with the notion of freedom. The professional musician may be looked down upon because he must perform when ordered and play whatever his patron wishes to hear at whatever length is desired. An amateur, who plays for his own pleasure and for his friends, may make these decisions himself, and particularly those that involve the modal system and improvisation. Considering that in Persian music the selection of mode, or dastgah, has a lot to do with the musician's mood, as each mode has its own character, the notion of freedom gives amateur status its higher prestige. And since improvised music has the greatest prestige but requires the greatest degree of freedom for the performer, the amateur (assuming he is really as well trained and as knowledgeable as the professional) is able to indulge his own musical desires best.

One other group of individuals in Islamic society is particularly associated with music—the Sufi. Sufism is a mystical movement in Islam, which is able to overcome the disapproval of music by saying, in effect, "Music is just another way of knowing and being close to God." Thus many Middle Eastern musicians, if they are Muslims, are members of Sufi sects.

In rural or small-town culture of the Middle East, the classical-music systems are hardly known. But the kinds of music used in the countryside are not principally performed by the general population (as they are in some of the world's rural societies), but rather by specialists. Individuals are not known as "musicians" per se, but there are various genres of music and each is the province of a particular specialist class with a name.

In his study of the Khorasan music, Stephen Blum identified a large number of musician-types, recognized as such by society, each of whom specialized in one genre or context. The naqqal recited the Shahnameh in teahouses. The darvish (any of a number of different kinds of individual all associated with Sufism), might recite the same work, and recent religious poetry, on the streets. The bakhshi performed narratives dealing with war and romance at weddings and similar events. The rouzeh-khan performed rouzeh, songs of the martyrdom of Hossein; the monaqeb-khan sang about the virtues of Ali and his descendants. The motreb performed vocal and instrumental music at teahouses, using instruments such as those shown in Fig. 3–9; the asheq sang romantic narratives in towns and encampments. One person could perform several functions and have several of these designations, but the point was that none of them associated himself with music as such, none was a "musician." The relationship between art and folk music is quite different from that found in Western Europe, where folk music is performed by people who are not specialists. In the Middle East, folk music is the province of the specialist; art music, ideally of the amateur. All this comes, of course, from the different kinds of value placed on music in the two culture areas.

MIDDLE EASTERN CULTURE AND HISTORY

A Culture Area: Common Features and Diversity

The Middle Eastern culture area is centered in the region of Iran. Turkey, and the heartland of Arabic culture—Saudi Arabia, Syria, Iraq, Lebanon, and Egypt. It is in these nations that the cultural characteristics of the area are most pronounced, and

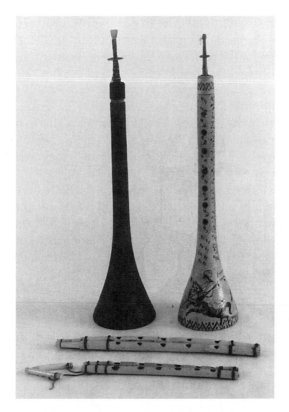

Figure 3–9 Middle Eastern wind instruments. **Top:** Two zornahs, double-reed instruments used throughout the Middle East. **Bottom:** Arabic zummarahs, double clarinets with parallel finger-holes. *Photo: Wanda Nettl.*

from which they radiated over a period of more than a thousand years in several directions. What most characterizes the culture is the religion and general way of life of Islam. Islam is monotheistic and basically egalitarian—all people are equal before God—while insisting on greatly differing cultural roles for men and women. The culture places emphasis on urban life, and trading and business are the ideal occupations. The extended family and, in more traditional Arabic societies, the tribe play a major role in social life, and ethnicity is associated with small population units rather than peoples. It is a culture in which quality of speech, elegance in writing, and direct verbal exchange among individuals play a major role. It is important for people in positions of authority—everyone from kings to religious leaders to teachers—to be directly accessible to those under them, as one looks for leadership and guidance directly to the figure of authority, not to intermediaries.

With the Islamic religion which was brought by the Arabs to the Persians and other peoples of Iran and to the various Turkic peoples of the area came the Arabic alphabet, now long held in common by most peoples of the area. The Middle Eastern heartland is an area of major literary, and particularly poetic, accomplishments, and of great architecture and abstract art such as carpets, as well as grand traditions of miniature painting. What may appear as a lower level of musical accomplishment results from the culture's ambivalence toward music.

But the Middle Eastern heartland is certainly not completely homogeneous. There is much cultural, linguistic, and religious diversity. To speak simply of "Arabs" neglects the existence of many Arabic-speaking cultures, from tribal units to urban societies. Then there are a number of different Turkic-speaking peoples, as well as Kurds, Armenians, Baluchis, and many more ethnic groups. Furthermore, while most Middle Easterners are Muslims (largely Sunni Muslims in Arabic and Turkish areas, Shi'ites in Iran), there are also Armenian, Nestorian, and Assyrian Christians, as well as Jews, Baha'is, and Zoroastrians (Zoroastrianism being the original religion of Iran).

The Middle East stretches in several directions and has no precise boundaries. What we label here as the Middle Eastern culture and music area goes beyond the heartland and includes North Africa, all the way to Morocco (a largely Arabic-speaking area); the Caucasus, largely in the former Soviet Union; and Afghanistan and Central Asia, areas with largely Persian and Turkic speakers. Furthermore, some of the characteristics of Middle Eastern music are held in common with South Asia, and it would be difficult to draw a precise line separating the musics of Iran, Afghanistan, and Pakistan. Finally, because of its proximity but also because of a period of some five hundred years of occupation by the Turkish Empire, much of the Balkan peninsula has music clearly related to and often even definitely a part of the music of the Middle East.

History of Music in the Middle East

Since Middle Eastern music, like most musics, lives in oral tradition, we know much more about its workings in the twentieth century than we do about its history. But as the Middle East generally has long been an area of special interest to Europeans and Americans, its history has been greatly explored by archaeologists and historians. We have some knowledge of its cultures long before the Christian era, and we know a bit about its music history. Archaeological sites indicate that the entire area had a large variety of instruments some three thousand years ago. There is evidence that the Sumerians, around 2000 B.C.E., had a rather complex system of musical notation. The Bible suggests that in ancient Jewish society music was regarded as a joyful activity, and that the ambivalence about music that is characteristic of Islam came to this culture area later on.

We can get some sense of the age of the Middle Eastern system of modes (maqams or dastgahs) by looking at the modal system of ancient Greece, which in its time was culturally and closely associated with Egypt and Persia and should probably be regarded as part of the Middle Eastern rather than the European culture area at that time.

The ancient Greek modes—Dorian, Aeolian, Phrygian, Lydian, and so on—whose names are still used in modern modal analysis in Western music, appear to have been units somewhat like maqams or dastgahs. They were units with scales, but named after regions and probably derived from the folktune types of geographic areas in the Greek world, and they were thought to have some specific character. Though it was only in Greece that theorists and philosophers wrote about the modes, it seems likely that this system of making music was known throughout a far broader area, probably all the way to India, and that the present-day modal systems of South and West Asia are descendants of long standing traditions.

After Islam became established about 622 C.E., empires led successively by Arabic, Turkish, and Persian forces dominated the area for a thousand years. At the courts of these empires, art-music establishments were developed (despite the Muslim ambivalence about music), and famous individual musicians such as the Persian Barbod (who lived in the tenth century C.E.), Yunus al-Katib (d. 765), and Ibrahim al-Mausili (d. 850) flourished even during the Middle Ages. Except for verbal descriptions, we have no knowledge of the sound of their music.

More influential on the later tradition was the large body of music theory that was produced in hundreds of treatises written by musicians, scientists, and philosophers, many of them attached to the courts of the Middle Eastern empires. These treatises dealt principally with two topics, the value and acceptability of music and the tuning of the modal scales. Interestingly, however, the precise measurements of pitch that these treatises imply may never have played much of a role in performance, in which intonation is less emphasized than the appropriate musical themes and motifs. Among the authors of these treatises, however, are some of the great names in Arabic philosophy—Al-Farabi, Al-Kindi, and Ebn-e Sina (Avicenna)—who included music among the components of the system of knowledge to be described.

An important aspect of Middle Eastern music history is the interaction of the area with neighboring culture areas. In the Middle Ages, probably as a result of the Crusades, Arabic musical ideas and theories came to Europe, as did the oud, the Arabic lute with short neck, which became the European lute so widely used in art music of the Renaissance. In the sixteenth century, the Moghul emperor Akbar brought Persian musicians to India, and they are said to have had a major impact, establishing a musical system in north India distinct from the possibly older South Indian or Karnatak. In the nineteenth century, Western musical culture began to play a major role, and Western institutions such as concerts, conservatories of music, notation, and musical technology, along with Western ideas about music such as the eminence of the composed piece as compared to the improvised, began to affect the Middle East substantially.

One of the major events in the area in the twentieth century was the establishment of the state of Israel in 1948. The gathering of representatives of Jewish populations from many cultures and countries stimulated the development of a distinctive folk and popular music culture based mainly on a combination of Eastern European and Middle Eastern elements. At the same time, the arrival of many Jewish musicians from Middle Eastern Muslim countries encouraged the preservation and also the interaction of Middle Eastern traditions within Israel.

A Musical Area

This very large area—which does not, incidentally, take in the entire region of Islam, as Pakistan, Bangladesh, and Indonesia are actually the nations with the largest Muslim populations—is surely quite diverse musically, but it nevertheless holds in common certain characteristics of musical culture and musical style. We have described important elements of musical thought; what now of the musical sound?

Whether classical or folk, urban or rural, Middle Eastern music has a very distinctive sound. It is almost always monophonic—there is only one melody, not several melodies proceeding together, as might be the case in a European chorus, and no system of harmony to guide or accompany the melody. This statement is generally correct but also an oversimplification, as one sometimes does hear more than one pitch at a time. A vocalist improvising may be accompanied by an instrument that follows a note or two behind him or her; or there may be parallel polyphony, that is, two voices or instruments playing the same melody at different pitch levels, say a fifth apart. But in principle, Middle Eastern music is monophonic.

With this goes a prevailingly ornamented style of singing and playing. Many if not most tones are "bent" or are embellished with trills, glissandos, or short secondary notes—all kinds of techniques to transcend a simple, straightforward rendering of a pitch. Middle Eastern musicians consider that this ornamentation gives the music its special regional character and accounts for its emotional impact. The more ornamented a passage, the better and more expressive its audience perceives it to be.

Along with the ornamentation comes a characteristic singing style or instrumental tone color. The basic way the voice is used, the kind of sound made by singers and instrumentalists—in other words, the ideal musical sound—is one of the most important characterizing features of any musical style. It is also something that tends to be, on the whole, the same within any one culture, no matter how varied the structure of the music may otherwise be. Thus, singers of Persian, Arabic, and Turkish classical music and of the many regional folk and tribal musics of the area tend to sound rather alike. It is difficult to describe the ideal sound, much easier to grasp it by hearing the music. But we could attempt to convey its effect by saying that Middle Eastern singing is tense-sounding and has a harsh, throaty, nasal tone, with a certain flatness. It has ornaments, but no vibrato. Men sing high in their range, and women usually low. The kinds of sound made by the human voice are usually imitated by instruments. Thus, the traditional spiked fiddle, kamancheh, has a flat, nasal tone without vibrato. This is in contrast to the fuller and vibrated sound of the Western violin.

MELODY AND RHYTHM

Melodic Modes: Maqam, Makam, Mugam, and Dastgah

The most important structuring device for composers and improvisers is the modal system. Musicians and musicologists argue unendingly about the definition of "mode," but for our purposes we may say that it is a pattern or set of rules for composing melody. Modes are found in many of the world's culture areas, but particularly in European art music of earlier periods, in South and Southeast Asia, Indonesia, and of course, the Middle East. In the Arabic world, the term for mode is maqam, and also in Turkey, where it is respelled makam. In the Caucasus, the term for the Azerbaijani version of the system is mugam, and in Central Asian Uzbekistan, a more limited body of material called Shashmakom (six makams) is used. In Iran, it is the term dastgah. A unit like a maqam has a particular scale, that is, a collection or group of pitches (somewhat like the Western major and minor scales) from which the composer draws and to which he is limited when creating one piece.

Generally speaking, the Arabic and Turkish manifestations of Middle Eastern classical music constitute one stream, and the forms found in Iran, Azerbaijan, and Afghanistan together form a second stream.

The tones are separated by distances in pitch called intervals. In Western major and minor scales, the consecutive intervals are major and minor seconds, also called whole- and half-tones. (You can identify them on the piano: Half-tones are made by playing adjacent keys, whole-tones by skipping a key, but be sure to include the black keys in your calculation.) In Middle Eastern music, however, there are, besides these intervals known in the West, others not compatible with the standard Western system. They are three-quarter-tones, slightly larger than our half-tone, and five-quarter-tones, slightly larger than our whole-tone. From various combinations of these, the scales of maqams and dastgahs are made up.

But there is more to a maqam: Along with a scale, there are typical kinds of order in which the tones should appear, and short three- or four-note motifs or musical gestures that a composer or improviser must use, bringing them back every ten, twenty, or thirty seconds to maintain the proper character of the mode. To play just anything with the use of a prescribed scale is not enough.

Every maqam or Persian dastgah has a name. Some give place of origin (somewhat like the Greek modes). Thus, there is Isfahan (name of a city in Iran), Rak (probably a Persian form of the Indian word "raga," thus indicating Indian origin), Hijaz (a section of Saudi Arabia), Nahawand (a village in Turkey), and so on. The name may instead suggest something of the character of the music: Homayoun (royal), Shur (salty), and the like. In some cases, notions from technical music theory play a role; for example, Mokhalef ("opposite," indicating that the scale is, as it were, turned around), Chahargah ("fourth place," or "fourth fret"), Segah ("third place"), Panjgah ("fifth place"). The systems of Turkish, Arabic, and Persian music are quite different, but they share many of these terms, a preponderance of which comes from the Persian language. While it is impossible to know whether the name of a maqam or dastgah really indicates musical relationship to a place or nonmusical character, there is no doubt that Middle Eastern musicians consider each mode to have a particular character. And so, while much of the music of this area is improvised, it is a matter of music making within rather specific sets of rules and patterns.

If you are performing in one mode, you may wish to change, or modulate to another; and in Arabic and Turkish music, each maqam has certain others to which a musician would typically move. Thus, if you perform in Nahawand, you are likely to move to Rast, Hijaz, and Ajam, but not typically to others. In twentieth-century Iranian music, the system has become formalized, with each dastgah including within its purview several gushehs, units that are like the Arabic maqams and are performed one after the other. If, for instance, you want to play the dastgah of Chahargah, you will not only tend to move to particular other modal units as in Arabic music, but you must select your modulations from the gushehs belonging to Chahargah—Zabol, Mokhalef, Hesar, Mansuri, and others. Examples of some of the Persian dastgahs are provided in the accompanying recordings: Shur in Example 4B, Mahour in Example 4S, and Chahargah in CD 1, #7 and 8.

A number of the most important Arabic maqams are illustrated in Example 10, the maqams named Nahawand, Rast, Bayati, Hijazkar, Sika, and Saba. Telling them apart is not easy for the uninitiated listener, but one may learn to identify a maqam by its special quirks such as the three-quarter tone that sounds slightly out of tune to the Western ear in Rast; the augmented second of Hijazkar making it sound, again only to Western ears, sad and exotic; the compressed diminished fourth in Saba; the fact that in Sika it is hard to decide which tone is the fundamental tone, or tonic; and the rather conventional Western minor sound of Nahawand.

Rhythmic Structure

The modal system of Middle Eastern music is complex and fascinating, and has been the focus of musicological attention. Rhythm has received less attention, but it is equally complex. Take the matter of metric and nonmetric music. In standard Western music, we assume that there is always a metric cycle of beats, possibly with subdivisions, which organizes the rhythmic experience. It is usually rather simple, with the main stress on the first beat and secondary stress halfway through; for example, "1 2/3 4" or "1 2 3/4 5 6." In twentieth-century Western art music, other cycles and combinations are sometimes found; and in liturgical chant, such as Medieval Gregorian chant, there is no meter. And so we tend to classify non-Western music as either metric or nonmetric. Although some Middle Eastern music can be described in this way, it actually has a more complicated system of rhythm.

For one thing, Middle Eastern music is metric, or nonmetric, or somewhere in between. One can say about the chanting of the Koran (CD 1, #4) that it is nonmetric; but when we get to singing in the Zurkhaneh, by a morshed who chants epic poetry to percussion accompaniment, we have to admit that while it too is nonmetric it has more of a metric feel. The same is true of the improvised avaz in classical music, in which varying degrees of "metricness" can be found at various times and a performer can switch almost unnoticed between short metric and nonmetric passages. The stately, introductory ensemble pieces are definitely metric; but fast virtuoso pieces such as the Persian chahar mezrab are not only metric but are dominated by a short rhythmic pattern (such as 1 2 3 4–6/1 2 3 4–6), which gives an even greater degree of rhythmic predictability than the meter alone.

In Arabic and Turkish music—and evidently in Persian music too, before the twentieth century—the metric part of the music was organized by rhythmic modes of a sort. They are not too different from the talas of Indian music and involve a series of beats—up to twenty or twenty-five, but usually from seven to sixteen—some of which are stressed to provide a set of subdivisions. These rhythmic modes, which are called iq'a or wazn in Arabic and usul in Turkish, have names, like the melodic maqams, and serve as an underlying structure articulated by the drum, which uses different kinds of strokes on the drumhead for stressed and unstressed beats. The melodies that the drums accompany fit in with the rhythmic mode, but sometimes so subtly that one can hardly tell just what the relationship is. Just as the concept of melodic mode has been widespread, extending from Europe (in the Middle Ages) to Southeast Asia, systems of rhythmic modes are found in the same area. But they have been abandoned in European music, and now play less of a role in the Middle East than formerly; they remain important only in the two classical music systems of India.

WAYS OF MAKING MUSIC

Improvisation, Form, and Process

One of the central features of Middle Eastern music is improvisation. We have stressed that much of the music is composed. The music is put together by a known or unknown composer, memorized, and then taught to others who perform it more or less precisely as they have learned it, and also more or less exactly the same way each time they render it. Whether this music is written in notation or not is not really relevant. Until the twentieth century, Middle Eastern musicians did not use notation, but they composed pieces. Even so, much of the music is indeed improvised.

Improvisation is a central feature of many of the world's musics. A great deal of African music is improvised in the sense that musicians create, in the course of performance, variations on a short theme or musical unit. And in many African cultures, no sharp distinction is made between performance of memorized music and the spinning-out of improvised variations. In most of Western musical culture, improvisation is regarded rather as a craft, subordinate to the concept of composition and performance carefully worked out in advance. In jazz, however, a set of chords, or a popular tune, becomes the basis of improvisation. In the gamelan music of Java and

Bali, members of the ensemble improvise variations on a theme that is being played at the same time by other instruments. In the classical musics of India and the Middle East, improvised and composed musics coexist, and the two are regarded as distinct processes. The general system of Indian improvisation is rather related to that of the Middle East, except that different types of improvisation—slow, fast, metric, and nonmetric (vistar alap, jor, jhala in North India; alapana, tanam, kalpana svaram in South India) are recognized. Such differences are found in the Middle East as well, but they are not recognized by separate terminology.

As in all musics in which there is improvisation, Middle Eastern musicians do not simply perform any old thing that comes into their minds. Their improvised pieces have more or less predictable form and musical content.

The rules by which one improvises fall into two categories. One may be termed form, the overall design of a performance. The most widely known Middle Eastern improvised forms are the taqsim of Arabic and Turkish music and the avaz of Persian. Although it was not possible to provide an entire avaz or taqsim among the accompanying recordings, their styles are illustrated. CD 1, #5 and 8 are all excerpts of avaz and show the listener the general sound of this genre. CD 1, #11, showing several maqams, are actually excerpts of Arabic taqsims. An entire taqsim is typically five to ten minutes long and consists of six to twelve separate sections. CD 1, #10 gives the first two sections of a taqsim in the maqam of Nahawand, performed by A. Jihad Racy, one of the outstanding Arabic musicians living in North America.

An avaz or a taqsim—or any of the other improvised genres—is cast in a mode (maqam, makam, or dastgah), which tells the performer the scales, the identities of the pitches, and the typical motifs that must be used. Moreover, the rhythmic structure—not consistently metric, though metric bits may appear—is predetermined. Beyond this the performer has certain choices, but if we analyze many recorded performances we see that they follow a limited set of patterns. The performer may decide to move from the main mode into others; and in the case of Persian music, one is almost obliged to do so, moving gradually from a low part of the range to a higher part. He may also decide to how many and which secondary modes he may modulate, in what order, and just how long to stay with each one. The overall form is set, but the details are determined by the improviser.

But beyond the matter of overall form, there is a matter of style on a more detailed level. It is this aspect of the music that causes it to sound Middle Eastern or Iranian, or from a particular place, or by a particular performer—in the first place. It is the way in which musical materials are handled, repeated, changed, developed, alternated. In Middle Eastern music, it is important to repeat a motif two or three times but not more. It is important to present a highly characteristic motif occasionally and to surround it with more general material. Most melodic movements should take place in accordance with the scale of the maqam or dastgah, with few large intervals that skip tones. It is expected that the music be ornamented, that one moves from lower to higher areas of the scalar range. These are general rules of style, but how they are applied in detail is up to the improviser. And yet Arabic and Persian improvisations have a very consistent style. How does such a system live, with its balance of freedom and restriction?

Learning to Improvise

In the case of Iran, it has much to do with the way musicians learn the classical system, and the way in which they learn to improvise. They do this by studying the repertory of music known as the radif. It is not quite right to speak of the radif, because each musician, each teacher has one's own version of it. But all of these versions have a great deal in common; they are different only in the way that different American or English folk singers have different versions of one folk song. A radif consists of some three hundred pieces of music, most of them quite short—thirty seconds to four minutes—and they are organized in the twelve modes, or dastgahs, of Persian music. Thus, each mode has a section of the radif devoted to it. For example, the dastgah of Shur has some thirty pieces. The first is Shur itself, that is, a piece that has the main scalar and thematic characteristics of Shur. Then come others clearly related to Shur but with their own peculiarities; these are called gushehs (corners). Some have the same names as Arabic maqams, and there is reason to believe that the way Arabic musicians combined maqams informally in a performance of a taqsim, for example, was codified by Iranian musicians into the much more formal radif.

A student memorizes the radif; it takes about four years to learn, and some eight to ten hours to play through all the way. The radifs for various instruments are essentially alike, the vocal ones slightly different. The radif teaches a musician how to improvise. How can a piece of music do this? It incorporates the various techniques Iranian musicians need, ideas of how to take a musical motif and transform it into various versions, ways of moving gradually from metric to nonmetric rhythm, ways of repeating and then extending a theme, notions of when to present a memorable theme or motif of highly distinct character, and when to "noodle around." The content and structure of the radif isn't really different from the improvised avaz, but once you are an accomplished musician you should not perform the radif in public, but rather practice it and use it as a model, a point of departure, for improvisation.

CD 1, #7 illustrates the Persian radif; two of the three hundred or so pieces are provided. They belong to the section called Daramad of Chahargah, and CD 1, #8 gives excerpts from six performances all based on this bit of music from the radif and shows how several improvisers, all using a part of the radif as a point of departure, can produce quite different kinds of music. And the third and fourth excerpts in CD 1, #8, performed by the same violinist two weeks apart, as well as the fifth and sixth excerpts, played by a famous setar player a decade apart, indicate the range of improvisatory interpretation within the purview of individual musicians.

One may ask how it was that the Iranians established this large, formal radif as a basis for its classical music system when Arabic and Turkish musicians did not. Questions of this sort are always difficult to answer, and one cannot be sure that one's speculation is right, but the following is a possibility.

Iranian culture has for a long time developed a sense for large, complex structures. The complicated carpet designs, the tendency of literary artists to produce grand, compound works, including a very long national epic, and the complexity of the imperial political system show us this. But until the twentieth century, music and art that was looked down on did not partake of such development. In the late nineteenth century, Iranians became acquainted with European music, as the emperor brought French and Italian musicians to modernize the music of his military establishment. Iranian musicians saw Western music as a grand design—a system with a unified theory, notation, and great control over the sonic environment—and they also saw Western musicians as more respected members of their society. This, it would seem, stimulated them to develop the radif, a large, complex work. Organized by musicians who were members of the middle class, it reflected certain important values of Iranian culture—the tension between equality and hierarchy (that is, equality of all before God in Islam and the hierarchy of a political empire), the value of individualism and surprise, and a characteristic way of ordering the subdivisions of an event.

Take an example from Iranian social life as a model. In ordinary relationships between members of a family or close friends, what is important comes first: a father goes through the door before his son, an older friend before the younger, and this is done without much ceremony. In a more formal relationship, people shuffle around deciding who should go first (although it really has been settled in advance that the older, more prestigious, higher placed must precede). In a truly formal event, the amount of introductory behavior preceding the main substance is substantial. A formal dinner, for example, will be preceded by hours of chitchat and tea-with-cookies. The radif is like the family: what is important, main dastgahs, gushehs, motifs, comes first. When the radif is transformed into a more formal performance, the most prestigious part, the improvised avaz, comes later and is preceded by less prestigious composed compositions. In this way, the radif itself and the music derived from it reflect important values of Iranian culture and principles of social behavior.

The general structure of Middle Eastern art music is complex, perhaps most so in Iran. But the rural and vernacular repertories are based on similar principles. Take a major genre of folk music sung in Khorasan, the northeastern province of Iran. It is called chaharbeiti, which means something like "four lines," and it is a poem with four lines dealing with any of a variety of subjects, ordinarily lyrical and expressing a mood or sentiment. There are many hundreds of these poems. But ordinarily they are sung to one of the variants of one tune, which is actually called the "chaharbeiti tune." Variants are alike in that they follow the same general melodic contour, use the same selection of pitches, and emphasize the same notes. They are like variations on a theme. Musicologists call this a "tune type." But the fact that the society recognizes them as closely related and gives them a collective name is significant. Probably much of the radif was built up by the inclusion of such tune types, perhaps abstracting them into standardized short tunes. If one listens to Middle Eastern folk music in general, one finds a relatively small number of distinct tunes, but many, many variations on each of them. Probably many of these tune types became the bases of the maqams.

Serious and Ritual Genres

There are many other kinds of music in the Middle East. Classical music in the Middle East is often performed in suites or sequences of pieces. In North Africa, a widespread name for such a suite is naubat; in Iraq, it is simply known as the Iraqi maqam. Egyptian sufis or darvishes practice a complex ritual, with music, known as zikr.

In Turkey, the ceremony of the Mevlevi (Sufis following in the tradition of the founder of Sufism, the Persian poet Mowlavi or Rumi, who lived in Turkey) is in the form of such a suite. The form consists of several movements. Some of them are composed, some improvised; some are soloistic, others for ensemble; some are usually vocal, others always instrumental. It is during the performance of this suite that one may see the so-called dancing dervishes, who, while whirling to the music for periods over a half hour, achieve a state of trance.

Among the types of pieces that make up a Middle Eastern suite, the best known are the taqsim (Turkish, taksim), an improvised, usually nonmetric solo instrumental number in which the musician may move from the main maqam to others, eventually returning to the original; and the beshrav or peshrev, a metric, composed piece usually performed by an ensemble.

In Western classical music, opera, a play in which the characters sing rather than speak, is one of the most valued genres. In the Middle East there is no similarly complex form, but there is a type of play in Iran, called ta'azieh, in which the characters sing as well as speak. Like Middle Eastern music generally, it is monophonic, and since it has religious content there is no instrumental accompaniment. The plots ordinarily involve the martyrdom of the Imam Hossein, the son of the prophet Mohammed's son-in-law, in a battle in 680 C.E. at which the lines between the two main sects of Islam, Sunni and Shi'ite, were drawn.

Although not classified as "music" in the Middle East, the singing, reciting, or chanting of the Koran requires some attention. It is structurally very much like classical nonmetric improvisation. Anyone may sing the Koran, but in the mosque it is professionals who render the holy word. There is a system of modes similar to the maqam system, but different in terminology. There are different ways of chanting, schools with different practices, for example, the Meccan, Egyptian, Damascus, and

Western North African. The chanting is improvised, but the Koran may be written with a kind of notation that indicates whether a tone is to be ornamented or not, and in which direction the melody should move. Among musicians, the explicitly musical aspect of the Koran may ostensibly play a major role, but it is important to remember that the entire system of musical values, the high value of nonmetric, vocal, texted, improvised music and the low esteem of metric, instrumental, composed music is based on the relative similarity to or difference from the sound of the Koran.

Vernacular and Popular Music

At the other end of the spectrum of acceptability is the music for belly dancing, performed by a group called takht (literally, "platform"), which consists ordinarily of a hammered dulcimer, a violin, a lute, a goblet-shaped drum, and a tambourine. The music is rapid and is accompanied by fast, complex, but repeated drum figures. While belly dancing has recently become a genre of popular and somewhat vulgar entertainment, it was traditionally a high art performed by highly trained dancers and musicians.

And while Western music in its many aspects—concerts and opera, nightclubs, rock groups and jazz ensembles, instruments, notation, the mass media—is making the Middle East in certain ways a subdivision of the Western cultural system, there are many forms of music that combine traditional styles of music with features of Western music to create new forms.

Among the characteristic kind of venue is the traditional music hall, as found in some of the large cities in the period around 1970. Here a large audience (mostly of men, and often from the same social or occupational group) may attend a long series of entertainment numbers while eating a standard supper and drinking beer. The entertainment may consist of some twenty to thirty acts, some of them political or humorous skits, others folk dances and acrobatics, but the most prominent being musical. Typically, a female singer will be accompanied by a small ensemble of traditional and Western instruments that plays in unison with her while also providing some very simple, rudimentary Western harmony.

Some of these singers went far beyond those music halls. In the period since World War II, a small number of Middle Eastern singers—more women than men—gained great prominence, contradicting the Islamic ambivalence toward music and particularly toward public performance by women. Most prominent among these was Umm Kulthum (1908–1975) illustrated in a short excerpt on CD 1, #9, an Egyptian musician who achieved international prominence, becoming a star of radio and film as well as of stage and the record industry. Her songs, composed for her by prominent composers, became widely known throughout the Islamic world, and thus qualify as "popular" music. But her singing was based on classical Arabic models and included improvisatory passages. At the same time, she was accompanied by orchestras consisting in large part of Western instruments playing in a European-derived style. For almost four decades, she gave monthly concerts lasting four hours. Other singers, far less well known such as the Egyptian Abdel-Wahab, the Lebanese Fairuz, and the Iranian Delkash achieved similar fame on a more local level.

The words of these songs are about love, devotion to God, protest against unfairness in society and politics, the expression of grief. The structure of the poetry greatly affects the rhythmic form of the melodies.

Songs of the sort heard in the music halls could also be heard on radio or bought on 45 r.p.m. disks, and some come from films. They constitute the Middle Eastern version of urban popular music, a type of music that almost everywhere combines indigenous and Western elements and employs certain Western instruments and Western harmony. In general, the popular music of the Middle Eastern cities has a homogeneous style; what one could hear in Cairo, Beirut, and Tehran in the 1970s was very much one kind of music. The culture of the Middle East of centuries past was a relatively unified combination of the confluence of Arabic, Persian, Turkish, and other elements, and its popular music in the twentieth century constitutes to reflect this homogeneity.

In the period after 1980, a number of styles of popular or vernacular music reflected modern social agendas. The genre known as Rai, found in Algeria and Morocco, combines traditional singing styles, vocal virtuosity and Arabic modes with Western-style chordal accompaniment on synthesizer. In Turkey, a music called Arabesk draws young people back from strictly Western popular music to a more traditional Middle Eastern sound, as a way of symbolizing the Turkish people's association with Islam and to older cultural traditions of the area. Throughout the area, popular music combines Western-derived elements—simple chordal harmony, tuning of instruments to the European tempered scale, amplification and echo-chambers, Western keyboard synthesizers, guitars, violins—with traditional Middle Eastern sounds, nonmetric singing with heavy ornamentation usually alternating with metric pieces with a strong beat articulated by traditional hand drums, with words expressing allegiance to traditional cultural values and anticolonial political agendas. Middle Eastern musicians and their music have played a major role in the development of the phenomenon known as "World Music" or "World Beat," in combination with elements from modern American, African, and Indian film music.

In the Diasporas

In the history of the world's diasporas—when people in large numbers are forced, usually as a result of poverty or political persecution, to emigrate and settle in foreign "host" countries—music has traditionally played an important cultural role. As illustrated in detail in Chapter 11, the various European ethnic groups who settled in the United States—Italian Americans, Hungarian Americans, and so on—have used their traditional folk music to hold themselves together as communities. The Italian parade in Hartford, Connecticut; the German choir concerts with folk music arrangements in Chicago; the Czech polka bands in Wisconsin all have the purpose of showing their own people that they have a worthwhile culture—and showing this to their foreign neighbors as well. Immigrants who had no interest in music in their home country began to understand its value after they had left home. This applies to Arab Americans and Iranian Americans as well, or perhaps even more significantly, as music was not necessarily a favored activity in the traditional culture. The Arab American community has many musicians who perform at formal concerts, in night clubs, at weddings and parties. While the Arab American community may participate fully in mainstream American culture, its strives to keep an Arabic flavor in its musical life. A significant feature is a reduction on the importance of boundaries in the musical taxonomy. While society in Cairo and Beirut gave prominence to the separation between classical, popular, devotional, and folk music, these distinctions play a smaller role in North America, where an Arabic musician may play classical taqsims in concerts one day and perform in a night club for dancing on the next.

The Arab American community was already sizable early in the twentieth century, but Iranian immigrants did not come in large numbers until the 1970s and 1980s. In the cities in which there are many Iranians, night clubs with popular music abound and recordings by popular singers who live in America, or in Europe, or are able to tour from Iran, are readily available. But the classical music has played a greater role in the Iranian diaspora than in others. Concerts of Persian music—by masters on tour, or by less significant local figures—are important social events. People dress formally, arrive early to socialize, gladly travel two or three hours for the privilege of attending. Concerts of classical music are the most important ethnic social events in this culture which, on its home ground, thoroughly de-emphasized music. Iranian engineers and doctors living in Illinois and Iowa tell a common story: In Iran they took no interest in traditional music, but at most, went to hear the Tehran Symphony Orchestra. In America, Persian music reminds them strongly of home, and they purchase instruments and try to find opportunities for learning the radif.

The radif plays a role even in the music composed by Iranian musicians who are part of the international "new music" movement, and thus belong to the Western art music world. Alireza Mashayekhi, the first Iranian composer of electronic music, named his first piece "Shur," the name of the first dastgah of the radif; and another piece of his, for computer and flute, is named "Mahur," although its sound has only the vaguest similarity to that dastgah. The Chicago businessman and patron of music, Kiu Haghighi, composes music for santour and piano vaguely based on, but definitely named after, sections of the radif. There are Iranian musicians living in Los Angeles and San Francisco who make their living teaching young people santour, setar, and kamancheh, teaching the radif. Thus, Middle Eastern culture has reached out, a bit unexpectedly, with its music.

The appropriateness of musical activity came into sharp focus again after the 1979 revolution in Iran, when public musical performance—especially by women— was outlawed for several years and continued to be rigorously controlled into the twenty-first century. More radical prohibitions were exercised by the Taliban government of Afghanistan in the 1990s. But the first years of the twenty-first century saw, in the context of political and social reform and the easing of restrictions, a vigorous resurgence of traditional musical life in Iran, Afghanistan, and Azerbaijan. For example, the government of Iran has encouraged the development of Persian as well as Western classical (but not popular) musics, permitting concerts and tours and sponsoring research and attempts at preservation. Music is a subject of intense debate in the Middle Eastern artistic and intellectual circles, the issues including the concept of authenticity, the recovery and preservation of older folk and classical traditions, the participation of female musicians, and the desirability or avoidance of musical modernization and westernization.

MIDDLE EAST BIBLIOGRAPHY

Middle Eastern Music as a Whole   Kristina Nelson, *The Art of Reciting the Qur'an* (Austin: University of Texas Press, 1985); Harold S. Powers, ed., "Symposium on the Status of Traditional Art Musics in Muslim Nations," *Asian Music 12/1* (1980); Owen Wright, *The Modal System of Arab and Persian Music* A.D. *1250–1300* (London: Oxford University Press, 1978); Hans Engel, *Die Stellung des Musikers im arabisch-islamischen Raum* (Bonn: Verlag für systematische Musikwissenchaft, 1987); Amnon Shiloah, *The Dimension of Music in Islamic and Jewish Culture* (Brookfield, Vt.: Ashgate, 1993); Amnon Shiloah, *Jewish Musical Traditions* (Detroit: Wayne State University Press, 1992); Amnon Shiloah, *Music in the World of Islam: A Socio-Cultural Study* (Aldershot, England: Scolar Press, 1995); Amnon Shiloah, *The Theory of Music in Arabic Writings c. 900–1900* (Munich: Henle, 1979); William P. Malm, *Music Cultures of the Pacific, the Near East, and Asia*, 2nd ed. (Englewood Cliffs, N.J.: Prentice Hall, 1977), Chap. 3; Peter Manuel, *Popular Musics of the Non-Western World* (New York; Oxford University Press, 1988), Chaps. 5 and 6.

Iran   Ella Zonis, *Classical Persian Music: An Introduction* (Cambridge, Mass.: Harvard University Press, 1973); Bruno Nettl and others, *The Radif of Persian Music: Studies in Structure and Cultural Context* (Champaign, Ill.: Elephant & Cat, 1987); Stephen Blum, "Persian Folksong in Meshhed (Iran), 1969," *Yearbook of the International Folk Music Council* (1974); Hormoz Farhat, *The Dastgah Concept in Persian Music* (Cambridge, U.K.: Cambridge University Press, 1990); Jean During and others, *The Art of Persian Music* (Washington, D.C.: Mage Publishers, 1991); DariushTala'i, *Traditional Persian Art Music: The Radif of Mirza Abdollah* (Costa Mesa, Calif.: Mazda Publishers, 2000).

Arabic Music   Lois Ibsen al-Faruqi, *An Annotated Glossary of Arabic Musical Terms* (Westport, Conn.: Greenwood, 1981); Jürgen Elsner, *Der Begriff Maqam in Aegypten in neuerer Zeit* (Leipzig: Deutscher Verlag für Musik, 1973); Henry

George Farmer, *History of Arabian Music to the XIIIth Century* (London: Luzac, 1929); Habib Hassan Touma, *The Music of the Arabs* (Portland, Ore.: Amadeus Press, 1996); Earle H. Waugh, *The Munshidin of Egypt: Their World and Their Song* (Columbia: University of South Carolina Press, 1989); Virginia Danielson, *The Voice of Egypt: Umm Kulthum, Arabic Song, and Egyptian Society in the Twentieth Century* (Chicago: University of Chicago Press, 1997).

Afghanistan and Central Asia   Hiromi Lorraine Sakata, *Music in the Mind* (Kent, Oh.: Kent State University Press, 1983); Mark Slobin, *Music in the Culture of Northern Afghanistan* (Tucson, Ariz.: Viking Fund Publications in Anthropology, 1976); John Baily, *Music of Afghanistan* (Cambridge, U.K.: Cambridge University Press, 1988); Theodore Levin, *The Hundred Thousand Fools of God: Musical Travels in Central Asia* (Bloomington: Indiana University Press, 1996).

Israel   Eric Werner, *A Voice Still Heard . . . The Sacred Songs of the Ashkenazic Jews* (University Park: Pennsylvania State University Press, 1976); Philip V. Bohlman and Mark Slobin, eds., "Music in the Ethnic Communities of Israel," Special Issue, *Asian Music* 17/2 (Spring/Summer 1986); Philip V. Bohlman, *The Land Where Two Streams Flow: Music in the German-Jewish Community of Israel* (Urbana: University of Illinois Press, 1989); Robert Fleisher, *Twenty Israeli Composers: Voices of a Culture* (Detroit, Mich.: Wayne State University Press, 1997).

Turkey   Laurence Picken, *Folk Music Instruments of Turkey* (London: Oxford University Press, 1975); Karl Signell, *Makam: Modal Practice in Turkish Art Music* (Seattle, Wash.: Asian Music Publications, 1977); Béla Bartók, *Turkish Folk Music from Asia Minor* (Princeton, N.J.: Princeton University Press, 1976); Martin Stokes, *The Arabesk Debate: Music and Musicians in Modern Turkey* (Oxford: Oxford University Press, 1992).

MIDDLE EAST DISCOGRAPHY

Iran   *A Persian Heritage* (Nonesuch H-72060; 1974); *Tradition Classique de l'Iran: Le Tar* (Harmonia Mundi, France HM 1031; 1980); *Iranian Dastgah,* UNESCO Collection Musical Sources (Philips 6586–005; 1971); *Iran.* 2 disks UNESCO Collection: A Musical Anthology of the Orient (Bärenreiter Musicaphon BM 30 L 2004; ca. 1965); *The Kamkars: Nightingale with a Broken Wing* (Womad Select WSCD009); *Musique Iranienne* [D. Chemirani, M. Kiani, D. Tala'i] (Harmonia Mundi HMA 190391); *Majid Kiant: Santur* (Ethnic B 6756); *Radif: The Integral Repertory of Persian Art Music.* Dariush Tala'i, setar. 5 CDs (Al Sur ALCD 116–120, 1992).

Arabic Nations   *Iraq: Ud Classique Arabe par Munir Bashir* (Ocora OCR 63: 1983); *Arabian Music: Maqam,* UNESCO Collection Musical Sources (Philips 6586–0006; 1971); *Tâqâsim: The Art of Improvisation in Arabic Music* (Lyrichord

LLST 7374; ca. 1984); *The Music of Arab Americans: A Retrospective Collection* (Rounder CD 1122); *Mystical Legacies: Ali Jihad Racy Performs Music of the Middle East* (Lyrcd 7437); *Om Kalsoum (Enregistrement Public) Lesa Faker* (Sono Cairo 115); *Mystical Legacies: Ali Jihad Racy Performs Music of the Middle East* (Lyrichord LYRCD 7437).

Turkey   *Musik aus der Türkei*, 2 disks (Museum Collection Berlin-West MC1; ca. 1985); *Turkey; An Anthology of the World's Music* (Anthology AST 4003; 1971); *Turkish Village Music* (Nonesuch H-72050; ca. 1969); *The Necdet Yasir Ensemble: Music of Turkey* (Music of the World CDT 128).

Other Areas   *Heritage: Authentic Songs of Ambience and Ritual from the Musical Heritage of Jewish Communities in Israel* (CBS 63437; ca. 1970); *Jewish Music*, UNESCO Collection Musical Sources (Philips 6586 001; 1971); *Afghanistan: An Anthology of the World's Music* (Anthology AST 4001; 1969); *Azerbaijani Mugam*, UNESCO Collection Musical Sources (Philips 6586 027; 1975); *Anthologie du Mugham d'Azerbaidjan*, vols. 1 and 2. (Maison des Cultures du Monde, Inédit W260012/15.); *Turkmenistan: La musique des bakhshy/Music of the Bakhshy* (Archives internationales de musique populaire, Geneva CD-651); *Khaled, King of Rai* (NYC Music NYCD1221-2).

4

The Music of China

Isabel K.F. Wong

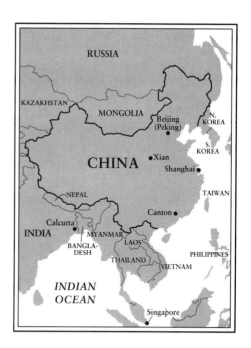

THE CONTEMPORARY SCENE

A huge millennium altar had been set up on Beijing's Tiananmen (pronounced Tyan An Mun, and meaning Gate of Heavenly Peace) Square for a New Year's eve spectacle to send off 1999 and to welcome 2000. Several hours before midnight the square was already filled with thousands of spectators who fixed their gaze on the millennium altar which was brightly lit with many multicolored and moving spot lights. Hundreds of colorful banners fluttered on the altar as a backdrop for the dozens of female dancers who wore glistening costumes in hard to define styles. One dancer wore a metallic overall that brought to mind the protective suit worn by astronauts, and this was topped off by a head gear with a pair of antennas; she looked like some outer-space creature from "Star Trek." While these dancers gyrated to a synthesized melody played over a heavy disco beat, the lead female singer stood before them wearing a colorful evening dress. Reminiscent of the traditional Chinese woman's garment know as "qipao," the neckline had a high, stiff collar, but it covered only one of her shoulders while the other was bare. Below this was a full-length and wide hoop-skirt. Holding a wireless microphone close to her mouth, the lead singer belted out her song. While the event had the visual effect of a Las Vegas spectacle, the lyrics of her song, which frequently declared "ai wo zhonghua" ("love my China"), immediately dispelled the illusion and made it clear that this was a spectacle made by the Chinese government for the Chinese people and for TV viewers of the world.

As if further to reinforce the patriotic message of the song and the official status of this production, a large corps of male dancers appeared on the stage, performing yangge (pronounced yahng ger, meaning "rice harvest dance"), a cultural product of the Yan'an years during the Chinese War of Resistance Against Japan (1937–1945) when members of the newly formed Chinese Communist Party (CCP) and their idealistic intellectual supporters set up their wartime headquarters in Yan'an, a desolate hill town situated in Shaanxi province in north-central China, as a base to conduct guerilla warfare against the invading Japanese forces. During the Yan'an period, the CCP was attempting to put into practice the theories of Marxism-Leninism and the emerging thoughts of Chairman Mao Zedong. These ideas advocated a revolution based on the practice of "class struggle," through which the establishment was to be pulled down and replaced by a leadership coming from the most downtrodden segment of the Chinese society, the peasants. Under the CCP leadership in Yan'an, far-reaching experiments took place to produce cultural products with a message of class struggle, based on cultural expressions of the peasants. Yangge, derived from a peasant dance accompanied by drums, gongs, and cymbals, was the most famous result of these cultural products. It became the icon of revolutionary idealism, patriotism, and class struggle after the CCP established the People's Republic of China (PRC) in 1949. Until the late 1950s, yangge was a stable feature in the programs of government sponsored song and dance troupes, and an integral part of the many anti-imperialist and anticapitalist parades and rallies. Students were required to practice yangge as compulsory extracurricular activity.

Beginning in the early 1980s, China ushered in a limited open-door policy and some measure of economic reform after the devastating Cultural Revolution (1966–1976), and social change became increasingly rapid. Because of a weak financial infrastructure, economic reform created many loopholes that allowed rampant official corruption, thus creating widespread discontent among the vast have-not segment of society. The students' demonstration at Tiananmen Square in 1989 gave expression to such discontent. The new open-door policy, initiated with the purpose of enticing foreign investment and of encouraging technological transfer from developed countries, also inadvertently brought in pop culture from outside. Pop and rock music from the West and from Japan, Hong Kong, and Taiwan, together with synthesizers and other paraphernalia, also became increasingly accessible to the mainland Chinese, and young people embraced these new forms eagerly. The dancers' and singer's performance on the millennium altar gave recognition to these new forms.

But along with these new influences, around the early 1990s, a revival of yangge performances began to take place in many old and ramshackle neighborhoods in the southern part of Beijing where most people had been left out of the new economic prosperity. The participants were primarily retired male and female workers (fifty-five years of age and above) who belonged to the generation that had witnessed and experienced the communist revolution. They organized neighborhood yangge clubs, and during the summer months members of these clubs danced yangge along street corners with the accompaniment of gongs, cymbals, and drums. The participants' enthusiasm was so great that the dance frequently lasted well after midnight, and the loud banging of the percussion could be heard miles away. The noise kept many people awake, and the many onlookers surrounding the dancers frequently blocked traffic. Whenever I was in Beijing during the summer, I often went to a southern Beijing neighborhood to watch the yangge dance. The atmosphere was very much like a carnival. The onlookers clapped their hands and moved their bodies with the rhythm of the beat and chatted with one another. Many Chinese political commentators paid acute attention to this phenomenon, interpreting it as a nostalgic expression for Yan'an idealism.

Unlike the retired workers dancing on the street corners in everyday clothes, the yangge dancers performing on the millennium altar wore light colored tunics tied with a red waistband, loose trousers, and red headbands in the traditional style of Chinese peasants, and each carried a small, two-headed barrel drum, suspended from his left shoulder and resting on his right side, which he beat with sticks. The drum is known as "you gu" (waist drum). The dancers beat their drums in a very showy way, while simultaneously performing acrobatic dance steps that involved high leaps and kicks and somersaults. The accompaniment provided by drums, cymbals, and gongs used simple but loud ostinato patterns, which were overlaid on the synthesizer music and the lead singer's patriotic song declaring "love my China." It was indeed a spectacle. To me, at least, the yangge dancing and the sound of the accompanying percussion really brought back memories of the early days of the People's Republic when I was a young student and was, like almost all young people in those days, thoroughly caught up with a revolutionary fervor. The Chinese spectators of the millennium show gave the yannge dancers a loud cheer, and many started to clap their hands and dance to the yangge beat.

Watching this spectacle on television on the eve of the millennium, I could not help recalling a very different scene on the Tiananmen Square in June of 1989, when thousands of Chinese university students demonstrated against official corruption and demanded greater democratic freedoms. Ignored by the government, the students went on a hunger strike. Before the tanks moved in successfully to crush the demonstration, the striking students, led by a student leader, sang in unison and in a low and dignified voice, the famous revolutionary song "Internationale." This song originated in France in the late nineteenth century during the Paris uprising popularly know as the Paris Commune. It was then adopted by the Bolsheviks in Russia for their revolutionary struggles, and eventually it became the signature song of world labor and communist movements. One of the founders of the Chinese Communist Party translated the lyrics of "Internationale" from Russian to Chinese in 1923, two years after the establishment of the Chinese Communist Party, as a signal of the Chinese communists' participation in the world communist movement. After that the "Internationale" was frequently sung in leftist gatherings at Yan'an during the war years, and after the establishment of the People's Republic in 1949 it was sung all over China. The beginning of the "Internationale" also inspired China's current national anthem, popularly know as "qi lai!" ("Arise!"). The lyrics of "Internationale" call forth the oppressed people of the world to rise to fight tyranny and state that internationalism based on a universal ideal of egalitarianism will prevail. In the charged context of the Tiananmen Square demonstration in 1989, however, the student-demonstrators' singing of this song could not possibly be interpreted as a celebration of these ideals, but rather, to my mind, as an ironic reminder to the leaders that they, yesterday's oppressed, had become today's oppressors.

Today, more then ten years after this incident, few Chinese care to talk about Tiananmen, even though human rights activists in the West continue to decry it. The twenty some years of economic restructuring have changed the outlook and aspiration of many Chinese people from that of political fixation to that of economic well-being. Young people, in particular, dream of making a lot of money and aping a version of a Western life style that concentrates on material consumption. Western inspired pop music is the choice of young people, and indigenous rock bands and pop bands have arisen in many cities. As the fierce 1999 demonstration in front of the U.S. Embassy in Beijing against the U.S. bombing of the Chinese embassy in Belgrade, Yugoslavia, has shown, however, there is a hardcore of modern Chinese nationalism in the psyche of Chinese people that could explode under provocation, and the veneer of political apathy is only skin deep. I find this ambivalent attitude well revealed in the nationalistic spectacle staged on the millennium altar with its many elements borrowed from the West.

The Creation of "Songs for the Masses" in Modern China

When I was a young student in the PRC in the early 1950s, the sole musical diet for my contemporaries and myself consisted of nothing but "Songs for the Masses." These songs, whose origins may be traced back to Western Protestant hymns and school songs, modern Japanese and Chinese school songs, Chinese folk songs, and Russian revolutionary songs, are short and simple, use the diatonic scale, and have texts that are sloganlike ideological messages of communism and nationalism. We sang these songs in music classes and numerous political rallies and demonstrations; we sang them during the labor sessions in the countryside that every student had to participate in; and we sang them in our leisure time to amuse ourselves.

Songs for the Masses had their foundation laid at the beginning of this century by educational reformers. At the outset of education reform, famous scholars and reformers like Kang Youwei (1858–1927) and Liang Qichao (1873–1929) had advocated the use of a new type of school song, with simple melodies and didactic texts, somewhat similar to those used in Western or Japanese schools, to inculcate a new ethic of discipline and nationalism. The reformers contended that traditional Chinese music was languid and passive and therefore unsuitable for school use. These opinions touched off a debate between the traditionalists and the reformers on the pros and cons of traditional music versus modern school music. The reformers' most representative views were summed up in a 1903 article entitled "On the Reform of Chinese Music," written by the pseudonymous Fei Shi. Fei Shi strongly attacked the two dominant kinds of traditional music: the yayue, or ritual music of the court, and the popular entertainment music of the theater. The yayue, said Fei Shi, was an antiquated vehicle of the state, bolstering the prestige and authority of the ruling monarch, and as such it had no relevance to the common people. The popular theatrical music, on the other hand, was too narrowly confined to entertainment and therefore also not suitable for the education of children. Fei Shi argued that China at this time of change needed to have her music reformed, or to create new music that would be accessible to a large segment of the Chinese people, including children, and capable of arousing in them a new morale of self-strengthening. Furthermore, he argued that China's habitual fondness for antiquity and disregard of things contemporary was suicidal, according to the evolutionary theory of social Darwinism. Fei Shi's view anticipated the development of modern Chinese music from the following decades up to our own time.

As didactic school songs were urgently needed when education reform first began in the beginning of the twentieth century, a selective adaptation of school songs from missionary schools in China and those from Japan brought back by Chinese students studying there was put into practice. By the end of the first decade of the century, however, Chinese songwriters, many of whom had received some elementary music training in Japan, began themselves to write didactic school songs. The three most notable were Zeng Zhimin (1879–1929), Shen Xingong (1869–1947), and Li Shutong (1880–1942), all of whom had been trained in Japan. The songs they wrote were simple and short, with a limited range and a square, march-like rhythm, and were predominantly syllabic, reflecting the influence of early Japanese school songs. The song texts have simple and direct messages concerned with patriotism, self-discipline, military readiness, and civic spiritedness, reflecting the national concerns of the Chinese intellectuals of that time. With these early songs, the modern genre of Chinese song emerged. In the following decades, the descendants of these didactic songs became the main musical diet of the majority of Chinese students.

After the fall of the Qing emperor in 1911 and the establishment of a republic in 1912 under the leadership of Dr. Sun Yat-sen, a parliament was formed. In the same year a new political party called the Guomindang (Kuomintang, or Nationalist Party, often abbreviated as KMT) was brought into being by Dr. Sun. Lacking an army, Sun was impotent to compete with the powerful new army chief, Yuan Shikai, the founder of the modern Imperial army who soon became the dictator of China. Yuan's death in 1915 left the central government in a weak position, and warlords came to power in various parts of China. In 1914, when World War I broke out, Japan on the allied side moved to take over the German concession in Shandong province in northern China, and in 1915 set before the central government in Beijing its Twenty-one Demands, which would have placed China under Japanese protection. Immediately, the Chinese people expressed their outrage in protests, demonstrations, and strikes. Songs denouncing Japanese aggression and the weak central government were part of the protest movement; they circulated widely in schools, universities, and nationwide demonstrations. The musical style of these protest songs resembled that of the didactic school songs, but what set them apart was the messages of the texts. Whereas the texts of school songs usually expounded the general principles of good citizenship, discipline, patriotism, and nationalism, those of the protest songs focused on the current political issues and used terse, sloganlike language. These protest songs may be regarded as the predecessors of the later political songs known as Revolutionary Songs, or "Songs for the Masses," which were developed by the Chinese communists.

In 1917 China entered World War I, declaring war on Germany in the hope of recovering Shandong province, then claimed by Japan. The confirmation of the Japanese claim to Shandong by the Western powers at the Versailles Peace Conference of 1919 brought a storm of protest in China. Protest songs denouncing the Conference and Western and Japanese imperialism immediately appeared and circulated in nationwide strikes and demonstrations. On May 4, 1919, the intellectual and political ferment culminated in a mass student demonstration at the National Peking University. This was the first time that the new intellectual class, educated along modern non-Confucianist lines, was able to make its mark on Chinese politics. The political activities and the intellectual currents set in motion by these modern students developed into a broad national intellectual awakening known as the May Fourth Movement.

The May Fourth Movement affected the development of modern Chinese music profoundly. The hub of the Movement was Beida (National Peking University), which under the administration of its remarkable and liberal Chancellor Cai Yuanpei (1867–1940) was fostering freedom of thought and education. Cai was a scholar well versed in the tenets of Confucianism as well as in Western philosophy; his thinking represented an attempt to synthesize the Chinese classical tradition and the libertarianism of the modern European West that characterized the May Fourth Movement. When he became Chancellor, Cai endeavored to create opportunities for the students to receive an aesthetic education that included music and art, which he maintained were essential subjects in modern education.

Like his contemporary Fei Shi, Cai felt that the reform of traditional Chinese music was necessary in order to bring it up to date, and that elements in Western music should be borrowed to modernize Chinese music. In 1916 Cai established at Beida an extracurricular music study group, staffed by both Chinese and Western teachers, which offered students instruction in Chinese and Western vocal and instrumental music; the teachers were also charged with the responsibility of finding ways to modernize traditional Chinese music. This music group eventually was reorganized and expanded to become China's first academic music department. Under the leadership of the composer Xiao Youmei (1884–1940), who was trained in Japan and Germany, this music department offered instruction in music theory, composition, as well as the academic study of music, in addition to instrumental and vocal instruction. Sharing Cai's enthusiasm and belief in modernizing Chinese music, Xiao pioneered in the reform of Chinese music by borrowing Western elements, notably harmony, and by so doing he put into musical practice for the first time the realization of the self-strengthening slogan of 1898, "Chinese culture as the essence, and Western learning for practical use."

Another development initiated at Beida during the May Fourth period that had significant implications for the future development of the field of Chinese musicology was the Folk-Song Campaign. Inspired by the Russian Narodniki Movement of the 1870s, it called for educated youth to go to the countryside to educate the peasants, and a group of Beida students did just that. Through the process of discovering rural problems, the young intellectuals encountered folk song and folk art (which were considered unworthy of attention by most of the members of the elites of the old regime); they came to recognize their value and realized that they were important areas to be studied. Out of these efforts eventually came the systematic collection and scholarly research of folk song, which laid the foundation for the future collection and study of other types of Chinese music and contributed to the development of the modern field of Chinese musicology.

The May Fourth Movement also affected the development of modern Chinese music by promoting the use of Chinese vernacular language as a written medium of communication in all fields, including scholarship, in place of the cumbersome literary Chinese that had continued as the language of literature and scholarship for millennia. Using the vernacular, the young writers introduced a new popular literature that emulated Western forms and spread it through numerous periodicals and newspapers. Inspired by this development, some songwriters began to set new vernacular poems to music. The pioneer in this endeavor was Zhao Yuanren (Y. R. Chao, 1892–1982), an internationally known linguist and a composer trained in the United States. Combining elements of traditional Chinese music with Western ones such as harmony, Chao wrote songs with vernacular poetic texts and piano accompaniment. He is now considered the creator of the modern Chinese art song.

One of the most enduring aspects of the May Fourth Movement was the change in the ideology of China's educated class, brought about by the attack upon Confucian values. Using newspapers and journals such as The New Youth, modern scholars condemned as tyranny the subordination of subject to ruler, of wife to husband, of son to father, and of individual to family, all of which were regarded as remnants of a feudal society. As the stories portrayed in the traditional Chinese musical theater adhered primarily to the values of the feudal society, a debate on the merits of the traditional theater was touched off by the journal's editors and contributors. Some writers advocated the total elimination of traditional theater; others advocated reform by emulating the theater of the West. Though these debates lasted only a few years (mainly from 1917 to 1919) and failed to produce any immediate, tangible reform, they may rightly be regarded as having initiated a lasting trend toward theater reform, which came to fruition after the establishment of the People's Republic in 1949 and reached a climax of extremism during the Cultural Revolution.

At the time of the May Fourth Movement, authoritarian parties were proving successful in Europe. The Fascists came to power in Italy during the period after World War I, and the Russian Revolution had just concluded with the triumph of the communist party there. Marxism-Leninism found adherents among many of the leading writers and thinkers of the May Fourth Movement; it also affected music activities. In 1921 members of a Marxist study group at Beida attempted to organize the railroad workers of Beijing and to introduce Marxism to them. They established an adult school and a recreation center for these workers, and the activities in these facilities included the teaching and singing of protest songs, which were later used in strikes by the workers.

The Chinese Communist Party (CCP) was founded in 1921 by a leader of the May Fourth Movement. There began a competition between the two groups, the KMT, or Nationalists, and the CCP, or Communists, for control of China that was to last for several decades.

By 1923 the impact of Marxism-Leninism on Chinese thought and on Chinese arts and music began to be felt. Arts and music are regarded by the Marxists as political tools for propaganda. The introduction of the "Internationale" (CD 1, #12) to China in 1923, a song closely identified with the European labor movement of the 1890s and with the Bolshevik Revolution in Russia, came to be regarded as the signal of China's entrance into the world communist movement.

The increase of Japanese aggression in China in the ensuing years stimulated many more protest songs against Japanese aggression, and Russian revolutionary songs began to be heard in leftist circles. The war of resistance against Japan from 1937 to 1945 stimulated a further outpouring of songs with patriotic themes; composers of all political persuasions joined forces to produce songs in support of the war. Through being sung in war films, many of these songs became very popular with general audiences, thus constituting a true mass medium. After the establishment of the People's Republic in 1949, the production of thousands of "Songs for the Masses" became one of the important functions of the propaganda machine, and one of the outstanding examples of the 1950s is "We Workers Have Strength" (CD 1, #13).

Western Art Music

Western art music has been imported to China since the early twentieth century. The first conservatory of music in China, the Shanghai Conservatory of Music, was founded in 1927. In the 1930s and 1940s a couple more conservatories of music were founded in Guangzhou (Canton) and Fujian province. In 1950, the CCP established the Central Conservatory of Music, first in Tianjin and then in 1958 moving it to Beijing.

Today, Western art music has a sizable audience in the big cities. Since the government instituted an open-door policy in the early 1980s, it has become rather common to have performances by visiting Western orchestras and virtuosi in big cities such as Beijing, Shanghai, and Guangzhou. Since the mid-1990s, big cities such as Beijing, Shanghai, and Guangzhou have built new concert halls with good acoustics. The audience for Western classical music performances is made up mainly of members of the modern educated classes, as well as influential government officials (called cadres in China) and their families. Tickets are quite expensive, yet they are always in great demand.

Some Chinese people genuinely enjoy Western art music, but others come to these performances with extramusical motives. For example, one of my friends, a university professor who had been to the United States as a visiting scholar recently, told me that he attends these concerts because they make him feel that he still has some link with the outside world; another friend, the daughter of a high official, told me that she likes to attend Western art-music concerts because they represent prestige and status.

I have often had opportunities to attend Western art-music concerts during my frequent visits to China in recent years. I particularly remember a concert in Beijing by a famous opera singer from the West, whose program consisted of arias from popular Italian operas such as *Madama Butterfly, La Traviata, Tosca,* and *Aida,* which are among the great favorites of Chinese concertgoers. Chinese audiences respond to performances of works like these with great enthusiasm. They applaud whenever they feel like it, which is often; they exchange appreciative remarks with their friends about the quality of the singing, often loudly; and they also move about a great deal during the performance. The singer graciously ignored all the commotion and gave a wonderful performance.

I remember thinking to myself: Someone must have informed the singer that most Chinese concertgoers, except the aficionados of Western art-music, are unaccustomed to listening to music in complete silence. The Chinese are used to talking and moving about a great deal during musical performances, because traditionally music has always served as background for a social gathering.

Popular Music

Shanghai, the modern metropolis of China, was the site where the first type of modern Chinese popular song, transmitted through recordings, radio, movie, and print, arose. Unlike Beijing, which is an ancient city and which has been China's political and administrative center for a long time, Shanghai is a young city built by foreigners as a colonial outpost on Chinese soil. The modern city of Shanghai, a port city on the banks of the Huangpu River, an estuary of the Yangzi River, was built in the mid-nineteenth century on a piece of farmland adjacent to the old Chinese walled town. This piece of land was ceded to the British after the Opium War (1839–1842), and on it the British built a Western-style city to serve as a toehold for commercial penetration to all parts of China. But China has also benefitted, for from here Western ideas and culture, including music, as well as technology and modern business practice were disseminated to all parts of China. Soon after modern Shanghai's establishment, people from other Western countries, such as Germany, France, Belgium, Russia, Italy, and the United States, as well as from Asian countries, such as India, Japan, Thailand, Vietnam, and the Philippines, all came to invest, live, and work here, thus vastly contributing to Shanghai's commercial and industrial development, and to its cosmopolitan atmosphere.

Right at the beginning, however, Chinese contributions to Shanghai's development were significant, both in the form of capital investment and of manpower. Large numbers of Chinese workers migrated to Shanghai to seek work in Shanghai's factories, providing a labor pool that fueled Shanghai's industrial development. Many could not find work, however, and the women among the unemployed frequently ended up as taxi-dance girls—women paid to dance with customers at cabarets for a short unit of time—or prostitutes. By the early decades of the twentieth century, Shanghai emerged not only as the financial, industrial, and cultural center of China and Asia, but also became Asia's entertainment mecca and a frontier for jazz in Asia. Shanghai served as the major distributing center of Hollywood movies in Asia, and it was also the home of China's domestic movie industry. Cinemas showing Hollywood or Chinese movies were everywhere. Shanghai became a hot tourist stop, and famous jazz musicians from the United States frequently made a stop in its cabarets. Many aspiring jazz musicians from Japan and the Philippines came to Shanghai to gain their first authentic lessons in jazz. Since the 1920s, the city was home to some twenty domestic radio stations, and the number grew rapidly. It was also home to some major Western owned recording companies in Asia, such as Columbia Records, RCA Victor, and the French Pathé Recording Companies that later became part of EMI.

The inhabitants of Shanghai led a hedonistic life style, as described vividly in a 1930s Shanghai guidebook for Western tourists, which I quote below:

> Whoopee! What odds whether Shanghai is the Paris of the East or Paris the Shanghai of the Occident? Shanghai has it own distinctive night life, and what a life! Dog races and cabarets, hai-alai and cabarets, formal tea and dinner dances and cabarets, the sophisticated and cosmopolitan French Club and cabarets, the dignified and formal Country Club and cabarets, prize fights and cabarets, theaters and cabarets, movies and cabarets, and cabarets–everywhere, hundreds of 'em! . . ." [*All About Shanghai*, Hong Kong: Oxford University Press, 1983 [1934–1935], p. 73]

Shanghai popular song, known in Chinese as "liuxing gequ" ("popular song"), is a quintessential product of this environment. Arising between the world wars, when Shanghai was at it peak, the Shanghai popular song constitutes a body of songs having lyrics in modern vernacular Mandarin—the lingua franca of modern China—

and melodies and rhythms of a cosmopolitan flavor with traces of Broadway and Hollywood hit tunes, jazz, Latin American rhythms like tango and rumba, as well as Chinese folk songs, urban ballads, and modern Chinese school songs.

The melodies of Shanghai popular songs were composed by Chinese composers, but the instrumentation in some recordings was the product of a small number of White Russian musicians in the employ of recording companies who escaped to Shanghai from Russia during the Bolshevik Revolution. These composers, Western or Chinese, drew their sound materials from Shanghai's cosmopolitan soundscape and created a huge body of songs of infinite variety catering to a diverse Chinese bourgeois audience with a multiplicity of taste.

The lyrics of the Shanghai popular song were frequently written by noted popular fiction writers and newspapermen of the day. Drawing on their knowledge of and familiarity with the modern metropolis, both its opulent and seedy sides, these lyricists created a body of lyrics that show a kaleidoscopic picture of modern city life and people, rich or poor, often with wit and verve.

Shanghai popular song served many functions. It made up the stable repertory for nightclub singers in cabarets for dancing, with the accompaniment of jazz musicians, many of whom were Filipinos. It was used as theme songs for Chinese song and dance movies, and through such exposure it was transmitted nationwide. In some radio stations broadcast recordings of Shanghai popular songs made up the bulk of the program; some radio programs also featured live performance by pop song stars singing audience-requested songs. These songs also served simply for individual enjoyment, and for this purpose many inexpensive pocket-size songbooks were mass produced and made readily available in neighborhood newsstands, drug stores, and book stores.

Recordings of Shanghai popular songs were manufactured and marketed primarily by Western owned recording companies in Shanghai who employed both Chinese and European staff. The most important manufacturer of these songs was the Pathé Recording Company, which eventually monopolized the market.

One of the most representative Shanghai popular songs is entitled "Ye Shanghai" ("Night Shanghai"); it was the signature song of the most popular star called Zhou Xuan, and ever since its appearance it has been considered the symbol of colonial Shanghai.

> Night Shanghai, Night Shanghai
> A city that never sleeps.
> Neon-lights blazing, car horns blaring,
> Singing and dancing in blissful oblivion.
> Look at her, smiling and welcoming,
> Who knows her sorrow and frustration?
> Leading a night life, paying for clothing, food and lodging,
> Getting drunk with alcohol, wasting youth recklessly.

Dawn arriving brings drowsiness, eyes heavy with sleep,
Everyone leaving for home,
The heart churning with the turning wheels,
Making a new environment, pondering the former night life,
As if waking up from a dream.

(Translation by Isabel Wong)

In "Night Shanghai," a brief instrumental introduction imitates the sounds of car horns and city traffic, after which comes the vocal part whose diatonic melody is arranged in the A–A–B–A scheme of Western popular song of the era. The jazzlike accompaniment is provided by a small band with prominent saxophone and piano parts in the rhythm of the foxtrot, one of the most popular dance steps of the time. In the lyrics, every index of modernity is there: automobiles, traffic, neon light, cabaret. A life style that typifies Shanghai night life is encapsulated: alcohol intoxication, dancing, and the taxi-dance girl—the many nationalities of women selling sex for a living who personified colonial Shanghai. In the last two lines the concept of a change to a new environment is introduced, and the song ends with the implication that the taxi-dance girl actually left the metropolis for a new environment—presumably the countryside—as if waking up from a bad dream. These two lines touched upon two recurrent themes in the cultural imagination of modern China: an ambivalence toward colonial Shanghai as both a site of modernity and of corruption and destruction; the other having to do with the city/country antithesis. The city is often presented in literature as a transient place of dislocation and loneliness, while the countryside represents enduring traditional values and a place of continuity. Shanghai popular song truly captures the spirit of its bygone era.

After the establishment of the PRC in 1949, the Shanghai popular song was censored and denounced as "the dregs of imperialism, colonialism, and capitalism." But outside of the PRC, fans of Shanghai popular songs continued to enjoy and circulate them. In the 1980s, the EMI Recording Company in Hong Kong reissued many of them on CDs to satisfy popular demand. Also in the 1980s, as China embarked on economic reform and ushered in a more tolerant attitude toward popular art, a small selection of Shanghai popular songs was allowed to be reissued by the government: the original jazzy accompaniments of many songs, however, were replaced by more insipid and square versions for synthesizer. Although technologically more modern, these new versions nevertheless demonstrated the government's continuing suspicion of the original sounds with their cosmopolitan symbolism and association with a discredited era. Coincidentally, as Shanghai struggles to reemerge as an international city, a Chinese film about colonial Shanghai, entitled "Night Shanghai" has recently been produced. The recording of Zhou Xuan's rendition of this song was used extensively as background music. Obviously, the symbolism of this song for Shanghai has not been forgotten as even a CBS news report recently attested, for when President Bill Clinton visited Shanghai on June 29, 1998, the CBS report began by showing a nightclub scene with many couples dancing to a female vocalist's rendition of "Night Shanghai."

After 1949, new popular songs, somewhat reminiscent of Shanghai popular songs, were produced in Hong Kong and Taiwan and were sung by local singers. In the 1970s, however, their popularity in Hong Kong was eclipsed by the rise of Cantonese popular songs known in the West as "Canto Pop," which was inspired by White rock of the 1950s and uses synthesizers for accompaniment.

Meanwhile, the late 1970s saw China emerge from the ruinous "Cultural Revolution" (1966–1976). Beginning in 1979, the Chinese government attempted to transform its centrally planned economy to one that borrowed some measures of a market economy, and it cautiously began to encourage private enterprises. In order to attract foreign investment, the government pursued an open-door foreign policy. Political pressure on the Chinese people, which used to be quite severe, became somewhat relaxed, and some influences from overseas were allowed to slip in. Beginning in the early 1980s, pop songs of Taiwan and Canto Pop from Hong Kong took mainland Chinese listeners by storm, particularly among the younger generation, and soon some mainland song writers began to emulate the style of these imported models.

The transformation and expansion of the Chinese economy also stimulated the growth of China's fledgling popular song industry. Encouraged and controlled by the government, China's popular song industry began to recruit and produce its own composers, lyricists, and singers, and to manufacture and market its own product. By 1984, Chinese popular music had definitely became commodified, relying on the government mass media such as radio and television broadcasts and government sponsored song and dance troupes for its dissemination and marketing, and its dominant concern was profit.

In the ensuing years, Chinese popular music proliferated, growing in strength and complexity, and began to vie for the market with Hong Kong and Taiwan imports. Drawing their musical inspirations directly from North American and European models such as jazz, blues, country, rock, and even Baroque music, new styles like disike (disco) and jingge (energy song) began to appear and gained widespread appeal.

In 1988, another new style called xibeifeng (northwestern wind) became extremely popular; its music is a combination of a disco beat and synthesized accompaniment with folk tunes of the loess plateau of northwest China, an impoverished region that had once been the cradle of the Communist revolution; its lyrics are set deliberately in a simple, unsophisticated, and bucolic language addressing issues of feudalism and backwardness in rural northwest China. These songs were appealing to many urban dwellers who were overwhelmed by rapid changes and inflation resulting from the economic reform, and who yearned for the simpler life style of a bygone time evoked in the folklike music and simple lyrics of the "northwestern wind."

Shortly after, there appeared another popular new style called qiuge (jail songs) whose provocative lyrics lament the fates of youthful convicts in labor reform camps and of the rusticated urban youth of the Cultural Revolution. The most enthusiastic consumers of jail songs were China's new urban private entrepreneurs who first emerged in the mid-1980s and who were at that time still a marginal group in Chinese society. Many private entrepreneurs were once convicted delinquents, or rusticated youth of the Cultural Revolution, and jail songs tell of their common experiences and serve as an emblem of their group identity.

In spite of their diversity, these many new styles of popular songs, dubbed collectively by the government as tongsu yinyue (light popular music), have one thing in common, that is, they are produced by a government sponsored popular music industry, and the messages they impart are politically correct and therefore, sanctioned by the government.

In contrast, there is a small group of "underground" rock musicians who first appeared on the scene around the mid-1980s. In spite of the government's disapproval and its efforts to marginalize rock music and musicians, Chinese rock nonetheless was able not only to survive but to attract a significant number of devoted young followers from the urban, educated circles. The most famous rock musician, Cui Jian, made his U.S. appearance in New York in September 1995.

Chinese rock traces its ancestry directly to Anglo-American rock in terms of melodic styles, rhythms, performing behavior, instrumentation, and ideology. The rock musicians compose their own music and write lyrics that are intensely personal. While a majority of the lyrics tends to focus on individual expression of strong inner emotion, others tend to address contemporary cultural and political issues in a deliberately idiosyncratic and ambiguous language.

Rock musicians and their audience form a very tight-knit social group. Concerts, never publicized and usually featuring many bands performing together, are named using the English word "parties." There are now about half a dozen bands in existence. Some label themselves as "zhong jinshu" (heavy metal), and others call themselves "benke" (punks).

INSTRUMENTAL PERFORMANCE AT A TEAHOUSE IN SHANGHAI

Traditional Chinese music includes instrumental music (both solo and ensemble), musical theatricals, and musical narratives. Each of China's three great topographical regions, northern, western, and eastern, has its own forms and styles of these genres.

One kind of traditional instrumental music I often go to hear in Shanghai is the chamber ensemble of winds and strings called Jiangnan sizhu. Jiangnan, meaning "south of the river" (the river being the Yangzi), is the designation for the Yangzi Delta region in southeastern China, of which Shanghai is a part. Si literally means "silk," and it denotes stringed instruments because strings used to be made of silk (nowadays the strings are usually made of steel for greater volume). Zhu literally means "bamboo," and it denotes wind instruments because they are made of bamboo.

Instruments belonging to the "silk" category include plucked strings, bowed strings, and struck strings. The plucked strings of the ensemble are one pipa (a pear-shaped, four-stringed plucked lute with a short, bent neck and twenty-four frets), one or two sanxian (a three-stringed lute with a long, fretless neck and an oval-shaped sound box), and one qinqin (a two- or three-stringed plucked lute with a long, fretted neck). The bowed strings are one or two erhu (two-stringed fiddles with hollow wooden cylindrical sound boxes having one side covered by snake-skin, Fig. 4–1). And the struck string is the yangqin (a dulcimer struck with a pair of bamboo sticks).

Instruments of the ensemble belonging to the "bamboo" category include one dizi (a transverse bamboo flute with six finger-holes, a mouth hole, and another hole

Figure 4–1 A Chinese visiting scholar playing the erhu at a Chinese New Year party at the University of Illinois at Urbana-Champaign.

Figure 4–2   Prof. Frederick Lau (University of Hawai'i) playing the dizi.

covered by a thin membrane which vibrates to give the instrument a reedy sound, Fig. 4–2), one xiao (an end-blown bamboo flute with five frontal finger-holes, one hole in the back, and a blowing hole on the top), and one sheng. (The sheng is a free-reed mouth organ made of a series of bamboo pipes arranged in a circle, each with a reed on its lower end, and all inserted into a base made of copper, wood, or gourd, to which a mouthpiece is attached. Two or more tones may be produced simultaneously on the instrument.)

The Jiangnan sizhu ensemble (Fig. 4–3) also includes an assortment of percussion instruments. These are: a small flat drum called the gu, a paired wooden clapper called the ban (the gu and ban are played by one person), a muyu, or "wooden fish" (a carved, hollow, wooden instrument struck with a pair of wooden sticks), and finally a pair of small hand-bells called pongzhong, which may be used in certain pieces in the repertory.

Jiangnan sizhu was formerly a favorite pastime of the gentry and educated classes of the urban centers in the Jiangnan region. There were many private clubs

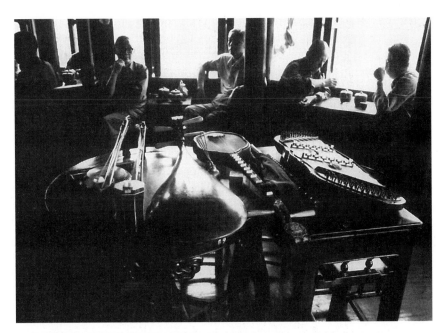

Figure 4–3   Instruments are put on tables before a performance; from **right** to **left**: the hammer dulcimer yanqqin, the plucked lute qinqin, the back of the plucked lute pipa, the two-stringed fiddle erhu, and an unidentified instrument.

where people gathered to play and while away a pleasant evening. As a rule, the performers of Jiangnan sizhu are amateurs; they perform not for payment but for their own enjoyment. In Shanghai today there are still half a dozen or so Jiangnan sizhu clubs whose members are retired urban workers; many belonged to the gentry class before 1949.

Jiangnan sizhu performances usually take place in neighborhood teahouses. The teahouse where I usually go to listen to Jiangnan sizhu is located in the Square of the Temple of the City God in the Old City of Shanghai, a picturesque area lined with many small shops selling all kinds of traditional wares and souvenirs. The old teahouse, always thronged with people, is an elegant structure built on an artificial lake teeming with goldfish, and it is approached via a zigzag footbridge. It is a hexagonal wooden building of two stories, lacquered with dark-brown paint, with intricate latticework windows open on all sides. It has double-tiered black tile roofs with elongated eaves swooping out in a complex pattern of upturned curves.

As an entrance fee, customers are required to pay a modest price for a pot of tea—they can choose their favorite kind of tea leaves—but there is no extra charge for the Jiangnan sizhu, which is played on the second floor every afternoon from 1:30 to 5:00. Tea is served to the customers seated at the dozen or so teakwood tables by a waiter who brings a very elegant, small, brown ceramic pot and matching cup. One may also order snacks such as watermelon or sunflower seeds.

Every afternoon before playing time, the players arrive one by one, place their instruments on a big table situated at one side of the teahouse, and then wander off to chat with friends, waiting for the rest of the ensemble to gather. Around 1:30, they sit down around the big table and start to play. The string players and the player of the drum and clapper sit in an inner circle, while the rest sit in an outer one. There is no conductor, but the player of the drum and clapper (gu ban) beats time. Everybody plays from memory, and no written music is used (Fig. 4–4).

There is no formal announcement of the program, nor are there program notes, for the audience is familiar with the small repertory, which consists of only about two dozen pieces that all have descriptive titles (the composers are anonymous). The first piece for the afternoon is always a short, slow, and simple piece, and is always played by novices. Pieces played during the afternoon progress from simple to complex. Each piece usually lasts ten minutes or more, and some may be played more than once. After one piece is finished, some players may get up from the table, and other players sitting among the customers may come up to the big table to join

Figure 4–4   A Jiangnan sizhu performance; the instruments are (**counterclockwise right from front**): the horizontal flute dizi, the hammer dulcimer yanqqin, the end-blown flute dong xiao, the plucked lute pipa, the mouth organ sheng, the two-stringed fiddle erhu (partially shown), the percussion muyu slit drum, and the plucked lute qinqin (partially shown).

the performers. There is no formal intermission between pieces. Around 4:30, the most skillful and respected players of the club will join in to perform pieces that are fast and require great skill.

When the novices are not playing, they usually sit around the big table listening to and watching the more skilled players. This is how the music is transmitted. There is no formal instruction, and learning is entirely by imitation. When it is felt that some novices are ready to join the more skilled players to play complicated pieces, they will be asked to do so. After they have finished playing a piece, the skilled players will give them criticism or suggestions.

Like most traditional Chinese instrumental music, Jiangnan sizhu pieces always begin slowly and gradually accelerate, ending in a fast tempo. The piece "Hua San Liu" ("Embellished Three-Six" CD 1, #14) is a good example. In this and other pieces of the repertory, there are no fixed tempo indications associated with any of the pieces; the tempi are left up to the discretion of the players. The drum-and-clapper player is supposed to provide the beat for the music, but the players typically are not overly concerned with rhythmic exactitude.

As in other pieces of Jiangnan sizhu, in "Hua San Liu" all the instruments play together most of the time. The overall timbral quality of this music is a combined strings-and-winds sound (the strings being plucked, bowed, and struck) in a relatively high register. A variety of musical temperaments exists because individual instruments are tuned differently. The resultant sonic quality of the melody is slightly fuzzy and thick, which is characteristic of traditional Chinese music.

When I first heard Jiangnan sizhu music, I could discern no break within a given piece; it seemed to me that, once started, it went on without break until the end. I later found out that every piece is divided into sections, but because the end of a section is always overlapped by the beginning of the next, a piece usually gives the impression of being seamless.

Another characteristic of Jiangnan sizhu, I later learned, is the extensive use of improvised embellishments on the basic melody. Every melodic instrument plays the same basic melody, but each player applies the improvised embellishments according to the idiomatic conventions of that instrument, creating a complicated texture of heterophony, which—like the variations in tuning—gives a kind of "thickness" to the melody. Because of this freedom in adding improvised embellishments, no two performances of one piece are exactly alike, and the more skilled the performers, the greater the differences may be.

The teahouse where Jiangnan sizhu is performed is always noisy. The customers chat among themselves and some of them play chess, while others come and go during the performance. The waiters crisscross between tables constantly, bringing tea to new customers and adding hot water to pots whose lids have been left open—an unspoken sign they are quick to notice. The players are oblivious to the commotion, and when some of them are not playing they also chat with their friends. Jiangnan sizhu, like many other kinds of traditional Chinese music of a popular nature, is considered a kind of background music to enhance the ambience of a pleasant social environment.

THE QIN AND ITS MUSIC

The qin (pronounced "chin"), a seven-stringed zither, is the most highly regarded of Chinese musical instruments because of its antiquity and its rich legacy of associations with scholars and poets. Made from a hollowed, slightly convex board approximately four feet long and eight centimeters deep, the qin has seven strings of varying thickness stretched over the entire length of the board. It has neither frets nor bridges. The most common tuning is C–D–F–G–A–c–d. The body is painted with layers of lacquer. Thirteen studs or position markers, called hui, made of mother-of-pearl or other semiprecious material, are embedded along the outer edge of the instrument and indicate finger positions for stopping the strings. The flat, smooth underside of the instrument has two openings called "sound pools" and is usually engraved with the name of the owner and the given name of the instrument. This indicates that the qin is a highly personalized instrument (Fig. 4–5).

Qin playing involves various ways of plucking the strings with the fingers of the right hand (except the little finger) and stopping them with the fingers of the left hand (except the little finger), as well as the use of ornaments such as portamento,

Figure 4–5   The famous qin master, the late Professor Wu Jing-le, giving a qin lesson to his student at the Central Conservatory of Music in Beijing.

vibrato, mordent, glissandi, and harmonics. Around the sixth century C.E., a type of directions for qin playing was devised, which explained in detailed prose the techniques required for producing each and every sound; this type of prose tablature is known as wenzipu (prose tablature). Later, in the Tang dynasty (618–906 C.E.), a new type of tablature was created that consisted of clusters of abbreviated symbols derived from Chinese characters; these specified the string number, the stopping positions, and the hand, finger, and direction of plucking. This tablature is called jianzipu (abbreviated-character tablature), and its later form is still in use today.

The qin enjoys great prestige because all through Chinese history it has been associated with sages and scholars. The earliest mention of the qin is found in the Shujing (Book of History), which contains references to the many ideas and concepts associated with the qin that were further developed later. Learning the qin was already a requirement for scholars and gentlemen before the third century B.C.E. At that time, however, the qin was employed primarily to accompany poetry recitation, as a member of the large orchestra for the court ceremonial music known as yayue (elegant music) or to form a duet with the se (a twenty-stringed plucked zither). A duo of qin and se symbolized a harmonious spousal relationship or friendship. After the Han dynasty (206 B.C.E.–290 C.E.), as ceremonial music at court gradually declined, the qin emerged as both a solo instrument and the accompanying instrument for chamber vocal genres. During the end of the Han period and thereafter, the literati initiated the scholarly study of the qin and wrote compositions specifically for the solo qin, and thus its status and prestige were established. In the subsequent periods of the Sui and Tang dynasties and the Five Dynasties (581–618, 618–907, 907–960), the playing of qin and qin scholarship were restricted to court circles only; outside of the court, the qin was neglected.

It was not until the Song dynasty (960–1027) that there was a renaissance of qin music. An ideological system for the qin was developed by fusing Confucian philosophy with Daoist (Taoist) and Buddhist mystical symbolism. According to this ideology, the playing of the qin is an act of contemplation, self-purification, and self-regulation; hence it should be played in private, amidst charming scenery, under pine trees and beside running creeks, in the privacy of one's garden, or in the cloister of one's own library with incense burning.

The qin vogue among the scholars reached its height in the Ming dynasty (1368–1644), when numerous treatises and handbooks of qin music were printed. Prince Zhu Quan, the sixteenth son of the first Ming emperor, was a qin scholar and the first person to print a qin handbook in 1425. But in the early twentieth century, rapid social change brought about a sharp decline in interest. Good qin players were very few, and qin scholarship came to a virtual halt. After the establishment of the People's Republic in 1949, under government encouragement, research in qin music and its history reached a higher level of competence, particularly during the 1950s. In recent years, the qin has been brought into the new context of the modern concert stage; and with the appearance of a younger generation of qin virtuosi, interest in the qin has been revived among members of the educated circle. Among the general populace, however, the qin, with its associations with past literary and philosophical traditions, is too exclusive and inaccessible and has, therefore, been totally neglected.

The earliest extant qin manuscript, dating from the Tang dynasty, contains the composition "Youlan" ("Orchids in a Secluded Valley"), which is written out in prose tablature. The first printed qin handbook, the *Shenqi mipu* (The Mysterious Secret Handbook), compiled by Prince Zhu Quan of Ming, appeared in 1425 and was followed by numerous other woodblock handbooks, together comprising more than three thousand compositions notated in the abbreviated-character tablature. Only about eighty pieces, however, have survived in the oral performance tradition.

In qin handbooks tempo is indicated by terms such as "Slow down," or "Speed up," but durational symbols are totally absent. Such omissions indicate the importance placed upon oral tradition and the realization and interpretation of the music by the performing artist. A process of reconstructing ancient pieces from qin tablature through the aid of oral tradition is called dapu (literally, "to obtain from the notation"). This recreating process, done by the qin player, has been a venerable qin composition/realization tradition. Qin meters vary among free meter, duple meter, and sometimes triple meter, often within the same piece.

Qin notation is very difficult to read, even for those who are literate and cultivated, and this contributes to the exclusive nature of the qin. In the famous eighteenth-century novel *The Story of the Stone* (also known as The Dream of the Red Chamber) by Cao Xueqin (d. 1763), there is a passage that conveys this well. This greatest of Chinese novels depicts in meticulous detail life in a very wealthy and influential family, in particular the love and fate of the hero Jia Baoyu and his cousin Lin Daiyu, two extremely talented, cultivated, and precocious teenagers. In Chapter 86, Baoyu seeks Daiyu out in her quarters and learns something about qin tablature and the philosophy of the qin although his wry concluding comment seems to indicate he takes it all with a grain of salt.

Daiyu was sitting at her desk reading. Baoyu approached her, saying cheerfully, "I see that you left Grandmother's place early." Daiyu responded with a smile and said, "Well, you wouldn't speak to me, so why should I stay any longer?"

"There were so many people there, I didn't have a chance." As he replied he tried to see what she was reading, but he couldn't recognize a single word. Some looked like the character for "azalea," some looked like the character for "hazy." Some had the radical "big" on the left, the character for "nine" next to it, and a large hook underneath them with the character for "five" written inside. . . .

Baoyu was curious and puzzled. He said, "Sister, I am more and more impressed by you. You must be reading a secret Book of Heaven!"

Daiyu couldn't help laughing. "Here is an educated man! Don't tell me you have never seen a musical score!"

"Of course I have," he replied, "but I don't know any of those characters. . . . Why don't you teach me to read some of it? . . . For example, what do you make of this character 'big' with that long hook and a character 'five' stuck in the middle?"

With a laugh Daiyu replied, "This character 'big' and the character 'nine' mean that you press on the ninth stud with your left thumb, and this big hook with the character 'five' inside means that you hook inward the fifth string with your right hand. This whole cluster is not a word; it stands for a musical note. There is really nothing to it. You have also many kinds of left-hand techniques such as the quick vibrato, broad vibrato, upward glide, downward glide, trill, quick glide, and so forth."

Baoyu was hopping with joy, saying, "Come on, dear sister, since you know so much about it, why don't we try it out?"

"It is said that the zither is synonymous with the word for self-restraint. The ancients intended it to be used for discipline, for tranquilizing one's emotions, and for suppressing excessive and frivolous desires. In playing the zither, you must select a quiet and secluded place. It could be in the top story of a building, in the forest among the rocks, at a mountain precipice, or at the edge of the water. The weather should be calm, with a light breeze or a clear moon. You have to burn some incense and meditate for a while. . . .

"As to the performance itself, the fingering and the intonation have to be good enough . . . the position of your heart should be in a line with the fifth stud on the instrument. . . . Now you are ready, bodily, and spiritually. . . ."

Baoyu said, "Can't we just do it for fun? It's next to impossible if we have to go through all that rigmarole!"

(Adapted from a Translation by Rulan Chao Pian)

Practically all qin compositions have programmatic titles either deriving from common poetic and mystical images or alluding to Chinese history or legends. The titles serve to evoke a mood or atmosphere familiar to the Chinese.

A typical qin composition usually contains several sections. The first part, known as sanqi (introduction), begins slowly in free rhythm. Its function is to introduce the principal notes of the mode used in the following particular piece. In the second part, known as rudiao (entering the music, or exposition), the meter is established and the principal motives of the piece are introduced, which are then varied by means of extension, reduction, and changes in timbre, tempo, and register. This part is usually the longest and musically the most substantial. During the third part, known as ruman (becoming slower), the principal motives undergo further rhythmic variation, and modulation to other keys may occur. In some larger compositions, motivic materials occuring in the second part may be restated and reinterpreted here; this is called fuqi (restatement). Finally, in the fourth part, a short coda known as weisheng (tail sounds) concludes the composition. The coda, always played in harmonics and in a slackening tempo, reiterates the important notes used in the composition.

The famous qin piece "The Drunken Fisherman" (CD 1, #15) is constructed in a four-part structure based on themes of a variation scheme. It consists of six stanzas with a coda. Stanza one, the "introduction," introduces two of the three basic themes in two basic tonal centers, the second one is a fourth above the first. Stanzas two, three, four, and five constitute the "exposition"; in stanza two all three themes, appearing in their entirety and in sequence for the first time, are introduced in the second tonal center; and these three themes undergo further tonal variations, expansion, and reduction in stanzas three, four, and five. Stanza six is the "restatement" in which the three themes are reinterpreted in different rhythmic configuration. Finally, in the coda, themes one and two come to an abrupt ending, followed by new materials in a slow and staggering rhythm, and at the end there is a passage in harmonics.

THE PIPA AND ITS MUSIC

The pipa is a four-stringed, fretted Chinese lute with a bent neck. It was introduced to China from Persia through present-day Afghanistan and India around the fourth century C.E., and became extremely popular from the seventh century C.E. onward. All through its history the pipa, an instrument associated with music for artistic entertainment rather than for ceremonies and rituals, has been played as a solo instrument, as a member of an instrumental ensemble, and to accompany musical narrative and drama.

The pipa is placed upright on the player's crossed knees and played with the fingers. The strings are usually tuned to A–d–e–a, and the entire chromatic scale can be produced. The pipa player employs a large variety of playing techniques, the most distinctive of which are: harmonics, a tremolo produced by rapidly and continuously plucking a string with all five fingers consecutively, a portamento produced by deflection of a string before or after it has been plucked, a percussive pizzicato produced when a string is plucked violently enough to cause it to snap against the body of the instrument, and a percussive strumming of all four strings.

The music of pipa, characterized by flexible tempi and frequent use of crescendo-diminuendo, encompasses many moods ranging from the contemplative and the lyrical to the heroic and even to the comical. Chinese musicians divide the pipa repertory into two categories according to structure: the "big pieces," and the "small pieces."

"Big pieces" are usually quite long, and there are three kinds: (1) pieces that are not divided into sections but are continuous; (2) pieces having many sections that follow a theme and variation structure whose themes derive from preexistent materials; and (3) pieces having many sections alternating songlike material with percussive material.

"Small pieces" are usually quite short, each containing about sixty to one hundred beats or so. Most of these pieces are in sectional form.

Pieces in the traditional pipa repertory are also divided into the wen (lyrical) and the wu (martial, percussive) categories. Wen category pieces are lyrical and expressive in nature in a slow or moderate tempo, and they tend to employ various kinds of finger techniques to produce embellishments and microtonal changes. Wu category pieces tend to be percussive and often loud and in fast tempo: fast strumming techniques are often employed to produce a martial effect.

Sectional pipa pieces, be they "big" or "small," frequently employ a rondo-variation principle in which basic melodic material returns periodically, but in a more improvisational manner than is usual in the Western rondo or variation form.

Pipa pieces usually have programmatic titles and some of these contain clearly descriptive musical elements directly related to their titles; others, however, are more abstract and have only a poetic relationship to their programmatic titles.

Pipa notation combines symbols indicating pitches of the diatonic scale and an additional set of symbols indicating various finger techniques. There are approximately a dozen printed collections of music for the pipa, the earliest of which date from the early nineteenth century. Prior to that time, music for pipa circulated in manuscripts, some of which still exist today. Notation has always been a secondary aid for the transmission of the repertory, as it exists primarily in oral tradition.

In traditional society, pipa playing was usually performed in an intimate surrounding, either in a private banquet or in a teahouse. Nowadays, pipa performance usually takes place in a modern concert hall. The pipa tradition is still very vital today. Many young pipa virtuosi are being produced in China.

PROMINENT FEATURES IN CULTURE AND MUSIC

In the foregoing descriptions of performances of music in varying contemporary Chinese contexts, I have already touched on some salient features of Chinese music and of Chinese attitudes toward music and music performance. In the following I shall give a more detailed description of these features under separate headings.

The Value and Functions of Music

Since ancient times, the Chinese have equated enjoyment of music with the natural human desire for aesthetic and sensual gratification such as the taste for food, the need for sex, and the satisfaction of seeing beautiful things. Music has traditionally been treated as one of the component phenomena that make up an environment for living. Thus, music has not only served as a means of expressing emotions such as joy and sadness or as a vehicle for spiritual or religious contemplation, but it has also always been integrated into events such as rituals, banquets, weddings, funerals, festivals, harvest celebrations, and so forth. In addition, music has always been conceived of as an integral part of other performing arts such as dance and drama. Furthermore, reference to some types of music has conventionally been used to evoke certain moods and atmospheres in literature, poetry, and painting. This complex and integral view of music and its functions had already become well established in the Zhou dynasty in the first millennium B.C.E.

Kong Fuzi, or Master Kong (551–479 B.C.E.), known to the West as Confucius, who founded the school of philosophy (popularly called Confucianism) that had the greatest effect on subsequent Chinese thought, maintained that music has positive and negative power to stimulate allied behavior and desire. Positive music, or shi yin (proper sound), which he believed to have attributes of harmoniousness, peacefulness, and appropriateness, was to Confucius an important educational tool capable of inspiring virtue and appropriate attitudes; whereas negative music, or chi yue (extravagant music), which had the attributes of inappropriate loudness (like thunder and lightning) and wanton noisiness, stimulated excessive and licentious behavior.

Confucius, who lived during the end of the Zhou period in a time of constant warfare and chaos, sought to restore China to the peaceful feudalism of the early Zhou years, but felt that the only way the hierarchical system could be made to work properly was for each person to correctly perform his assigned role. "Let the ruler be a ruler and the subjects be subjects," he said, but he added that to rule properly a king must be a virtuous person, setting an example of proper ethical conduct. To Confucius, social stratification was a fact of life to be sustained by morality, not force. He laid much stress on the possibility of remolding men's minds through education (in which music and dance were important parts of the curriculum), and taught that proper inner attitudes could be inculcated through the practice of rituals (which, to be effective, must have proper ritual music) as well as through the observance of rules of etiquette and decorum.

In the twentieth century Mao Zedong, Chairman of the Communist Party from 1949 to 1976, like Confucius, viewed music and the arts as important educational tools. But Mao's practical application of this view was vastly different from that of the Confucianists. To Mao, music and the arts were important tools in the propagation of state ideology. Couched in the language of Marxism-Leninism as interpreted by Mao, the state ideology plays a key political role in the People's Republic; it defines, explains, and rationalizes the whole range of human activities and thinking in the society. Endowed with the sanctity of unchallenged truth, the state ideology constitutes the basis and substance of political values and is buttressed by the fullest extent of coercive power inherent in a sovereign political system. Few in China are able to ignore the all-pervasive influence of ideology. Propagation of ideology is a premier function of the Communist Party acting on behalf of the state, and music and the arts are important components of this propaganda machine.

Mao, like Confucius, also defined music as being of proper and improper kinds. The proper or "correct" kinds are those that have been sanctified by the state and which contain "correct" ideological messages. The "Songs for the Masses" that I sang as a student in the various politically charged contexts I have described belong to this kind. (When the students in the pro-democracy movement of the spring of 1989 sang these sanctioned songs at Tiananmen Square, the irony, to me at least, was inescapable—the students were singing these songs of high-flown political rhetoric to remind the Communist Party and the state of their failures and unkept promises after forty years of rule.) Improper kinds of music are those which have been construed by the state to contain "poisonous" influence, either from the discredited "feudal" society of the past or from the capitalistic, decadent West, and as such they must be censored or eliminated. The pre-1949 popular liuxing gequ, and the more recent Chinese rock certainly belong to the "poisonous" category.

Authorship and the Creation Process

Only a few traditional Chinese pieces have any attributed authorship. The sources for most traditional Chinese music were anonymous folk or popular materials transmitted orally or through written notation in manuscripts rather than printed books, and the idea of an original composition identified with a particular person was foreign to the Chinese before the twentieth century. This may have something to do with the traditional method of composition, which involved rearrangement of often anonymous preexistent materials, resulting in a newly recomposed version of the older model. The rearrangement process, however, is genre-specific; that is to say, each genre has its own procedures and rules regarding rearrangements.

Some genres of music require a measure of improvisation during performance, such as the adding of improvised embellishments simultaneously in Jiangnan sizhu, which I have already described. By adding improvised embellishments and varying the dynamics and tempi of the music according to established conventions during a performance, and most important of all by extending or subtracting portions of the thematic materials in a spontaneous fashion, a performer is in fact acting as a composer as well.

With the introduction of Western ideas to China in the twentieth century came also the Western musical repertory, compositional processes, and techniques, and the idea of composership. Like their Western counterparts, modern Chinese composers nowadays regard themselves as individual creators of original music; the idea and emotion associated with a particular piece of music are regarded as the unique, individual expression of the composer alone.

Amateur and Professional Musicians

Before 1949 the status of a musician was determined by his education and his occupation. Professional musicians, who relied on music for their livelihood and usually had little formal education, had rather low social status, particularly those who performed entertainment music catering to members of the unlettered class. Unlike the professional musician, the amateur who did not rely upon making music for a livelihood but was accomplished in music, well educated, and cultivated was regarded as the ideal gentleman. In Chinese history, many distinguished amateur musicians such as players of the qin, who usually came from the leisure class, were given high acclaim as musicians and mentioned in historical documents. Records of professional musicians, on the other hand, were few and far between until the twentieth century.

After 1949, the Communist government endeavored to create a classless society, and the stigma on professional musicians was removed. For nationalistic and propagandistic purposes, many forms of traditional entertainment music and folk music that had been frowned upon by orthodox Confucians in the past were elevated as China's national heritage, and the status of their practitioners was also elevated as a result. The government established many modern conservatories, whose curricula included Western art music as well as traditional Chinese music. Distinguished performers of traditional music, both amateur and professional, were hired as equals to teach in these conservatories.

REGIONAL STYLES

Although the Chinese people are relatively homogeneous, China comprises diverse ethnic groups and languages, and the many regional styles of Chinese music reflect this diversity. The Han ethnic community, which accounts for 95 percent of the population, speaks a number of related Sinitic languages that are known collectively as Chinese, of which the major form is Putonghua (Mandarin); other forms are Wu, Xiang, Min, Hakka, and Yue (Cantonese). These various forms are mutually unintelligible when spoken, but the use of a common written language and ideographic writing system enables any literate Chinese to communicate with any other. The rest of the Chinese population is made up of some sixty groups of non-Han people, the "minority nationalities" (chief among them the Tibetan, Mongol, Hui, Korean, Manchu, and Miao), whose homelands have been absorbed by the Chinese state. The languages of the minority nationalities also are unintelligible both to the other groups and to the Chinese, and each group has very distinctive musics which we do not have space to touch on here.

Musically, each major linguistic region possesses its own vocal styles and forms. The major types of vocal music of the Han, such as musical narratives and musical theatricals, have been profoundly influenced by the linguistic characteristics of each region. According to Chinese statistics, there are about 317 regional dramatic genres in China today. Instrumental music is also regional in character; for example, the Jiangnan sizhu is predominantly a genre of the Jiangnan region, while the Fujian province in the south has its own instrumental ensemble style called the Fujian nanqu (Fujian music ensemble), and the Guangdong province in the deep south has its own Guangdong yinyue (Guangdong music ensemble). Some of the same instruments, however, are used in most major instrumental ensembles, for instance, the dizi (transverse flute) and the yangqin (dulcimer).

In spite of the regional differences, there are some common stylistic characteristics shared by music of various regions, and one of the reasons for this commonality is the extensive borrowing of musical styles from region to region. When a particular regional style like the famous Peking opera becomes widely adopted throughout the country, a national style is formed.

The Musical Theater JINGJU

Jingju, meaning "the theater of the capital" (i.e., Beijing) is the proper name for the well-known Chinese musical theater in the West commonly called "Peking Opera." This is a rather misleading name, because singing, though a prominent feature in Jingju, is by no means the sole feature as in Western opera. Crystallized into the form we know today around the mid-nineteenth century, Jingju is a form of musical theater combining plots, stylized gestures and movements, acrobatics, fanciful makeup, elaborate costumes, and simple props into a unified whole; it is a conglomeration of several northern and southern regional music-theater styles from Beijing. It is a sophisticated genre offering diverse attractions such as virtuosic singing in romantic scenes involving young lovers, stylized battle scenes on land or at sea featuring breathtaking acrobatic skills, comical slapstick often having the bite of political satire, and dramatic scenes having themes of betrayal and revenge, retribution, and the triumph of loyalty and justice. Since its inception in the mid-nineteenth century, the Peking opera theater has been enjoyed by a wide spectrum of Chinese audiences all over the country.

The sources of the plots of Peking opera come mainly from popular legends, historical events, novels, and other narratives. At present there are some two hundred traditional plays in the repertory that are still performed frequently, and new plays are also occasionally created. The nature of the individual plays varies; depending on their purpose or focus, the Chinese classify them as lyrical plays, warrior plays, acrobatic plays, virtuosic vocal plays, virtuosic acting plays, and so forth.

Personages in Peking opera are divided into five main categories and their subcategories according to sex, age, social status, and character. Each role type is defined by the costumes and makeup the actor wears. All the characters sing, but each employs distinct vocal techniques, timbres, and singing styles. The characterization of each role is thus defined by costumes, makeup, and timbral quality and style of singing and speech. The five main categories and their subcategories are described as follows:

1. Sheng: Male role.
   a. Xiaosheng: A young-male role; usually a romantic and dandyish scholar. A xiaosheng actor must have a good singing voice; he sings in a delicate manner and uses both falsetto and chest voice.
   b. Laosheng: A major old-male role; usually a serious, loyal, and just character who may be royalty, a minister, or a respected family retainer. A laosheng actor must possess good singing and acting skills; he sings with chest and throat voice, and his singing style should be steady and vigorous.
   c. Wusheng: Male warrior; someone with consummate acrobatic ability and extremely skilled with sword and spear. A wusheng actor sings with a throaty voice; acrobatic skills, however, are more important than singing ability.

2. Dan: Female role.
   a. Qingyi: A major female role for a mature woman. Qingyi literally means "blue gown"; the sedate color of her gown exemplifies the Confucian ideal of virtuous womanhood. A

qingyi character sings in falsetto voice exclusively, in a steady and delicate manner and with clear articulation. He (i.e., a female impersonator) or she must be a consummate singer as well as a good actor or actress (Figs. 4–6, 4–7).

b. Huadan: Young female role; usually a frivolous, flirtatious young lady, a prostitute, or a pert young maid. A huadan sings in falsetto voice in a manner full of infectious nuances and innuendos and must possess both good singing and good acting skills.

c. Daomaodan: Female warrior; someone with acrobatic skills.

d. Laodan: Old female.

3. Jing: Painted-face role; played by a male whose face is painted with intricate colored patterns indicating his character and psychological makeup; a heroic character who may be a general or a leader of a rebel or bandit group. A jing character sings with a throaty voice and in a very forceful manner (Fig. 4–8).

4. Mo: A minor old-male role.

5. Chou: Male comic role; someone with quick wit and verbal skills who is also a good mimic. A chou actor does not sing very often, and when he does, it is usually in an exaggerated and ironical manner.

Figure 4–6   Performance of a scene from the Peking Opera play Huan Shan Lui (Tragedy in the Deserted Mountain) in Beijing. The role-types are (**from left to right**): the dan role (qingyi, or "bluegown"); the actor is the well-known female impersonator Zhao Rongshen, the wa wa sheng role (male child role), and the jing role (painted face role).

Figure 4–7   A dan role (young female) played by Hua Wenyi, National Heritage Awardee, in a scene of the romantic play Mou dan ting (Peony Pavilion).

The basic musical elements of Peking opera are arias, musical speech, and instrumental music. These elements, together with movements, are systematically organized into a simple structure making up a play. In the following, the individual musical elements are discussed in some detail.

Instrumental music in Peking opera has many functions first and foremost, to accompany the singing and the physical movements and dance. To an audience familiar with the conventional musical code of Peking opera, it may also describe a dramatic situation and action, indicate the spatial dimension of the setting, convey the moods and psychological makeup of characters, and provide soundscape or sound effects connected with a particular dramatic moment. With musical clues, an educated Peking-opera audience will be able to form a mental picture of the temporal and spatial aspects of the drama and respond to it with appropriate emotion and understanding.

The instrumental ensemble is made up of two components: the melodic, or wenchang (civic instrumentation) ensemble, and the percussion, or wuchang (military instrumentation) ensemble. In the musical communication of information, the percussion ensemble plays a more important function than the melodic ensemble. In addition, the percussion ensemble also provides rhythmical punctuation for movements and singing, and it serves to combine all the discrete elements of a play, musical as well as gestural, into a complete whole.

Figure 4–8   The jing role (painted face) actor in the ghost play Zhong Kuei Jai Mei (Zhong Kuei Marrying His Sister).

The percussion ensemble is made up principally of five instruments: danpigu (a single-headed drum), ban (a paired wooden clapper; danpigu and ban are played by one person, who functions as the conductor), daluo (a big gong that produces a falling pitch), xiaoluo (a small gong that produces a rising pitch), and naoba (a small pair of cymbals). In addition, there are a few other percussion instruments for special effects: datangu (a big barrel drum), xiaotangu (a small barrel drum), several other gongs and cymbals of different sizes, a muyu (a "wooden-fish" slit drum), and a pair of small handbells (Fig. 4–9).

The music of the percussion ensemble includes some sixty conventional rhythmic patterns, each of which is identified by a proper name and a specific onomatopoeic syllabic pattern. The five principal instruments are combined in different ways to indicate different kinds of dramatic situations, atmospheres, or moods. There are three basic percussion combinations.

1. A trio made up of the big gong, the small gong, and the cymbal, with the big gong being the principal instrument. This combination is usually employed in scenes of pageantry featuring a big crowd of actors, and also in dramatic scenes that require strong emphasis.

Figure 4–9   Students of the Peking Opera percussion ensemble at a training academy in Beijing rehearsing. The instruments are (from **left** to **right**): small gong, cymbals, gong, drum and clapper (hung on the drum stand).

   2.   A duo made up of the cymbal, as the principal instrument, and the small gong. This combination usually accompanies tragic scenes.
   3.   A small gong solo. This is generally used in scenes of a tranquil or lyrical nature.

Besides these basic combinations, other additional combinations include a duo of the big and small barrel drums (used in acrobatic and fighting scenes), a duo of the small gong and the big cymbal (played in a specific way to indicate underwater and thunder sounds), and so forth.

   The sixty-or-so named conventional percussion patterns, each requiring different instrumental combinations and varying tempi, perform many functions. The most common are:

   1.   to indicate entrances and exits of dramatic personages and their social status;
   2.   to indicate and emphasize certain emotional situations;
   3.   to emphasize a word, a phrase, a person's name, or a place name;
   4.   to punctuate sentences;
   5.   to increase the rhythmic liveliness of certain words or phrases;
   6.   to accompany an interlude between actions or arias;
   7.   to accompany specific stylized miming movements;
   8.   to accompany fighting scenes;

9. to produce special sound effects; and

10. to introduce arias and melodic interludes.

The instruments of the melodic ensemble of the Peking opera are mostly strings and winds, as well as a set of ten small, suspended pitched gongs called the yunluo. The strings are the jinghu (the leading melodic instrument, a two-stringed bamboo spiked fiddle with very high and piercing pitch), the erhu, the yueqin (a four-stringed plucked lute with a round sound box), and a small sanxian. The winds are the dizi transverse flute, the sheng, and the big and small suona (conical double-reed oboes).

The primary functions of the melodic ensemble are to play introductions and interludes for arias, to accompany arias, and to play incidental music for dance and miming movements. The strings and the winds perform somewhat different functions. The strings, with the jinghu as their principal instrument, accompany the two main types of Peking opera arias known as the xipi and the erhuang, which were derived from some folk predecessors of Peking opera. (These arias will be explained further.) In addition, the strings also play various incidental pieces—all of which have proper names—to accompany some miming movements such as sweeping, changing clothes, putting on makeup, walking, and to accompany scenes of banqueting and general pageantry, celebration, and dance. Each individual piece of named incidental music has an association with specific dramatic situations and moods, and each requires different playing techniques on the various strings for the production of varying volumes and timbres.

The winds—the dizi and the sheng only, without the suona—sometimes in combination with the sanxian and the erhu, accompany arias in scenes derived from the repertory of the aristocratic theater called kunju, another predecessor of the Peking opera, which uses the dizi as its principal melodic instrument. Kunju-derived scenes are usually lyrical in nature, and in these scenes the yunluo gong set is also used. The winds are also used to accompany arias derived from folk tunes that have been absorbed into the Peking-opera repertory. Furthermore, the winds play specific named incidental pieces to accompany dances derived from the kunju.

Finally, the big and small suona are always employed in combination with the percussion ensemble exclusively to accompany arias sung by a chorus. Named incidental pieces specially associated with scenes involving military maneuvers, fighting, marching, hunting, or processions are also played by the suona-and-percussion ensemble.

The instrumental ensemble of Peking opera is organized with great economy. There are only nine players in the entire ensemble. The performers, who are very versatile, usually play more than one instrument. For example, in the percussion ensemble, the conductor, who plays both the single-headed drum and the clapper, also plays the big or small barrel drum. One person plays the various sizes of cymbals, and another plays the various sizes of gongs. In the melodic ensemble, the jinghu and erhu players also play the big cymbals when the music only involves the wind players, and sometimes they may have to play the suona and the dizi as well. The yueqin and sanxian players also play the suona, the dizi, the sheng, and even the yunluo or the barrel drums.

Now let us turn our attention to vocal music. Vocal music in Peking opera comprises arias, recitative-like short phrases, and heightened speech, which is a type of stylized stage speech having steeply rising and falling contours. The arias express the lyrical sentiments of the character; the recitative-like phrases and the heightened speech propel the narrative of the dramatic actions. Heightened speech is used exclusively by important characters and characters of high social status, while everyday speech in the Peking dialect is used by the comics and characters of lower-social status. In general, arias, recitatives, and speech are performed as solo numbers, but there are exceptions when these are done by an ensemble.

The term "aria" used in the context of Peking opera requires further explanation. All Peking-opera arias derive from a group of some thirty preexistent skeletal tune-and-rhythm pattern types called ban (literally "beat," but best translated "melody-rhythmic type"). By setting the same melodic-rhythmic type to a different text, a new aria is produced.

Most arias contain a two-phrase unit that sets a rhymed couplet; the constituent lines, which are of equal length, may have either seven or ten syllables. The syllables in each line are always grouped into three prosodic units; the prosodic grouping for a seven-syllable line is 2 + 3 + 2, and that for a ten-syllable line is 3 + 5 + 2. The melody for each phrase, however, is always arranged in a five-bar structure, juxtaposed with the three-prosodic-units-per-line textual structure.

Defined in terms of their rhythm, tempo, and corresponding dramatic functions, five main aria types can be identified:

1. the narrative aria in 4/4 meter and moderate tempo is usually used to provide narration in an unemotional manner (CD 1, #16);
2. the lyrical aria in 4/4 meter and slow tempo is used at lyrical moments and is usually melismatic (CD 1, #18);
3. the animated aria in measured rhythm and fast tempo is used to reveal a character's psychological state;
4. the dramatic aria in free rhythm, always accompanied by a steady beat from the clappers and the fiddle, is used to propel the dramatic action or to add tension to spoken dialogue (CD 1, #17); and
5. the interjected aria, usually very short (only one phrase) and in free rhythm, is sung at a highly dramatic moment as a signal or a call.

Musically, the melody-rhythm types of Peking opera are divided into more than ten categories, each of which has different melodic characteristics. The two most important ones are the xipi and the erhuang; the former derives from a northern regional theater, and the latter from a southern regional theater. In addition, folktunes of various regions and arias of the Kunju have also been absorbed into the Peking opera.

Arias in the erhuang category are in a moderate tempo and are usually employed in tragic or lyrical scenes. Erhuang arias are arranged in a seven-tone diatonic scale, with a raised fourth degree and a lowered seventh degree; the raised fourth and lowered seventh are usually used as neighboring or pivotal tones, and they serve to identify erhuang arias. For erhuang, the two strings of the jinghu are tuned a fifth apart (i.e., Sol-re). In all metered arias, the first and last textual syllables of each phrase is articulated on beat 1 of each measure.

Arias belonging to the other melodic category, the xipi, are rhythmically more varied and lively than those in the erhuang category and are used in a greater variety of dramatic situations. Xipi arias are arranged in either a five-tone or a seven-tone scale. For xipi, the pitches of the two strings of the jinghu are tuned a fifth apart (i.e., La-mi). In metered xipi arias, the articulation of the first textual syllable in each phrase always coincides with the beat 3 of a measure, and the articulation of the last textual syllable of each phrase always coincides with beat 1 of a measure.

In Peking opera, the aural and visual elements are of equal importance. The conventions of Peking opera require that an actor should master highly stylized acting techniques just as thoroughly as singing. Just as knowledgeable Chinese audiences would not excuse bad singing, neither would they excuse bad execution of movements on stage. For a Peking-opera actor, the appearance demanded by his conventional role, his capacity for wearing the costume pertaining to it, and the scores of strictly defined movements and gestures are of vital importance. The actor is the focus of attention, the central point of that harmony of movement which is the essence of a theatrical performance. The costumes are designed to assist and emphasize that movement, together with instrumental music, speech, and arias, all interdependent on the others.

Such a highly stylized and conventional theater requires an audience that possesses "the art of watching and listening" to appreciate it fully. Unfortunately, in recent decades such audiences have been rapidly shrinking. The conventions of Peking opera are deeply rooted in an old society based on Confucian moral precepts and political outlook, and these have been thoroughly discredited by the contemporary socialist state. It is small wonder that young people who have grown up in this state find the art archaic and alien; they prefer programs on television and pop music. The government has tried to remedy this situation by taking certain reform measures, which include the creation of libretti with modern themes, reorganizing troupes in order to streamline the companies, giving more financial incentives to able actors, and introducing electroacoustic instruments, but these measures appear to have met with little success.

CHINA BIBLIOGRAPHY

Robert H. Van Gulick, *The Lore of the Chinese Lute*, rev. ed. (Vermont and Tokyo: Charles E. Tuttle, 1969); Fritz Kuttner, *The Archaeology of Music in Ancient China* (New York: Oaragon House, 1990); Mingyue Liang, *Music of the Billion: An Introduction to Chinese Musical Culture* (New York: Heinrichshofen, 1985); Mingyue Liang, *The Chinese Chi'n: Its History and Music* (San Francisco: Chinese National Music Association and San Francisco Conservatory of Music, 1972); Bell Yung, *Cantonese Opera: Performance as Creative Process* (Cambridge: Cambridge University Press, 1989); Colin P. Mackerra, *The Rise of Peking Opera, 1770–1870* (Oxford: Clarendon Press, 1972); Kenneth J. DeWoskin, *A Song for One or Two: Music and the Concept of Art in Early China.* Michigan Papers in Chinese Studies No. 42 (Ann Arbor: Center for Chinese Studies, University of Michigan, 1982); Rulan Chao, *Song Dynasty Musical Sources and Their Interpretation* (Cambridge, Mass.: Harvard University Press, 1967); J. Lawrence Witzleben, *Silk and Bamboo Music in Shanghai: The Jiangnan Sizhu Instrumental Ensemble Tradition* (Kent, Oh.: Kent State University Press, 1995); Andrew F. Jones, *Like A Knife* (Ithaca, NY: Cornell University Press, 1992); Andrew F., Jones, *Yellow Music: Media Culture and Colonial Modernity in the Chinese Jazz Age* (Durham, N.C.: Duke University Press, 2001); Frederick Lau, "Forever Red: The Invention of Solo Dizi Music in Post-1949 China," *British Journal of Ethnomusicology* (1996) 5:113–131; Jonathan P. J. Stock, *Musical Creativity in Twentieth-Century China: Abing, His Music, and Its Changing Meanings* (Rochester: University of Rochester Press, 1996); John E. Myers, *The Way of the Pipa: Structure and Imagery in Chinese Lute Music* (Kent, Oh.: Kent State University Press, 1992); Stephen Jones, *Folk Music of China: Living Instrumental Tradition* (Oxford: Clarendon Press, 1992); Isabel K. F. Wong, "Geming Gequ: Songs for the Education for the Masses," in Bonnie MacDougall, ed., *Popular Chinese Literature and Performing Arts in the Peoples' Republic of China, 1949–1979* (Berkeley and Los Angeles: University of California Press, 1984); Isabel K. F. Wong, "From Reaction to Synthesis: Chinese Musicology in the Twentieth Century," in Bruno Nettl and Philip V. Bohlman, eds., *Comparative Musicology and Anthropology of Music* (Chicago: University of Chicago Press, 1991); Isabel K. F. Wong, "The Incantation of Shanghai: Singing a City into Existence," in Jim Craig, Richard King, eds., *Global Goes Local: Popular Culture in Asia* (Vancouver: University of British Columbia Press); J. Lawrence Witzleben, ed. "China," in Robert C. Provine, et al. eds., *The Garland Encyclopedia of World Music*, Vol. 7: East Asia (New York and London: Routledge, 2002).

CHINA DISCOGRAPHY

General   *Anthology of the World's Music: The Music of China*, Vol. 1: Chinese Instruments, ed. and with notes by Fredric Lieberman (Anthology); *Chine Populaire, Musique Classique* (instrumental music) (Ocora); *Chinese Classical Music* (instrumental) (Lyrichord LL 72).

Peking Opera   *The Chinese Opera* (Lyrichord LLST 7212 sides A and B); *The Peking Opera* (Seraphim SER 60201 sides A and B); *Ruse of the Empty City* (Folkways FW 8882 sides A and B); *Traditional Peking Opera* (Folkways FW 8883 sides A and B).

Kunjü   *Youyuan Jingmeng* (A Dream in the Garden) (Art Tune Co. CO 228 & 229);[1] *Kunqü Changduan Xuancui* [Selections of Wellknown Kunqü Excerpts] (in six cassettes, Shanghai Audio Production).

Qin (Ch'in) Music   *Ch'in Music of Ten Centuries* (Museum Collection Berlin MC7 A&B); *Chinese Master Pieces for the Ch'in* (Lyrichord LLST 7342 A&B); *The Drunken Fisherman* (Lyrichord LL 72 B/3); *"Youlan"* ("Orchids in a Secluded Valley") (Art Tune Co. ATC 73 A/1); *Wumen Qin Music* (Compact disc, Hugo Production, HRP712-2).

Pipa Music   *Floating Petals . . . Wild Geese, Lui Pui-yuen, pipa* (Nonesuch Explorer Series, H-72085); *China, Music of the Pipa* (Complex Disc, Elektra Nonesuch 9 72085-2); *Ambush From All Sides* (Compact Disc, Bailey Record, BCD 90028, band 1); *Autumn Moon Over the Han Palace* (Compact Disc, Bailey Record, BCD 90029, bands 5 & 6); *Autumn Recollection* (Compact Disc, Bailey Record BCD 90030, bands 6 & 7).

Jiangnan Sizhu   *"Chunjiang huasyueye"* ("The Moonlit Spring River") (Art Tune Co. ATC 16 A/1); *"Sanliu"* ("Three Six") (Art Tune Co. ATC 16 B/1); *"Huanlege"* ("Song of Happiness") (Art Tune Co. ATC 16 A/2); *Popular Jiangnan Music* (Hong Kong; under license from China Records Co., Peking).

Regional Ensemble Music   *Music of Amoy* (Art Tune Co. AST 4002 A & B); *Shantung Music of Confucius' Homeland* (Lyrichord LLST 7112 A & B); *Chinese Masterpieces for the Erh-hu* (Lyrichord, LLST 7132 A & B).

"Songs for the Masses"   *The East Is Red* (China Records M 982); *Commune Members Are All Like Sunflowers* (China Records M 2265).

The Legendary Chinese Hits   Vol. 5 Chow Hsuan, EMI FH81005 2.

---

[1]Recordings released by the Art Tune Company can be ordered through World Music Enterprises, 717 Avondale Street, Kent, Ohio.

5

The Music of Japan

Isabel K.F. Wong

HOGAKU PERFORMANCE IN TOKYO

Tokyo, Japan's capital, is a crowded, bustling modern city with almost twelve million people. It is the political and financial center not only of Japan but of Asia, and increasingly of the world as well. Although a formidable city at first glance, Tokyo can be seen at a second glance to be more like a conglomeration of small towns and neighborhoods clustered together, each with its own shops and narrow, winding streets.

Tokyo is both new and old, Eastern and Western. The variety of Japanese, Asian, and Western musical performances that take place in Tokyo during the concert season (spring to fall) is a reflection of this fact. Any day during the concert season, the visitor is likely to find concerts of Western art music or popular music, as well as performances of hogaku, Japan's traditional music. Some hogaku performances may take place in the concert halls clustered around the Tokyo Station, others in the recital halls inside great department stores in the Ginza area, Tokyo's chic shopping district, and still others in the National Theater, situated across the street from the grounds of the Imperial Palace.

During one of my recent visits I attended two musical performances at the National Theater, which was opened in 1966 for the promotion and development of traditional Japanese performing arts. It actually comprises two theaters: a large one seating nearly 1800, which is used principally for the performance of kabuki musical drama; and a small one seating about 630, which is used to stage a variety of concerts of hogaku music and dance, as well as performances of puppet musical plays known as bunraku. There are also two restaurants attached to the National Theater: a larger one on the second floor that serves a set menu for dinner, and a smaller one at the front of the theater grounds that serves snack food.

A Mixed Concert

One of the hogaku concerts I attended at the National Theater was a gala event commemorating the sixtieth birthday of a respected hogaku master. It took place in the small theater and started at 6:30 P.M., but most of the audience arrived before curtain time in order to have dinner at the restaurants. It was a sold-out concert, and I was lucky to have obtained a standing-room ticket—the least expensive kind—at 4000 yen (equivalent to about U.S. $40 in 1995). As in a Western concert, the audience was greeted by ushers at the door of the theater and handed program notes (in Japanese) about the four items to be performed; this included song texts and instrumentation, and was followed, as in the West, by many advertisements. The inside of the theater was very similar to a Western one, with a proscenium stage and rows of seats. The members of the audience were primarily well-dressed Japanese men and women wearing Western-style clothing, but there were some older women who wore the kimono.

The relatively long concert, lasting more than three hours, began with three pieces for a chamber ensemble consisting of six musicians. The final piece of the program, coming after an intermission of about twenty minutes, called for a chorus and orchestra each consisting of a dozen or so performers, as well as dancers. All the performers wore traditional attire and knelt on the floor of the stage with low music stands placed before them.

As each piece began, the performers picked up their instruments from the floor in front of them in a deliberate and uniform fashion. Their erect posture and great decorum was complemented by the attentiveness of the audience. At the end of each piece the performers replaced their instruments on the stage floor in the same deliberate and uniform manner in which they had taken them up, and only then did the audience applaud. They acknowledged the applause by bowing very formally, and then remained stationary until the curtain had descended completely.

The first piece in the program was an ensemble played by three kotos (long thirteen-stringed zithers) and three shamisens (three-stringed lutes played with a plectrum). The musicians, who included both men and women, sang as they played; I noticed that the first and last sections were sung with instrumental accompaniment, while the middle section, which was the longest, was entirely played by instruments. I also noticed that the music was primarily pentatonic but with occasional auxiliary pitches. The voice, the kotos, and the shamisens seemed to share a basic melody, but each performed the melody in a somewhat different fashion, rhythmically as well as melodically, resulting in a texture that may be described as heterophonic (Figs. 5–1, 5–2, and 5–3).

Figure 5–1   The Japanese-American musician Yoko Hiraoka playing the thirteen-stringed long zither koto. *Photo courtesy Yoko Hiraoka.*

Figure 5–2   The Japanese-American musician Yoko Hiraoko playing the three-stringed plucked lute shamisen. *Photo courtesy Yoko Hiraoka.*

Figure 5–3   Ralph Samuelson playing the end-blown flute shakuhachi. *Photo courtesy Ralph Samuelson.*

The second piece was a jiuta. Broadly speaking, the term denotes a type of vocal piece having a lyrical text that is accompanied principally by the shamisen, sometimes by a koto as well. This performance included both shamisen and koto accompaniment, the former being supplied by the vocalist herself. Like the previous piece, this too had three sections, of which the middle was a purely instrumental interlude.

The third piece was a trio for solo voice and two shamisens that was derived from a narrative genre called shinnai-bushi. The vocalist, who did not play any instrument, sang with a penetrating voice. The shamisen used in this piece had a thicker neck than those used in the previous pieces. One shamisen played the basic melody while the other played a lighter and higher part, heterophonically elaborating the melody. In contrast to the others, this piece was divided into six sections.

During the intermission, people who had not had dinner before the concert—I among them—went to the theater restaurants to have a quick bite. The food was delicious and was served in beautifully decorated lacquered bowls and plates; but when the bell rang indicating that the curtain was about to go up, I hurriedly finished my dinner and returned to the auditorium.

The final piece, featuring some two dozen musicians, made me realize how much a foreigner to Japanese music I was. Despite the magnificent costumes of the dancers I had difficulty concentrating on the performance, yet I noticed how most of the audience appreciated the piece greatly. Many different types of instruments were used, including a number of kotos and shamisens and various types of flutes such as the fue (horizontal flute), shakuhachi (end-blown flute), nohkan (a horizontal flute closely associated with the noh drama), and ryuteki (a horizontal flute closely associated with the gagaku court music). In addition, there was a double-reed oboe called the hichiriki, which has a very distinct and penetrating sound; a mouth organ called the sho; plus a small percussion ensemble (a small pair of cymbals, a small drum, a paired wooden clapper, and a small gong). A modern attempt to combine various kinds of traditional music in a new composition, this piece included the jiuta (played by a trio made up of shamisen, koto, and shakuhachi) from the nagauta ensemble, lyrical shamisen music with chorus also associated with the kabuki theater, the Buddhist chant shomyo, a shamisen duet, and finally materials deriving from folk song and dance. At the end of what seemed to this foreigner a tediously long piece, the audience gave the performers a standing ovation. As soon as the curtain fell, however, the audience disappeared quickly, and clearly no encore was expected.

A Kabuki Appreciation Class

The second performance I attended at the National Theater was an appreciation class for the kabuki theater, which was extremely interesting and educational.

Kabuki, Japan's main popular theater, is regularly performed in several theaters in Tokyo; among these the most famous and best known is the Kabukiza (za means "seat," but today it has come to mean "theater"), which is situated in the Ginza and contains, aside from the theater, six restaurants. The Kabukiza has about eight or nine kabuki productions a year, each of which lasts about twenty-five days. Usually two different programs are performed daily; matinees run from about 11:00 A.M. to 4:00 P.M., and evening performances run from 4:30 P.M. to 9:00 P.M. The Kabukiza was built in 1887 and has been reconstructed many times since then. It is an impressive theater with more than 2000 seats, a wide orchestra, and two balconies. The stage, almost ninety-three feet wide, is equipped with revolving platforms and trap lifts. In addition, there is a long runway connecting the stage with the rear of the theater, which is also part of the stage. In the lobby, various kabuki recordings and cassettes, books about kabuki (in both Japanese and English), and various souvenirs are sold. Foreigners who do not understand Japanese, or are novices to the theater, can rent earphones and listen to a simultaneous translation of the libretto.

Kabuki performances are also held several times a year at the larger hall of the National Theater, which also runs an annual "Kabuki appreciation class" every summer for young people. There are two appreciation classes daily at 11:00 A.M. and 2:30 P.M., and I bought a ticket for the morning one.

When it was time for the class to start, all the lights in the theater were turned off except those on the bare proscenium stage. An actor in a kimono appeared on the stage. "Hello everyone, I am a kabuki actor called Iwai Hanshiro. I am going to tell you something about the kabuki theater today so that you can appreciate it better," he said. "It is a pity that too many Japanese people nowadays cannot appreciate kabuki because they do not understand it. The purpose of this appreciation class is to tell you some of the fun and secrets of the kabuki theater, so you will come to the theater again and again.

"Let me first tell you a bit of the history of kabuki. The first kabuki performance was done entirely by females and took place in 1596 in Kyoto. The government immediately banned female performance of kabuki, so the stage was taken over by a troupe of young males. Since 1652, kabuki has been performed by adult males, as it still is today. Female roles are impersonated by male actors. In the eighteenth century, when Japan was ruled by a succession of military strongmen known as shoguns and entered a long period of peace, kabuki developed into a definite cultural form for urban dwellers (chonin). You must remember that kabuki is predominantly a dance theater with musical accompaniment; it makes use of extensive and elaborate scenery, costumes, and properties, which I will show you later. Kabuki borrowed a lot from other types of theater, such as the classical noh theater and the puppet theater bunraku. It has also absorbed folk dance and popular dance. How many of you have been to the noh theater?" Only a few hands were raised. "How many of you have seen the bunraku?" More hands were raised. "Let me demonstrate some kabuki gestures that were derived from the bunraku and the noh."

At this point our lecturer made a vigorous gesture with his arms and legs, which was very masculine, abrupt, and angular. "This gesture is an adaptation of puppet movement of the bunraku theater, known as aragoto, meaning 'rough business.'" He then walked in stately, gliding steps, moving without any perceptible upper-body motion. "This gentle and refined movement came from the noh theater."

"Dance is very important in kabuki theater. A kabuki actor is primarily a dancer, and kabuki dance is essential movement toward a climactic static posture." He now struck and held a dramatic pose, and then turned to us and said, "Now, this is the time for you to applaud me. We kabuki actors like to know that you appreciate what we do!" The young audience, encouraged by the lecturer, giggled and applauded enthusiastically. At that moment, a middle-aged woman sitting next to me shouted, "Bravo!" in Japanese, which was acknowledged by our lecturer with a deep bow in her direction. The young audience turned to look at her with puzzled expressions on their faces, whereupon our lecturer said, "This is a very appropriate and common way to give praise to actors. You may try it yourselves!" "Bravo! Bravo!" shouted the audience, greatly energized. Our lecturer bowed graciously to them.

"It is now time to show you something about the kabuki stage. The kabuki stage is equipped with several trap lifts, which are used to bring scenery or musicians from below the stage to the level of the stage floor, and vice versa." As he spoke, several men, who were holding musical instruments in their hands, suddenly rose up through the stage floor on a trap lift. The young audience, obviously loving this, burst into applause. "There are more fun things to follow. The stage is also equipped with two revolving stages in the center, an outer one and an inner one, which are capable of being moved in opposite directions. These revolving stages are used to change the entire set at once and have been in use since the sixteenth century." As he spoke, a realistic set depicting a large rice field complete with stacks of grain, trees, and thatched huts suddenly revolved into the center of the stage. A few seconds later, this set disappeared from sight, and another one showing the inside of a house, with cooking utensils and straw mats on the floor, appeared in front of us (Fig. 5–4).

Then our lecturer pointed in the direction of the raised runway connecting the stage to the rear of the auditorium, and asked: "How many of you know the name of this runway?" A few treble voices shouted, "Hanamichi!" "Good!" our lecturer said. "You have been studying this in school, no doubt! The hanamichi is a unique feature of the kabuki theater. It serves as an additional acting space for the actors, and it also serves as a more intimate acting area. There is a passageway built beneath the floor of the theater for actors to go from the dressing rooms behind the stage to the entrance of the hanamichi without being seen by the audience." Suddenly, a man dressed in the costume of a peasant appeared on the hanamichi at the rear of the theater. He walked a few steps, paused, gently moving his head from side to side as if hesitating, and finally moved forward to the stage proper with an attitude of determination.

"Meet Hayano Kanpei, the hero of the play you are going to see after my lecture! Have you guessed that Kanpei is no peasant? He is really a ronin—that is, a samurai who has lost his master. He is disguised as a peasant in order to avenge his master's death. If you have been observant, you should have noticed that before he

Figure 5–4 A scene in the Kabuki play Kagami Hishi (Lion Dance), with on-stage musicians. *Photo courtesy Mr. Shozo Sato.*

finally proceeded to the stage proper, he moved his head gently from side to side. A peasant does not move in such a refined fashion! The connoisseur would know from this gesture that his real social status is higher than that of a peasant." At this point, the actor who portrayed Kanpei gave the audience a bow and exited.

"Another important element of kabuki theater is music, and it is time to introduce the musicians! Many musicians and instruments are used in the kabuki theater. I will show you some of them later. In general, there are two groups of musicians: those who appear on the stage, and those who do not. The onstage musician group is called the degatari, and the offstage group is called the geza." He gave a signal, and a pair of men were elevated from below to stage left. Both were kneeling, and one was holding a shamisen. "This is the chobo, a pair of onstage musicians borrowed from the puppet theater. One is a narrator; the other one accompanies him on the shamisen. Even though they may sometimes participate musically in the events taking place on the stage, the chobo musicians are not actors. Let me give you an example. Suppose that I am a character in a play who is sobbing; the chobo narrator can take over the sobbing for me without a break, and the shamisen player in turn can imitate the sound of sobbing on his instrument, while all the time the sobbing is supposed to be that of the character on stage and the accompanists do not participate in the action. The chobo musicians not only participate musically in the events on the stage, they also narrate and explain the plot to the audience; you could say that they are story tellers.

"Sometimes a character in a play may want to sing about his feelings, or another may want to perform a dance. Who will provide musical accompaniment? Another group of onstage musicians is called the debayashi, meaning 'coming-out orchestra.' These musicians are singers as well as instrumentalists, and their number varies according to the needs of the drama." He gave a signal, and from the rear of the stage a trap lift raised up a two-tiered platform covered with red cloth on whose upper tier knelt six men holding shamisens; below them, on the level of the stage, six singers knelt behind low music stands. "Let us hear their music!" the lecturer commanded, and the ensemble played nagauta, a kind of unison chorus with shamisen accompaniment (CD 1, #21).

"Now let us bring on the geza musicians." At this moment both the chobo and the debayashi musicians were lowered beneath the stage by trap lifts, and downstage left there appeared another group of instrumentalists and a large drum. "These are offstage musicians called the geza," we were told. "They normally sit in a room situated at stage right, where they can look out to the stage and the hanamichi through a bamboo curtain, and the audience cannot see them. Their job is to provide sound effects for the dramatic action. The instruments are: the o-daiko (big drum), shamisen, nohkan, and gongs and bells. Let me show you the strokes of the o-daiko." As he was talking he picked up the two drumsticks and hit the drum with several types of strokes. "Some strokes indicate curtain calls; others create different atmospheres and moods; some strokes represent raindrops, the sound of wind or thunder, and others represent the appearance of a ghost."

When the demonstration was over, the geza musicians disappeared from the stage. "I know you are very eager to see today's play, but I have yet one more important instrument to show you, and that is the hyoshigi." Immediately, a man appeared at the corner stage right, holding two rectangular woodblocks in his hand; he knelt and began playing the blocks in a series of accelerating beats. "The player is called the kyogenkata; he is a stagehand, and the rhythmic pattern he just played announces the rise of the curtain." With this final demonstration, the actor concluded his introduction and called for the play to begin.

The play, about Kanji's revenge, employed all the devices, mechanisms, and musical groups we had just learned about, and using the simultaneous translation of the dramatic dialogue and explanation of the plot in English transmitted through the headphones I wore, I found that I could readily understand the plot and enjoy the drama.

The music for the chamber vocal and instrumental recital described and for performances of kabuki can be heard and seen in Japan nowadays with some frequency, particularly in the four major cities—Tokyo, Kyoto, Osaka, and Nagoya. These types of hogaku music are essentially products of Japan's most recent "ancient" period—that is, the time from the seventeenth to the nineteenth century known as the Tokugawa or Edo period, when Japan, ruled by the Tokugawa clan in the capital Edo (present-day Tokyo), experienced a period of uninterrupted peace. Cities such as Edo and Osaka grew into populous centers of trade and government where a large and prosperous bourgeoisie developed—tradesmen and artisans who vigorously supported the developing arts and culture. It was under the patronage of this bourgeoisie that the kabuki theater and the many chamber vocal-instrumental genres involving the koto, shamisen, and other instruments came into being and flourished.

THEATER MUSIC

The culture of the bourgeoisie, essentially urban and popular, was characterized by a taste for romantic or comic novels, for salacious or witty lampoons, for brightly colored prints and paintings, and above all, for lavish theatrical entertainment. The kabuki theater, with its lavish costumes and staging, its elaborate stage machinery, and its fondness for plots of romantic love, is representative of this culture.

The Bunraku Puppet Theater

The other important popular theater of the Edo period, which can also be seen today, principally in Osaka and in Tokyo's National Theater, is the puppet theater called bunraku. Growing up at about the same time as kabuki and under the same circumstances and patronage—primarily that of the bourgeoisie or chonin of Osaka—the bunraku both borrowed from and exerted influence on the kabuki theater.

The bunraku puppet, made of wood, is moved by three puppeteers who manipulate its arms, fingers, legs, body, head, eyes, mouth and even eyebrows. These movements are so realistic that the spectator can easily forget the actor is made of wood, even though the puppeteers are not hidden behind or above the stage. The two junior puppeteers are, however, completely shrouded in black and hooded, and only the senior puppeteer's face is visible.

The narration of the bunraku, both sung and spoken, is provided by a narrator/chanter who is accompanied on shamisen, a three-stringed, long-necked, fretless lute whose sound box is covered with cat or dog skin front and back, and whose strings are plucked with a large plectrum; this is the same combination as the chobo ensemble we encountered in the kabuki demonstration. When a kabuki play is derived from the bunraku theater, the narrative and music accompanying the dramatic actions are provided by the chobo, in the same manner as in the bunraku theater.

The narrative style used in bunraku is called gidayubushi, after its developer, Takemoto Gidayu (1651–1714) of Osaka. The vocal style of gidayubushi includes chants, heightened speech, and lyrical songs. The shamisen, whose music is made up of various arrangements of stereotyped patterns, plays preludes, interludes, and postludes to the singing. Bunraku rose to its artistic and popular height when Takemoto collaborated with the famous playwright Chikamatsu Monzaemon (1653–1725).

The Noh Theater

Edo-period musical theatricals are by no means the only kinds of traditional stage genres one can hear and see in Japan today. Among genres originating in other historical periods of Japan, the noh theater is particularly important. Combining various folk dances, musical theatricals, and religious and courtly entertainment of medieval times, the noh was transformed into a serious Buddhist art by the performer Kannami Kiyotsugu (1333–1384), and into a refined court art by his son Zeami Motokiyo (1363–1444). Wearing a mask, brocade robes, and white socks, the chief actor moves and dances slowly on a bare stage with perfectly controlled and restrained movements; accompanied by a male chorus and a small instrumental ensemble made up of a flute and three drums, he carries the spectator into the austere world of a medieval Japan deeply influenced by Zen Buddhism.

The noh was a product of the Muromachi period (1333–1615), which was marked by continuous military strife among the various clans of warriors (samurai). Exclusively an art of the ruling samurai class from the fifteenth to the nineteenth century, the noh, with its performing style of elegant simplicity and restraint and its major themes of redemption of human suffering through the love of Buddha, is a direct antithesis of the flamboyant, colorful, and lavish theatrical entertainments of the Tokugawa bourgeoisie such as kabuki and bunraku.

In Zeami's day, a performance of noh consisted of at least five plays—a god play, a warrior play, a female-wig play, a possession play, and a demon play—interspersed with comic plays called kyogen for a change of pace. Today the usual program consists of two or three noh plays (each lasting about an hour) and one or two kyogen (lasting about thirty to forty minutes).

Supported mainly by intellectuals now, noh is performed in major cities in special indoor theaters that are owned and operated by live traditional schools of noh performance. In addition, noh plays are performed on various festival occasions throughout Japan on outdoor stages that are built in the compounds of Shinto or Buddhist temples.

The main element and action of a noh play is linked closely with its major actor, the shite. The supporting actor, or waki, provides a foil for the revelation of the shite's character and the explanation for his actions.

Noh plays are typically in two acts. Thematically, these acts can be organized into five major dan (sections or units). The first act—comprising the first dan, which is an introduction, and the second, third and fourth dan, which together make up the exposition of the play—ends with a dance called kuse, its high point. The act provides a full exposition of the spirit of the shite. The second act consists of only one dan; in this denouement the shite is transformed into a new character (usually a supernatural being), sings a couple of songs, and performs another dance, called the mai, which reveals his new essence after his spiritual transformation.

Music for the noh consists of songs (solo and choral) sung by the actors or chorus, recitativelike heightened speech for the actors, and instrumental music played by an instrumental quartet (a flute and three drums). The functions of the instrumental ensemble are to play introductory music and interludes, to set the scene or mood of individual units within the two acts, to accompany entrances and exits of actors, to accompany songs and dances, and to provide a rhythmic background for dialogue and action. The songs (uta), sung by either the actors or the chorus, are of two types: the sageuta, which are short, slow, and in low range, and the ageuta, which are longer and higher.

The instruments making up the instrumental quartet for noh are a flute called nohkan and three drums of different sizes.

Unlike most bamboo flutes, which simply consist of a tube of dried bamboo, the nohkan is constructed from such a tube split lengthwise into strips that are then turned inside out, wrapped with cherry bark, and lacquered. It has seven fingerholes and a mouth hole. Other elements of its construction and playing technique lend this flute a distinctive, piercing sound, and rather than blending with the other components of noh, like them it retains a strong individuality.

The music of the nohkan is made up of various arrangements of a large number of stereotyped patterns; different pieces are produced by rearrangement of the sequential order of these patterns, and the use of certain sequences is determined by the dramatic conventions of the noh theater. The music for the nohkan serves as a marker for certain subunits of a dan, sets the tempo for the dances and accompanies them, adds a melodic layer to the drum patterns, sets the pitches for the chorus and accompanies it, and provides emphasis for certain lyrical passages of the songs.

The nohkan and the three drums used in noh are collectively called hayashi (a generic term for ensembles of flute and drums). The three drums are: the ko-tsuzumi, the o-tsuzumi, and the taiko. The first two are hourglass-shaped drums, while the taiko is a shallow barrel drum. Of the three, the smallest but most important is the ko-tsuzumi; although it derives from Chinese and Korean models, the manner of playing it in the noh theater is entirely a Japanese development.

All the noh drums have wooden bodies, with two skin heads that are stretched over iron rings and then stitched, and two sets of ropes that hold the skins to the body. The special tone of the ko-tsuzumi, is achieved by carving special patterns on the inside surface of the body and affixing bits of damp paper to the rear head, which is not struck, and the ropes holding the heads to the body may be squeezed to increase tension on the heads. The tension of the head of the o-tsuzumi is always at a maximum and thus cannot be altered by further tightening the ropes; in fact, before a performance the drumhead is heated over a hibachi to increase the tension still further, and during a performance a newly heated drum may be substituted. All this tension creates a dry, hard sound that may be increased by the use of hard thimbles on the player's fingers.

The taiko is played with two thick sticks instead of the hand. Instead of being held by one of the player's hands, the drum is placed on a special stand that grips the encircling ropes, lifting the drum off the floor for better resonance. The taiko is used sparingly, normally joining the other instruments for dance sections.

All three drums are capable of producing several basic sounds, and their varying combinations form stereotyped patterns that are identified onomatopoeically.

An additional but integral part of noh drumming is the use of drum calls by the drummers. These kakegoe, as they are called, may have originated as practice devices, but they are now part of the overall sound of the music for noh and are certainly one of the distinctive elements that add to its strangely rarefied atmosphere (Figs. 5–5 through 5–9).

Like the chobo ensemble of gidayubushi, the noh hayashi, too, has been adopted for some kabuki performances, where it always introduces a reference to classical, courtly culture.

The vocal part of noh, called yokyoku, is sung by both the actors and the onstage chorus. The melodic style of yokyoku is solemn and spare, betraying its origin in Buddhist chanting of medieval Japan. The articulation of every textual syllable is deliberate and prolonged, and their pronunciation is based on a stage convention different from everyday speech. Together with the actors' stately bodily movements and gliding steps, which I described in conjunction with the kabuki appreciation class, the music of yokyoku and hayashi contribute to the overall impression that the noh theater is ethereal and otherworldly.

Figure 5–5 and 5–6 Sakiji Tanaka
playing the noh drum taiko. *Photo
courtesy Shozo Sato.*

Yokyoku has two basic styles: the heightened speech called kotobe (words) and
the aria called fushi (melody). Fushi is sung in two basic ways: the yowagin (soft)
style, which is delivered softly and is used in lyrical scenes, and the tsuyogin (strong)
style, which is delivered with strength and is used in masculine and warlike scenes.

The tonal system of the yokyoku is based on the interval of the minor seventh,
coinciding with the same interval when the uniquely constructed nohkan is
overblown. (Most flutes produce the octave when overblown.) Within this minor
seventh, three notes making a conjunct pair of perfect fourths provide important
tonal centers. If we designate the minor-seventh interval as being from A down to B,
then the three tonal centers are A-E-B, in that order of importance. Around each of
these tonal centers there is a cluster of notes forming a tonal system for melody.

The rhythmic structure of noh singing, like that for the hayashi, is based on an
eight-beat framework, but in a very flexible manner. The number of textual syllables
in each poetic line to be sung within these beats varies, but a five-syllable line is most
common.

The individual musical elements of noh are conceived in a linear fashion, and the
key to appreciating noh is to follow the various lines of the voices and the instruments.

Figure 5–5 and 5–6   (continued)

For example, the chorus and the nohkan may be involved in two completely separate melodic lines, while the drums may be playing a rhythmic pattern of a different length from either. As mentioned, the strong individuality of the components of noh is a characteristic feature, and relying on this, noh can create a complex art from few resources. The center of this art is the poetic text, and the musical elements revolve around it.

Noh plays are produced by a group of people: the poet supplies the text, and the actors, the chorus, and the hayashi compose their own parts according to the text. Such a creative process works for noh because the music is highly systematized.

One of the most famous Noh plays is "Hagoromo" ("The Robe of Feathers," CD 1, #22). Belonging to the category of "female-wig plays," this one act play in two scenes tells the story of a fisherman (portrayed by the waki actor) who stole an

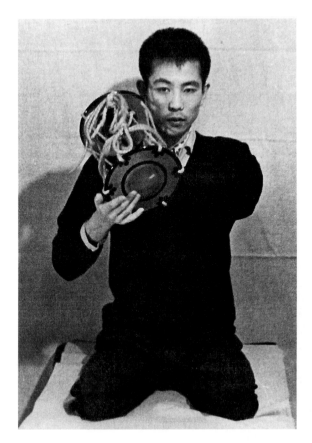

Figure 5–7 Sakiji Tanaka playing the noh drum ko-tsuzumi. *Photo courtesy Shozo Sato.*

angel's (portrayed by the shite actor) feathered robe and thus prevented her return to heaven; however, he was so moved by her distress that he agreed to return it if she would dance for him. The second scene, consisting of a series of dances accompanied by choral chanting and the hayashi, is considered the high point of the play.

THE RELIGIOUS TRADITIONS

Shintoism and Shinto Music

Among the ancient types of Japanese music that can still be heard today are court Shinto music, or mikagura; court orchestral music, or gagaku; and the Buddhist chant, or shomyo. The latter two were originally Chinese-inspired, while the first one is entirely indigenous.

The earliest Japanese religion shared many elements with the religions of other peoples of East Asia, and only became designated Shinto ("the way of the

Figure 5–8   Sakiji Tanaka playing the noh drum o-tsuzumi. *Photo courtesy Shozo Sato.*

gods") when confronted with Buddhism and Confucianism. Shinto is a loose agglomeration of local and regional cults with a diversity of gods and spirits, and it includes a variety of religious elements such as nature worship, animism, shamanism, ancestor worship, hero worship, fertility rites, phallicism, fortune-telling, and so on.

Constant change and adaptation is the norm of Shinto. It adopted and adapted gods and cults with ease, and there has seemed to be no clear conception of divinity and no real attempt to articulate a theology on a rational basis, nor is there an organized, hereditary priesthood.

Five elements or objects stand out in Shinto worship: the sun (or fire), water, mountains, trees, and stones. In ritual practice, Shinto ceremony consists essentially of attendance upon a god and offerings to him or her, accompanied by invocations and prayers. Festivals represent special occasions for honoring the gods and establishing good rapport with them by offering food, drink, and music and dance. Shinto

Figure 5-9 The noh drum o-tsuzumi. The ropes holding the heads to the body may be squeezed to increase tension on the heads. *Photo courtesy of Shozo Sato.*

rituals generally take place during important occasions of life and of the agricultural year, such as birth, marriage (always celebrated at a Shinto shrine), the New Year, plowing, planting, and harvesting. Shinto has nothing to do with death, however.

Until the Edo period, musical creation was regarded as a gift from god, and like the beauty of nature, a miracle. Thus in the Shinto view, an appreciation of music sprang from admiration and awe at what is "natural," pure, and simple, rather than from a rational admiration of the artfully organized.

One type of ancient Shinto music that can still be heard today is that performed in court Shinto ceremonies, called the mikagura. It is performed by a male chorus and accompanied by the wagon (a six-stringed zither), the kagura-bue (a transverse bamboo flute with six holes), the hichiriki, and the shakubyoshi (a pair of wooden clappers). Fifteen songs are still preserved in the present-day repertory, and they are of two main types: the torimono, songs paying homage to the gods, and the saibara, songs meant to entertain the gods. Since the nineteenth century, mikagura songs have been performed by two choruses, each having its own repertory. The performance is initiated by the leader of each chorus, who sings the initial phrase of a song and accompanies himself on the clappers, followed by a unison chorus accompanied by the rest of the instruments. In Shinto ceremonies, dance is an integral part of the ceremony.

In folk Shinto rituals, the music used is called satokagura. There are two main types: the one used in shamanistic rituals paying homage to the gods involves a priestess who sings and dances and is accompanied by the wagon, the transverse flute, and the suzu (bell-tree); the other, used in Shinto festivals called matsuribayashi (festival music), is performed by a hayashi consisting of the o-daiko, two taiko, and a transverse flute. This music is characterized by a lively syncopated drum rhythm which accompanies a repeated melodic line played by the flute.

Buddhism and Buddhist Music

Buddhism came to Japan in the sixth century C.E. from Korea and China. By this time it was already a thousand years old, and a highly developed religion.

The essential tenet of Buddhism concerns suffering and the elimination of suffering through the cessation of desire—the achievement of Nirvana. When it came to Japan, Buddhism gave the Japanese a means of dealing with death and suffering, something that Shintoism had not provided. It affected the Japanese deeply, but their innate delight in the simple joy of life also modified Buddhism by infusing it with an appreciation for life and nature.

During the Nara (553–794) and Heian (794–1185) periods, when Japan's capitals were in Nara and Kyoto respectively, the great aristocratic clans adopted the Mahayana form of Buddhism. Great monastic systems were established and integrated into the court and its civil administrative system. The theology of Mahayana Buddhism asserted that salvation from suffering and death was open to all, and it attracted a huge following among the populace. The government decreed the building of many great monasteries and demanded religious services praying for peace and prosperity for the state. Sutras were chanted in these ceremonies to secure good harvests and the welfare of the state.

The chanting of Buddhist sutras is called shomyo; it is performed by a male chorus in responsorial style, and the texts are in several languages: those in Sanskrit are called bonsan; those in Chinese, kansan; those in Japanese, wasan. The music consists of a series of stereotyped patterns belonging to two different Chinese-derived scales, the ryo and the ritsu, each of which has five basic notes and two auxiliary notes. Shomyo chants may be syllabic or melismatic, and their rhythm may be more or less regular or free. A chant usually begins slowly and gets faster.

During the Nara and Heian periods, the aesthetic aspect of Buddhism predominated, not only because of native Japanese sensitivity but because the aristocrats admired beauty and elegance above all things. Aesthetic cultivation (the playing of music being one of the requirements), together with physical training and psychological discipline—all aspects of one personality—were involved in the attainment of Buddhahood, which was the goal of the Esoteric Buddhism practiced in the Nara and Heian periods. Consequently, ritual, art, and music were as important as scriptures and meditation. It was not just a matter of enlightening the mind but of affecting and transforming the whole world. This view of the world and of man gave great impetus to Buddhist art (including images of Buddha and mandala paintings) as well as Buddhist music.

The collapse of the Heian court and its civil administration in the eleventh century brought about profound changes in Buddhism. Religious institutions bound up with the fortune of the court nobility declined, while a highly aestheticized and sentimentalized religion, based on the refined enjoyment of beauty, could not meet the challenge of the difficult time ahead. With the constant warfare, famine, pestilence, and social disruption of the ensuing Kamakura (1185–1333), Muromachi, and Azuchi-Momoyama (1333–1615) periods, a new form of Buddhism arose, whose primary mission was to bring salvation immediately within reach. This Buddhism for the masses, called *Amida Buddhism*, had little to do with the arts and aesthetics.

Another form of Buddhism that arose during this difficult period was Zen Buddhism, whose roots were in China and India. Zen emphasizes personal enlightenment through self-understanding and self-reliance by means of meditation, using practices related to the yoga practice of ancient India. In Japan, Zen Buddhism was supported by the military class during the Azuchi-Momoyama period.

Aesthetically, Zen inspired many of the traditional arts of Japan, such as landscape painting, landscape gardening, swordsmanship, the tea ceremony, and noh drama. It was under the patronage of the Ashikago shogun that Zen and its allied arts, including noh, evolved and developed.

A CONCERT AND A COURT TRADITION

Sokyoku

Popular koto-and-vocal music of the Edo period is known under the generic name of sokyoku. The koto is a long zither whose thirteen strings are stretched over movable bridges. The player places the instrument on a mat or low table and plucks the strings using plectra on the thumb and the first two fingers of the right hand. With the left hand, the player presses on the strings to the left of the bridges in order to create ornaments and new pitches by altering the tension of the strings.

There are two types of sokyoku. The first, kumiuta, is a koto-accompanied song cycle; the verses of each individual song, called uta, are derived from pre-existent poems whose subjects are unrelated. Typically, an uta has duple meter and is in eight phrases, each divided into four measures. The second type, danmono, for koto alone, is in several sections (dan), each consisting of either 64 or 120 beats. The structure of danmono is akin to a loose rondo-variation form. The famous piece "Rokudan" (Six

Sections) is a classic example of this form. A basic theme is presented and within each of the six dan the theme undergoes variation with interpolation of new material (CD 1, #20).

Jiuta is an important hybrid form of koto music that combines the techniques of both kumiuta and danmono. It is sometimes called tegotomono, after the tegoto, the important instrumental interludes between vocal sections. Tegotomono usually contain three parts: a foresong (maeuta), an instrumental interlude (tegoto), and an aftersong (atouta). This basic structure may be extended.

Today, jiuta is played by an ensemble called sankyoku (trio) consisting of koto, shamisen, and shakuhachi (an end-blown bamboo flute with four finger-holes and one thumb hole, with a notch cut in the lip to facilitate sound production). The koto plays the main melody, while the shamisen and shakuhachi play an elaboration of the main melody, producing simple heterophony.

One of the most famous koto pieces is called "Chidori" (CD 1, #19). It is set in a four part jiuta form (introduction-song-interlude-song) and can be heard as a solo piece, a koto duet, or a kotos and shamisen ensemble; it is also employed as geza music in the Kabuki theater.

The koto tradition is perpetuated by various schools, the most important of which are the Ikuta School of Kyoto and the Yamada School of Tokyo, while the Meian and Kinko schools, also based respectively in Kyoto and Tokyo, are the main traditions of shakuhachi performance. The latter have an interesting and colorful origin; they were founded in the Edo period by masterless samurai who combined the profession of street musician with that of spy and informer and used their heavy bamboo flutes not just as musical instruments but also as clubs!

The music of the koto and the shamisen best represent the music of the Edo era. While the shamisen belongs primarily to the world of the theater, with its colorful and exciting entertainments, the koto, by contrast, developed out of a court tradition and gradually entered the home, played by members of the rising merchant class as an emblem of cultural accomplishment. In the modern era, the koto maintains a position in Japan similar to that of the parlor piano in nineteenth-century America. It is a popular instrument for middle-class Japanese girls, who play it as a sign of good breeding.

Gagaku

Gagaku, meaning elegant or refined music, is the instrumental and choral music and dance that has been under the continual patronage of the imperial court for more than a thousand years. Influenced by the ancient music of China, Korea, and Sinicized Indian music, it has been carefully transmitted by generations of court guild musicians to the present day and is perhaps the oldest ensemble music in the world. Gagaku is also used to accompany dance; in this role it is called bugaku.

Gagaku was first initiated in the Nara period (553–749)—the first major historical period in Japan, during which the Japanese struggled to establish a national government modeled after the Chinese government of that time. Prior to the Nara period, Japan was ruled by various rustic clans, among which the Yamato, who originated from the southern island of Kyushu, were dominant. Up until the Nara period, the history and mythology of Japan were concerned primarily with the gradual northern extension of the imperial Yamato power and the justification for Yamato hegemony over other lesser clans of the land.

The construction of the city of Nara was begun in 708, and the court was moved there in 710. Fashioned as a miniature of the Chinese capital of Changan (present-day Xian), it captured perfectly the spirit of an age in East Asian history dominated by the pervasive influence of the great empire of the Chinese Tang dynasty. Nara was the first urban center in Japanese history.

The founding of Nara was accompanied by a great burst of economic, administrative, and cultural activities. One of the administrative measures taken was the establishment of a music bureau staffed by musicians from Korea and China. Musicians in the music bureau performed music and dance for court entertainments and rituals.

The founding of Nara also ushered in the age of the court nobles, a period that lasted until the later twelfth century. Members of the imperial household, court ministers, and Buddhist priests contended for political power at court. The constant court intrigues suggest a fundamental instability in the ruling institutions. A century later, this instability was exploited by one dominant court family, the Fujiwara, who were able to dominate the throne and subsequently the political affairs of the country for a long time.

The emperor Shomu and his consort, who was a Fujiwara, were fervent Buddhists, and they greatly helped the perpetuation of this foreign faith. In 737, Shomu ordered the construction of the Todaiji (Great East Temple) in Nara. Housed within the central building of the Todaiji is the huge bronze statue of the Buddha. The casting of the Great Buddha was an impressive technological feat for eighth-century Japan, and it also represented the first Japanese artistic representation of the human form.

At the "eye-opening" ceremony for the Great Buddha in 752, during which the statue was symbolically given life by having the pupils of its eyes painted in, all the great dignitaries of the Nara court were in attendance. In addition, there were visitors from China, India, and other distant lands, and some 10,000 Buddhist priests. It was without doubt one of the grandest occasions in all of early Japanese history. Hundreds of musicians and dancers performed, and many instruments dating from this occasion are still preserved in the imperial treasury of Nara, the Shosoin. Music thus became a part in important rituals pertaining to religious and court affairs.

The court music of the Nara period was all of foreign origin and was played primarily by foreign musicians in its original style. In the subsequent Heian period

(794–1185), there were signs that the Chinese influence was beginning to be assimilated and modified.

Heian (Kyoto), the newly constructed city to which the government moved in 794, remained the capital of Japan for more than a millennium (until the Meiji Restoration in 1868). At the end of the Heian period in 1185, a new military national government was established in Kamakura by the warrior family of Minamoto, bringing an end to the age of the court nobles and ushering in nearly seven centuries of dominance by the warrior class, until the restoration of the Meiji emperor in the late nineteenth century.

During the Heian period, great changes occurred in the governmental system, with the power of the emperor becoming eclipsed by that of the regent, who was controlled by the Fujiwara family. Buddhism continued to flourish in the Heian period, and it had become the principal intellectual system and one of the most important institutional systems in Japanese life. The nobles of the Heian court were preoccupied with etiquette and ritual, and they lived in a world governed by formal standards of beauty and the cultivation of poetry and music.

The court music of the Heian period still employed a host of Chinese instruments and forms, but the musicians themselves were mostly Japanese. In the ninth century, a standard gagaku orchestra was created under order of the emperor, and a repertory of two main categories was standardized. The togaku repertory includes music of Chinese and Indian origin, while the komagaku includes music of Korean and Manchurian origin.

Gagaku music was extremely popular in the Heian court. Not only was it a necessary component of all court ceremonies, but it was also practiced by the court nobles themselves. Amateur gagaku clubs flourished at court. The famous novel of the Heian period, *The Tale of Genji*, is full of descriptions of musical activities of the noblemen. Today there are about twenty gagaku musicians maintained by the emperor who are descendants of musicians of the professional guilds, and there are also amateur ensembles outside the court.

The ensemble for gagaku consists of percussion, strings, and winds. The various instruments used in gagaku are described briefly under separate headings.

Percussion

1. The da-daiko, a huge drum struck by two thick sticks. It is only used in bugaku.
2. The tsuri-daiko, a suspended two-headed drum, only one side of which is struck with two sticks. It is a "colotomic" instrument—that is, it serves to mark off the larger phrase units.
3. The shoko, a small suspended gong played with two sticks. It is usually played on the first beat of every measure.
4. The kakko, a small drum whose two heads are struck with thin sticks. The kakko is the leader of the togaku ensemble. Its three basic rhythmic patterns are two types

of rolls (a slow roll done with both sticks and a faster roll done on the left skin) and a single tap with the right stick. These patterns are played to regulate the tempo of the piece, and they are found mostly in free rhythmic sections; they are also used to mark off beats or phrases. The kakko is only used in togaku.

5. The san-no-tsuzumi, an hourglass-shaped drum with two heads, only one of which is struck. Korean in origin, it is played only in komagaku, by the leader of that ensemble.

Strings

1. The wagon, a six-stringed zither used in kagura.

2. The gaku-so, a thirteen-stringed zither, a predecessor of the koto. The strings are plucked by the bare fingers or with finger picks. The music for the gaku-so is made up of two basic patterns that are played to mark off sections.

3. The biwa, a pear-shaped lute with four strings and four frets played with a small plectrum. It is also used to mark off sections in a piece. The music for the biwa consists primarily of arpeggios, which may end with short melodic fragments. The effect of biwa music in gagaku is primarily rhythmic.

Winds

1. The hichiriki, a short, double-reed bamboo oboe with nine holes, originating from China. Through use of the embouchure and fingering technique, tones smaller than a half-step can be produced, and this is the salient characteristic of the hichiriki. Its tone quality is penetrating and strong, and it is the center of the gagaku ensemble.

2. The kagura-bue, a six-holed bamboo flute that produces a basic pentatonic scale; other pitches may be produced by using special fingerings. The length of this flute varies, and thus also its actual pitch. It is used for Shinto ceremonies.

3. The ryuteki, a seven-holed bamboo flute of Chinese origin used for togaku music. It is the largest of the gagaku flutes.

4. The koma-bue, a six-holed flute of Korean origin used for komagaku music. It is the smallest of the gagaku flutes.

5. The sho, a mouth organ with seventeen reed pipes (two of which are silent) in a cup-shaped wind chest with a single mouthpiece. Its predecessor was the Chinese sheng. Chords are produced by blowing into the mouthpiece and closing holes in the pipes. Its primary function is harmonic. Typically, each chord is begun softly and gradually gets louder, whereupon the next chord is produced with the same dynamic swelling; this process is repeated continuously by inhaling and exhaling air.

The wind instruments are the heart of the gagaku ensemble; they play roles analogous to those of the strings in a Western symphony orchestra.

Different instrumentations are used for togaku and komagaku. The former uses three sho, three hichiriki, three ryuteki, two biwa, two gaku-so, one kakko, one shoko, and one taiko. Instrumentation for komagaku is basically the same, except that the komabue is used instead of the ryuteki, the san-no-tsuzumi is used instead of the kakko, and the strings are not used.

The musical style of gagaku is characterized by smoothness, serenity, and precise execution without virtuosic display. The major melody, played on the hichiriki and the flutes, is supported by chords produced on the sho. An abstraction of this melody is played on the gaku-so in octaves and on the biwa in single notes. While smaller sections of a piece are marked off by a biwa arpeggio, larger sections are delineated by tsuri-daiko and shoko strokes. Drum patterns played by the kakko or san-no-tsuzumi serve similar colotomic functions and also regulate the tempo of a piece. When a chorus joins in the major melody of gagaku, it sings in a natural voice using very little ornamentation.

The melody of the gagaku is based on six modes theoretically based on the Chinese-derived ryo and ritsu scales; the rhythm is organized so that slow pieces have an eight-beat rhythm, moderately fast pieces have a four-beat rhythm, and fast pieces have a two-beat rhythm.

Gagaku music, like most music that came after it, was conceived in an aesthetic scheme of introduction–exposition–denouement known as jo-ha-kyu, which has also influenced the aesthetic of noh. In gagaku, jo is the netori, a slow beginning section that is meant to set the mood of the mode in which the piece is written. In a full-blown gagaku piece, the sho generally starts the netori (prelude), followed in turn by the hichiriki, the flute, and finally the kakko. The mood of the netori is generally subtle and serene and has a tentative feeling like a warming-up (CD 1, #23).

During the ha section, the rhythm becomes regular. Here the main body of the composition begins. The hichiriki and fue play the basic melody, the sho provides a harmonic background, and the percussion provides accompaniment; shortly, the strings also join in. Once the entire ensemble is playing together, there is no further change in the full ensemble sound.

Kyu is the rushing to the end. Here the tempo gets very fast; toward the end, the pace slackens, the instruments drop out one by one, and the texture becomes thinner. Finally, only the biwa and the gaku-so are left; they play two or three very slow notes, the biwa ending with plucking the dominant or the tonic of the mode, and the gaku-so completing the composition with one stroke on the tonic.

Listening to the archaic sound of the gagaku, one may imagine going back into the rarefied time of the Heian court nobles and sharing with them, for a brief moment at least, their profound preoccupation with aesthetic self-cultivation.

GENERAL TENDENCIES AND CHARACTERISTICS OF HOGAKU

Before closing, it may be helpful to provide some summary observations on the general tendencies and characteristics of traditional Japanese music, hogaku.

The rise and fall of a particular style of music through Japanese history has been closely linked with changes in political life, social conditions, and religious developments. For example, the gagaku of the Nara period was regarded as a symbol of authority and power of the newly evolved imperial and national government, and no effort was spared to increase its grandeur.

The noh theater, with its themes of redemption of human suffering through the love of Buddha, was exclusively an art of the ruling samurai during the long ages of military strife; it is, in particular, an expression of the samurai class's preoccupation with Zen Buddhism, which emphasizes simplicity and personal enlightenment through self-understanding and self-reliance. Noh was also a political symbol of the samurai class. During the Edo period, it continued to be performed in the Edo castle, the political center of the Tokugawa military government. Finally, the popular rise of the kabuki and the bunraku theaters was due entirely to the rise of the urban bourgeoisie and their patronage. As the bourgeois arts par excellence, they represent a fondness for popular entertainments, and in particular, lavish theatrical entertainments.

Japanese music is closely tied with ritual, literature, and dance, and these ties have remained unbroken through the ages. It was said that in ancient times, when the emperor or his courtiers asked for the pronouncement of an oracle, it was habitual to offer a musical performance first; therefore the court has always kept musicians in its service.

In hogaku, vocal music predominates. Music serves primarily as a vehicle for words and literature. All Japanese instruments were developed to emulate the human voice. It is noteworthy that the first significant instrumental solos, the tego-tomono, were created to serve as interludes to the verses of songs.

Among Japanese music genres, theatrical music is the most important. The course of Japanese music history is marked by a steady growth of theatrical music. This is due again to the Japanese love of storytelling and preoccupation with ritual.

Finally, we have already noted at some length the basic Japanese aesthetic concept of jo-ha-kyu, and the application of this concept in various kinds of music. We have also noted the propensity of the Japanese to use stereotyped melodic patterns in creating new compositions. It remains to be noted that Japanese music is predominantly a chamber music in its conception; even the gagaku ensemble is essentially a chamber orchestra.

JAPAN BIBLIOGRAPHY

William P. Malm, *Japanese Music and Musical Instruments* (Rutland, Vt: Charles E. Tuttle, 1959); William P. Malm, *Six Hidden Views of Japanese Music* (Berkeley: University of California Press, 1986); William P. Malm, *Nagauta: The Heart of Kabuki Music* (Rutland, Vt.: Charles E. Tuttle, 1963); Francis Taylor Piggott, *The Music and Musical Instruments of Japan*. 2nd ed. (London: B.T. Barsford, 1909; repr. New York: Da Capo, 1971); Eta Harich-Schneider, *A History of Japanese Music* (London: Oxford University Press, 1973); Robert Garfias, *Music of a Thousand Autumns: The*

Togaku Style of Japanese Court Music (Berkeley: University of California Press, 1975); Willem Adriaansz, *The Kumiuta and Danmono Traditions of Japanese Koto Music* (Berkeley: University of California Press, 1973); Bonnie C. Wade, *Togotomono: Music for the Japanese Koto* (Westport, Conn.: Greenwood, 1975); James R. Brandon, William P. Malm, and Donald H. Shively, *Studies in Kabuki: Its Acting, Music, and Historical Context* (Honolulu: University Press of Hawaii, 1978); Kunio Komparu, *The Noh Theater: Principles and Perspectives* (New York, Tokyo: Westherhill/Tankosha, 1983); Christine Reiko Yano, *Tears of Longing: Nostalgia and the Nation in Japanese Popular Song* (Cambridge, Mass.: Harvard University Press, 2002); Shuhei Hosokawa, et al., eds., Mitsui Toru, trans., *A Guide to Popular Music in Japan* (Kanazawa: IASPM-Japan, 1st printing, 1991; 2nd printing, 1993).

JAPAN DISCOGRAPHY

General   *Nihon No Ongaku*, 2 disks (Polydor MN-9041–9042) (notes in Japanese).

Instruments   *Traditional Music of Japan*, 3 disks, with notes in English and Japanese by Shigeo Kishibe (Nihon Victor, JL 52–54); *Japan: Semi-Classical and Folk Music*, with notes in English, French, and Italian by Shigeo Kishibe (Odeon 3 C064–17967); *Classical Music of Japan* (Elektra EKS 7285).

Shomyo   *Shomyo-Buddhist Ritual from Japan, Dai Hannya Ceremony-Shigon Sect* (UNESCO Collection Musical Sources, Philips); *The Way of Eiheiji, Zen-Buddhist Ceremony* (Folkways FR 8980) (everyday chanting of shomyo).

Shinto Music   *Edo No Kagura To Matsuri Gayashi* (Nihon Victor SJ 3004) (shinto festival and dance music).

Gagaku   *Gagaku Taikei* (Nihon Victor SJ 3002) (instrumental gagaku; another disc (SJ 3003) contains vocal gagaku); *Gagaku: Ancient Japanese Court Music* (Everest 3322); *Gagaku* (The King Record KC 1028).

Noh   *Noh*, 2 disks (Nihon Victor SJ 1005, 1006) (the most complete albums for noh; with history, music theory, libretti, photographs, and explanatory commentaries for each piece); *Hogoromo and Kantan* (Caedmon TC 2019) (contains two major noh dramas, sung and performed by players of the Komparu and Kanze School of Noh, Tokyo); *Japanese Noh Music* (Lyrichord LL 137).

Koto Music   *Sokyoku To Fiuta No Rekishi*, 4 disks (Nihon Victor SLR 510–513); *Japanese Koto Music, with Shamisen and Shakuhachi* (Lyrichord 131) (performed by masters of the Ikuta School).

Kabuki   *Azume Kabuki* (Columbia WL 5110); *Kanjincho* (Nihon Victor JL 105) (a complete Kabuki play); *Kabuki Geza Uta Shusei*, 4 disks (Nihon Victor SJL 2091–2095) (off stage kabuki music explained in detail).

6

The Music of Indonesia

Charles Capwell

JAVANESE MUSIC IN CHICAGO

A subtly glowing array of bronze ingots, pots, and gongs in intricately carved wooden cases painted indigo and red with flashes of gold leaf—this was the dazzling sight that greeted us, a small group of university students and faculty who had come to the Field Museum in Chicago for an afternoon's introduction to the performance of gamelan music (Figs. 6–1 and 6–2). Gamelan—an Indonesian word meaning "musical ensemble"—can be variously constituted, but the one at the Field Museum is representative of those used at the princely courts on Java, the most heavily populated island in the nation of Indonesia. Nowadays, similar gamelan are to be found in many universities and colleges in the United States and Europe. The Field Museum gamelan, however, has a special history: a couple of Dutchmen who owned coffee and tea plantations on Java brought the gamelan to Chicago, along with a group of Javanese musicians and craftsmen, for the Columbian Exposition of 1893, a great world's fair. The same entrepreneurs had arranged similar contributions to an exposition in Amsterdam a decade earlier and to another in Paris in 1889. At the latter, the composer Claude Debussy was enchanted by the music he heard and later tried to capture what appealed to him in pieces of his own such as some of the Preludes and Images for piano.

Now that dozens of Indonesian gamelan of various types are to be found scattered around the United States in private and institutional collections, dozens of

Figure 6–1   The Sundanese gamelan at the Columbian Exposition in Chicago, 1893, *Photo courtesy of The Field Museum of Natural History, neg. #A106223, Chicago.*

Figure 6–2   The Columbia Exposition gamelan as it looked after it was restored in 1978. *Photo courtesy of The Field Museum of Natural History, neg.#A106838c,* Chicago.

Americans have become competent performers and scholars of different types of Indonesian music. At the time of our visit to the Field Museum, Dr. Sue Carole DeVale, an ethnomusicologist with a special interest in the study of musical instruments (organology), took charge of our instruction. She had been fundamental in getting the museum to restore the gamelan, which had been more or less forgotten in storage for many decades, and had convinced them to make it available for use under her direction.

THE JAVANESE GAMELAN

Instruments in the Javanese Gamelan

Like most high-quality gamelan, this one consists largely of metallophones—in this case, instruments of gleaming bronze, but it also includes a chordophone (rebab, a two-stringed fiddle), a xylophone (gambang), an aerophone (suling, a notched vertical flute), and a couple of membranophones (kendang, drums).

Sitting among the metallophones, we became aware that the bronze had been fashioned in several different ways to make the various types of instruments. The sarons, for instance, had keys shaped like rounded ingots (Fig. 6–4, in front); these were pinned through the holes in their ends to the edges of a shallow trough made in a wooden case that thus served both to hold them in place and to increase their resonance. There were three different sets of sarons, each in a different octave. The highest, the peking, had a delicate but piercing tone; that of the middle range, barung, was mellower and longer-lasting; and the set in the lowest range, demung, had a powerful clang. The peking was sounded by striking the keys with a mallet of water-buffalo horn, but the others were played with heavier and less bright-sounding wooden mallets.

A similar three-octave range was found in the differently constructed bonangs, although there were only two of these. The lower pitched b. barung and the higher b. panerus each spanned two octaves, with the higher octave of the lower instrument duplicating the lower octave of the higher one. The "keys" of the bonangs resembled overturned bowls with knobs protruding from the tops, which is where they were struck with a pair of batonlike mallets wrapped with string. Each instrument had two rows of bowls resting on strings that were stretched in wooden frames.

The kenong also had bowllike individual components, but these were fewer and much larger than those of the bonangs, and each one was supported in its own case on a web of string. A single bowl, closer in size to one from the set of bonangs but flatter in contour, sat by itself and contrasted with all the other instruments mentioned so far because of its curiously dull-sounding "clunk"; this was the kethuk.

The most impressive bronze instruments, for both their size and their sound, were the hanging gongs. ("Gong," by the way, is a Malay—that is, Indonesian—word.) The largest, gong ageng, was nearly a meter in diameter, and its slightly smaller mate, gong siyem, hung by its side. These can be seen in the 1893 photo presiding over the whole ensemble from their privileged position at the back and in the center. On the end of the same rack that holds these gongs, a smaller gong has been suspended that is named kempul; like other names such as gong or kethuk, kempul is onomatopoetic and calls to mind the sound of the instrument it names.

In addition to these common instruments, the Field Museum gamelan also contained two others—the jenglong, similar to the kenong, which is found in gamelan from Sunda, the western part of Java; and the gambang gangsa, similar to the wooden gambang but having bronze keys like those of the saron instead of wooden ones. All in all, this original group of about twenty-four instruments was as impressive for its size as for its beauty; nevertheless, it lacked certain other instruments at the time of its use at the Columbian exposition that have since been added.

Perhaps the gender (pronounced with a hard "g" as in "good") could be considered the most important of these. Coming in two sizes (g. panerus and g. barung, like the bonang), they group thin, slablike bronze keys in a slightly larger range than the saron (Fig. 6–3). Much thinner than the ingots of the saron, the keys of the gender are struck with a pair of mallets having padded disks at their ends, and they produce a delicate, muffled ringing that makes up for their soft volume with longer lasting resonance. The secret to the long-lasting sound is that each key has its own individually tuned amplifying resonator in the form of a tube, above which it is suspended by strings so that it is not damped by resting directly on the case (the saron keys rest on pads of rubber or rattan to lessen the damping).

Originally, the kempul in the Columbian Exposition gamelan, as described, had been a single hanging gong, but additional gongs have been added to complete a full scale, as was also done for the kenong. While the two-stringed fiddle, the rebab

Figure 6–3   F.X. Widaryanto, playing the gender barung.

(Fig. 6–4), was part of the original ensemble, the plucked string instrument celem-pung, a type of zither, was among the additions.

Tuning and Scales

Having familiarized ourselves a bit with the components of what at the start had seemed a bewildering array, we still had one further thing to learn before taking up our mallets to attempt our first piece: the instruments came in pairs. A complete Javanese gamelan is in fact two orchestras in one, for there are two different types of scales used in Javanese court music, one of five tones (pentatonic) and another of seven tones (heptatonic). Since the gaps (intervals) between pitches in one scale are different from those of the other, it is not possible to select five tones from the hepta-tonic scale to produce the pentatonic, and therefore there is a separate collection of instruments for each tuning system (laras). To play in laras slendro (pentatonic sys-tem), for example, the saron players faced front, and to play in laras pelog (hepta-tonic system) they had to make a quarter-turn to the left. (You could get a general idea of the contrast between these by playing on the piano C-D-E-G-A as 1-2-3-5-6 of slendro and E-F-G-Bflat-B-C-D as 1-2-3-4-5-6-7 of pelog.)

Although the Western scale, like that of the white piano keys, is heptatonic, too, we soon discovered that the seven pitches in pelog formed a different set of intervals from the regular half- and whole-tones on the piano. The difference was not so simple as merely being one between Javanese and Western scales, however,

Figure 6–4   F.X. Widaryanto, playing the rebab.

because each gamelan has its own unique slendro and pelog scales, unless it has been constructed purposely on the model of an existing gamelan. It is a bit as though each symphony orchestra in the West used slightly different forms of major and minor and as a result their performances of standard works like Beethoven's Ninth Symphony would all sound subtly distinct from one another.

Instrument Functions and Formal Principles

When we finally took up our mallets to play, we began with a piece in pelog called "Golden Rain" (heard on Nonesuch H-72044). As the sarons attempted the first section of their melody, we sang along with them using numbers for the pitches and following our instructor: "6-5-3-2" we sang out as the sarons sounded the tones, all of equal duration. After repeating this phrase, we learned the third, "3-3-2-3," and then returned to the original for the conclusion. On the last tone, the player of the gong agneg was given the signal to strike, and the awe inspiring sound left little doubt that we had arrived at an important juncture. The role of the gong was just to furnish this most important punctuation at the end of every completed melody—a melody, in this case, having sixteen beats, with a single pitch on every beat. Two distinct musical functions were illustrated in this beginning: the sarons provided a "skeletal melody" (balungan) whose periodic punctuation (the "colotomic structure") was provided by other instruments like the gong ageng (Fig. 6–5).

Figure 6–5   The University of Illinois gamelan performance group during a rehearsal.

The other colotomic instruments were the next to join in as the sarons grew more confident: the kenong sounded the appropriate pitch at the end of every group of four beats (gatra), and so every fourth kenong stroke sounded with the gong; in the same manner, the kempul sounded the pitch every fourth beat midway between strokes of the kenong, omitting the second beat, however, so as not to interfere with the continuing resonance of the gong. Finally, on every odd-numbered beat the "clunk" of the kethuk was heard, so the beats in between kempul and kenong were marked, too.

The next instruments to be added were the bonangs, which added a third functional component to the music, that of elaboration of the balungan. Because their music was more elaborate, it also required more dexterity and skill to play than did the other instruments, and while we had been pleased at the ease with which we had picked things up to start with, it became clear as we patiently waited for the bonang players to start getting the hang of their parts that things were getting rapidly more complicated and demanding. While the bonangs required more skill to play, the principle behind their basic method of melodic elaboration was easy enough to understand: as the kenong and kempul played every fourth beat, the b. barung did the opposite and divided the beat in two, and the b. panerus divided it into four, doubling or quadrupling each pair of balungan pitches. The peking (highest-pitched saron) was also told to double the number of pitches to a beat by anticipating each balungan note. Thus, the first gatra (four-beat phrase of the balungan) came out like this:

```
bonang panerus   6  5  6  .  6  5  6  5  3  2  3  .  3  2  3  2
bonang barung       6     5     6     5     3     2     3     2
peking              6     6  5     5     3  3     2        2
SARON                     6           5           3           2
kempul                                5
kenong                                                        2
gong                                                          X
```

When we got the whole sixteen-beat phrase together, it sounded like a marvelous clock whose music was the actual time-keeping mechanism, and just as with a clock, the sounding of the gong signaled a conclusion that could also be the taking-off point for another cycle.

Whether we were to repeat or not was indicated to us by the drum player, our instructor, who, in regulating and supporting the pulse and rhythm of the music, fulfilled the fourth function in the ensemble so that the melody, its elaboration, and its punctuation were controlled from this instrument rather as the conductor in a Western orchestra controls the rest of the group. (In the eighteenth-century Western orchestra, in fact, the "conductor" was actually a performer, too—usually the first violin or the harpsichord player.)

When we had at last become comfortable with this first phrase, we went on to complete the piece with a second, similarly constructed phrase (7567 5672 2765 6765) which we now learned to call a gongan, that is, a phrase punctuated with a stroke of the big gong. As we have seen, each gongan was divided into four 4-beat kenongan (punctuated with a kenong stroke), and each of these was further subdivided by a kempul stroke on the second beat and kethuk strokes on beats 1 and 3. Because this colotomic pattern is a fixed structure, it is common to a number of pieces differentiated from one another by, for example, their balungan, but similar in their colotomy, and these make up a general category of small, simple pieces called bubaran. The particular piece we had learned, as was mentioned, has the title "Udan Mas" ("Golden Rain") and is used to send people off at the end of a ceremony or concert. It served as our farewell, too, as we had used up most of the afternoon and decided not to press our luck in attempting another piece.

The Variety of Styles and Forms

Although we came away feeling we had accomplished quite a bit in one afternoon, we had, of course, barely scratched the surface of this one type of Indonesian music. We hadn't even touched some of the instruments such as the genders, for example, because we played a "loud-style" piece in which gender, rebab, celempung, gambang, and suling do not participate; these difficult instruments are used for the elaboration of "soft-style" pieces, which may also include singing by a chorus of men (gerongan) and one or two female soloists (pesindhen).

We had naturally learned to play a short, simple type of piece, but among the types of other pieces for gamelan there are some whose gongan, for example, have sixteen times as many beats as our sixteen-beat bubaran. And instead of playing just twice for each beat, the saron peking might play four times in order to fill in the great gap between one beat and another—so it might be as much as ten minutes between strokes of the gong ageng instead of the approximately ten seconds of our bubaran.

As an example of a small-scale, soft-style piece, we could consider ketawang "puspawarna" laras slendro pathet manyura. This is a work entitled "Kinds of Flowers" ("Puspawarna") that has a gongan of sixteen beats, like a bubaran, but it is divided into only two eight-beat kenongan, and therefore it falls into the class of ketawang. It employs the scale of the pentatonic tuning (laras slendro) in one of three particular ways or pathet, that is called "peacock" (manyura). (There are also three distinct pathet for laras pelog.)

"Puspawarna" is a very popular piece (cf. Nonesuch H-72044 and H-72074) played not only on the precious gamelan of princes but also on the modest two- or three-piece ensembles of itinerant street musicians. Despite its wide use for a variety of circumstances and audiences, however, it is not merely a piece intended for listening pleasure; it also has particular associations and prescribed uses, and even its title can tell us something about the political and cultural history of Java.

THE CULTURAL AND HISTORICAL SIGNIFICANCE OF JAVANESE GAMELAN MUSIC

Ketawang "Puspawarna": A Piece for the Prince

Just as "Hail to the Chief" played by the Marine Band has sometimes been used to announce the arrival of the President at a function or ceremony, "Puspawarna" was played by the gamelan of the two subsidiary central-Javanese courts to announce the presence or the arrival of their respective princes. The main courts of the Sultan of Yogyakarta and of the Susuhunan of Surakarta (Solo) were established in the mideighteenth century when the Dutch succeeded in supporting their trade interests by asserting political control over much of the Indonesian archipelago. The central-Javanese kingdom of Mataram was divided at that time between two ruling families centered at Yogyakarta and Solo, with a secondary court, the Mangkunegaran, attached to Solo. Later, in the early nineteenth century, the Paku Alaman court was established as an adjunct to Yogyakarta, and the various princes all had their own particular identifying pieces of music, "Puspawarna" serving both of the subsidiary courts and symbolizing a family connection between them.

Since political power was largely in the hands of the colonial overlords, the wealth and energy of the courts was expended on the development of cultural matters like music and dance as a means of both establishing and justifying their precedence and prestige. Mataram had been the last great native power in Java, a Muslim kingdom in a land where Islam had steadily been increasing its influence for several centuries. As the Sanskrit words in the title "Puspawarna" and in the name of pathet

"Manyura" reveal, however, the culture of India and its Hindu and Buddhist religions had considerable influence on the elite and ruling classes in Java and other parts of the Indonesian region for a millennium or so before the establishment of Islam, which itself had been introduced in large part by traders from northwestern India. While a segment of Indonesian society may follow a strict and conservative Islam that, among other things, condemns most musical and performing arts, the aristocracy of Java, while accepting the "new" belief, continues to prize the older spiritual and cultural concepts and also to accommodate indigenous practice and beliefs that antedate any of the imported ones.

Some Spiritual Aspects of Javanese Gamelan Music

We may discover something of the complex relationship between Islam and music that obtains in Java by citing some observations the ethnomusicologist Jaap Kunst made about sixty years ago:

> The gamelan, found by the Islam on arrival in Java as an indispensable element of all Hindu ceremonials, has never become . . . an integral part of Mohammedan religious rite. Accordingly during the month of fasting, as well as on Fridays, all orchestras in the whole of the Javanese territory are expected to remain silent. (This rule is not strictly adhered to in the kraton [court]. All that is done there is to avoid beating the gong ageng, and to play the gong kemodong [a substitute gong] instead. The princes, for that matter, are regarded as above the adat [customary law]. When, for example, one of their memorial days falls in the fasting month, then the prohibition of gamelan-playing, it seems, is raised entirely. Then, however, a sum of money is paid into the mosque cashbox as a compensation of this breach of the religious adat.)[1]

Princely privilege was partly related to the use of music in rites and ceremonies, and to do away with music altogether would have undermined the privilege as well; yet acceptance of Islam required some recognition of its precepts. So a fine was paid to the mosque when a princely anniversary requiring musical performance to ensure its success violated the prohibition against playing the gamelan, or alternatively, the most imposing and important instrument in the ensemble was kept silent and a simpler substitute was used. In the latter case, the gong ageng no doubt stood as a metonymical symbol for the whole ensemble which could be considered silent, too, if it were absent.

The Power of the Gong

But another reason for silencing the gong might also be offered. In many cultures the blacksmith has had a special position, not simply because of his technological

---

[1]Japp Kunst, *Music in Java: Its History, Its Theory, Its Technique*, 3rd enlarged ed., ed. Ernst Heins (The Hague: Martinus Nijhoff, 1973), Vol. 1, pp. 266–267.

expertise but also because of his spiritual power.[2] Metallurgical skill was considered to require supernatural cooperation, and the smith, therefore, had to be possessed with special powers to accomplish his extraordinary task of converting earth and stone into metal. In Java, the smith in charge of forging a new gamelan used to prepare himself by fasting and other acts of purification so that he could become fit for possession by the spirit of Panji, a culture hero who figures in many traditional Javanese stories. If the forging of the instruments were successful, they too would become the abode of a spirit, and the gong ageng, the most difficult instrument to make, would contain the greatest spiritual power. Especially fine old gamelan—or their spirits—have even been ennobled; one at the Yogyakarta kraton, for example, that actually antedates the founding of the Sultanate in 1755 and that is used for special celebrations like those accompanying the birthday anniversary of Mohammed, is referred to as "Kangjeng Kyai Guntur Madu," or "Venerable Sir Torrent of Honey." For this reason, it remains proper etiquette when entering the gamelan to remove one's shoes and to avoid the rudeness of stepping over an instrument. Further, the spirit of the gamelan, embodied in the gong ageng, is paid homage with offerings of food, flowers, and incense. A rigidly orthodox Muslim might find such behavior to be verging on idolatry, so it is not surprising that even in the more flexible attitude found at the kraton, the gong ageng should be singled out for silencing on the Sabbath.

A Christian, too, might object to venerating the spirit of the gong, but just as different attitudes prevail among the Muslims, Christians can also accommodate old patterns of behavior. Consider, as an illustration, a story told to me by a dancer whose family had been performers connected with the Yogyakarta kraton and whose father had converted to Christianity. Once when he was rehearsing with a gamelan, the gong was disturbing him by its poor tone quality, even though it was supposed to be a very fine instrument. It was suggested that the spirit of the gong was disturbed and that an offering of incense and flowers should be made to it; when this was done, the dancer was pleased and surprised to notice that the gong began to sound resonantly and clearly again.

The spiritual power that is invested in old gamelan by tradition in turn invests power in their owners, for which reason they are important components of princely regalia (pusaka), over which battles have been fought in the past. The gendhing (musical work) played on these gamelan, too, may have such power that, for example, it was in the past forbidden to hum them casually; in transcribing them into notation—a practice initiated as a result of European influence in the nineteenth century—it used to be considered advisable to make an occasional mistake in order to prevent the power of the tune being used inappropriately.

[2]Mircea Eliade, *The Forge and the Crucible*, 2nd ed. (Chicago, University of Chicago Press, 1978), p. 238.

The Sacred Dance Bedhaya

The tunes accompanying the sacred dance bedhaya, for example, are considered especially powerful because of the reputed origin of the music and dance and their association with kingship, as recounted in this paraphrase of a story from the *History of Gamelan* by Warsadiningrat:

One night in the year 1643, Sultan Agung (the last great ruler of the kingdom preceding the establishment of Yogya and Solo) was meditating when he heard music that was so beautiful it gave him goosebumps. The next day he decided to form a dance troupe and called together musical experts to arrange the melodies for the accompaniment. Suddenly Kanjeng Sunan Kalijaga appeared; one of the nine saints legend credits with introducing Islam into Java, he was a noble Hindu by birth who first became a notorious bandit and then converted to Islam after a lengthy period of continuous meditation in the manner of a Hindu holyman. Kalijaga congratulated the Sultan on his plans to create the gendhing bedhaya, for it was clearly a gift from He Who Is Great and Holy and meant to be a pusaka for the kings of Java that would bring blessings of peace, supremacy, and strength until the end of time.

Nine young girls from noble families were selected for their beauty and grace to dance the bedhaya. The bedhaya dance is important because (1) it contributes to an understanding of Javanese culture by providing a guide to meditation; (2) it explains certain strategies of war; (3) it contributes to an understanding of music that portrays deep and noble emotions.

Just as the dance lessons were to begin, Kanjeng Ratu Kencana Sari, queen of all spirits, good and evil, suddenly arrived from her palace in the South Sea, in the dress and make-up of a bride. She appeared every day at dusk for three months to teach the dance because she loved the noble and majestic melodies, and she still appears for this reason. Because of this, when the bedhaya is performed, complete offerings of many kinds are prepared and a great deal of incense is burned continuously throughout the performance, and all the performers—dancers, singers, and musicians—must be pure and clean.[3]

As we see in this story, bedhaya is a remarkable example of the eclectic nature of Javanese elite culture and the way in which it is used to assert status. Music and dance that conjure an indigenous Javanese goddess from her home in the sea and receive the blessing of a legendary Muslim saint whose conversion was accomplished through yogic meditation constitute one of the special heirlooms that buttress the powers of the king (Fig. 6–6).

[3]Paraphrase of pp. 80–83 of "Wedha Pradangga" by Raden Tumenggung Warsadiningrat, trans. Susan Pratt Walton, in *Karawitan: Source Readings in Javanese Gamelan and Vocal Music*, Vol. 2 ed., Judith Becker, Michigan Papers on South and Southeast Asia No. 30 (Ann Arbor: Center for South and Southeast Asian Studies, University of Michigan, 1987). Description of Kalijaga based on pp. 25–29 of Clifford Geertz's *Islam Observed: Religious Development in Morocco and Indonesia* (Chicago: University of Chicago Press, 1973).

Figure 6–6   A performance of bedhaya at the kraton of the Sultan of Jogyakarta.
*Photo from Tari di Mangkunagaran . . . M.A. Thesis (1990) for Gadjah Mada University
by B. Suharti.*

The Shadow Play—Wayang Kulit

The shadow-puppet theater, or wayang kulit, is another Indonesian performance medium using music that has achieved special prominence in Javanese culture and that may also be associated with extraordinary power. While stories of Javanese and Islamic origins are performed in shadow plays, the stories derived from the Indian epics the Mahabharata and the Ramayana have the greater popularity and prestige, particularly the Mahabharata. Performed during the course of a whole night, the plays generally depict a battle whose turmoil is reflected in a disturbance of nature that, towards morning, is resolved when order is restored to human society and the world.

While the stories of the wayang kulit revolve around Indic characters, they have been Javanized by the introduction of a number of comic characters who act as servants to the protagonists and incidentally serve as translators for the audience, since their masters speak a Sanskritized and highfalutin poetic Javanese that is not commonly understood. This differentiation according to language reflects the situation in contemporary Javanese, which has many styles of speech based upon social class distinctions. (In Indonesia, whose motto is "Unity in Diversity," the Indonesian language—Bahasa Indonesia—has rapidly gained acceptance throughout the country as the lingua franca, since it helps to overcome regional, ethnic, and class differences.) The chief of the clowns, Semar, is a fat, lazy, wily, lascivious, and obstreperously flatulent fellow, but he is also a mysteriously all-knowing sage who even takes precedence over the Hindu god Siva himself. Java may have been awed by exotic Indian culture, but it seems that autochthonous wisdom still earns the greater respect. Since Semar speaks colloquially, he has the advantage not only of entertaining the audience with his wit and shenanigans but also of giving good advice and wise counsel.

In fact, all the familiar characters in wayang communicate, at least by their actions, the various modes of human existence and manners of behavior. The shadow play has thus long been a medium for moral and ethical instruction and for discussion of contemporary events, and today it is often a medium for explaining government social programs as well.

All the different skills and knowledge needed to perform the shadow play come together in the dhalang, the puppeteer, a man (rarely a woman) who commands a thorough knowledge of karawitan (musical repertory and practice), who is familiar with the many different stories of the plays and their appropriateness for particular occasions, who speaks with a host of voices suited to everyone from the most refined gentleman to the crudest villain, who can skillfully move his puppets to convey an equal range of refinement and crudity, who knows archaic languages and the full range of contemporary social dialects, who is a repository of spiritual and cultural values, and who is acquainted with the latest political events and social problems. No wonder he is often thought to be a kind of superman!

Seated between a light source and a thin screen, the dhalang casts the shadows of flat leather puppets against the screen, all the while giving the appropriate signals to the gamelan for the pieces of music needed to accompany the scene, be it a moment of comic relief with Semar dancing or a tremendous battle between the forces of good and evil. Sometimes he sings, too, to set the mood for an upcoming scene.

Now that dhalangs can learn their art in schools (just as gamelan musicians do), an abbreviation and standardization of the wayang stories and of the puppeteers' skills is occurring. This inevitably lessens the special aura of the wayang and of the dhalang but helps to ensure them a continuing role in the cultural life of modern Indonesia.

MUSIC IN BALI

The arts of Indonesia, especially music and dance, have undergone many changes over the centuries as political and social circumstances have created different requirements and possibilities for performance. Among recent influences, the impact of tourism is certainly one of enormous significance, particularly for the arts of Bali, the small island just to the east of Java in the Indonesian archipelago. A jet airport that was opened there in 1969 has made possible easy accessibility to Bali for tourists from around the world, who since then have come in ever-increasing numbers. Not that tourism is new to Bali: some of its most famous visitors—painters, composers, anthropologists—arrived there in the decades prior to World War II and often stayed long enough to leave their indelible imprint on Balinese life.

Some Historical Events Influencing Balinese Culture

Before we touch upon the impact of tourism on the music of Bali, let us first consider a couple of political events of singular importance in the history of Bali. Earlier, we mentioned the Islamic kingdom of Mataram in the discussion of bedhaya. This kingdom was the predecessor of the central Javanese courts, founded in the eighteenth century through intervention of the Dutch, that still continue to exist in a ceremonial way in the present-day Republic of Indonesia. Mataram itself had earlier displaced the Hindu kingdom of Majapahit, refugees from which migrated to Bali in the fifteenth century. The culture these refugees brought with them casts an attenuated shadow over the arts of Bali today, but the aura attendant on all things connected with Majapahit casts all other cultural criteria into the shade. The elite Hindu-Buddhist-based culture of Majapahit introduced a new layer into the cultural fabric of Bali, and those who resisted its caste-based hierarchy and monarchical organization retreated to remoter areas of the island where so-called Bali Aga or "old Bali" villages continue many of the pre-Indo-Javanese ways.

The other overwhelming event in Bali's history took place in 1908 when the kingdoms that had dominated the island for the last several centuries were finally dissolved by the Dutch, who invaded the island and took over its administration. The effect of Dutch intervention on Bali was quite different from its effect on Java. In Java the newly established courts, provided with financial resources but given limited responsibilities of governance, evolved an elegant way of life that fostered the development of the arts as the most effective means of retaining exalted status. In Bali the courts were dissolved, and the descendants of nobles, who were often employed as agents of Dutch rule, rarely had the financial resources to maintain the elaborate musical establishments associated with courtly life.

Music in the Balinese Courts

Among the several different ensembles maintained by Balinese kings, with their different instruments, musicians, repertories, and functions, was the gamelan gambuh, a kind of opera derived from Majapahit models. Quite unlike the large gamelan of metallophones we encountered in discussing Java, this one is smaller and consists of several extraordinarily long, vertical flutes (suling gambuh) and a rebab, with a few percussion instruments for punctuation and rhythmic control. The melodies of the flutes and fiddle are elaborately ornamented like those of the corresponding instruments in the Javanese gamelan, but rather than being part of a much denser and richer texture that competes with them, these flute melodies are the sole focus of attention. The flutes, whose tones have an ethereal and otherworldly quality, are played in such a manner that the melody is never interrupted when the player takes a breath. Using his cheeks as a kind of bellows, he inflates them before taking a breath so that he can continue to sound the flute with air from his cheeks while breathing in. The long-winded melodies and unfamiliar orchestra, the stately progress of the action, and the archaic language of the actors and general lack of comic episodes have given gambuh the status of a venerated relic of the past, even though it has recently undergone something of a revival. Much more popular today is the gamelan arja theater, another type of operatic performance not associated with courtly ceremony. It too has a small ensemble with flutes of a shorter, more common type and a few percussion instruments, but it also employs a greater variety of stories (including some on modern, topical subjects), female as well as male actors, and a lot of comedy.

Now rather rare, the "gamelan with the big gongs" (gamelan gong gede) is another ensemble that played an important role in the old courts. In its construction, it is more similar to the large instrumental gamelan of central Java than the g. gambuh is. It was regularly played for public ceremonies and temple festivities and performed pieces with regular structures whose melodies, elaboration, colotomy, and rhythm were realized in ways broadly similar to those discussed earlier for Javanese gendhing. An important difference, however, is the fact that, like the majority of Balinese ensembles, the gamelan gong gede is a single orchestra with but one tuning system, pelog; further, the version of pelog used is pentatonic—a selection of five pitches from the heptatonic pelog system scale. Like gambuh, this gamelan has a more popular and modern counterpart that we will discuss later.

A third court ensemble, gamelan Semar pegulingan, is a sizeable orchestra consisting largely of metallophones that was used to play purely instrumental arrangements of gambuh for the private enjoyment of the court. Since gambuh melodies employ heptatonic scales, some gamelan Semar pegulingan used to have fully heptatonic instruments, but others played pentatonic versions of the melodies. Today this ensemble, with its peculiarly delicate sound, has been revived to play a variety of old-style, classically structured pieces as well as new compositions and arrangements.

A very modest ensemble, the gender wayang, has not suffered a loss of popularity or been in need of revival because of its association with the shadow play based on stories of the Mahabharata and Ramayana. This quartet of gender, similar in construction and playing technique to the gender of Java and tuned in laras slendro, is the sole accompaniment, other than the voice of the dhalang, for the Mahabharata; some percussion and colotomic instruments are added to it for the stories of the Ramayana. The quartet consists in fact of two pairs of gender distinguished from one another by being in different octaves. Within each pair, moreover, one instrument is distinguished from the other by being slightly "out of tune," that is, a particular key on one instrument is purposely made slightly higher or lower than its twin in order to create a sensation of acoustical beats that gives a shimmering quality to the pitch when the keys are struck simultaneously. As the instruments of a pair are often played in unison, the result is a constantly throbbing resonance that almost seems to be breathing. While particularly effective in the Balinese wayang quartet, this principle of purposeful "mistuning" is evident in other bronze ensembles as well, and is especially noticeable when an octave is played.

The gender wayang continues to be a vitally important component of Bali's musical life, but the gamelan gambuh, Semar pegulingan, and gong gede have a more attenuated role as reminders of the past. With the passing of the courts, the patronage needed for the maintenance of the large numbers of instruments and for the support of the musicians, actors, and dancers disappeared. The common people of Bali, however, responded by filling the gap left by the absence of noble patrons, and this provided the impetus and stimulus for developing new types of performing arts. When Western intellectuals began to discover Bali between the World Wars, there was an efflorescence of the arts as they adjusted to the passing of old forms while accommodating new influences from the people and from contact with foreigners.

A Modern Form of Dance and Music—Kebyar

The most vibrant of the new styles was the result of the reshaping of the gamelan gong gede into the gamelan gong kebyar, by dropping some instruments and modifying and borrowing others. Village gamelan clubs often bought older-style gamelan no longer maintained or needed by the courts and recast them into the new form, and the new music developed for these was a revolutionary departure from the sedate and majestic pieces of the repertory for the gamelan gambuh or gamelan gong gede. In the latter, predictably familiar formal structures, conventional instrumentation, stable rhythms, and relatively unvaried dynamics created a sense of classical elegance; but the music of kebyar was a revolutionary change—virtuosic, mercurial, flashy, and unpredictable (Fig. 6–7).

In an old-style gendhing for the gamelan gong or Semar pegulingan, the introduction would normally be a somewhat tentative solo on the trompong, an instrument similar to the Javanese bonang. Kebyar music, on the other hand, immediately asserts its independence of older formal traditions by beginning with a loud, confident unison for the whole ensemble like that heard on CD 1, #24. Instead of the classical elegance and refinement of former times, it displays a willful exuberance, progressing in fits and starts with sudden dynamic contrasts, jerky syncopations, and breathtakingly rapid figuration. No wonder many older connoisseurs found kebyar a disturbing phenomenon when it first took Bali by storm around the time of World War I.

Figure 6–7   The Gamelan gong kebyar "Tjarman Wati" of Sebatu, Bali. *Photo reproduced courtesy of Mel Howard.*

Originally a purely orchestral music ideally suited for musical competitions among different villages, kebyar was given a new twist when it began to accompany dance. About 1925, a young dancer named Mario made a particular impression with his version of a dance to go with this exciting music. Like the fixed structures of the classical gendhing, the various dances done by trained court dancers or by people making offerings at the temple were based on traditional movements and gestures, and the stock characters of dramas like gambuh were confined to expressing the limited range of moods suited to them. But Mario's kebyar mirrored the fleeting moods and unpredictable contrasts of the music. Performing in an unusual crouched position, the dancer was on the same level as the seated musicians with whom he sometimes interacted directly, seeming to tease and cajole. Alternately rising onto his knees and squatting, playing with a fan, flashing a bizarre series of glances that registered astonishment, pique, enticement, and fury in rapid succession, the dancer would interpret the music's every change, and to top things off he might conclude by joining his accompanists in a choreographically performed solo on the obsolete trompong, all the while continuing to bob up and down and back and forth on his knees, twirl his mallets like a drum major, and register a bewildering series of moods on his face (Fig. 6–8). While originally danced by boys or young men, today kebyar is also danced by young women dressed as men; this kind of cross-dressing in dance performance is nothing new, however.

Figure 6–8   A typical dance pose in kebyar. *Photo reproduced courtesy of Mel Howard.*

The individual nature of kebyar gave a new importance to the role of the composer and choreographer, and for a while compositions were jealously guarded as the special property of a particular club. The concept of the "composition" in the view of the Balinese gamelan club, however, is hardly equivalent to the Westerner's idea of a piece, say, by Beethoven. We can get an idea of how a Balinese composition is realized and treated from a memoir written by John Coast, an impresario who arranged the first world tour of the gamelan from Peliatan village in 1951. For this occasion, Coast wanted a special new piece for the repertory of the tour, and he commissioned Mario to choreograph a new dance to go with it. Here is his account of how the gamelan learned the piece.

When we arrived about nine o'clock that night in the village we found the gamelan well into the first melody of the new dance [which they were learning by having each part demonstrated, as is customary, rather than from a score]; and it was Kebiar music, though new, Mario told us, having been composed originally by Pan Sukra for a club in Marga, near Tabanan, but it had never been used. And anyhow, these tunes were arranged for a girl dancer, while the original ones had been for a man.

It took about three weeks for the thirty minutes of music to be perfectly mastered by Pliatan, and at the end of that time Pan Sukra went home to his village. Then Anak Agung, Made Lebah, and Gusti Kompiang grinned freely. "Now it is our turn," they said.

"What do you mean?" we asked.

"Aggh! This is crude music. Now it is a matter of tabuh—style. You will see. It must be rearranged and polished by the club.[4]

In light of this, we might think of the Boston Symphony Orchestra playing a composition originally composed for the New York Philharmonic and, when the composer had turned his back, rewriting it according to their own tastes! No doubt some instrumentalists in Boston would respond with that expressive "Aggh!" to a newly commissioned work, but it is highly unlikely they would have the temerity to suggest altering the piece once it was completed, even if the composer had once asked for their advice on how to arrange the parts for their particular instruments.

Even in matters of interpretation, the initiative is apt to be that of the music director and conductor rather than of the rank-and-file instrumentalist. But in Peliatan as in other Balinese gamelan, the repertory was shaped by the contributions of all the club members although decisions may have been made by acknowledged leaders like the Anak Agung, a nobleman, and Made Lebah, a commoner, both of whom were respected performers and teachers.

In his account of the creation of the dance to go with the new music, Coast again reveals the cooperative nature of the work.

And we saw the story of the dance unfold, as Mario had told us it would, creating itself bit by bit, with ideas thrown in from us all. We saw Raka as the little bumblebee sunning herself in a flower-filled garden, in moods of surprise, delight and fear; we saw the gaudy male bumblebee enter, and Sampih could pick up Mario's ideas with the speed with which a western ballet dancer follows an enchainement in class; we saw him spy the delectable little bee, zoom toward her, court her, frighten her by his advances till she fled from him. Then Sampih danced alone in baffled fury as the Kebiar music raged around him, and in the last rollicking melody he danced a Kebiar of sheer frustration around the whole gamelan, flirting desperately with its members. This was a development out of Mario's original Kebiar, and he called it now: Tumulilingan Mengisap Sari—the Bumblebee Sips Honey.

Luce was meanwhile busy with the costumes. . . . All our Pliatan family were engrossed in this dance, for it was a new thing and it was ours.[5]

[4]John Coast, *Dancers of Bali* (New York: Putnam, 1953), p. 109.
[5]Ibid., p. 110.

To the creation of this new piece—which soon became a standard item in the repertory of the gamelan gong kebyar—even Coast and other members of the entrepreneur's retinue were able to make contributions as part of the "Pliatan family."

THE INFLUENCE OF FOREIGN ARTISTS AND TOURISTS

The Revival of Gamelan Angklung

Coast and his entourage were hardly the first outsiders to have an influence on Balinese arts, though. In 1938, for example, the Canadian-American composer Colin McPhee had, among other things, inspired the resuscitation of a moribund type of gamelan angklung. This multipurpose ensemble, often having only a four-tone scale, was a common feature of most village ceremonies and festivities, and at the time McPhee was in Bali only a few gamelan angklung in remote villages any longer included the instrument for which it was named. A kind of bamboo rattle, each angklung produces a single pitch in two, three, or four octaves, depending on how many bamboo tubes are loosely mounted in the frame that is shaken back and forth to make them sound. Ingeniously constructed, each tube is sliced in half over the greater part of its length to form a "key" that produces the desired pitch while the remainder of the tube is left intact to form a tuned resonator. Taking an interest in this obsolete instrument, McPhee attempted an experiment that he recalls in his book *Music in Bali*.[6]

> Bright young musicians from central Bali who accompanied me on my expeditions to these remote villages found their old-fashioned orchestras utterly absurd. They would sit in polite silence while the musicians played, but could hardly wait until we drove off to comment on the "plain" . . . style of the music, the "stiff" . . . way of playing, and to gaily parody the preposterous accompaniment of the angklungs.
>
> Nevertheless, when in 1938 I organized in Sayan a gamelan angklung composed entirely of small boys, I decided to include a set of angklungs in the orchestra. At first the children ignored these instruments entirely, but they soon became intrigued with their unusual sound, and there was much discussion—in which I took no part—as to who should play them. I engaged a young musician from Karangasem [the remote area where angklungs were still used] to teach the club and train the four boys to whom the angklungs had been assigned. These latter caught on to the unfamiliar style with surprising rapidity. Within a few months this club of children—a complete novelty in Bali—had acquired a repertory of compositions, some short, some of considerable length, which they played with complete assurance. Their first public appearance at a temple odalan [festival] in Sayan created a local sensation, partly because of the youth of the musicians, some of whom were no more than five or six, but especially because of

---

[6]Another of McPhee's books, *A Club of Small Men*, is a full account of the history of this ensemble. Written for children, it is also enjoyable reading for adults. Colin McPhee, *A Club of Small Men* (New York: J. Day Co., 1948), pp. 48, 61.

the novelty of the angklungs. The word spread, and soon the club was in demand for festivals in other villages; the gamelan with angklungs had proved a success. Today [1966], I am told, these almost forgotten instruments have become familiar to everyone, and have been adopted by other angklung orchestras in central Bali.[7]

While the angklung may have been on the verge of extinction in Bali when it was revived by McPhee's intervention, in Sunda, West Java, (where the Columbian Exposition gamelan came from) the angklung has always retained its popularity. But there, too, it has experienced interesting changes. Often combined with oboelike tarompets in ensembles accompanying street entertainments such as martial-arts duels or trance dancers, the angklung is now also found in school orchestras, where it is tuned to the Western diatonic scale for performing tunes like "Waltzing Matilda" in complete harmonic arrangements.

The evidence for change as a result of external influence in the Sundanese use of the angklung is obvious, but in the Balinese example it is hidden, since the music it performs had a continuous tradition. Without the intervention of McPhee, however, the angklung might have remained an archaic curiosity in Bali.

A Ramayana Performance—Kecak

McPhee's friend Walter Spies, with whom he toured Indonesia playing two-piano recitals, was also involved in bringing about changes in the arts of Bali. Primarily a painter, Spies had a profound influence on the visual arts as well, but his involvement in the development of kecak is of particular interest because this unusual performance medium has become a "must-see" item for tourists, who are often unaware that they are witnessing an art form specifically created to satisfy them. Being strange and disturbing in terms of the Westerners' usual experience of performing arts, it has indeed satisfied millions of tourists as an experience of something powerfully exotic, without which the time and money we spend in getting to new and distant places might seem poorly spent.

The kecak takes its name from the brusque, staccato monosyllables shouted by a large chorus of men in rapid and intricately interlocking rhythmic patterns. A few other men imitate with their voices the sound of a small gamelan, and these two elements accompany a drastically shortened version of the Ramayana acted out by a few actor-dancers. The basic story is this: Sita, wife of King Rama, an incarnation of the god Vishnu, has been abducted by the demon Ravana, who carries her off to his palace in Sri Lanka, but Hanuman, general of the monkey army and devotee of Rama, pursues them and rescues Sita. Since the chorus of men intermittently takes

---

[7]Colin McPhee, *Music in Bali* (New York: DaCapo, 1976), p. 243.

on the role of Hanuman's monkey army and sounds like chattering monkeys, the performance is also called the "Monkey Chant."

The rhythmic shouting of the men is traditionally associated with rituals of divination, in which young girls are entranced in order for questions to be put to the spirits (sanghyang) that take possession of them. While music and dance are frequently part of these rituals, dramatic stories from the Ramayana are not. Thinking that the kecak was an exciting and unusual kind of music, Spies suggested using it as the foundation for a concise presentation of the Ramayana that would give tourists, who were already discovering Bali before World War II, a professionally arranged and attractive means of experiencing it.

A Trance Dance—Barong

Performers in the Ramayana form of kecak do not go into trance as do the mediums in the sanghyang type, and in fact there is no indication in the former of the original association with trance. Barong, another kind of trance ritual adapted as a regular performance medium for tourists, is a kind of dramatic presentation accompanied by the gamelan gong or kebyar that represents the struggle between Good (in the being of the barong, an awesome but benevolent lion) and Evil (impersonated by a horrendous and malevolent witch). At the high point of the story, the supporters of the barong attack the witch with their krises (wavy daggers) and are forced by the witch's magic to turn them instead upon their own bodies, but the magic of the barong protects them from injuring themselves. During performances at village temples, many participants may fall into trance during and after the battle; indeed the spirits that are normally thought to reside in the masks of the barong and of the witch may possess the men who wear them as well.

In temple rituals for the Balinese themselves, the barong is certainly an event of supernatural import, but that does not prevent it from being an entertainment as well. One village, in fact, may visit another to perform its particular version of the barong and be appreciated for the style with which it performs as well as for the evident power of its barong and witch. There are, in fact, trance performances in Bali and elsewhere in Indonesia in which the trancers are said to be possessed by animals or even inanimate objects and that seem to have as their sole or main purpose the presentation of a bizarre entertainment. In such circumstances, the entertainment of tourists with a barong performance seems to fit in with the Balinese view of things, but it should be clear that such a performance cannot mean the same thing as one in which the primary object is to create a sense of well-being and security for the community rather than, for economic gain, to satisfy the curiosity of outsiders. While many of the tourists may regale their friends back home with stories of the "authentic" rituals they witnessed, the Balinese probably have a clearer idea of the distinction between the different types of authenticity involved in the performance of barong for themselves and for tourists.

Although changes in the motivations and presentation of performances like kecak or barong may be regretted by many for whom their original associations have strong meaning, such regret is surely an inevitable part of human experience, as no society is static and all culture must evolve and change or cease to exist. As the Sun Dance and other festivities of the Plains Indians in North America evolved into pan-Indian powwow celebrations or as the Medicine Dance of the San people of Botswana has evolved into a performance for others as well as for the San themselves, barong may be undergoing an evolution from an organic and vital part of specific Balinese communities to a "cultural performance" meant to help shape the idea of "Baliness" for the modern Balinese and for the outside world. Musical performances like barong, after all, can help mediate not just the contact between the human and the otherworldly but also the contact between groups of human beings, and we may hope that this latter role is no less powerful a validation of an art form than the former.

FOUR KINDS OF POPULAR MUSIC IN JAVA

Gambus

Entertainment and monetary gain are often thought of as the only reasons for the existence of many types of popular music. But when we think, for example, of how some people enjoy rap and willingly pay for the pleasure of listening to it while others dislike it but are vehemently devoted to reggae or heavy metal, it becomes clear that more powerful motivations must also be involved. Like barong, such music can shape an identity—for an individual or a group—and present it to the world. In Indonesia, one of the pop musics that succeeds in doing this as well as providing its consumers a good deal of enjoyment is gambus, a genre named for an Arabic instrument that signifies connection with the homeland of Islam. Nowadays the gambus may be present only by virtue of having lent its name to the genre, the instrument itself having been replaced by the 'ud, which has wider currency in the music of the Middle East.

Not just the instruments of gambus—which may include, for example, qanun and dombak (Middle Eastern type of zither and drum)—but the musical style itself reflects Middle Eastern origins, with its short, often sequentially repeated phrases and simple, catchy, and danceable rhythms; even the vocal timbre is often more that of Middle Eastern than of Indonesian singers. And the dress of the performers as depicted on the sleeves of cassettes may include such articles as the kaffiyeh and agal, the Arab headdress worn by men (Fig. 6–9). Although the texts of gambus may have Islamic subject matter, the songs are very much appreciated for their musical qualities—too much so in view of the more puritanical Muslims. As one Javanese

Figure 6–9 Cover for cassette recording of gambus.

Muslim told the anthropologist Clifford Geertz in response to a query about gambus, "It's like Africa in Java," by which he meant to say (being ignorant of the spiritual and communal values in much African music) that the music was not conducive to leading a proper Islamic life since it was primitive and sensual. Perhaps one could imagine a similar confrontation in the United States between supporters of Christian rock and their adversaries.

Dangdut

Dangdut is another popular music that is an extraordinary mix of Western rock and Indian film song (CD 1, #25). Its Indonesian texts have usually dealt with homiletic advice about leading a better, more productive and uprightly Islamic life although secular love lyrics are becoming increasingly common now. Its infectious rhythms have earned it the onomatopoetic name dangdut that represents its characteristic drum sounds and, for those who deride it, its suspiciously worldly appeal.

Transformed into a popular medium for broadcasting Islamic values to the public in the seventies under the influence of the superstar Rhoma Irama (originally called Oma, he added the "R" and "h" from Raden Haji, a title given those Muslims who, as he did, perform the pilgrimage to Mecca), it has become the dominant pop music in the nineties, and like the Indian songs from which it borrowed so much, it has been featured heavily in films.

Kroncong

While dangdut, a relatively recent phenomenon, has had a fairly swift rise in popularity in the manner of many kinds of commercial pop, kroncong, another popular style, has a long history in Indonesia stretching back to the first contact with European colonialism. The Portuguese ports in the East such as Goa in India, Macao in China, Malacca in Malaysia, and the Portuguese areas of southern Africa and the Azores, linked Europe of the sixteenth and seventeenth centuries to the spice-growing areas of Indonesia. Before the Dutch established colonial hegemony in the Indonesian archipelago, the Portuguese outposts on the islands served as entrepôts for the shipment of spices to Europe; of mixed ethnic and racial background, these communities nevertheless maintained aspects of Portuguese culture such as the Christian religion and some types of folk music. In Indonesia, this music came to be called kroncong, and during the late nineteenth and early twentieth centuries it had a somewhat unsavory reputation associated with urban violence and glamorous toughs called buaya kroncong (kroncong crocodiles), who were like the Malay pirates of some Hollywood movies in the twenties and thirties.

The typical instruments accompanying kroncong are of European derivation— violin, cello, flute, and plucked strings of various types; one of the strings, similar to a ukulele, has given its name to the genre. These provided a simple, harmonically based accompaniment to vocal melodies sung with a mellifluous sweetness Americans might think characteristically Hawaiian, but the tunes often had disjunct progressions that exaggerated their crooningly sentimental quality in a distinct way. When kroncong began to attract the interest of a more polite section of middle-class Javanese society in the twenties and thirties, it underwent a kind of acculturation to central Javanese style, and while the instruments were the same they took on functional qualities similar to those of gamelan music. The flute and violin became like the suling and rebab, providing free, heterophonic elaboration of the melody; the cello, while continuing to provide a foundation for the harmony, was played pizzicato in rhythms resembling kendanglike drum patterns; and the kroncong, with its regular offbeat plucking, had a resemblance to the kethuk.

Some kroncong during this period also took on the typical 4 X 8-bar structure of Tin Pan Alley ballads, with a repeated first phrase that also returned after an intervening and contrasting second phrase—AABA; and, too, they acquired a jazzy feeling with the addition of "blue notes." What had been an indigenously evolved, traditional popular music, based on very old importations, had evolved into a more internationalized commercial music at the same time that it was becoming more "Javanized."

With its variety of styles appealing to different ethnic groups and social strata, kroncong became a music of broad appeal, and its popularity was consolidated during World War II when the Japanese banned foreign popular music, thereby helping it become a vehicle for the expression of national solidarity and nationalist sentiment. While newer styles like the rock-oriented kroncong pop have developed more recently, the powerful nostalgia evoked by the music from the war and prewar period gives it a strong appeal for an older crowd, even as the young turn to more sensational music like dangdut.

Jaipongan

The Jaipongan style of pop music has the unique characteristic of being derived from a type of professional folk entertainment of Sunda (West Java) and does not betray the foreign derivations or influences of gambus, dangdut, or kroncong. The Sundanese kethuk tilu (three kethuk) is a small ensemble of musicians playing rebab, gong, three kethuk, and drums, who accompany a female dancer/singer (and sometimes prostitute) in a kind of audience-participation performance during which various men get up to dance with her. Many similar types of dance entertainments exist or existed in Java and Bali as well as other parts of Indonesia, and troupes were often hired for private parties or for celebrations connected with occasions like weddings or circumcisions.

Like "dangdut," the word jaipongan was made up from syllables representing drum sounds, and flashy Sundanese-style drumming is basic to jaipongan. To the instruments derived from kethuk tilu a saron is generally added, and this accounts for another characteristic equally as attractive as the drumming and as typically Sundanese, for the saron is in slendro while the singer and rebab usually perform in another tuning such as pelog, adding ornamental pitches as well. According to Philip Yampolsky, it was a young musician named Gugum Gumbira who was responsible for introducing the amalgamation of various Sundanese musical components that started the jaipongan craze in 1974, and the popularity of the style soon caused it to spread beyond his original troupe to other parts of Java outside Sunda, as well as to take on the nature of a popular dance fad for couples.

> [Jaipongan] was taught in schools and private dance classes, and was performed in dance-halls and nightclubs, at parties and festivals, in the streets and on TV. A 1982 newspaper report describes some of the places in Jakarta and Bandung where one might find Jaipongan; a dance-hall, where the women hired by the management danced with paying customers; an exercise club for rich women; an open-air stage near

the railroad tracks in a seedy area, where peddlers and pedicab drivers danced with prostitutes.[8]

While the social-dance fad has waned in recent years, Gugum Gumbira has concentrated on creating staged performances, and as Philip Yampolsky remarks later in the disk-jacket notes also quoted above: "Today, Jaipongan is accepted as a 'national' stage dance." It is even included in cultural performances by Indonesian students in the United States for national-day celebrations.

UNITY IN DIVERSITY

"Unity in Diversity," as we pointed out earlier, is the national motto of Indonesia, a nation created within the memory of many of its present-day citizens. Creating unity is a primary concern in any attempt to form a nation—or to maintain one, as events in the Soviet republics, the former Yugoslavia, recently reunited Germany, struggling to reunite Korea or fissiparous Great Britain remind us every day. But the chore is a remarkably daunting one in a country with the topography of Indonesia and a population ranging from the industrialized city dwellers of Java to recently contacted groups of former headhunters in Irian Jaya (the Indonesian part of Papua-New Guinea) and Kalimantan (the Indonesian part of Borneo). In the scholarly view of music, the unity of the area is often related to the use of bronze-casting technology and cyclical musical structures that also link Indonesia to the Southeast Asian mainland, to southern China, to northeastern India, and to the Philippines. Valid and interesting as such a system of relationships is, it does not accommodate many other types of musical phenomena in Indonesia such as, for example, the various pipe ensembles of people in Kalimantan, whose music might be reasonably discussed in comparison with that of similar ensembles among the Andean Aymara or South African Venda.

The necessity of national "unity," evidenced in music by the establishment of government conservatories with standardized curricula, will present a challenge to the more marginal components of Indonesian society and to their cultural forms; these components of Indonesia's "diversity" will likely be neglected—as we have neglected many of them in this chapter—but their lack of importance for the national scene does not necessarily indicate the inevitability of their disappearance or impoverishment. Thanks to the inexpensive and widespread technology of audio-cassette recording, many types of regionally circumscribed musics find a locally supportive market that helps to perpetuate them at the same time as it may alter their uses and associations. Rather than propagating a narrow range of musical product, the cassette industry in Indonesia has in effect created the audio equivalent of the country's motto, a wide range of music in the uniform medium of the audio cassette.

[8]Notes by Philip Yampolsky for *Tonggeret*, compact disc Nonesuch 79173-2, [4].

Recorded sound has demonstrated the variety of Indonesia's music today, but it has also made a record of the sound of its past as well, for the gamelan brought to the Columbian Exposition of 1893 was recorded not only on film but also on wax cylinders, the audio-recording medium of the day. Although these are not the first recordings of an ethnomusicological nature—some earlier ones were made of Native Americans—they are among the earliest, and they help to lend a special aura to the instruments now housed in the collection of the Field Museum. What would those musicians recorded in 1893 have thought, I wonder, if they had been able to hear the performance of bubaran "Udan Mas" that was described at the start of this essay?

INDONESIA BIBLIOGRAPHY

Java   Judith Becker, ed., *Karawitan: Source Readings in Javanese Gamelan and Vocal Music*, 3 vols., Michigan Papers on South and Southeast Asia No. [29?], 30, 31 (Ann Arbor: Center for South and Southeast Asian Studies, University of Michigan, 1984, 1987, 1988); Mantle Hood, *The Nuclear Theme as a Determinant of Patet in Javanese Music* (New York: Da Capo, 1977); Susan Pratt Walton, *Mode in Javanese Music*, Monographs in International Studies Southeast Asia Series No. 79 (Athens, Oh.: Ohio University Center for International Studies, 1987); Claire Holt, *Art in Indonesia: Continuity and Change* (Ithaca, N.Y.: Cornell University Press, 1967); Judith Becker, *Traditional Music in Modern Java: Gamelan in a Changing Society* (Honolulu: University of Hawaii Press, 1980); Jaap Kunst, *Music in Java: Its History, Its Theory and Its Technique*, 2 vols., ed. Ernst Heins (The Hague: Martinus Nijhoff, 1973); Peter Manuel, *Popular Musics of the Non-Western World* (New York: Oxford University Press, 1988); Bronia Kornhauser, "In Defence of Kroncong," in Margaret J. Kartomi, ed., *Monash Papers on Southeast Asia No. 7* (Clayton, Victoria: University of Monash, 1978); Ward Keeler, *Javanese Shadow Puppets, Images of Asia* (Singapore: Oxford University Press, 1992); Jennifer Lindsay, *Javanese Gamelan: Traditional Orchestra of Indonesia*, Images of Asia, (Singapore: Oxford University Press, 1992); Michael Tenzer, *Balinese Music* (Berkeley: Periplus Editions, 1991); Ben Brinner, *Knowing Music, Making Music* (Chicago: University of Chicago Press, 1995); Sumarsam, *Gamelan: Cultural Interaction and Musical Development in Central Asia* (Chicago: University of Chicago Press, 1995); R. Anderson Sutton, *Traditions of Gamelan Music in Java: Musical Pluralism and Regional Identity* (New York/Cambridge: Cambridge University Press, 1991).

Bali   Colin McPhee, *Music in Bali: A Study in Form and Instrumental Organization in Balinese Orchestral Music* (New York: Da Capo, 1976); Colin McPhee, *A Club of Small Men* (New York: John Day, 1948); Colin McPhee, *The Balinese Wajang Koelit and Its Music* (1936; repr. New York: AMS Press); I Made Brandem and Frederik deBoer, *Kaja and Kelod: Balinese Dance in Transition* (Kuala Lumpur, New York: Oxford University Press, 1981); Urs Ramseyer, *The Art and Culture of Bali* (New York: Oxford University Press, 1977); Michael Tenzer, *Gamelan Gong*

Kebyar: The Art of Twentieth-Century Balinese Music (Chicago: University of Chicago Press, 2000); Michael B. Bakan, *Music of Death and New Creation: Experiences in the World of Balinese Gamelan Beleganjur* (Chicago: University of Chicago Press, 1999).

INDONESIA DISCOGRAPHY

Java   *Java Palais Royal de Yogyakarta: Musiques de Concert* (Ocora 558 598); *Java Historic Gamelans*, Art Music from Southeast Asia IX-2 (Philips 6586 004); *Musiques et Traditions du Monde: Une Nuit de Wayang Kulit Légende de Wahju Tjakraningrat* (CBS 65440); *Java Court Gamelan from the Pura Paku Alaman Jogyakarta* (Nonesuch H-72044); *Java Court Gamelan Istana Mangkunegaran Surakarta* (Nonesuch H-72074); *Java Court Gamelan Kraton Yogyakarta* (Nonesuch H-72083); *Sunda: Musique et Chants Traditionnels* (Ocora 558 502); *Tonggeret* (Jaipongan) (Nonesuch 79173-2).

Bali   *Semar Pegulingan: Golden Gong of Bali* (Grevillea Records GRV 1020); *Gamelan of the God of Love: Gamelan Semar Pegulingan* (Nonesuch H-72046); *Bali: Musique et Théâtre* (gender wayang, gambuh) (Ocora OCR 60); *Golden Rain* (kebyar) (Nonesuch H-72028); *Bali: Le Gong Gede de Batur* (Ocora 585 510); *The Balinese Gamelan: Music from the Morning of the World* (Nonesuch 72015); *Gamelan Music of Bali* (Lyrichord LLST 7179).

General   *Music of Indonesia*, series of twenty compact discs issued by Smithsonian Folkways.

7

The Music of Sub-Saharan Africa

Thomas Turino

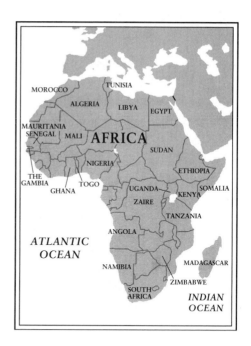

A SHONA MBIRA PERFORMANCE IN ZIMBABWE

Heading toward the roundhouse after dark, I heard the powerful sound of people playing hosho (large maraca-like shakers) from some distance down the path. As I entered the dimly lit kitchen hut where the ceremony was being held I could make out other people clapping, singing, talking, and drinking; one frail old woman was dancing by herself in the center of the room. Beneath all of this there was still another sound, soft yet deep and moving like the combination of water and bells. This was the mbira. Two men, leaning against the far wall, sat with their hands hidden inside large calabash gourds playing mbira. They were the foundation of the musical activity, and the singers, dancers, and hosho players created their rhythmic patterns and improvised vocal parts based on the many simultaneous melodies that the mbira played.

During a break in the music I asked the mbira players to show me their instruments. Twenty-two slightly rusted metal keys were tightly fastened over a metal bridge on a wooden soundboard, with bottle caps attached to a metal plate on the board (Fig. 7–1). A necklace of bottle caps was also strung around the gourd resonators, creating the buzzing sound a torn stereo speaker makes. The musicians explained that, without the gourds, the mbiras were too soft to be heard in occasions for communal music making, such as the bira ceremony that we were attending, and without the buzzing of the bottle caps they would not sound like mbira.

Figure 7–1   Shona instruments (**left to right**): karimba; hosho rattle; 22-key mbira in calabash gourd; 22-key mbira, side view.

Belonging to a general class of instruments known as lamellaphones (plucked tongues or keys mounted on a soundboard or soundbox), the mbira is referred to as "thumb piano" and sometimes thought of as a toy in the United States. Yet the mbira that these men were playing is one of the most highly developed classical instruments of the Shona, a Bantu speaking people of Zimbabwe in southeastern Africa. Although different types of lamellaphones are played all over Africa, this class of instruments has been most highly developed by the Shona and other groups in southern Africa. The Shona play a variety of lamellaphones associated with different regions of Zimbabwe including the karimba, the njari, and the matepe, but presently, the 22-key mbira is the most popular type (Fig. 7–1). Shona mbira players often specialize on one variety of instrument, each with its own distinct scale pattern and playing techniques; changing from a karimba to an mbira or njari is like switching from a guitar to a mandolin or a banjo.

The musicians sat down and began playing another piece. Listening more closely to the mbira this time, I could hear distinct bass, middle, and high melodic parts coming from the two instruments. I watched their hands closely. They would play the same patterns for a long time before changing, perhaps, only one or two pitches by striking different keys, and then would repeat the new variation many times. But even when they were playing the same patterns, I sometimes thought that

I heard changes in the melodies. During their next break the musicians explained that it was always like that. Even simple mbira pieces contained many "inner melodic lines" that resulted not from changes in the keys played but rather from the particular combination of right- and left-hand parts that the listener focused on. They explained that mbira music was an art of creative listening as well as playing, and that the mbira itself seemed continually to suggest new inner melodic lines to the musician even when his hands continued to play the same keys. They told me that this was one reason why mbira players can perform the same pattern for a long time without getting bored or feeling the need to create constant contrasts. It was almost as if the mbira itself magically created its own variations; one simply had to have patience and learn to hear what it had to offer. I enjoyed talking to these musicians, and was learning something of the art of listening to Shona music, but it was time for them to return to playing for the ancestral spirits in the bira ceremony (Figs. 7–2, 7–3).

The Bira

In the local Shona religion there is the belief that one's ancestors continually interact with and affect the lives of the living. As in many places, Shona people emphasize maintaining good relationships with their parents, grandparents, and other elder relatives; for the Shona, however, such relationships do not cease when someone dies. Interactions with deceased relatives take place through spirit possession when an ancestor enters and speaks through the body of a living person—a spirit medium.

Figure 7–2 Shona mbira players Emmanuel Chidzere and David Mapfumo with singer and hosho player Pyo Murungweni, Murehwa District, Zimbabwe.

Figure 7–3 Shona women of Mhembere singing and playing hosho, Murehwa District, Zimbabwe.

Not everyone who dies comes back as a spirit. However, those that do return select one person to be their medium for life. (Family spirits are usually within the past three generations.) Once spirits make themselves known in this way, family members can call them back to speak with them at family-sponsored community events known as bira. Misfortunes such as illness or losing a job are sometimes interpreted as the result of offending a particular ancestor. People also commonly turn to their ancestors for advice during times of trouble. Even when there isn't a specific problem, some families periodically hold ceremonies to honor an ancestor or simply to keep in touch (just as we might feel the need to call our parents when living away from them). These ceremonies often involve mbira music and dance in central ways, although in various Zimbabwean regions drums are used instead of mbira.

As the bira begins people arrive gradually, those already present casually talk and joke together to the music of the mbira and hosho which will play all night. Mbira players (and drummers) are musical specialists who are invited to perform at the ceremony. They supply the musical foundation, but as the evening progresses, family and community members join in by clapping different patterns and dancing in the center of the room. Men and women also may contribute to the performance by singing melodies that weave in and out of the mbira's bass part, or by performing in a high-pitched yodeling style. (These types of singing do not often involve words, only nonsemantic syllables.) Both well-known verses and improvised words are also sung to fit the occasion, and the poetry moves people as do the dance and the music at this participatory event. After one piece has ended, the two mbira players begin again, each with his own specific part, and again the different participants add what they will, until the performance becomes a dense, rich fabric of sound, movement, and feeling. As the spirit medium shows subtle signs that the ancestor is coming, the rest of the participants often begin playing, dancing, and singing more intensely. This collective energy helps to bring on possession.

Good mbira playing and concentrated communal effort are essential for the success of the bira, because music is one of the main attractions that call the spirit into the ceremony. As the intensity mounts and the energy within the room becomes right, the spirit enters the body of the medium. Spirits are particularly attracted by the music that they enjoyed while they were living. Thus, playing the right tunes is important for bringing on possession. Once possessed, the spirit medium is usually dressed by an attendant in a special robe. The medium then follows the will of the spirit and may continue singing, dancing, or she or he may become quiet and withdrawn. After the spirit has participated in the event for a brief time, the music comes to a halt. The host of the bira welcomes the spirit with a formal greeting as they sit in the center of the hut. He also offers special beer, brewed by the family for seven days, and snuff. The host and other people then consult the ancestor about the problem or issues that occasioned the bira, and a discussion ensues between the spirit and concerned participants. After the consultation, the music, singing, and dancing start up again and continue until morning, even if the spirit decides to leave the medium some time during the night.

THE MBIRA AND SOME GENERAL PRINCIPLES OF AFRICAN MUSIC

A closer look at Shona mbira performance reveals a series of features and aesthetic preferences that are common to many Sub-Saharan musical traditions. These include the practice of interlocking: fitting your pitches and beats into the spaces of other parts, or alternating the pitches or phrases of one part with those of another to create the whole. As we will see, this occurs at a variety of levels in mbira performance and in the other African traditions we will study. Call-and-response—the alternation of leader and chorus parts, or of a vocal and instrumental part—illustrates the principle of interlock at the macrolevel of musical organization. Call-and-response is a very common practice all over Sub-Saharan Africa. A second general feature of African music is the aesthetic preference for dense overlapping textures and buzzy timbres that contribute to a dense sound quality. Third, African music is often cyclical and open-ended in form involving one or more repeated melodies or rhythmic patterns (ostinatos) as the basic foundation of a performance. These repetitive, cyclical pieces are often repeated for a long time with gradual variations added as a performance progresses. Community participation is valued in many African musical traditions; repetition and long performances facilitate participation by giving nonspecialized participants a chance to get their bearings and to enter the performance.

African music is famous for its rhythmic complexity. At the most basic level this involves the juxtaposition or simultaneous performance of duple and triple rhythmic patterns (patterns of two against patterns of three). The multiple layering of different rhythmic patterns creates a tension and, at times, an ambiguity such that a listener can hear and feel the same music in a variety of ways depending on which rhythmic part or pattern he or she is focusing on. A final general characteristic is that African music, and musical ensembles, often involve "core" and "elaboration" parts. The "core" musical roles and parts are those that must be in place for a performance to go forward. Core parts are the foundation, the vehicle, that make other contributions, variations, and improvisations possible. In mbira performance, core roles include the basic rhythmic flow maintained by the hosho, and the basic melodic-harmonic ostinato played in the midrange and bass of the mbira. The "elaboration" parts, no less essential to an artful performance, include clapped patterns, vocal lines, high mbira melodies and bass variations, and dancing.

Interlocking

The longest, lowest keys on the mbira are found in the center; they become shorter and higher as they fan out to each side. The keys on the left side are played by the thumb of that hand and the right thumb and forefinger play the keys on the right side (Figs. 7–1 and 7–2). Mbira pieces are constructed so that the left thumb alternates with the right thumb and forefinger to play a single midrange melody. These notes played by the two hands interlock to create a single melody. On many pieces, the left thumb also alternates between the midrange keys of the upper-left manual and the bass keys of the lower-left manual to produce an independent bass line which interlocks with the midrange melody. Finally, the right forefinger plays the smallest, highest keys (far right) to produce additional descending high melodic lines; these pitches are, again, alternated with the left hand part in interlocking fashion. The bass, midrange, and high melodies create a variable polyphonic texture, and a listener's perception of the piece can change substantially by shifting attention from one line to another, or to the resultant melodic patterns that emerge from the relations between different parts (CD 1, #26).

While the mbira can be played solo, a piece is not really considered complete unless two players are present to play their separate complementary parts which interlock to create the whole. One part is called the kushaura, ("to lead the piece" to play the basic piece), and the other is called kutsinhira, a second accompanying part. On many pieces the kutsinhira part is almost exactly the same as the kushaura but it is played a beat behind so that each pitch played by the first part is doubled by the second. This doubling effect produced by the two instruments can be heard on the high descending lines of *Nhemamusasa* (CD 1, #26). With the exception of the high melodies, however, *Nhemamusasa* (cutting branches for a shelter) involves a second type of kushaura-kutsinhira relationship in which a completely different accompanying part is composed to interlock with the kushaura part.

The hand-clapping patterns, dance movements, and vocal melodies performed by participants at the bira and other occasions frequently do not simply reproduce the basic beat and, typically, are not performed in unison. Rather, each participant may add his or her own clapped patterns, sung parts, or dance movements, so that they fall in between or around central beats and pitches—in the spaces—of other people's parts, thereby providing another series of interlocking aspects. A basic musical value among the Shona, and in many African societies, is the ability to add one's own distinctive part to the ensemble while making it blend with the whole. Call-and-response singing is also very common in Shona musical culture.

Density

The final polyphonic, polyrhythmic character of a communal Shona performance results from the interlocking and dense overlapping of the participants' contributions. The Shona, like many African peoples, prefer dense, rich sounds. Bottle caps or shells attached to gourd resonators and mbira soundboards create a buzzing aura around the discrete pitches that contrast with the clear, "pure" instrumental timbres (tone qualities) preferred in the European classical tradition. The multiple layers produced in a communal performance also add to the density of sound, as does the very nature of the mbira, on which keys previously struck continue to ring through the following pitches sounded, with each key producing multiple overtones.

Cyclical Form and Variation

The form of classical mbira music is a melodic-harmonic cycle, or ostinato, of 48 quick beats; the particular ostinato of any classical mbira piece is divided into four 12-beat phrases resembling 12/8 meter; (CD 1, #26). As an mbira performance progresses, small variations, including traditional formulas and improvised lines, are gradually added to, and over, the basic ostinato. Mbira players say that a skilled musician must have patience and not rush the variations. It is not considered good playing to use overly apparent or dramatic contrasts; rather, one variation must be built on the last and subtly lead to the next within the ostinato cycle. Usually, each variation will be repeated a number of times before further development is attempted.

Conceptions of Music

The very definition of what constitutes a "piece" in Shona culture, and in many Sub-Saharan societies, suggests another characteristically African feature. Although mbira pieces have titles, the composition is conceived as an aggregate of musical resources that may be put together and improvised upon in different ways, making each performance recognizable as "the piece" and yet unique. Such resources include: the harmonic, temporal, and melodic character of the basic ostinato; a series of stock variations and motifs associated with the piece; and certain sung melodies and lines of text. The length of a given performance, the number of variations used and the order in which they are performed, the speed and character of development, and the improvisations on the basic patterns, however, make each performance fundamentally distinct, so that in a sense, a new piece is created in every performance. This approach resembles that of jazz, blues, and of some rock performers, indicating one way that people working in these styles may have been influenced by the African heritage.

In Shona villages, "the piece" and music itself are conceptualized as a process linked to specific people and particular moments or contexts, whereas for some musical traditions in the West, music has become a reproducible sound object that can be, and is, isolated and abstracted as a thing in itself. Recordings and written scores perhaps facilitate thinking about music as an object that can be purchased, consumed, collected, and copyrighted. It is significant that the Shona words for the two basic parts of a mbira piece—kushaura and kutsinhira—are not nouns, referring to things, but rather are verbs ("kushaura" means literally "to lead the piece"), underlining the notion of music as an interactive process.

AFRICA GENERAL AND AFRICA SPECIFIC

In the previous section I have tried to link certain features of Shona mbira playing with more widespread African musical characteristics, and indeed there is a tendency among North Americans and Europeans to think of Africa as one place, and African music as a single, identifiable phenomenon. The continent of Africa has over 50 countries, however, and linguists have identified at least 800 ethnolinguistic groups. In Nigeria alone, 386 different languages have been identified. The organization of Sub-Saharan Africa into modern nation-states is primarily a colonial legacy based on the way the continent was carved by the European powers at the end of the nineteenth century. It has little to do with internal ethnic divisions within these territories or with the single linguistic groups that cross national borders. (Mande societies, for example, span parts of Senegal, Gambia, Mali, Burkina Faso, Ivory Coast, Guinea, and Sierra Leone.) Because many musical traditions are linked to specific ethnolinguistic groups and cultures, it is often better to think about African music in these rather than in national terms.

In contrast to the stereotypic vision of small, so-called primitive tribes in Africa, it has been shown that there were various kinds of traditional indigenous political organization including: (1) complex, hierarchical, centralized states with political authority vested in the hands of hereditary rulers; and (2) more decentralized, smaller-scale societies where political power was regulated by interactions between kinship groups such as clans or lineages. Centralized kingdoms with highly developed political organization have existed in Africa from early times. One example is the state of Zimbabwe (the modern nation being named after this early empire) which was thriving by the twelfth century. On the other hand, small egalitarian bands of hunters and gatherers such as the BaMbuti Pygmies have lived for centuries in the central African rain forest. Hunter-gatherer groups such as the Pygmies and the San (Bushmen) are in a small minority, however. The majority of traditional African societies depended on agriculture and animal husbandry for subsistence— stable agriculture being important for state formation. Just as political and economic systems differ widely between specific African societies, family and social structures are also diverse.

Ethnomusicologists have begun to find that sometimes there are important correlations between economic modes of production, social structure, and musical practices and style. Given the socioeconomic diversity among African societies, we would expect musical diversity as well. Indeed, there are important differences in the styles, processes, and functions of music making between different African societies, just as there are differences in conceptions about music, the role and status of musicians, and the types of repertory, instruments, and dances performed. As I suggested earlier, however, there are some basic similarities in musical style, practices, and aesthetics that span the Sub-Saharan region, even among such diverse groups as the Shona in southeastern Africa, the BaMbuti Pygmies in the central rain forest, and the Mande peoples in the northwestern savanna region. Taken at the most general level, it is these similarities that allow us to speak of "African music" (much as the European harmonic system, among other general traits, allows us to identify mainstream "Western music"). Nonetheless, it is the facets that distinguish the different African musical cultures, rather than the similarities, that will probably appear as most significant to Africans themselves.

In the sections that follow, similarities with the major characteristics outlined for Shona mbira music will serve as a focus for the discussion of several specific African musical cultures. At the same time, differences between the musical cultures will be emphasized, and these will be considered in light of the distinct ways of life and worldviews that characterize different African societies.

MUSICAL VALUES, PRACTICES, AND SOCIAL STYLE

The Pygmies

Groups of Pygmies are found in the equatorial forest area stretching from Gabon and Cameroon in the west to Uganda, Rwanda, and Burundi in the east. The Ituri Forest, bordering on Uganda to the east and Sudan to the north, remains a major stronghold for Pygmies, and about 40,000 live in this region. The majority of groups maintain a semiautonomous hunting-and-gathering existence. Centuries ago, the Pygmies found their central forest region invaded from the north by Bantu (a major linguistic category in Sub-Saharan Africa) and Sudanic groups who were cultivators and pastoralist. The Pygmy languages were abandoned for those of the neighboring groups, with whom they entered into types of patron-client relationships. The anthropologist Colin Turnbull, however, suggests that the BaMbuti Pygmies of the Ituri Forest lead a kind of double life, maintaining their own traditional ways (with the exception of language) when alone in the forest and taking part in Bantu ritual and musical life on their visits to the villages. Here we will concentrate on Pygmy life and music in their forest home.

The BaMbuti net-hunters maintain a nomadic existence, setting up camps for a month or so in different places in the forest as they continue their search of game. Net-hunting, like most aspects of Pygmy life, is a communal affair, with male family members stringing their nets together in a large semicircle and the women and children beating the brush to scare game into them. The catch is shared. Bands are composed of nuclear families, and while certain individuals are considered to have more expertise in some realms of activity than in others, there is little specialization of social and economic roles within age and gender categories. A formalized hierarchical system of leadership is not present. Because survival is dependent on cooperation rather than competition, the keystones of Pygmy society are egalitarianism, consensus, and unity. Because of their nomadic existence, the ownership of goods and property is minimal among most Pygmy groups.

All of these aspects strongly influence their musical culture. The Pygmies have few musical instruments of their own. Pygmy instruments include whistles and end-blown flutes made from cane. They may be used to accompany singing, or in duets for informal music making. In flute duets, one instrumentalist plays a repeating ostinato pattern, while the other plays a part that interlocks and overlaps with the first, reminding us of the basic principles of Shona mbira performance. Rhythm sticks and rattles are found, as are several trumpet types such as the long, end-blown molimo trumpet. Some Pygmy bands also use a musical bow. A few other instruments such as small lamellaphones and drums, may be borrowed from their Bantu neighbors.

Vocal music is at the core of Pygmy musical culture. Some songs are sung by individuals informally such as lullabies and game songs, however, communal singing for collective ceremonies and occasions is considered much more important. Like most aspects of Pygmy life, musical performance is a nonspecialized activity. As in net-hunting, where men and women fulfill different roles, however, musical participation may be differentiated by gender, depending on the context. For example, men are the primary singers for the molimo ceremony, through which the benign relationship with the sacred—and living—forest is maintained. Women are the primary singers for the elima, a puberty ceremony. On other occasions, for instance, before almost every hunt, men and women sing together.

Except for the ritual occasions when gender and sometimes age distinctions are made, musical performance involves anyone in the band who wants to sing. Song forms are varied but follow two basic principles that we have already encountered in the Shona mbira music and the Pygmy flute duets: the use of ostinato and interlock. A standard organizational feature found in and among the BaMbuti Pygmies and in many other African societies is the use of a leader and chorus in call-and-response format. The leader, or one group of people, sings a melodic phrase and is immediately answered by a second group singing another phrase so that the two interlock to create the entire melody. Pygmy vocal practice frequently uses the hocket technique (singers alternating short melodic fragments to create a melody), reproducing the same practice of interlocking parts. Yodeling is also frequently practiced by some Pygmy groups and is often considered a hallmark of their vocal style.

In its simplest form, the call and response phrases are simply repeated continually, creating a cyclical ostinato pattern like that described for Shona mbira music. People within a Mbuti chorus help to create a dense, layered sound by simultaneously singing a number of individual variations of the basic melodic parts (CD 2, #1). Among the Pygmies of the Central African Republic, ostinatos without call-and-response organization constitute a basic structure. On top of the basic ostinato, singers may add a second complementary ostinato, and others will perform variations on both melodies, thereby creating a dense, overlapping contrapuntal texture (a texture consisting of different simultaneous melodic lines). The time span of the basic ostinato serves as the reference point for various clapped and percussion parts. Thus, one percussion part may be a six-beat pattern and another may last eight beats, dividing the overall time span of the song, say of twenty-four beats, into different-length cycles.

Certain individuals may begin or lead a song, just as different individuals are considered to have particular expertise in other realms of life. Once a performance is in motion, however, musical roles and leadership may shift, different voices may move in and out of the background. Hence, Pygmy musical style and practice grows out of, and reflects, the specific egalitarian nature of Pygmy social and economic life just as certain features (e.g., ostinatos, density, and interlock) are consistent with African musical practice in other societies.

As in Shona culture, Pygmy musical performances often involve communication with the spiritual world. What differs is the conception of the divine and humans' relations with it. According to Colin Turnbull, the Pygmies recognize that they cannot see, truly comprehend, or give a single name to God. Since they view the forest as the benevolent provider of their lives and livelihood, however, they associate divinity with the forest, itself living and divine. They believe that the world and the forest are basically good, and if misfortunes such as a bad hunting period, sickness, or death—come, it is because the forest is sleeping. Their response is to wake it by singing to it every night during a ceremony known as the molimo, which may last several months. The long, tubular, end-blown trumpet known as molimo is used to create the sounds of the forest and answer the men's singing, thereby realizing, through ritual, the relationship the Pygmies feel with their natural surroundings and the divine.

Unlike the Shona, who use elaborate and varied sung poetry in performances for the ancestors, communicating with the divine occurs among the Pygmies primarily through musical sound alone; song texts are kept to a minimum, even to a single line such as "The forest is good." Since the Pygmy conception of the divine cannot be formulated with words, it may be that music, whose existence and meaning are likewise both concrete and diffuse, provides a more direct mode of relating to and representing God. Nonetheless, it is interesting that the Pygmies emphasize singing much more than instrumental music and yet grant so little attention to sung poetry and the power of the word. In this and other important respects these people of the forest are very different from the Mande on the savanna in West Africa.

The Mande of West Africa

The Mande represent one of the most important ethnolinguistic groups in Sub-Saharan Africa. A number of Mande subgroups, including the Mandinka of Senegal and Gambia, the Maninka of Guinea and Mali, the Bamana (or Bambara) of Mali, and the Dyula of the Ivory Coast all claim a common descent from the thirteenth-century Mali empire. Connected historically to the Mali state, Mande societies are characterized by a social hierarchy as well as by occupational specialization. While slavery once existed, the two main social categories in contemporary Mande societies are sula and nyamalo. Sula refers to "ordinary people," farmers, merchants, people in urban occupations, and it includes the aristocracy as well. According to Roderic Knight,[1] who has studied Mande music for many years, the term nyamalo

> designates those who rely on a specialized craft as a profession. In Mande culture this means metal smiths, wood and leather workers, and musicians, known by the term jali. The "material" that the musician works with is not the musical instrument (although they do typically make their own), but the *word*, whether spoken or sung.
>
> In the traditional hierarchy, the craft specialists, as "service providers" to the king and the general population, occupied various slots below the general populace, but as the sole providers of goods and services needed for both agriculture and war, they were at the same time regarded with awe and respect. All of the nyamalo, by virtue of their specialized knowledge, were regarded as having access to a special life force (the nyama) that gave them a certain power over others. The jali, with the power to manipulate words, had the greatest power. He or she (women being the prime singers) could praise when praise was due, or criticize if necessary, incorporating oblique commentary and poignant proverbs into their song texts if a public figure exhibited lackluster behavior.

At the present time the distinction between the sula and nyamalo social groups are not as strictly maintained as they once were. Yet the jali (pl. jalolu) still maintains many of his or her traditional roles as oral historian, musician, praise singer, genealogist, announcer for the aristocracy, and diplomat, and they still perform at important social events such as weddings, child-naming ceremonies, religious holidays, and affairs of state.

[1]Personal communication from Roderic Knight, September, 1995.

The Mande case clearly differs in some ways from conceptions about music and musicians within Pygmy society, where music making is a nonprofessional, largely nonspecialized activity. In contrast, the jali is a hereditary specialist working as a professional musician and verbal artist, whose status position derives from hierarchical rather than egalitarian social relations.

Another distinction between these two societies regards the power of the word and the importance of song texts. Although vocal music is very important in both societies, jali performance often emphasizes verbal artistry and elaborate texts, whereas some of the most important Pygmy music such as singing for the molimo ceremony involves very little text indeed. Nonetheless, certain features of Mande musical style are consistent with the general traits discussed for the Pygmies and the Shona.

The main instruments played by the Mande jali to accompany singing are the balo (a xylophone), the kora (a bridge harp), and the kontingo (a five-stringed plucked lute with a skin face like the banjo); male jalolu specialize on one instrument. The kora is unique to the Mande. It has twenty-one strings, and a range just over three octaves. Cowhide is stretched over the gourd sound box, and strings come off the neck in two parallel rows perpendicular to the face of the sound box (Fig. 7–4). The tuning is such that the scale series alternates for the most part between the

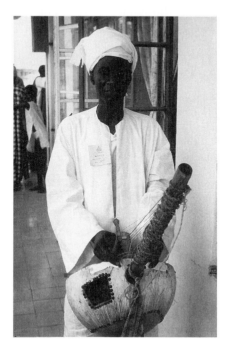

Figure 7–4 Manding kora player Kunye Saho, of the Gambia. *Photo: Roderic Knight.*

two rows and the two hands (right hand—do, left hand—re, right hand—mi, left hand—fa, etc.). The basic playing technique for the kora often involves the plucking of alternate notes by the right and left hands so that the melody results from the interlocking of these two, similar in principle to mbira playing and the principle of interlocking parts in general. Another similarity between the kora and the Shona mbira is the attachment of a metal plate with jangles to the bridge of the kora. This produces the buzzing timbral effect favored in so many Sub-Saharan societies.

Mande music performed on the kora consists of several components. Each piece has a basic vocal melody known as donkilo and a second kind of improvised, declamatory singing style called sataro. Sataro sometimes receives major emphasis in jali performance, as does text improvisation and the insertion of proverbs and sayings appropriate to a given context. It was traditionally through the performance of formulaic praise and proverbs for a given occasion that the jali earned his living—praising a patron, telling a story, or recounting history. The use of songs to fulfill these social functions is widespread throughout West Africa and in other parts of the Sub-Saharan region.

The jali accompanies his singing with the kumbengo part—a short ostinato, the most basic organizing feature of a performance—played on the kora. The kumbengo is played for long periods during which subtle variations are gradually introduced, as in Shona mbira playing. Improvised instrumental interludes known as birimintingo are inserted between the long ostinato sections. The nature of the four components of a jali performance—kumbengo (K), birimintingo (B), donkilo (D), and sataro (S)—will become clearer by listening to Ala l'a ke (CD 2, #2) and following along with the text.[2]

Kora	Voice	
K		(Instrumental introduction)
K	D	A, Ala l'a ke, silan jon m'a ke
		(Ah, God has done it, now it was not a man)
K	D	Kuo bee kari bai, (all things can be delayed,)
K	D	Kunfai kuno te baila. (but not the wishes of God.)
K	D	Ala ye men ke te baila.
		(What God has done can't be delayed.)
K	D	Kori bali ku la manso le (The omnipotent king)
K	D	Kun fara kina ngana nin tabisi nani.
		(head-splitting celebrity and . . .)
K	S	N'ali be nganalu lala, nganalu man kanyan.
		(If you are calling great people, they're not all equal.)
K	S	Damansa Wulandin nin Damansa Wulamba
		(Damansa Wulan the small, and Damansa Wulan the big [?])

[2]The text, designation of parts, and translation was kindly provided by Roderic Knight.

K	S	Moke Musa nin Moke Dantuma
		(Moke Musa and Moke Dantuma)
K	S	Tarokoto Bulai bangeta. (Tarokoto Bulai was born.)
B		(Instrumental interlude, with vocable singing)
K	D	Ala ye men ke te baila . . .

On this recording one can clearly hear the metal jangles buzzing and the relatively soft volume of the kora compared to the voice. As is apparent here, the birimintingo sections provide a greater degree of musical contrast, departing from the basic kumbengo ostinato. This type of instrumental interlude contrasts with Shona mbira performance or a Pygmy song where variations and improvisations are added to and over the basic cycle. Nonetheless, the conception of what constitutes a "piece," that is, a series of stock resources that are uniquely arranged and improvised upon according to the needs of a given performer and occasion are very similar between the Mande and the Shona.

The Ewe of Ghana

North Americans often have the general impression that African music primarily consists of drumming. As we have seen, vocal music, strings, and other types of melodic instruments such as the mbira and marimba may in fact have equally, or more, prominent positions in certain musical cultures. One of the most famous Sub-Saharan regions for drumming however, is the West African coast, and among the Anlo-Ewe of Togo and the southeastern coast of Ghana dance drumming is the most important type of musical activity.

The Anlo-Ewe, who remain musically and socially distinct from other Ewe groups farther north and inland, work primarily as farmers and fishermen. Southern Eweland is divided into autonomous political districts, with the Anlo district having the largest population and cultural influence. The district, which traditionally functioned like an independent state, was ruled by a paramount chief with largely ceremonial and sacred status, although he had the important role of mediating disputes. The chief stands at the pinnacle of a political hierarchy over geographically organized territorial and town chiefs and finally over clan, lineage, and ward (village subdivision) leaders. The clans and lineages (tracing descent to a common male ancestor) and wards thus form an important basis of the social system. Age sets (groups of people of similar age who identify with each other on this basis) are another important feature of social organization. Social organization is often a key to understanding basic aspects of a musical culture, because the formation of ensembles, the definition of genres, and even the organization of musical events are frequently shaped by local conceptions of social hierarchy as well as according to the groups (e.g., gender, age, lineage) that people use to define their social identity.

Among the Anlo-Ewe, voluntary dance clubs, organized by individual villages, wards, or age groups, are the primary institutions through which the all-important dance-drumming traditions are performed. As villagers migrate to the cities, new dance clubs are often created on the basis of hometown identity, and these clubs may serve as the basis for social networks and support systems in the urban environment. According to David Locke, an ethnomusicologist and performer of Ewe music, the organization of some dance clubs traditionally reflected the political structure of the ward and lineage, although European influences have also by now been incorporated.

The dance-drumming clubs are generally led by a committee of men and women consisting of a chairperson, a secretary, and the leaders of different subgroups within the institution (i.e., dance leaders, and leaders of the drummers and the singers). Club organization, then, may be seen as resembling the broader Ewe political hierarchy, which involves a paramount chief who presides over the leaders at the more specific levels of social organization (territorial, village, clan, etc.). Living in a hierarchical society ourselves, this might appear as a normal way to organize things, and yet we must remember that to the egalitarian Pygmies such a modus operandi might seem very strange. Besides the officers already mentioned, another key figure in the club is the composer, who is responsible for creating the distinctive music and song texts that serve as identity emblems for his institution.

Unlike the Pygmy band, where some kind of music is likely to be performed almost daily, musical performance is less frequent among the Ewe. Occasions for club performance include the welcoming of government officials, the promotion of a political party, the formal presentation of a new club, or occasions for recreation. One of the primary functions of the clubs is to support its members during crises, and especially on the death of a family member. Like the Shona, the Anlo-Ewe place great religious importance on the ancestors and the spirits of the dead, who are believed to intervene in the lives of the living. The Ewe thus place major emphasis on providing honorable funerals for the new spirits, and it is considered extremely prestigious to have a dance club perform at such events (Fig. 7–5).

In terms of musical specialization and professionalism, we might think of the Ewe dance clubs as midway on a spectrum between the highly trained, specialized, and professional jali and the nonspecialist, nonprofessional Pygmy musician. For example, rehearsing is an important part of an Ewe club's activities, and learning to perform the dance and music is relatively rigorous, whereas among the Pygmies learning to sing, like learning to talk, is a normal part of socialization. While the jali is a full-time musical professional, most members of the Ewe dance clubs can be thought of as semiprofessional at best. That is, except when fulfilling personal obligations to club members—such as performing for a funeral, or for recreation—the organizations expect payment for their musical presentations, but the members usually only derive a small portion of their income in this way.

As Alfred and Kobla Ladzekpo have suggested, the drumming, dancing, singing, and hand clapping in an Ewe performance must be thought of as a unified whole. If any individual part is changed the perception of the whole changes, because each part is heard as relative to and dependent on the others, as in an mbira

Figure 7–5   Ewe Drum Ensemble: Gideon Foli Alorwoyie of Ghana, lead drummer
for the Yewe Cult, funeral music. *Photo: Art Davis.*

performance. This characteristic, common to many African musical traditions, is a
result of the practice of interlocking multiple parts.

Among the Anlo-Ewe there are a number of different dances. Depending on
the specific dance tradition performed, each club uses various types of music. For
example, clubs involved in the takada tradition have different genres for processions,
for more leisurely types of dancing, and for the vigorous styles of dancing that are
accompanied by the full drum ensemble. The specific instruments used also depend
on the dance traditions performed by a given club, although certain instruments are
widespread (Fig. 7–6).

Typically, Ewe drum ensembles include a double-bell (gankogui), which often
plays a repeated ostinato within a twelve-pulse cycle, serving as the organizational
point of reference for the rest of the instrumental parts. A gourd shaker (axatse) performs a similar role. In addition, a series of four or more different sized barrel-
shaped drums (made of wooden staves and hoops, ranging from 55 cm to 124 cm in
length) may be used for a variety of functions. The large drums (e.g., atsimevu,
gboba) are used by lead drummers to create music from a repertory of established
and improvised patterns. The middle-sized drums (sogo and kidi) serve the function
of a chorus, playing a more limited variety of patterns in call-and-response fashion
with the lead drummer, and they interlock their patterns with other percussion

Figure 7–6   Ewe dondon drum player of Ghana, member of the Brekete Cult. *Photo: Art Davis.*

parts. In the takada tradition, the smallest drum (kaganu) plays a single repeated ostinato which, in combination with the bell and rattles, creates the ground of the overall rhythmic organization that consists of the combination of the different parts. In the Ewe Gadzo dance, the singers begin the piece and then the bells and shakers establish the basic time cycle before three drums enter with their interlocking parts to create a rich texture and wonderful rhythmic excitement (CD 2, #3).

Within these ensembles we thus find musical principles and aesthetic values that have already been discussed for other African societies: call-and-response, interlock, ostinato organization, improvised variation based on stock formulaic patterns, and density in the resulting sound of the entire ensemble. The drum ensemble accompanies both the dancing and the singing, and it is the songs themselves that are considered particularly important to Ewe participants for expressing the distinctive identity of the club. As elsewhere in Africa, the dance steps performed can be considered integral to the polyrhythmic fabric of the total performance.

The Buganda Kingdom

Buganda is the name of the country that was formerly the most powerful independent kingdom in the Lake Victoria region in East Africa; *Baganda* is the term for its Bantu-speaking people. The kingdom was particularly well-off economically

because of ecological conditions favorable to agriculture and particularly to the raising of bananas, the staple crop. Unlike many African kingdoms, the Ganda king, or
kabaka, did not have "divine" or sacred status. His notably strong, centralized power
was supported by a system in which the king directly appointed and could remove
subordinate chiefs, and by his ultimate control over many estates. (This contrasts
with other African kingdoms, where middle-level chiefs could appoint their own
subordinates, thereby creating an independent power base.) While individual citizens belonged to clans and other social groups, primary allegiance was to the state
and to the kabaka himself.

The kabaka's court was a major center for musical activity. The kabaka supported a number of different ensembles, and the musicians lived as retainers on land
granted by the king. One important court ensemble consisted of at least five side-
blown trumpets made of bottle-shaped gourds. The different gourd-trumpets each
produced different pitches necessary to complete a melody and were thus played
strictly in interlocking fashion. Like most of the Buganda instruments, the trumpets
were associated with a specific clan. Another court ensemble, of less prestige than the
trumpets, consisted of five or six end-notched flutes accompanied by four drums.
Specific to the court was the akadinda, a large twenty-two key xylophone in which the
keys were freely set on two supporting logs running perpendicular to the keys. A single akadinda was played by six different musicians, three sitting on each side of the
instrument. The most important royal ensemble of all was the entenga; this consisted
primarily of twelve drums carefully graded in size and tuned to the local pentatonic
(five-tone) scale, thus actually serving as melodic instruments. These were played by
four musicians; they were accompanied by three other drums played by two drummers. The performance of the entenga was strictly limited to the royal enclosure.

The same principles of interlocking parts and ostinato organization that have
been described for the Shona, Ewe, Pygmies, and Mande are also basic to entenga
and akadinda performance. Each piece contains two distinct melodic rhythmic parts
known as okunaga (meaning "to start") and okwawula ("to divide"), each of which is
composed of two or more phrases. On the akadinda xylophone, the three players for
one of the parts sit across the keys facing the three musicians who play the other. The
pitches of the starter and divider parts literally alternate, thereby reproducing the
basic hocket or interlocking technique between the players on opposite sides of
the keys. The parts themselves involve ostinato patterns. A third part comprising
only two pitches, called the okukoonera (or "binder") emphasizes composite patterns formed by the interaction of the okunaga and okwawula. The okukoonera
helps the players orient themselves within the dense ensemble texture.

The political importance of the royal drums and the demise of an African court
tradition in the postcolonial period is dramatically illustrated by the story of the
Buganda kingdom. During the colonial period, African kingdoms were often left in
place within the European colonies, since the native political systems could be
used to rule African populations indirectly. Under an agreement with the British

colonizers, the kabaka of Buganda was officially recognized in 1900 as the ruler of his semi-autonomous state, with the provision that he obey the British Governor of the Uganda Protectorate.

After independence, many new African states had to deal with the threat to national unity and state sovereignty that independent kingdoms within their boundaries might pose. While such problems have been handled variously in different African countries, in Uganda violent means were used to suppress the powerful Ganda king. Only a few years after gaining independence in 1962, troops under Uganda's first leader, Apollo Milton Obote, stormed the kabaka's palace and sent him into exile in an effort to stamp out the independent kingdom.

It was no accident that the royal drums were among the things destroyed in the attack on the palace. Traditionally, the drums were such central symbols of the kabakaship that potential heirs to the throne were known as the "Princes of the Drum." In *Desecration of My Kingdom* (London: Constable, 1967), a book written in exile by the last kabaka, he says that

> Among the sad news of who is dead, who is in prison and what is destroyed comes the confirmation that the Royal Drums are burnt. I saw this work begun and feared that it must have been completed. These drums, of which there are more than fifty, are the heart of Buganda, some of them hundreds of years old, as old as the Kabakaship. To touch them was a terrible offense, to look after them a great honour. A Prince is not a Prince of the Blood but a Prince of the Drum and his status is determined by which Drum. They all had separate names and significance and can never be replaced.[3]

With the destruction of the former political system and way of life in the name of nationalism came the demise of musical traditions that were central symbols of that kingdom. Although often less dramatic in nature, transformations of African musical cultures have taken place, and are still occurring, throughout the sub-Saharan region under the pressures of capitalism, nationalism, urbanization, and influences from cosmopolitan culture.

A SAMPLING OF INSTRUMENTS

Judging from the few musical cultures already touched on, we can see that African musical performance includes all the major instrument types (percussion instruments, skin-headed drums, winds, and strings), and the importance of given instruments may vary from one society to another. Vocal music, however, seems to be emphasized by a great majority of African societies, with the sung poetry often considered as important as the musical accompaniment—if not more so.

We have also seen that aspects of the social and economic organization influence the number and types of instruments used within a given society. For example,

---

[3]Mutesa II, King of Buganda, *Desecration of My Kingdom: The Kabaka of Buganda* (London: Constable, 1967), p. 193.

the Pygmies and the San of the Kalahari Desert have relatively few permanent instruments and a minimal material culture generally because of their nomadic way of life. In societies where the royal court was an important site for musical performance, the number, size, and elaborateness of instruments may be greater because of both available wealth and a more stable environment for performance. This was the case for the large Ganda drum-chime (entenga) and xylophone (akadinda) ensembles as well as for court traditions of other East and West African kingdoms.

The tremendous variety of specific African musical instruments, either played solo or combined in various types of ensembles, makes even a partial list difficult. Here it may be useful to highlight some of the most important instrument types as well as some that are less well known.

Percussion Instruments

Classified as percussion instruments, lamellaphones (known as mbira, karimba, kisaanj, likembe, and by many other names depending on the region) and xylophones are two of the most widespread and important instrument types in the Sub-Saharan region. Although it has diffused to the Americas, lamellaphones like the mbira are instruments uniquely of African origin. Rattles, bells, cymbals, rhythm sticks, stamping tubes (hollow tubes with an open end made to sound when struck against the ground), and scrapers are also among the most common instruments found. For each of these general types, however, there are many different varieties, each with a specific local name. For example, there are rattles with the seeds inside the gourd (the Shona hosho) and those on which beads are sewn into a net stretched around the outside of the gourd (the Ewe axatse, and the sekere of the Yoruba of Nigeria). New materials such as soda bottles and cans are becoming increasingly important for the construction of percussion instruments.

Although percussion instruments such as bells, scrapers, and rattles primarily serve rhythmic functions, the aspects of pitch and timbre are important considerations in their construction and incorporation into a given ensemble. The parameters of pitch and timbre allow the given percussion instrument to contrast with and complement the other instruments used. For instance, the clear, high-pitched, metallic bell in Ewe ensembles contrasts in both pitch and tone quality with the drums, and the hosho both provides a timbral contrast and serves to augment the density in mbira performance.

Drums and "Drum Languages"

The variety of African drums and their social importance in many societies is striking. In Ghana, for example, the relative status of Akan chiefs of different communities and regions is indicated by the size of their atumpan drums; a subordinate chief cannot have drums larger than his superior's drums. Among the many Yoruba kingdoms of Nigeria, each court was said to have its own dance rhythms provided by a special set of royal drums. The very power of the drum music, and the styles played, were supposed to express the elevated nature of the aristocracy. Also among the Yoruba, some of the most important orisas (deities) have specific types of drums and repertories associated with them. Drumming is used to call the gods into their mediums during Yoruba spirit-possession ceremonies, much as was described for Shona ceremonies. Thus, in these societies, drums are tied to both political and spiritual sources of power.

African drums are usually carved from a single wooden log (e.g., the Ganda entenga, Yoruba dundun and igbin, and Akan atumpan, and the Shona ngoma) but may also be constructed with wooden staves and hoops, as described for the Ewe. Drums are also made from ceramics, gourds, and even tin cans and oil drums. Both double- and single-headed types are found in hourglass, conical, cylindrical, and bowl shapes, among others. Metal jangles, shells, or seeds are attached to drums among West African groups such as the Hausa, Dagbamba, Yoruba, and Akan peoples to create the same type of buzzing effect described for the kora and mbira.

The attention paid to the pitch of drums is notable in many African societies, and it may involve the combination of different-sized, fixed-pitch drums in ensemble. Some drums, like the Yoruba dundun and the lunga of the Ghanaian Dagbamba, however, are used to produce multiple pitches. These are hourglass-shaped tension drums; the different pitches are produced by squeezing the lacing that connects the two drum heads under one arm while the other hand beats it with a curved stick. The importance of pitched drums goes beyond merely creating contrasts; as we have seen, it is sometimes extended to making tuned drums serve as melodic instruments (e.g., the entenga). More interesting still, pitched drums are used in many African societies to imitate speech.

Many languages in the Niger-Congo family, including the Bantu languages, are tonal; that is, the meaning of a word depends on the relative pitches applied to given syllables. Drums, lamellaphones, and even instruments such as the guitar are used by the Yoruba of Nigeria to articulate verbal formulas—for example, proverbs or praise names—by imitating the tonal patterns of the words. Longer messages can be played by drumming the tonal contour of different well-known stereotypic verbal formulas. Since many words may share the same number of syllables and tonal contours, the meaning of a given "word" (drummed tonal pattern) can be clarified by following it with a formula of its own (e.g., "cat" might become "cat walks quietly at night"), the tonal patterns of the whole phrase being easier to recognize. The social and "linguistic" contexts are crucial to interpretation. The Akan atumpan, a set of two large tuned drums, are used as speech surrogates, as are the Dagbamba lunga, the Yoruba dundun, and wooden slit drums and paired skin-headed drums in the Congo region, among other examples.

Wind Instruments

In some societies, wind instruments, especially horns, are also used for signaling. Trumpets, made from metal or animal horns and often side-blown, are particularly prevalent throughout the Sub-Saharan region, and are frequently played in interlocking fashion, as was described for the Ganda. Side-blown and vertical flutes are widespread African wind instruments. It is perhaps less well known that panpipes are also found in different parts of Africa, including among the Venda of southern Africa, the Soga of Uganda, the Yombe of Zaire, the Shona, and in Mozambique. Ranging from a single tube closed at one end and blown like a bottle to instruments with multiple tubes and pitches, panpipes are usually played collectively in interlocking fashion, the tones of the scale being divided among the various instruments of the ensemble so that each performer inserts the pitches that he or she has with those of others to create a complete melody.

Stringed Instruments

While we usually think of the banjo as the most American of instruments, it was brought by slaves during the colonial period. The banjo was modeled on West African lutes, which are known by various names depending on the linguistic group and region (e.g., tidinit in Mauritania, halam among the Wolof in the Senegambia area, kontingo among the Mande). The sound box is made from a gourd or a carved wooden back with a stretched skin for the face. A neck is attached, and these instruments have between two and five strings depending on the region.

A wide variety of harps exist in different African societies. The kora, which we have already discussed, combines features of the lute (with a sound box and neck) and the harp. Instruments of this type with both straight and curved necks are found all over the Sub-Saharan region. Single- or multiple-string fiddles made with round sound boxes and skin faces are also important in West Africa (e.g., the goge of the Hausa people of Nigeria) as well as in central and eastern Africa.

The oldest and one of the most widespread stringed instruments of Africa is the musical bow. Like the bows used to shoot arrows, it consists of a single string attached to each end of a curved stick. Depending on the tradition, either a gourd attached to the stick or the mouth cavity of the player serves as a resonator. The string is either plucked or, alternatively, struck with another stick; it is sometimes stopped with a hard implement to raise the pitch. The playing technique results in a percussive and yet beautiful and delicate sound. One of the newest and most widespread stringed instruments is the guitar. There are local acoustic guitar traditions all over Africa, and electric guitars have become central to the new urban styles.

POPULAR MUSIC IN THE TWENTIETH CENTURY

Over the course of the twentieth century, new popular music styles emerged in countries throughout the Sub-Saharan region alongside the indigenous musical traditions that continued to be performed. African musicians combined European, North American, and Latin American musical instruments, scales, harmonies, rhythms, and genres with local musical instruments and styles to create their own distinctive forms of popular music. Local elements and musical sensibilities made each emerging style unique while the cosmopolitan elements served as a kind of common denominator among them. During the first half of the twentieth century, European colonialism generated institutions and social attitudes that led to the emergence of new musical styles. Mid-century, African nationalism became a primary force for local musical creativity. By the 1980s, in the context of the "worldbeat" or "world music" phenomenon, African musicians were attracted by international markets and thus shaped their styles to cater to cosmopolitan audiences in Europe, North America, Japan, Australia, and elsewhere.

Through military conquest, various European powers colonized the Sub-Saharan region in order to control resources and labor for production, and ultimately to expand capitalist markets. Along with the use of force, colonial governments and missionaries also used legislation and education to teach Africans to accept European "civilization" as superior to their own ways of life, and thus to accept their own subservient position. Through colonial education, a small African middle class began to emerge in the different colonies. Serving as clerks, teachers, foremen, and in other low-level administrative positions, this group understood European education as the means to upward social mobility within the colonial order. In the process, middle-class Africans internalized colonial values and aesthetics and became attracted to European and cosmopolitan music and dance styles.

European musical instruments and styles were first taught to Africans through two colonial institutions, military bands and schools. Particularly in the British colonies, Africans were trained in military band music and these musicians often went on to form dance bands that played cosmopolitan styles such as European popular music and jazz; it was often these musicians who also created new local popular styles. In the process of Christian conversion, missionaries taught school children religious songs and hymns, which were sometimes translated into their own languages. Through singing in school and church, Africans learned how to read music, they became accustomed to European diatonic melodies (i.e., melodies based on the standard do-re-mi scale) and harmonies with basic Western chords (I, IV, V). They also learned very different aesthetic values. For instance, instead of the dense overlapping sounds typical of indigenous performance, school children were taught to value clear, precise phrasing (e.g., everyone singing the same notes at exactly the same time), and precise vocal diction. These values influenced certain urban popular styles such as highlife in Ghana, and "concert" music in Zimbabwe that especially pertained to the African middle class.

In addition to schools and the military, commercial interests also played a key role in diffusing cosmopolitan instruments and styles in Africa. By the 1920s, a variety of relatively inexpensive instruments such as mass-produced guitars, harmonicas, concertinas, accordions, autoharps, and banjos became available in dry good stores in larger towns, cities, and in mining centers. These instruments became popular among the emerging working class who, through wage labor, had some money to spend. Commercial recordings of European popular music, Latin American and Caribbean styles (especially Cuban son, and Trinidadian calypso), and U.S. popular music including jazz, country & western, and popular groups such as the Mills Brothers became available by the 1930s and 1940s, as rock 'n' roll, soul, and rap would become later.

By mid-century, local acoustic guitar styles had emerged in many parts of Sub-Saharan Africa. Sometimes the guitar was simply adapted to styles formerly played on local indigenous instruments. For example, in Zimbabwe and South Africa, the guitar was used to play mbira and bow music, or in West Africa to play music formerly performed on indigenous lutes (e.g., halam, or kontingo). In other cases, African musicians used the guitar to play foreign styles; surprisingly, early American country & western performers such as Jimmie Rodgers and Tex Ritter were popular models for African guitarists in many regions. The acoustic guitar, usually accompanied by percussion instruments, was also used to play new styles that were fusions of foreign and local musical elements Examples include West African "palmwine" guitar music and various acoustic guitar styles in the Congo region, and in southern and eastern Africa. Common to African guitarists in many places, a two-finger (thumb and index) picking style was used to play independent bass and melody lines within simple chord progressions (e.g., I, IV, V; I, V; I, IV, I, V; I, IV, ii, V) in first position (on the first three frets of the guitar). By the 1960s, electric guitars had begun to replace acoustic instruments in popularity.

West Africa

In West Africa, dance-band highlife music originated on the Ghanaian coast, where the training of local African musicians in the brass-band idiom had begun as early as the eighteenth century, and where port life had introduced the locals to many international musical styles. By the 1920s, big bands using brass instruments and playing European popular dance genres like the waltz and fox-trot began performing at upper-crust social affairs for the westernized African elites and Europeans. During this period local Akan melodies and rhythms began to creep into the highlife repertory, thereby Africanizing what was more or less a Western musical style in terms of rhythm and orchestration.

It was not until after World War II, however, that the fusion of Western and African elements became more integral in big-band highlife. According to David Coplan, E. T. Mensah, the "King of Highlife," was the first to orchestrate both traditional themes and indigenous rhythms for dance band in conjunction with the use of North and Latin American genres such as swing, the samba, the Cuban son, and calypso (see Chapter 9). By this time the electric guitar had been incorporated, and Mensah's group used that instrument as well as trumpet, trombone, saxophone, string bass, and a Cuban-style percussion section. While these groups were playing for higher-class patrons, a parallel development of "guitar-band" highlife grew up among the lower classes in urban centers. This style fused the techniques and repertories of local Ghanaian instrumental traditions with those of the guitar and songs learned from sailors. The music of West Indian sailors, whose rhythms were originally based in African lamellaphone and string techniques, came full circle and began to influence West African highlife.

"Palm-wine" music, played on acoustic guitar and accompanied by various percussion instruments, spread throughout British West Africa. In Lagos, Nigeria, palm-wine and other syncretic urban working-class styles served as a basis for jùjú music. Now associated with the names Ebenezer Obey and King Sunny Ade, jùjú has become one of the internationally best-known "African-pop" styles. Christopher Waterman suggests that after World War II, the use of amplification influenced jùjú's evolution to include both more modern and increasingly traditional African features simultaneously. With the use of electric guitars and amplified vocals, it became possible to reintroduce larger and more complex percussion sections using the Yoruba sekere (rattle) and the hourglass-shaped "talking drum," among other instruments. The pedal steel guitar has also been added to jùjú instrumentation, an element that might be traced back to the popularizing of North American country and Hawaiian music on 78-rpm records in earlier decades. The highly polished "studio" sound of contemporary jùjú bands is also aided by the use of synthesizers. Jùjú groups combine the traditional functions of praise singing and social-dance drumming, and perform both at urban bars and neotraditional Yoruba ceremonies (naming ceremonies, weddings, funerals). Although Western harmonies are used, jùjú music is organized around a series of interlocking ostinato parts played by the guitars and drummers and leader-chorus call-and-response singing.

Congo-Zaire

Within the Sub-Saharan region, there is no doubt that the urban-popular guitar music of the Congo-Zaire region has had a more profound impact than any other single African style. Leading exponents of the style include Franco and his band O.K. Jazz, Docteur Nico, and Kanda Bongo Man among others. Local likembe (lamellaphone) dance music (accompanied by struck bottles and a drum) and Afro-Cuban music served as the foundations of the Zaire-Congo style. By the mid-1950s, the likembe had been replaced by acoustic guitar, and by the late 1950s Caribbean music became a primary model, with electric guitars as well as saxophones, trumpets, clarinets, and flutes sometimes being used. Different international "dance crazes" involving Afro-Cuban music were fueled throughout the Americas, Europe, and Africa by the recording industry. For some reason, the Afro-Cuban son and the distinctive Cuban "clave" pattern (see Chapter 9) took hold in the Congo region.

At first, groups copied the Cuban recordings to the extent that some even imitated the original Spanish texts. As time went on, however, the Congolese groups began to develop their own distinctive sound as well as incorporate new foreign influences such as riffs from North American soul music. Less rhythmically complex than jùjú, the Congolese style is organized around one or more guitar ostinatos, which serve to accompany the high, sweet singing style of performers like Franco. This style is now known internationally as soukous. A performance usually includes long improvised guitar solos as well as the sparse, orchestrated entrances of the horn section over a danceable rhythm in duple meter. Perhaps inspired by the Congolese sound, the use of Cuban-style rhythms and rhythm sections can be heard in East and West Africa as well as in the modern music of Mali where, as in the style of the Super-Rail Band, such elements are fused with electric-guitar ostinatos and solos that are clearly based on kora music.

South Africa

The urban-popular music of South Africa—a particularly early European settlement—differs in various ways from the styles created in other countries. The traditional music of the Nguni (Zulu-, Swazi-, Sotho-, Xhosa-speaking) peoples of the region is itself stylistically distinct from the music of other African areas. For example, in contrast to all the African musical styles that we have discussed so far, Nguni music is a predominantly choral-vocal style using slower tempos and lacking the polyrhythmic percussion accompaniments found in, say, West Africa. The music taught by Christian missionaries, also a choral tradition, had a particularly strong impact in South Africa, as did North American urban-popular musical traditions.

Various related syncretic choral styles were created using these sources in the context of the dismal living conditions of rural African migrant workers, who were forced by harsh circumstances to seek employment in the mines and cities. Within the workers' compounds, vocal-dance groups formed and participated in competitions, which became a primary social outlet. Styles such as mbube, bombing, and isicathamiya blended the harmonies taught by missionaries with the slow Zulu choral style characterized by multiple overlapping ostinatos. The music of Ladysmith Black Mambazo and the earlier 1939 hit of Solomon Linda, popularized internationally by Pete Seeger, "Mbube" ("Lion," or "The Lion Sleeps Tonight") are examples that come out of this line of development. In addition to the vocal traditions, urban-Black South African music was also highly influenced by African-American instrumental traditions, including the music of minstrel shows, ragtime, jazz, and more recently rock. Black jazz and rock groups flourish in the cities, as do artists who play locally created variants blending indigenous and international styles. Contemporary Zulu "jive" or mbaq'anga bands blend electric guitars, bass, and trap drums with accordions, violins, and penny whistles for a straight ahead, driving dance beat in 4/4 time.

Zimbabwe

Like elsewhere in Africa, "Zairian rumba" has been popular in Zimbabwe since the late 1950s, and South African styles such as mbaq'anga have also been very influential among local musicians as have North American rock and soul. Two urban-popular guitar genres, however, stand out as unique to Zimbabwe. The most famous of these involves the performance of classical mbira music by electric dance bands; the second genre, known as *jit* or jiti, is associated with dance drumming and songs performed in informal gatherings in Shona villages. Both mbira music and jit were played by solo itinerant acoustic guitarists by at least the late 1940s (at the time jit was called marabi, tsaba, and by other South African names). Similar to much Shona village music (but unlike mbira music), jit has a two-phrase ostinato, each phrase being 12 quick pulses with beats 1, 4, 7, and 10 receiving equal accents. These characteristics remain regardless of whether jit is performed by village drummers and singers, solo acoustic guitarists, or electric dance bands.

By the mid-1960s, young Zimbabwean "rock" bands began to add a few Shona village songs to their typical repertoires of Zairian rumba, South African mbaq'anga, and North American rock and soul. It was in the 1970s, however, during a period of heightened black nationalism and the violent war to end white rule, that urban audiences began responding to electric band renditions of Shona village music. Inspired by positive audience reactions, a number of Zimbabwean guitar bands began to play increasingly more local Shona music, especially mbira-based songs and jit, in symbolic support of Shona identity and the war effort. This Zimbabwean guitar style continued to be refined throughout the 1980s by artists such as Thomas Mapfumo.

Mapfumo's music is a wonderful example of the blending of indigenous African and Western-popular musical elements. He began his professional career in the 1960s playing cover versions of English and American rock and soul music, as well as some Shona village songs. He recorded his first song based on classical mbira music in 1974. On this recording and throughout the 1970s his bands played mbira and jit songs with electric guitars, bass, drums, and horns. In the mid-1980s, when he began to tour internationally, however, he added an actual mbira player, and by the early 1990s he had three mbira players in the band.

Classical mbira pieces like *Nhemamusasa* are used as the basis for many of Mapfumo's pieces. Electric guitars play the basic four-phrase kushaura ostinato as well as melodic lines that would be on the higher mbira keys; the electric bass plays the part of the lower mbira keys of the kushaura. In recent recordings, according to Mapfumo, the keyboard often plays the kutsinhira mbira part, and the mbiras divide these parts as they normally would (see Mango MLP 9848 in the discography). The drummer plays a rhythm on the highhat that sounds like the traditional hosho used to accompany the mbira, and Shona hand-clapping patterns and an actual hosho are also added. Mapfumo sings in Shona village style including the high, yodeling technique and low-pitched singing of vocables; he also sings traditional lyrics as well as texts of his own composition. While Shona people who remain in the villages and who have migrated to the cities still play mbira and hosho, or drums, at spirit-possession ceremonies, Mapfumo's music, like that of urban-popular bands all over

Africa, illustrates the creativity and adaptability of African musicians in the context of ever-changing social conditions.

SUB-SAHARAN AFRICA BIBLIOGRAPHY

African Music, General   Robert Kauffman, "African Rhythm: A Reassessment," *Ethnomusicology* 24 (3), 1980; Alan P. Merriam, "Traditional Music of Black Africa," in Phyllis M. Martin and Patrick O'Meara, eds., *Africa* (Bloomington: Indiana University Press, 1977); J. H. Kwabena Nketia, *The Music of Africa* (New York: W.W. Norton, 1974); Ruth Stone, ed., *Garland Encyclopedia of World Music, Vol. 1: Africa* (New York: Garland Publishing, 1998).

Ewe and Ghana   John Miller Chernoff, *African Rhythm and African Sensibility: Aesthetics and Social Action in African Musical Idioms* (Chicago: University of Chicago Press, 1979); Alfred Kwashie Ladzekpo and Kobla Ladzekpo, "Anlo Ewe Music in Anyako, Volta Region, Ghana," in Elizabeth May, ed., *Musics of Many Cultures* (Berkeley: University of California Press, 1980).

Ganda Music   Lois Ann Anderson, "Multipart Relationships in Xylophone and Tuned Drum Traditions in Buganda," *Selected Reports in Ethnomusicology*, [Volume 5:] *Studies in African Music* (Los Angeles: Program in Ethnomusicology, Department of Music, UCLA, 1984); Peter Cooke, "Canada Xylophone Music: Another Approach," *African Music* 4 (4), 1970.

Mande Peoples   Roderic Knight, "Music in Africa: The Manding [Mande] Contexts," in Gerard Béhague, ed., *Performance Practice: Ethnomusicological Perspectives* (Westport, Conn.: Greenwood, 1984); Eric Charry, *Mande Music* (Chicago: University of Chicago, 2000).

Pygmies   Colin Turnbull, *The Forest People: A Study of the Pygmies of the Congo* (New York: Simon & Schuster, 1962); Michelle Kisliuk, *Seize the Dance! BaAka Musical Life and the Ethnography of Performance* (New York: Oxford University Press, 1998).

Shona of Zimbabwe   Paul F. Berliner, *The Soul of Mbira* (Chicago: University of Chicago Press, 1993); Thomas Turino, *Nationalists, Cosmopolitans, and Popular Music in Zimbabwe* (Chicago: University of Chicago Press, 2000).

Studies in African Urban-Popular Music   John Collins, "Ghanaian Highlife," *African Arts* 10 (1), 1976; John Collins, *African Pop Roots* (London: Foulsham, 1985); David Coplan, *In Township Tonight! South Africa's Black City Music and Theatre* (London: Longman, 1986); David Coplan, "Go to My Town, Cape Coast! The Social History of Ghanaian Highlife," in Bruno Nettl, ed., *Eight Urban Musical Cultures* (Urbana: University of Illinois Press, 1978); Veit Erlmann, *African Stars:*

Studies in South African Performance (Chicago: University of Chicago Press, 1991); Ronnie Graham, *The Da Capo Guide to Contemporary African Music* (New York: Da Capo, 1988); Christopher Waterman, *Jùjú: A Social History and Ethnography of an African Popular Music* (Chicago: University of Chicago Press, 1990).

AFRICA DISCOGRAPHY

Anthologies   *Musical Instruments 1: Strings*, Music of Africa Series No. 27 (GALP 1322); *Musical Instruments 2: Reeds (Mbira)*, Music of Africa Series No. 28 (GALP 1323); *Musical Instruments 3: Drums*, Music of Africa Series No. 29 (Kaleidophone KMA 3); *Musical Instruments 4: Flutes and Horns*, Music of Africa Series No. 30 (GALP 1325); *Musical Instruments 5: Xylophones*, Music of Africa Series No. 31 (GALP 1326); *Musical Instruments 6: Guitars 1*, Music of Africa Series No. 32 (GALP 1327).

Ewe and Ghana   *Folk Music of Ghana* (Folkways FW 8859); *Drums of West Africa: Ritual Music of Ghana* (Lyrichord LLST 7307); *Ewe Music of Ghana* (Asch Mankind Series AHM 4222); *Songs of War from the Slave Coast: Abutia-Kloe Ewe* (Ethnic Folkways FE 4258).

Ghana   *Uganda 1*, Music of Africa Series (Kaleidophone KMA 10).

Mande   *Kora Manding: Mandinka Music of the Gambia* (Ethnodisc ER 12101); *Mandinka Kora par Jali Nyma Suso* (Ocora OCR 70); *Rhythms of the Manding Adama Drame (Jembe)* (UNESCO Collection, GREM DSM 042); *Malamini Jobarteh & Dembo Konte, Jaliya* (Rounder 5021); *Sounds of West Africa: The Kora & the Xylophone* (Lyrichord LLST 7308).

Pygmies   *Music of the Rain Forest Pygmies* (Lyrichord LLST 7157); *Pygmies of the Ituri Forest* (Folkways FE 4457); *Music of the Ituri Forest* (Folkways FE 4483).

Shona   *The Soul of Mbira: Traditions of the Shona People of Rhodesia* (Nonesuch H-72054); *Africa: Shona Mbira Music* (Nonesuch H-72077); *The African Mbira: Music of the Shona People of Rhodesia* (Nonesuch H-72043); *Rhodesia I*, Music of Africa Series (Kaleidophone KMA8); *Ephat Mujuru: Master of Mbira from Zimbabwe* (Lyrichord LLST 7398).

Urban-Popular Music   *Ju Ju Roots: 1930s–1950s* (Rounder 5017); *King Sunny Ade and His African Beats; Juju Music* (Mango 9712); *Zulu Jive* (Earthworks ELP 2002); *Viva Zimbabwe* (Earthworks ELP 2001); *Voices of Africa: Highlife and Other Popular Music by Saka Acquaye and His African Ensemble from Ghana* (Nonesuch Explorer H-72026); *Black Star Liner: Reggae from Africa* (Heartbeat 41556); *Mbube Roots: Zulu Choral Music from South Africa, 1930s–1960s* (Rounder 5025); *Thomas Mapfumo and The Blacks Unlimited; Corruption* (Mango MLP 9848).

8

The Musical Culture of Europe

Philip V. Bohlman

MUSIC IN THE LIFE OF MODERN VIENNA

Streets and Stages: A Musical Stroll

As we stroll through the streets of Vienna on a June evening, the sounds and symbols of music envelop us and persuade us that Austria derives much of its identity from the musical past and present of its capital. Music is everywhere, and Vienna has found a remarkable number of ways to make its own musical persona obvious. Grandiose edifices, monuments, and statues attest to the masters of the past and the extravagant performances of the present. The sounds of street musicians intermingle with insistent scales wafting from an open window in a music academy. Wall placards announce abundant upcoming concerts, and musicians with violin cases or armsful of musical scores scurry into buildings on the way to rehearsals or concerts. Even restaurants and the foods they serve bear the names of composers and musicians. This is an image of Vienna as the quintessentially musical city in a fundamentally musical nation in the heart of Europe, an image to which we are well accustomed. It is an image reproduced by recordings and movies, history books and tourist literature, all conspiring to convince the world that Vienna is, above all, a musical city.

Continuing our stroll, we begin to see that the larger image of Vienna as a musical city is considerably more complex than we had inferred from its surface. The map of Vienna in our hands tells a great deal about the interaction between the cultural core—symbolized by the city center (First District), which the Ringstrasse, with its governmental and cultural buildings, surrounds (Fig. 8–1)—and the concentric ring streets that ripple outward toward the Alps in the west, the Czech and Slovak Republics in the north and east, and Hungary and Slovenia in the east and south. The major highways radiating from the center connect it with these other countries and cultures, which until little more than a half-century ago constituted an empire ruled by Austria. The Habsburg Empire is no longer a political reality, but Vienna still has the look and the sound of an imperial capital, for we see many cars from the countries of Eastern Europe, and we hear street musicians singing in Hungarian or playing Slovak instruments. As stylistically different as they are, CD 2, #6–10 all represent musics heard in the Habsburg Empire at the beginning of the twentieth century. After the transition from communism to newly independent nation-states in the early 1990s, Austria's borders opened again, and musicians were among those who took advantage of the access to the cosmopolitan musical life of its capital. Vienna, it seems as we listen to the many contrasting musics, attracts musical diversity and provides it with ample opportunities to express itself, as in CD 2, #10, in which an Austrian folk-music ensemble plays a dance simply called "The Bohemian," referring directly to the western part of the Czech Republic.

The annual Vienna Festival is in full swing during June, so it is hardly surprising that, as we head in the direction of the Staatsoper (National, or "State," Opera), many people are funneling into the front doors to see the nightly performance. Opera is an elegant affair, and many attend this evening's performance, dining before the 5:30 P.M. curtain and going to the nearby Mozart Café for drinks and desserts between acts. We check a kiosk to see what opera is on this evening, thinking it might be *Le Nozze di Figaro*. It is instead Richard Strauss's *Rosenkavalier*, although we see from the schedule of Vienna Festival events that *Figaro*, a Viennese favorite, will be staged later in the month.

Many symbols of Vienna's musical past lie within a few blocks of the State Opera, and we decide to explore. We walk a few blocks to the Gesellschaft für Musikfreunde (Society for the Friends of Music), a large building with several halls for musical performances, a library, archives, even a showroom for the distinguished Austrian piano manufacturer Bösendorfer. We pass along Bösendorfer Street (the Austrians have a habit of giving musical names to just about everything) and enter the piano showroom. It is an imposing, even daunting place, filled with pianos so highly polished that one hesitates to touch them and draped with huge posters of great Austrian pianists (and a few non-Austrians) staring or smiling down at us. Somehow, we get the impression of music that we should see and respect, even worship, but touching and playing seem out of the question just now.

We consider the possibility of attending a concert in the Society for the Friends of Music—it hosts several evening concerts during the Vienna Festival—but every-

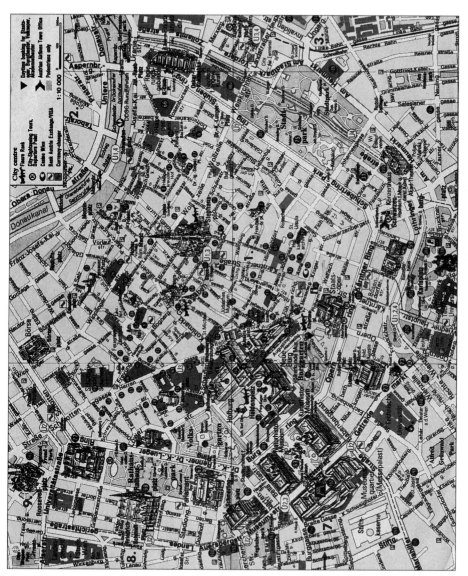

Figure 8–1   The Ring Area, or First District, of Vienna.

thing is sold out, and, anyway, we are a little underdressed. Still, it is early summer, and our disappointment fades quickly as we resume our walk through Vienna. Many people are walking toward St. Stephen's Cathedral, the middle of Vienna's downtown. Kärntner Street, Vienna's main shopping thoroughfare, leads in that direction, and it is not long before we encounter street musicians, in fact numerous street musicians. They are of many types, and accordingly they are performing a remarkable variety of musical repertories. Flower vendors are selling an array of plants from the countryside and some imported from Italy and Spain, and they hawk their wares with a singsong style characterizing work songs (cf. CD 2, #4–5). Several groups of street musicians have come to Vienna from Hungary, including a folk-dance troupe from a single village, whose performances are described by the local priest. The Hungarian musicians perform an amalgam of styles, mixing rural folk songs with contemporary popular hits (cf. CD 2, #7). The young dancers even perform entire rituals, for example, a mock wedding. Everything, however, bears the stamp of the Hungarian language and an awareness of Hungarian instrumental styles.

We encounter also the rather raucous sounds of a young American singing chestnuts from the folk-music revival of the 1950s and 1960s, and with some embarrassment we throw a few coins into his guitar case. At the edge of the square surrounding St. Stephen's, we pause to listen to an Andean panpipe ensemble, performing songs of political protest in Spanish and attracting the largest crowd of all the street musicians. Whether or not anyone understands the lyrics, the Andean ensemble (no one seems to know whether they are Peruvian or Bolivian) obviously earns a considerable amount of money, probably enough to draw them back to this square through the rest of the summer.

Finally, we conclude our excursion by entering St. Stephen's itself, there to be greeted by the magnificent sounds of an organ on which Bach is being played, the music of a North German Protestant in the cathedral of this largely Catholic Austrian city. The other visitors in St. Stephen's seem rather unsure whether the music accompanies a religious service, but they respond meditatively, remaining silent or only whispering nervously to their neighbors. Just as nervously, we leave the cathedral and decide to spend the rest of the evening at a local wine garden, a so-called Heuriger, where we will enjoy the wine of the season and the urban music called Schrammel-music, named after Johann and Josef Schrammel, two nineteenth-century musicians who made this style of "folklike" (volkstümlich) urban music famous and contributed to the compositions and performance practice of the tradition. By the end of the evening, we wonder whether there is any music that we did not encounter, and, if so, whether we might have happened upon it had we chosen a different route. Rumors fly about that there is good country-western music at a club called "Nashville." We hear, too, that some bands from the Celtic and Klezmer revivals are playing in the city this evening. Just where are the limits of Vienna's musical life?

The Many Musics of Vienna

The musical life that we discover during an evening's stroll through Vienna sharply contrasts with many descriptions of this quintessentially Central European city. Music-history books, for example, contain labels for musical styles that are distinctively Viennese such as "Viennese classicism," "Viennese waltzes," and even the "Second Viennese School" of avant-garde composers in the early twentieth century. Could we also observe a similar "Vienneseness" in our encounter with the vibrant musical life of the city on a summer evening? Surely there was no question that our expectation that Vienna would be a "very musical" city was fulfilled. It would hardly be an exaggeration to say that music—its presence as sound and idea—was everywhere. And yet it is not that easy to pin down what was especially Viennese about it, or even any unequivocally Viennese trait connected to style, repertory, or performers. The street performers were often not even Austrian, and the multitude of musical sounds was more often mixed than identifiably of Viennese origin. Vienna's presence, nonetheless, was essential to our musical encounter. The city attracted these musicians, sanctioned their performances, and brought together the conflicting histories and cultural contexts in a unique way. What we heard during our stroll—indeed, what we would have heard on any stroll—was Viennese music.

Our firsthand encounter with Viennese music reveals to us that there are many possible ways of understanding just what it is. One view seems anchored in the existence of a historical canon, a series of repertories created by gifted composers who lived in Vienna because of the ideal conditions it provided for both the creation and performance of music. Music symbolizes something unbroken and persistent in the history of the city, and the language used to describe music's historical role—notably the stubborn word "classical"—tells us that the past has been important in the present.

A contrasting view of Viennese music concentrates not on the central core but rather on the periphery, on the tendency of Vienna to attract outsiders. Relatively few of the composers generally associated with Vienna were originally from the city or received their musical education there; Mozart, Haydn, Beethoven, Brahms, and Mahler were outsiders, and their biographies demonstrate vividly that being accepted as an insider was no easy task. Clearly, the modern street musicians are not so different from the pantheon of Viennese composers in their relation to the city; the outsider status of the Hungarian folk-singers or the Andean panpipe ensemble at once privileges and impedes, while making their presence almost unexceptional.

A third view of Viennese music challenges the historical nature of the first two and poses what we might call postmodern arguments. Vienna, according to this view, forms the sort of cultural backdrop that permits unexpected, even jarring, juxtapositions. There are, accordingly, certain conditions that foster Viennese musics at particular moments, but these are almost random. Such a view helps to explain why the old and the new, the classical and the avant-garde, opera and street music exist side by side. Vienna is no less important to the various juxtapositions, for it provides a cultural template that encourages them. Its concert halls, its music academies, and its streets all become the stages for a music that, whatever else it might be, is unassailably Viennese. (Fig. 8–2 also represents musical juxtapositions, but on the streets of nineteenth-century France.)

EUROPE AS A MUSIC CULTURE

Europe as a Whole

There is no more commonly held assumption about music's relation to cultural and geographical areas than that something called "European music" exists. Other categories are created to contrast with European music, for example, Middle Eastern and Oriental music, whose positions in a world culture are determined by Europe's position, not their own. Throughout the world, students study European music; they call it by other names at times, perhaps "Western music" or "Euro-American music," but generally "European" became common parlance in the twentieth century.

Figure 8–2   Contemporary graphic of French street music, early nineteenth century. Vastly different styles and repertoires—from colportage to hurdy-gurdy to military music—are juxtaposed in the urban environment. *Graphics collection Deutsches Volksliedarchiv, Freiburg i Br., Germany.*

Just what European music is, of course, is another question. Despite the lack of consensus, relatively few writers on music concern themselves with stating the limitations of European music or defining what it is. It might be easiest to suggest that it is the music of Europe or the music created in Europe. Would, then, the Andean panpipe ensemble we heard in Vienna be European music? And would the music of Islamic Spain in the Middle Ages be European music? If we answer "no," we argue that Europe is more a shared culture than a unified geographic entity. If we answer "yes," we place greater importance on what happens within the geography, allowing even that the geography shapes the culture.

Europe is indeed unified in several ways. For example, it is a continent, largely though not completely bounded by water. Linguistically, most peoples of Europe are related, closely in several cases and more remotely in others. Those languages not related to the larger Indo-European family, such as Hungarian and Finnish, may demonstrate European interrelations of their own. The cultural history of the continent, too, has a sort of unity, although sometimes that unity results only from barricading the continent from Asia and Africa. Religion unifies Europe. Europeans are largely Christian, certainly to a degree that distinguishes certain aspects of shared culture; to travel from Europe toward Asia, the Middle East, or North Africa brings one immediately into contact with peoples who are not primarily Christian. At the beginning of the twenty-first century, more nations are joining the European Union, thereby responding to calls for political and economic unity. All these cases for unity contain exceptions, but together they justify studying Europe as a whole.

Europe as an Amalgamation of Cultural Areas and Peoples

Despite the acceptance of Europe's cultural wholeness, individuals do not always—or even most of the time—identify with it. Instead, individuals identify more often with the culture of the town, region, or nation in which they live. Similarly, at the individual level, most identify more closely with a regional musical style than with an abstract European unity. It has been characteristic of music in Europe that patterns of regional and cultural identity have remained especially pronounced, even as mass culture encroaches in the twenty-first century. The geographic area surrounding Lake Constance in Central Europe, for example, belongs to a single cultural area in which a single dialect of German is spoken, and its musical styles and repertories are related by a long history. This small area nevertheless includes parts of four nations (Germany, Switzerland, Austria, and Liechtenstein). Even though the folk musics of Germany, Switzerland, and Austria are distinct at a national level, the Lake Constance region plays the decisive role in determining musical unity.

The musical areas of Europe also result from groups of people who share a way of life and a distinctive music, even when these have little to do with national and political boundaries. Jewish, Saami, and Roma (Gypsy) music cultures in Europe, for example, are circumscribed primarily by boundaries that arise within these communities. Roma communities exist throughout Europe, having adapted to many different socioeconomic settings. Roma musicians have traditionally adapted to the music in countries where they settled, often fulfilling specialized roles as performers in the musical life of the non-Roma society. This flexible response to music in the surrounding society has not erased a distinctively Roma musical life. Bolstering that musical life have been the customs, languages, and social functions unique to the Roma community. It is not quite proper to speak of "Roma"—and surely not "Gypsy"—culture as a homogeneous whole. Instead, we must always keep in mind the distinctive linguistic and cultural communities that make up the whole.

If we were to generalize about the music of Roma and Sinti (another Gypsy culture) in Europe, we would always need to take into consideration a process of negotiation between the community and the larger nation or cultural area of which it was a part. We would also need to incorporate the ways in which Roma and Sinti make distinctions among their own musics and create their own typologies. Each supranational community generates its typologies in different ways. The Saami in northern Europe have traditionally responded relatively little to the music cultures of Norway, Sweden, Finland, and Russia, whereas Jewish musicians have often been active participants in the musical life outside the community, so much so that certain differences of style and repertory have disappeared. The Jewish klezmer musicians in CD 2, #9, for example, have incorporated Romanian sounds.

European Unity and Europeanness in the Music of Modern Europe

Many genres of European music reflect an underlying belief that unity of musical style is important. Hungarian and German folk-music scholars have created classification schemes that assert the historical presence and importance of Hungarian and German folk music. European folk music in general falls into repertories that have national, linguistic, or cultural designations, suggesting that those who describe such repertories feel that unity is fundamental to what folk music really is. Scholars in several countries have gone so far as to recognize patterns of unified history in their national folk musics. This historicization of a national music is particularly evident in Hungarian and English folk music; but elsewhere, too, we witness the ascription of unity based on the belief that the music of the past is related to the music of the present.

Folk music can reveal and articulate history in both musical and cultural (or, better, political and nationalistic) ways. The classification of Hungarian folk song is based on claims about whether musical style has been relatively unbroken since the time Hungarian people lived in Asia (old style) or whether it has absorbed influences from surrounding European peoples (new style). Musically considered, an old style song exhibited most of the following characteristics in one form or another: (1) a five-note, or pentatonic, scale, in which no half-steps were found; (2) melodies or phrases that started high and ended lower; (3) a melody in two halves, in which the second half repeated the first, only at the interval of the fifth lower; (4) a rhythmic style Bartók called parlando (speechlike); (5) a relatively steady tempo; and (6) ornamentation of the melody. The following example from Bartók's collections of Hungarian folk song demonstrates the characteristics of the old style in every way. You will hear these also in CD 2, #7. Each characteristic is bracketed and numbered according to the preceding list to help you identify the musical arguments Bartók and other Hungarian scholars brought to their understanding of history (Fig. 8–3).

The musical characteristics of the new style contrast in virtually every way with the old style. (1) Melodies are repetitive, and they form arches rather than descending contours, with four-line verses like the following (A^5 designates a phrase transposed a fifth higher); A A^5 A^5 A, A A^5 B A, A B B A. (2) The rhythm is not "speechlike" but rather "dancelike," demonstrating what Bartók called tempo giusto. (3) Whereas pentatonic scales are occasionally found, more common are the so-called church modes or major mode. (4) Non-Hungarian musical elements have been incorporated. (5) The influence of popular song, particularly Hungarian popular genres from the nineteenth century, is evident.

One of the first things we notice when we compare the musical traits of the old and new styles is that there is much more flexibility in those traits recognized as new. To fulfill the requisites for old style is very difficult, but virtually any Hungarian song—folk, popular, or even religious—fits into the new style. If the two are compared even further, we realize that, in certain ways, they are not so different. The transposition by fifths is as much old as it is new style, excluding the fact that a falling melody should somehow be older. Pentatonicism, too, is not excluded from the new style, and one might argue that the ornamentation in the old style has a tendency to fill in the gaps in its characteristic five-note scale. Figure 8–3, for example, is pentatonic when we consider only the main notes but has a seven-note scale when we add the ornaments, marked in Bartók's transcription with small noteheads.

This Hungarian construction of history out of folk-song style has clear nationalistic implications, and these are important to understand as ideas about European

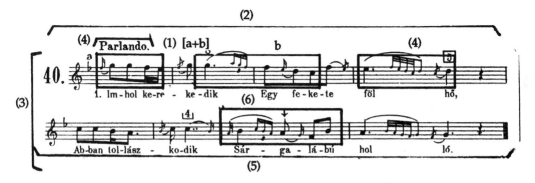

Figure 8–3   "Imhol kerekedik"—Hungarian Folk Song in the Old Style. *Source:* Bartók, Béla. *Das ungarische Volkslied.* Berlin: de Gruyter, 1925, p. 11, Example No.40.

music. Transposition by fifths was important to Bartók because it was quite rare in Western and Central European music, but more common in Central and East Asian traditions. A style of music that utilized transposition by fifths, therefore, proved that the integrity of the Hungarian people had been maintained to some measure, at least since they left Asia to settle in Europe. The close relation of the old style to speech (parlando) also reveals an attempt to link music to the uniqueness of Hungarian culture, for the Hungarian language is not a member of the Indo-European family. Clearly, identifying songs in the old style provided a strong argument for Hungarian nationalism. Recognizing that songs in the new style had been influenced from the outside—that their rhythms were regularized and loosened from their connection to language—made an equally strong nationalistic appeal. This interweaving of musical style, national history, and cultural ideology is such that we find it difficult to determine which characteristic of a song was determined for musical reasons, which for ideological reasons, and which for both.

The concept of "music history," itself a particularly European notion, asserts that unity is somehow central to the formation of musical repertories. French music, then, is more than just music that utilizes the French language or music created or performed in France; rather, it is music that occupies a position within French music history, in which successive musical styles develop in a consistent way, maintaining an essential style that is French. If we look at virtually any European country, we will find similar associations of national unity with a belief that musical style plays a fundamental role in music history.

Whether or not the patterns of stylistic unity sought by European scholars are real or not is open to question. Such patterns have sometimes produced rather unfortunate historical distortions, for example, when some German musical scholars sought to equate pockets of German folk-music style (in French Alsace-Lorraine, for instance, or in the so-called German "speech islands" of Eastern Europe) with colonialist expansion in the late nineteenth and early twentieth centuries. The need to equate musical style with national and regional unity in Europe remains one of the most noticeable traits of the continent even at the end of the twentieth century.

The "Europeanness" of music assumes many forms in modern Europe. We shall touch upon only a few here, keeping in mind that it would be possible to discover an infinite variety. An initial survey of the way Europeanness in music is articulated suggests that more traditional notions have survived relatively untouched. We find in the British Isles and Ireland general acceptance that there are English, Irish, Gaelic, Cornish, and Highland folk musics; all of these recognize regions, population groups, and political aspirations in ways that could be extrapolated to the diverse countries of the former Yugoslavia or the Iberian Peninsula. Classical music and its institutions also seem no less codified by nationalistic designations than they were a century or two ago; we find many people who accept that there is Polish music or a Czech national opera, even though most would be hard-pressed to identify the precise musical traits that justify these assertions. European popular music, though heard across national borders, becomes undeniably nationalistic at certain levels, for example, when performed in the annual "Eurovision" song competition, in which singers and ensembles from one country are pitted against those from another.

The more we choose examples to illustrate the persistence of older patterns of unity, the more we recognize that these are functioning in different ways in modern Europe. Motivations for retaining and expressing nationalistic or regional musical qualities have changed, as have the audiences who listen to popular and classical musics. A Polish popular singer must sing part of her repertory in English to assure success in Warsaw, but that success allows her to sharpen the bite of the political message in her songs, both Polish and English. The mass media link the different linguistic regions of Europe in new ways, thereby empowering indigenous languages to claims of greater importance while permitting international languages to encroach at an increasing pace.

The religious underpinnings of many repertories have become extraordinarily important, albeit not necessarily because the music retains an intimate connection with ritual. The German-speaking residents of northeastern Italy (Southern Tyrol), for example, find it especially significant that the liturgy of the Catholic Church is in their vernacular German, in fact, a transformation that occurred only with Vatican II, almost a half century after Southern Tyrol was absorbed by Italy in World War I. Identity with the music of the Catholic Church has an increasingly politicized meaning. The churches of Eastern Europe also functioned in this way prior to the fall of the Iron Curtain, providing a powerful voice—and in public, especially a musical voice—for East Germans, Poles, Lithuanians, or Ukrainians asserting the unity of their national identity.

The Europeanness of music today is not unlike the Viennese attributes we observed during our stroll through Vienna. Seemingly unrelated traditions are juxtaposed in unpredictable ways. Elements of indigenous and foreign music commingle, and in some cases they demonstrate an affinity for each other. Revitalizing old folk music is not an uncommon way of highlighting contemporary political issues. The old and the new coexist. Just as Vienna shaped its conflicting musical parts into a unity that reflected the history and contemporaneity of Vienna, so too does the Europeanness of music today assert itself so that the changing complexion of Europe has a powerful musical presence. That European music so often combines such diverse parts is, as we shall see, fundamental to the basic ideas that Europeans hold about music.

IDEAS ABOUT MUSIC

The Concept of "European Music"

Music is many different things to Europeans. Still, we recognize from many larger concepts that we employ in our speech about music that there are qualities that make music European and enable us to discuss a European music culture. We commonly employ the term "European art music" to describe the classical music of the Western concert hall. "European folk music," too, provides a way not only of stratifying shared musical activities but also of ascribing boundaries to these activities.

Earlier in the history of ethnomusicology, and to some extent today, music outside of Europe was defined by contrasting it with European music, calling it simply non-European. Implicit in such terms was not the notion that music was so much the same in different parts of Europe, but rather that certain experiences, both historically and culturally, had produced musical activities and ways of thinking about music that were more similar to each other than to those elsewhere in the world. Hungarian and Norwegian folk musics, therefore, do not sound like each other, but both fulfill certain expectations of what folk music should be in rural European society and in the construction of national cultures, musical styles, and art musics.

Music in Peasant and Folk Societies

European ideas about music have a great deal to do with shared historical experiences and the ways these experiences have formed modern European societies. At an early stage in these experiences social relations were relatively undifferentiated and rural, and yet a common culture—consisting of language, folklore, and belief system—provided cohesion. Music played a role in expressing the common culture of a people, and it could do so because it was in a language shared by the people and was a part of their daily lives and rituals. Music was thought to be inseparable from the essence of a culture. As such, it could express the culture's past, share traits of a language, and articulate religious belief. In doing so, music differentiated one society from another on the basis of national, regional, and linguistic styles (Fig. 8–4).

Music functioning in these ways is, of course, what we call folk music. Folk music is a particularly European concept. It is hardly surprising that a German, Johann Gottfried Herder, actually coined the term Volkslied (literally, "folk song") in the late eighteenth century and that the collection and study of folk music spread throughout Europe by the end of the nineteenth century, forming the basis for nationalism in music. The gap between a village folk song and a symphonic poem using it was massive, but it is significant for our consideration of European music that folklorists, composers, and many other intellectuals found it vital to bridge that gap. Folk music provided a means for understanding both the essence of, say, the Polish people and the ultimate expression of that essence in a national art music. Many twentieth-century European composers, such as Béla Bartók and Ralph Vaughan Williams, have continued to combine collecting and writing about folk music with composing in nationalistic styles (Fig. 8–4).

Music in Urban Society

Most European concepts of folk music portray it as the product of rural life. A certain irony lurks behind the need to privilege the music of rural life, because Euro-

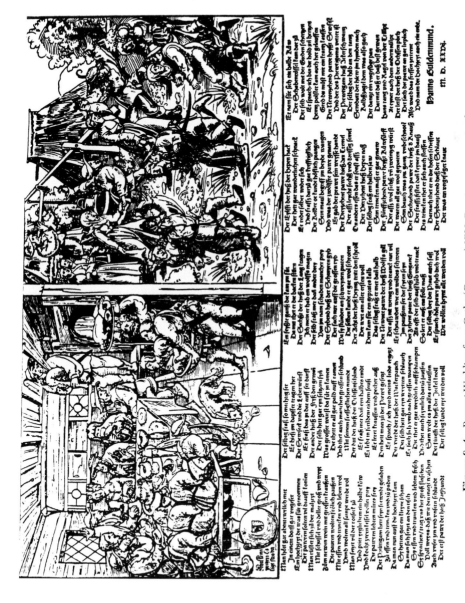

Figure 8–4 Peasant Wedding from Gotha (Germany) 1526. Bagpipe accompanies the meal; Schalmei accompanies the wedding dance. Text of the song is printed with the woodcut. *Graphics collection, Deutsches Volksliedarchiv, Freiburg i Br., Germany.*

pean society has a long history of extensive urbanization. Markets, seaports, monasteries, courts, and fortifications all served as the kernels from which great European cities developed during the Middle Ages. Ideas about music reflect this history. European cities, for example, have often served as the gathering points for people from other places, that is, people singing in different languages and performing on different instruments. As we might expect, musical "trade" has been as common in the city as mercantile trade. During the Middle Ages, troubadours, Minnesingers, and minstrels emerged as highly skilled musical specialists who traveled to urban centers, courts, and fairs, picking up new styles and repertories. Urbanization has also affected the manufacture of musical instruments and the mass production of music in all forms, ranging from printed broadsides (Fig. 8–4) in early modern Europe to recordings in the twenty-first century.

Cities may bring the musics of many different groups together, but by no means do they eliminate the distinctive qualities of these musics. The survival of communities that were relatively independent of national folk music or European art music helps us distinguish yet another fundamental European idea about music. Roma and Sinti musicians, for example, not only have a distinctive music culture, but they also perform as musical specialists in a variety of settings outside their own society such as in the small courts of southeastern Europe prior to the twentieth century. Similarly, a wide variety of musical styles and repertories exist in European Jewish communities, while Jewish musicians are known for the specialist roles they play in non-Jewish society. Even the klezmer ensembles that performed widely for the rites of passage in the Jewish shtetls of Eastern Europe occasionally traveled to play at Christian events and celebrations (cf. CD 2, #9).

Music within the Nation, Music outside the Nation

Music cultures such as those of the Saami and Jewish communities illustrate yet another characteristic of European music, namely the persistence of repertories that cross national borders. The boundaries of Saami music culture, for example, are effectively the same as those represented by the reindeer-herding routes in far northern Scandinavia and Russia. The Celtic folk-music traditions of Western Europe—traditions unified by the Gaelic languages and related stylistic traits, among them the harp and bagpipe in the instrumentarium—stretch from Brittany (western France) north through Wales and Ireland to Scotland. Modern political boundaries have failed to eliminate these traditions, and in fact the unity of musical style characteristic of such traditions has ensured their cultivation during periods of revivalism.

The twentieth-century political state has become a significant element shaping modern ideas about music in Europe. Governments have been particularly supportive of music, providing financial support for folk music as well as classical music and supporting festivals and broadcast media. When Bulgaria sought to create an international image of Bulgarian music in the 1980s, it would send its Bulgarian State Women's Chorus on tour throughout the world. State choral ensembles from the

Figure 8–5 Polish postcard from 1978, used to disseminate folk songs. *Postcard in the collections of the Deutsches Volksliedarchiv, Freiburg i Br., Germany.*

Baltic countries of Lithuania, Latvia, and Estonia tour widely, promulgating an officially sanctioned national sound. It is hardly surprising that there is no single model for national music in Europe. A national music may have a style that results from a unified history, or it may combine rather disparate styles from different parts of a country, symbolizing modern unity. Whatever the reasons for associating music with the state, politics has come to play a powerful role in twentieth-century ideas of European music (Fig. 8–5).

Music and Religion

Religious concepts and experiences often provide keys for understanding music in European society. Both folk and scholarly classifications include categories that specify some forms of music as religious, not infrequently relying on just two large categories, sacred and secular music. Classification schemes that simplify tend to mask a far more complex presence of religion in European ideas about music. If we consider the larger historical impact of Christianity on European culture, we see that systems of musical patronage often reflect the structure of Christian polity, that is, the organization of society within the hierarchy of the Church. Indeed, much of the music studied as European art music was created for specific use in religious services. Choral composers of the Renaissance, Johann Sebastian Bach, and the contemporary French composer Olivier Messiaen produced many of their greatest works for religious services, and it was not uncommon for musical style to respond to the requirements of the Church hierarchy, for example, the call during the sixteenth-century Counter-Reformation for a polyphonic style that rendered text as audible as possible.

Folk music that accompanies ritual or that embodies spiritual themes is overwhelmingly religious in many communities (cf. CD 2, #25). A harvest or wedding song, for example, may articulate a community's most fundamental sacred beliefs. Not only are Norwegian folk songs predominantly religious in thematic content, but many are actually variants of hymns that have entered oral tradition. Religious occasions such as pilgrimages have generated new songs and formed new communities that give such songs special meaning and function. During the Cold War, religious music became a primary voice for resistance, especially in Eastern Europe (Fig. 8–6). More recently, religious music has created venues for protesting violence against foreign workers and asylum seekers in Central Europe.

Figure 8–6   Folk Musicians at the Pre-Lenten Celebrations in Gusswerk. Austria, February 12, 1991. Hans Martschin and the Mariazeller Sparkassenmusi. *Photograph, Philip V. Bohlman.*

Concerts and Concert Stars

When most of us think about European music, we think also about how and where it takes place. In short, we equate European music with concerts. The concert is a specialized musical event, one in which the difference between performer and audience is very great and the focal point of most activity is the singing or playing of music. At one level, the concert suspends the ritual of folk or sacred music by privileging the music itself, and social behavior dictates that one listen carefully to a particular musical text. At another level, concerts have generated their own rituals in European society, and audiences behave according to social requirements specific to the concert setting: dressing in a certain way, refraining from conversation, and listening attentively.

Concerts have become a form of musical ritual particularly suited to modern Europe. Some concerts may preserve one type of musical ritual, while others become the moment for radical innovation. The European concert empowers musicians to recontextualize music, to bring rural folk music to the streets of the city, or to relocate sacred music in a public auditorium. Though an idea shared by all Europeans, the concert has nevertheless remained one of the major sources of musical diversity in modern times.

Concerts inevitably shift a certain degree of attention to the performer as a result of splitting musical participation into the two groups of music makers and audience. The performer acquires importance because of the skill he or she possesses, because of the role the audience wants the performer to play. Virtuosity often becomes one of the markers of this role, and accordingly outstanding musicians become extremely important in European ideas about music. The virtuoso has taken many forms. We think first of the performer who plays the most difficult passages in a concerto cadenza faster than anyone else—the early-nineteenth-century Italian violinist Nicolò Paganini, for example. There were those in the nineteenth century who speculated—a few even seriously—that Paganini's virtuosity resulted from other-worldly influences, perhaps some sort of pact with the devil. Stories about the nineteenth-century piano virtuoso Franz Liszt chronicle his amorous skills, which were linked to his ability as a performer when he tossed broken piano strings to adoring women in the audience.

Although many stories about virtuosi are apocryphal, they reveal a great deal about European ideas about music. The virtuoso is somehow superhuman and can achieve things that no mortal is able to achieve. A sort of cult-figure worship develops around this superhuman quality, and the usual requisites for behavior are suspended. We find these ideas embedded elsewhere in European music, such as the association of certain instruments, particularly fiddles, or musical structures, especially the "devilish" interval of a tritone, with supernatural forces. The German philosopher Friedrich Nietzsche canonized these ideas in his writings about cultural superbeings, and music historians have applied them to virtuosi in all aspects of classical music making—composer, conductor, and performer alike. European music has been inseparable from the presence of individuals who stood out from the rest of society.

The Individual and Society, Creativity and Community

As a social counterpoint to the musicians who stand out as exceptional, more communal forms of music making continue to thrive in European society. Musical ensembles in which the total musical product depends on a group's willingness to subsume individual identity into that of the ensemble reflect many ideals that Europeans associate with folk music. In the idealized folk society, all music theoretically belongs to the community, and because the means of producing music—family traditions, group interaction, community ritual—are shared, music becomes an aesthetic metaphor for communality. We recognize that this notion of communality is idealized, and yet we need not look far before discovering similar metaphors for other types of European music making. Chamber music, for example, is a genre of classical music in which each member of a small ensemble performs a part regarded as equal to all the other parts. The four voices of a string quartet, one of the most common ensembles, interact so that competition to make one voice dominate the others would undermine the performance. To symbolize this social equality, the chamber orchestra, the largest chamber ensemble in the classical tradition, often performs without a conductor. Not only does this avoid the symbol of power accruing to an individual, but it assures the performers that their musical and social survival depends on functioning as a whole with interacting parts.

The folk-music or chamber ensemble may appear as idealized models for European society, but the complexity of European society, in which the parts do not always function as a whole, can also be symbolized by the musical ensemble. Folk-music ensembles—the tamburitza of southeastern Europe, for example—derive their structure in part from the soprano-alto-tenor-bass structure of choirs. European classical music ensembles became relatively fixed in this format in the late eighteenth century and so we see that the tamburitza and the string quartet both symbolize a perception of gender roles in an otherwise egalitarian society.

German male choruses in the nineteenth century became a symbol for the power of nationalism embedded in and expressed by the *Volk*, the German people. Similarly, large choruses in socialist Eastern Europe during the second half of the twentieth century symbolized the achievement of the modern socialist state. Even though musical ensembles function in vastly different ways, their connection to the people as a collective society pervades European ideas about music. We witness a vivid portrayal of this in Mozart's *Le Nozze di Figaro*, in which the peasant folk together constitute the choruses, who gather on the stage at the culmination of significant scenes in the opera to serve as the final arbitrators of the actions of peasant, specialized laborer, and noble alike. In the end, it is the chorus that symbolizes the communal underpinnings of European society.

MUSICAL INSTRUMENTS

If we reflect back on our stroll through the streets of Vienna and take stock of the instruments we observed musicians playing, we might be struck both by the importance of instruments and their variety in this vignette of European musical life. The pianos in the Bösendorfer showroom were displayed as if in a museum, untouchable and expensive symbols of an elite. No less untouchable was the organ in St. Stephen's, whose sounds filled every corner of the Gothic cathedral, yet failed to help us locate the organist tucked away in a loft somewhere. The instruments of the street musicians were equally symbolic of identity and social function. The distinctiveness of the Andean panpipe players emanates most directly from their instruments; once considered a measure of music's universality, panpipes now serve as markers of a few musical cultures, especially those of the South American highlands.

Musical institutions in Vienna also bear witness to the importance of instruments. Museum collections juxtapose the so-called "period instruments" of early music with the experimental models of more recent times (which, too, may someday become "period instruments"), and folk-music archives assemble folk instruments to run acoustical experiments on them. The music academies are, in fact, metaphors for the learning and specialization that musical instruments demand. Musical instruments, therefore, are inescapable symbols of the unity and distinctiveness of European musical life. They may tell us that a musical style or repertory is European on one hand but Austrian, Hungarian, Sicilian, or Macedonian on the other. Instruments act as a vital material representation of musical life in Europe and as such embody its history and its great diversity.

Folk Instruments

Musical instruments have long served as some of the most commonly employed criteria for classifying music. The instruments of folk music, for example, were those constructed within the society or community where the particular repertory of folk music was performed. Indeed, many thought that a folk instrument was one built by its player, therefore functioning ideally for the player's needs. An instrument imported from elsewhere, even a neighboring village, did not belong to the musical life of the community in quite the same way. In the idealized folk society of Europe, then, an instrument is somehow the extension of the individual musician yet a marker of the community's musical identity. It is a specific product that we should be able to trace to its maker and the particular roles it plays in a given community. If this understanding of the folk instrument is idealized, it nevertheless underscores the importance of the instrument as a measure of European folk music itself as a product that comes into being according to a specified set of conditions.

There are performers of folk music who do make their own instruments, but today the norm is that instruments come from elsewhere and are probably the product of an unknown maker or an industrial manufacturer. The willingness of European musicians to borrow an instrument from elsewhere is by no means a modern phenomenon. Instrument types and names reveal a long history of instrumental peregrinations, both within Europe itself and across its borders. European instruments such as the lute and the guitar came originally from Islamic North Africa, and the Ottoman presence in southeastern Europe induced a particularly rich exchange with Turkey. The button-box accordion called the Grazer is no longer found only in Graz, a large provincial capital in southeastern Austria, but has become one of the preferred button boxes in many regions of Europe where they are played, such as Slovenia. Instruments like the bagpipe and the violin exist in countless variations in folk-music cultures throughout Europe; local communities everywhere have adapted these instruments to their own music cultures and individual musicians have personalized them. The Hardanger fiddle of Norway, a fairly recent adaptation of the violin, is indisputably Norwegian; a Swedish hummel, or dulcimer, is as likely to bear witness to the individual who performs it as is the gusle, or bowed lap fiddle (see Fig. 11–4; listen to CD 2, #6), of a Serbian epic singer. The ubiquity of such instrument types notwithstanding, they show that the tendency to use instruments to express individuality and community identity has not abated in modern Europe.

When Instruments Tell Stories

If musical instruments illustrate certain ways in which music is a product, many also participate in the means of production. Musical instruments become indispensable participants in a chain of events, and Europeans show a tendency to authropomorphize instruments, to regard instruments as music makers with human qualities. We refer to the parts of an instrumental piece as its "voices," and it is fairly common to relate these directly to human voice ranges. Europeans, like peoples throughout the world, ascribe human qualities to instruments (think of how many instruments have "necks," that part of the human body in which the vocal cords are located) and decorate instruments with human or animal figurations. Instruments become the musician's partner in music making.

Musical instruments in Europe often assist in telling a story. Narrativity is one of the functions that makes them humanlike. Among the earliest specialists who performed secular narrative song in Europe were those who sang by accompanying themselves on an instrument. The medieval Minnesinger, for example, recounted tales of history and great heroes, encounters with lovers and with enemies while wandering about the world, all the while relying on the narrative assistance of the lute. The importance of the lute to the German song tradition appears in a nineteenth-century interpretation in Richard Wagner's *Die Meistersinger von Nürnberg*, in which the mastersingers must prove themselves by playing the lute according to the rigorous rules imposed on the tradition.

Whereas Wagner's vision was particularly Romantic and German, the narrativity of epic traditions in southeastern Europe predate medieval Europe, evolving from the Homeric epic traditions of ancient Greece. The epic is a narrative genre in which the poet-singer performs tales from the life of a hero or heroine. The singer's instrument, the gusle, has become so closely identified with the genre that the singer's name, guslar (player of the gusle), is derived from the instrument itself (cf. CD 2, #6).

The instruments of classical European music also demonstrate narrative functions, often in such ways that we recognize a close relation to rural society and folk beliefs. The twentieth-century composer Igor Stravinsky used the narrative potential of the orchestra to transform the pagan ritual of *Le Sacre du Printemps* (The Rite of Spring) and the Shrovetide folktale of *Petrushka* into classical ballets. The narrative power of the piano, too, marks the work of many composers—for example, Robert Schumann, who told the tale of attending a pre-Lenten party (again Shrovetide) in his *Carnaval* (Figs. 8–6 and 8–7 depict pre-Lenten music making today). Narrativity also distinguishes the symphonic tone poems of late nineteenth-century composers and the nationalistic works of composers seeking to use the orchestra to tell the stories most characteristic of their own history.

Musical Instruments in an Industrial Age

Although personal, communal, and human qualities continue to influence European concepts about musical instruments, the modern European instrumentarium would be inconceivable without technology. Technology's influence is evident in the development of new areas of musical life—for example, the dependence of rock-music instruments on mass-produced sound and dissemination. Perhaps less evident is the previous development of new instrument types during the rapid technologizing of European society from the end of the seventeenth century on, when instruments we

Figure 8–7 Japanese musicians performing on St. Mark's Square in Venice during pre-Lenten celebrations in 1996. *Photograph by Philip V. Bohlman.*

now regard as standard—the piano, for instance—were invented and reinvented. The technology of musical instruments is also one of the primary musical exports from Europe, and we can recognize European influences on non-European musics by the adaptation of certain types of technology, such as the harmonium in North India and Pakistan. Moreover, technological developments have directly affected the reception of music, making it possible for larger audiences to hear a piano with a more powerful cast-iron frame or the amplified sounds of a folk-music ensemble using microphones.

No instrument symbolizes the impact of technology on European musical instruments as fully as the piano. Invented at the beginning of the eighteenth century in Italy, the piano transformed the direct striking or plucking action of the clavichord and harpsichord into a more powerful action by employing a series of levers connected by joints. The new machinery in the piano not only allowed for a broader palette of sound colors but made it possible for the piano to dominate the other instruments with which it was played. As the piano grew larger, so did its sound; as its machinery grew more complicated, the factories that manufactured it became more sophisticated and efficient. The technology to create pianos kept pace with the demand for an instrument that had its own solo repertory and a role in many other repertories. The piano both appeared on the stage of the largest concert hall and stood in the parlor of the bourgeois home.

A product of technology, the piano became the preferred instrument of the European "everyperson" by the mid-nineteenth century. It was an instrument that resulted from mass production and was capable of attracting mass audiences. Pianos followed Europeans as they settled elsewhere as both immigrants and colonizers. Yet the piano did not lend itself particularly well to other musics. Its technology was so highly developed that it could not be easily adapted to non-European scales. It stood apart in non-Western societies, effectively symbolizing the hegemony of European music in the colonial era.

Instruments and Musical Professionalism

Musical instruments often represent complexity, which is a musical quality highly valued in European society. Whereas both singers and instrumentalists do generally practice and study to acquire their skills, playing an instrument is often regarded as less natural, less a product of pure gifts than singing. The distinction between vocal and instrumental forms of music is, in fact, universal, and in many societies, such as those of the Islamic world, instrumental music may be criticized or even prescribed because it is less human, that is, not directly tied to words. Restrictions on instrumental music are not unknown in Europe, where periodic attempts to keep instruments out of Christian religious music are among the hallmarks of conservative religious movements. When they ascended to power in 1649, forming the English Commonwealth, the Puritans inveighed against instruments in churches and ordered that organs be destroyed. The medieval division of music into *musica humana, musica mundana*, and *musica instrumentalis*, a concept also fundamental to early Greek thought about music, persists in European musical thought today.

Instrumentalists therefore acquire the status of specialists and, very often, professionals. They stand out as exceptional in society because of the skills they command, and the best—that is, the most skillful—receive financial rewards for their labors. The exceptional role of instrumentalists does not always reflect public sanction; instrumentalists like the becar in southeastern Europe are sometimes regarded as ne'er-do-wells or troublemakers (and, not insignificantly, attractive lovers). The outsider status of the instrumentalist also empowers one to move with ease from community to community, or even to perform within several distinct societies. We have witnessed this already with Roma and Sinti musicians. Medieval minstrels, generally instrumental musicians, were also distinguished by relative mobility. In more modern times, this has obtained also for the klezmer ensembles of European Jewish society. Increased mobility ensured the profitability of the instrumentalist's trade. We see again the European willingness to view music as a product, indeed one that a consuming society is willing to pay to hear.

HISTORY AND SOCIAL STRUCTURE IN EUROPEAN MUSICAL LIFE

The Underlying Historicism of European Musical Thought

We have seen throughout this chapter that history is one of the primary forces unifying European concepts of music. Just as Europeans are aware of larger historical forces and moments—whether wars, religious transformations, or responses to other parts of the world—they also share a sense that a historical unity characterizes the musics of Europe. We witness such unity in phrases like "European art music" or "European folk music" (and conversely in phrases like "non-European music"). Though the presence of history in European musical life may seem abstract, Europeans constantly sense that presence when talking about music.

At least since the Renaissance, those who have written about music have largely concerned themselves with some musics of the past and the relation of these musics to a more recent time. It is hardly surprising that we commonly refer to scholars who write about European art music as music historians. The study of European folk music has been no less motivated by the urge to construct historical patterns. As we saw in Fig. 8–3 and heard in CD 2, #7, Béla Bartók and Zoltán Kodály created a model for Hungarian folk song in which musical style was entirely historical, emerging as "old style," "new style," or a mixture of these two styles and outside influences.

Individuals and Collectives in the History of Music

History does take a number of distinctive forms in European concepts of the relation of music to a given community, society, or nation. Music may be a part of and serve as a voice for a people's mentalité. In contemporary usage, the mentalité of a people is that cultural profile existing apart from the actions of armies and political figures; instead, it forms from the everyday acts, aspirations, and belief systems of an entire society. The concept applies particularly well to an interpretation of musical life that emphasizes folk music as a corpus of expressive activities shared by an entire cultural group; in effect, folk music becomes the product of the group's mentalité.

We find a similar sense of collectivity in Johann Gottfried Herder's eighteenth-century model for the shared music of a people, Volkslied. Herder and nineteenth-century folk-music scholars steeped their concept of Volkslied in historical potential. The "everyperson" in European society, therefore, continued to contribute to music history by sharing in a musical collective. Even attempts to reformulate the concepts of folk music into "people's music" (in Marxist thought) or "group song" (a formulation associated with the German scholar Ernst Klusen) retain the basic premise that it is a collective that shapes the formation, transmission, and history of music.

Few modern interpreters of European music history accept the notion that a folk song or any other form of popular music came into existence simply because of the will and collective action of the community. Instead, an individual, usually a musician with some specialized role in the musical life of the community, creates a piece of music, "composes" it, and establishes its position in a particular music history. Folk songs, for example, might begin their history in oral tradition by first being printed on a broadside and sold on the street, largely to earn profit for the composer, printer, and hawker. The broadside ballad, which often appeals because it captures the news of the moment, is only possible if it embodies certain aspects of the community's mentalité and relies on the community's knowledge of common melodies, yet it is the individual who composes these relationships in the ballad.

The broadside composer is often anonymous and represents one end of a continuum of individuals in music history. At the other end, we find the twentieth-century recording virtuoso, whose status as a cult figure would seem to stand outside of history (fans will regard the virtuoso's interpretations as superior to those fixed or limited by historical performance practice), except for the mediating role that history has also played in creating technology so that individual interpretations can be widely disseminated and idolized. The history of European music has gradually shifted more emphasis toward the individual. The notion of the individual musician standing out from his or her community was virtually unknown in the Middle Ages, but it began to form in the fourteenth century, when minstrels acquired names such as "Fiddler" or "Pfeiffer" (Piper) that help us to understand the relation between the musical specialist and the community. The designation of the individual as potentially exceptional, a musical genius, began only in the late Renaissance, but quickly became a primary impetus in European music history, and by the nineteenth century music historians were using "great composers" to mark the epochs of historical change (e.g., the "Age of Bach").

Modern Nations, Modern Histories, Modern Musics

Twice during the twentieth century, world wars radically redrew the map of Europe, creating new political entities while splitting and eliminating many old ones. The new face of Europe has had a profound effect on musical life in the continent. Just as new nations and cultural boundaries have developed, so too have new music histories emerged to interpret and, in some cases, to justify the widespread change. More than at any previous moment, the diversity of Europe's music at the beginning of the twenty-first century is a result of conscious historicism: the revitalization of a musical past in the present. On one hand, historicism interrupts the path of steady historical development by altering traditional social contexts. On the other, it collapses the differences between past and present, making it possible to combine musical styles and repertories in ways particularly appropriate to the political reality of modern Europe. Musical historicism recaptures the past in distinctly modern ways (Fig. 8–7).

Just what can musical historicism capture from the past? In what ways do elements from the past effectively serve as the music of the present? There are no simple answers to such questions. Modern European musical cultures have employed historicism with quite different motivations. One of the most common motivations is nationalism. This reflexive impulse explains the urge to search for Czechness in the music of the Czech Republic. A nation of quite distinctive regional and minority cultures, the Czech Republic has nevertheless endeavored to establish the criteria that make music Czech, finding little consensus among composers or folk-music styles of the past. If Czechness in music is itself elusive, the motivation to discover a distinctive nationalism is not unique to the Czech Republic.

We find similar tendencies among the inhabitants of Southern Tyrol in Italy, who have carved out repertories of music that consist entirely of German-language songs and pre-Italian Latinate dialects, called ladino locally, which also survive in the region today. Songbooks in the region simply do not contain songs in Italian, and the examples in German, Ladino, and English (the last usually from the American folk-song revival) reveal a clear pattern of choosing selectively from the past to build the repertory of the present. European institutions of classical music also arise because of the historicist impetus of the modern nation. The state or national academy of music, orchestra, or chorus has become normative throughout Europe. The new map of modern Europe, then, has relied on the historical underpinnings of musical life to reformulate that life, to modernize it, and to link it to new historical conditions.

EUROPEAN MUSIC AT THE BEGINNING OF THE TWENTY-FIRST CENTURY

The Eurovision Song Contest

For the Eurovision Song Contest the 2002 final competition—the "Grand Prix"—in Tallinn, Estonia, signaled the beginning of a new era for European popular music.

No one failed to recognize the historical fact that the Grand Prix was taking place, for the first time since the Eurovision Song Contest began in 1956, in a country in Eastern Europe. Already in 1989, in the midst of Eastern Europe's Velvet Revolution, the Eurovision (the contest's short name) was looking eastward, with the hope that it might win new national competitors and new audiences. In that year, the Yugoslav group, Riva, won the contest, the first Grand Prix for Eastern Europe. The first Eurovision in 1956 also had political significance, for that was the year in which Soviet troops forcefully ended the attempts of several Communist nations, particularly Hungary, to liberalize their economies and loosen their ties to the Soviet Union. Following its birth in Switzerland, the Eurovision embarked on its first chapter during a critical moment in the Cold War, and it is hardly surprising that every subsequent moment of political significance would be recorded in one way or another in the Eurovision, when the nations of Europe compete for the honors of the best popular song of the year. Popular music and politics could not be more tightly and more paradoxically intertwined.

The Eurovision Song Contest is a moment when Europe turns to popular song as a means of performing its national and global identities. On the Saturday evening each May when the Grand Prix ceremonies are broadcast by the member networks of the European Broadcasting Union, hundreds of millions of Europeans find themselves glued to their television sets to watch the national entries perform and to root for their favorite songs and national musical heroes. In many cities crowds of fans flood the main public squares to watch the Eurovision on massive screens and to root not only for their national entries but also for the entries from nations regarded as cultural and political allies. At the 2002 Eurovision in Estonia, a powerful undercurrent of support for the entries from the Balkan neighbor states, Latvia and Lithuania, and for the Scandinavian neighbors to the north and west flowed through the crowds in Tallinn's town square. Enmity for the historical enemy, Russia, was no less palpable.

In the world of popular music, the professional stakes for a good showing at the Eurovision are very high. The Eurovision played a signal role in launching the careers of the Swedish group, ABBA, the Canadian singer, Céline Dion (performing and winning for Switzerland in 1988), the Israeli worldbeat star, Ofra Haza, and the Celtic music phenomenon, Riverdance, which was catapulted to prominence after its Eurovision intermission performance in 1993. Winning, or even doing well in front of an international audience, can mean lucrative recording contracts and a string of appearances for the European media who sponsor the Grand Prix.

All this sounds more like media hype and crass commercialism than a response to the Cold War, the reunification of Europe, and the countercurrents of old and new nationalisms. Once the different singers and groups start performing, one after another in the alphabetical order of their countries, the evidence for national identities becomes even more perplexing. The Grand Prix took place in Tallinn in 2002 by virtue of the Estonian winners from the year before, Dave Benton and Tanal Pedar, whose song, "Everybody," plumbed Caribbean musical styles, especially Jamaican dancehall. Few listeners would be bothered by the absence of Estonianness in the Estonian entry, not least because Dave Benton is Afro-Caribbean, originally from Aruba. In 2002, after all, the three women singers constituting the Swedish entry, "Afro-Dite," were all of African descent.

European popular song at the Eurovision does not look particularly European, and it surely does not sound European. In 2000 and 2001, African American styles were particularly prominent among the national entries, ranging from the blues to Motown to hip hop. Why should this surprise us, we might ask, for other international and hybrid popular styles also dominated previous periods during the almost half-century history of the Eurovision Song Contest? Celtic influences were most palpable in the 1990s, and before that Mediterranean song dominated, following on the era of rock 'n' roll and French chanson. Turkey and several nations from Southeastern Europe wishing to draw attention to historical and musical connections to Islamic traditions often combine Middle Eastern instrumental and vocal improvisatory styles.

Lest we think there is conformity, we find ourselves confronted by alternative styles as the gala performance moves from group to group. The entries from Southeastern Europe seem unwilling to buy into the prevailing musical fashions. The entries from Bosnia-Hercegovina, Croatia, Macedonia, and Romania have something else to say about the history of Europe during the dozen years of its reunification efforts. Regional and local politics find their way into national entries, such as Norway's 1980 entry, the Saami Mattis Hætta, who, together with Sverre Kjelsberg, performed the song, "Saamiid Aednan," which was based on a Saami yoik and included extended passages of yoiking. In 1999, Germany's Sürpriz, herself Turkish-German, sang "Journey to Jerusalem," an acknowledgment of the cultural debt to and political difficulties of Germany's so-called guest workers from Turkey, who had historically been denied German citizenship. Eurovision entries that make political statements rarely win the contest or even place particularly high, but they are able to seize one of the most visible forums in the continent at a highly charged public moment.

History, politics, and music were all at stake in May 2002 when the twenty-four entries took to the stage of the Eurovision in Tallinn. The audience wore nationalism on its sleeves, or rather displayed it with a flurry of fluttering national flags, further evidence that popular song had embarked on a new, more nationalist path with Estonia's victory the year before. Longer political histories, such as Estonia's own opposition to Russian domination, mixed with recent flashpoints, particularly the Israeli-Palestinian conflict, which the Israeli entry, Sarit Hadad, did little to deflect with her vocal call for peace, "Light a Candle." The evening, however, belonged to the Baltic states and the other Eastern European nations vying for membership in the European Union. Tension grew in anticipation of the Latvian entry especially, Marie N singing "I Wanna," which many had recognized as the best chance to keep the Eurovision in the Baltic region. And they were right. Announced by a trumpet fanfare from a Spanish bullfight, Marie N swept across the stage, brilliantly dancing her way as a toreador from Spain to the Caribbean as an amalgam of Afro-Cuban rhythms emerged from its Spanish and African roots. When the song made its way back to Europe before the final refrain, it was through breathless transition to flamenco, punctuated by Marie N's instantaneous change of costume from male to female. "I Wanna" won the day, and Latvia won the Eurovision, focusing European cultural politics on Eastern Europe for another year at least.

A Viennese Waltz in Conclusion

The musical Europe of the twenty-first century that we witnessed while watching the 2002 Eurovision Song Contest was in many ways not unlike the musical Vienna we encountered during the excursion that opened this chapter. Issues of cultural identity were important, and music served to articulate these in varied but always striking ways. The Eurovision showed that nations took great pains to display the ways they wished to belong to Europe, even when this meant mixing the local, national, and global. The vital musical life of Vienna, too, was essential to its identity as a quintessentially musical city in the heart of Europe, but the more we listened to Viennese music the more we realized it was not one style or repertory but many. Just as the Eurovision incorporated Israel, Turkey, and Morocco into the continent's musical life, the shoppers on Kärntner Street adopted the Andean panpipe ensemble into the musical life of Vienna.

In European music history, "Vienneseness" has signified many different styles and repertories: the Viennese classicism of Mozart's time; the modernist experiments of Arnold Schoenberg and the "Second Viennese School"; the popular theater traditions of Viennese operettas; the nineteenth-century reform of Jewish liturgical music known as the "Viennese Rite" for the synagogue; and, last but not least, that symbol of the city of music, the Viennese waltz. We therefore realize that Vienneseness is nothing if not a construction, a whole with parts that are sometimes compatible and at other times contradictory. The classicism denoted by the Viennese label in European art music suggests a conscious awareness of the past, even a return to the past. Yet neither Mozart nor Schoenberg was a musical conservative. Were they both not progressives, visionaries, even radicals in their own day? The Viennese waltz, too, combines and reformulates musical styles, namely the diverse styles of Central European folk dance with the urbane culture of nineteenth-century Vienna. As the Viennese label affixes itself, music undergoes complex processes of negotiation: between past and present; between rural and urban; between Austrian and foreign; between the individual and the collective; between one musical style or genre and another.

The Viennese waltz is surely all of these; we can understand it as folk, popular, or classical, typically Viennese or international, socially conservative or liberal. As a juxtaposition of all these traits, it reflects a balance, and it is the nature of that balance that eventually establishes the relation of the Viennese waltz as a musical style to Vienna as a cultural setting. That balance—struck and forged among the conditions of history, society, politics, geography, language, style, performance, instrumentarium, and repertory—assumes myriad forms in other European cities and nations, and charts the path of European music history. That balance, in fact, provides the dynamic tension that makes it possible to understand the music of Europe as a whole that achieves its identity only from its diverse, composite parts.

EUROPE BIBLIOGRAPHY

Europe as a Whole   Theodor W. Adorno, *Introduction to the Sociology of Music*, trans. E. B. Ashton (New York: Seabury, 1976); Constantin Brăiloiu, *Problems of Ethnomusicology*, ed. and trans. A. L. Lloyd (Cambridge: Cambridge University Press, 1984); Bruno Nettl, *Folk and Traditional Music of the Western Continents*, 3rd ed. (Englewood Cliffs, N.J.: Prentice Hall, 1990); Timothy Rice, James Porter, and Chris Goertzen, eds., *Europe*, vol. 8: *The Garland Encyclopedia of World Music* (New York: Garland Publishing, 2000).

Cultural Life in Vienna and Austria   Walter Deutsch and others, eds., *Volksmusik in Österreich* (Vienna: Österreichischer Bundesverlag, 1984); Carl Schorske, *Fin-de-Siècle Vienna* (New York: Alfred A. Knopf, 1980); Michael P. Steinberg, *The Meaning of the Salzburg Festival: Austria as Theater and Ideology, 1890–1938* (Ithaca, N.Y.: Cornell University Press, 1990); Stephen Toulmin and Allan Janik, *Wittgenstein's Vienna* (New York: Touchstone, 1973).

Folk Music   Ralph Vaughan Williams, *National Music* (New York: Oxford University Press, 1954); Walter Wiora, *European Folk Song: Common Forms in Characteristic Modification* (Cologne: Arno Volk, 1966); Philip V. Bohlman, *The Study of Folk Music in the Modern World* (Bloomington: Indiana University Press, 1988).

Music of Eastern and Southern Europe   Béla Bartók, *Hungarian Folk Music*, trans. M. C. Calvacoressi (London: Oxford University Press, 1931); Béla Bartók and Albert B. Lord, *Serbo-Croatian Folk Songs* (New York: Columbia University Press, 1951); Béla Bartók, *Rumanian Folk Music*, 5 vols., ed. Benjamin Suchoff (The Hague: Martinus Nijhoff, 1967–1975); Zoltán Kodály, *Folk Music of Hungary*, trans. Ronald Tempest and Cynthia Jolly (London: Barrie and Rockliff, 1960); Albert B. Lord, *The Singer of Tales* (Cambridge, Mass.: Harvard University Press, 1960); Bernard Lortat-Jacob, *Sardinian Chronicles* (Chicago: University of Chicago Press, 1995); Paul Nixon, *Sociality, Music, Dance: Human Figurations in a Transylvanian Valley* (Gothenburg: Göteborgs Universitet, 1998); Svanibor Pettan, ed., *Music, Politics, and War: Views from Croatia* (Zagreb: Institute of Ethnology and Folklore Research, 1998); Timothy Rice, *May It Fill Your Soul: Experiencing Bulgarian Music* (Chicago: University of Chicago Press, 1994); Mark Slobin, ed., *Retuning*

Culture: Musical Changes in Central and Eastern Europe (Durham, N.C.: Duke University Press, 1996); Jane C. Sugarman, *Engendering Song: Singing and Subjectivity at Prespa Albanian Weddings* (Chicago: University of Chicago Press, 1996).

Music of Central Europe   Philip V. Bohlman, *Central European Folk Music: An Annotated Bibliography of Sources in German* (New York: Garland Publishing, 1996); Ludwig Erk, ed., *Deutscher Liederhort*, 3 vols., ed. and expanded by Franz Magnus Böhme (Leipzig: Breitkopf & Härtel, 1893–1894); Celia Applegate and Pamela Potter, eds., *Music and German National Identity* (Chicago: University of Chicago Press, 2002).

Music of Western and Northern Europe   Frances James Child, *The English and Scottish Popular Ballads*, 5 vols. (Boston: Houghton, Mifflin, 1882–1898); James R. Cowdery, *The Melodic Tradition of Ireland* (Kent, Oh.: Kent State University Press, 1990); Svend Grundtvig and others, eds., *Danmarks Gamle Volkeviser*, 12 vols. (Copenhagen: Akademisk Forlag, 1853–1976); Chris Coertzen, *The Normal Fiddle in Norway* (Chicago: University of Chicago Press, 1997); Olav Gurvin, *Norwegian Folk Music* (Oslo: Universitetsforlaget, 1958–); Dave Harker, *Fakesong: The Manufacture of British "Folksong" 1700 to the Present Day* (Milton Keynes, England: Open University Press, 1985); A. L. Lloyd, *Folk Song in England* (London: Lawrence and Wishart, 1967); James Porter, *The Traditional Music of Britain and Ireland: A Research and Information Guide* (New York: Garland, 1989); Cecil J. Sharp, *English Folk Song: Some Conclusions* (1st ed., 1907), 4th ed., rev. Maud Karpeles (Belmont, Calif: Wadsworth, 1965); Frances Vernillat and Jacques Charpentreau, eds., *Dictionnaire de la chanson française* (Paris: Larousse, 1968).

Music of Ethnic Groups or Communities Stretching across Several Nations Samuel G. Armistead, Joseph H. Silverman, and Israel J. Katz, *Judeo-Spanish Ballads in Oral Tradition* (Berkeley and Los Angeles: University of California Press, 1968); Philip V. Bohlman and Otto Holzapfel, eds., *The Folk Songs of Ashkenaz* (Middleton, Wisc.: A-R Editions, 2001); Bálint Sárosi, *Gypsy Music*, trans. Fred MacNicoll (Budapest: Corvina, 1978); *Old Jewish Folk Music: The Collections and Writings of Moshe Beregovski* (Philadelphia: University of Pennsylvania Press, 1982); Eric Werner, *A Voice Still Heard . . . The Sacred Songs of the Ashkenazic Jews* (University Park: Pennsylvania State University Press, 1976); Walter Wiora, *Europäischer Volksgesang* (Cologne: Arno Volk, 1953); Max Peter Baumann, ed., *Music, Language and Literature of the Roma and Sinti* (Berlin: Verlag für Wissenschaft und Bildung, 2000); Barbara Rose Lange, *Holy Brotherhood: Romani Music in a Hungarian Pentecostal Church* (New York: Oxford University Press, 2002).

European Musical Genres   Rolf Wilhelm Brednich, Lutz Röhrich, and Wolfgang Suppan, eds., *Handbuch des Volksliedes*, 2 vols. (Munich: Wilhelm Fink, 1973, 1975); Richard Middleton, *Studying Popular Music* (Milton Keynes, England: Open University Press, 1990); Leslie Shepard, *The Broadside Ballad: A Study in Origins* *and Meaning* (Hatboro, Penn.: Legacy, 1978); Lajos Vargyas, *Hungarian Ballads and the European Ballad Tradition*, 2 vols. (Budapest: Akadémiai Kiadó, 1983).

Instruments   Erich Stockmann and Ernst Emsheimer, ed., *Studia instrumentorum musicae popularis* (Stockholm: Musikhistoriska Museet, 1969–present; currently 11 vols.).

Nationalism and Music   Sidney Finkelstein, *Composer and Nation: The Folk Heritage in Music*, 2nd ed. (New York: International Publishers, 1989); Dieter Rexroth, ed., *Zwischen den Grenzen: Zum Aspekt des Nationalen in der Musik* (Mainz: B. Schott's Söhne, 1979); Philip V. Bohlman, *The Music of European Nationalism: Cultural Identity and Modern History* (Denver: ABC-Clio, 2004).

EUROPE DISCOGRAPHY

Discographical Note

Among the best surveys of national folk musics are those released on the Folkways label and rereleased on the Smithsonian label, with extensive critical notes geared toward students among others. A particularly good selection of Eastern European traditions is to be found on the Nonesuch Explorer label. The European recordings of the "Alan Lomax Collection" have been steadily appearing since the mid-1990s on the Rounder label, each of them with notes by well-known ethnomusicologists. The Rounder Lomax collections for Italy, Romania, Spain, and Yugoslavia were relatively extensive by 2003.

European academies of science and ethnological museums often produce recordings of extraordinarily high musical and educational quality, reproducing both modern field recordings and rereleasing historical collections from the first era of recorded sound. During the 1970s and 1980s, a period of widespread folk-music revival in Europe, and during the 1990s, when the European Union's political and economic influence spread, voluminous recordings of local, regional, and national folk-music traditions have appeared on CD.

The most comprehensive discographical guide to national and ethnic popular music is Simon Broughton, Mark Ellingham, and Richard Trillo, eds., *World Music: The Rough Guide*, vol. 1: *Africa, Europe and the Middle East* (London: The Rough Guides, 1999). The *Rough Guides* also have published CDs of national and regional music in Europe, emphasizing ethnic and national styles of popular music.

Students will also wish to consider recordings of European art music and popular music, which are available in large numbers in libraries and record stores. When studying and listening to these recordings, however, the student may wish to make comparisons in new ways and to examine new issues that their mass production reveals—for example, just how are these genres marketed in different ways, or how do different nations produce the "same" music but in different ways?

Deutsche Volkslieder, 2 discs (DGG 004-157, 004-160); *Electric Muse: The Story of Folk into Rock*, 4 discs (Folk 1001); A. L. Lloyd and Ewan MacColl, *English and Scottish Popular Ballads* (Washington 715-723); *Folk Music of France* (Folkways P 414); *Folk Music of Hungary*, collected by Béla Bartók (Folkways P 1000); *Folk Music of Portugal*, 2 discs (Folkways 4538); *Folk Music of Rumania*, collected by Béla Bartók (Folkways 419); *Islamic Ritual from Yugoslavia: Zikr of the Rafa'i Brotherhood* (UNESCO Collection, Philips 6586 015); *Le mystère des voix bulgares*, 3 volumes (Electra/Nonesuch 79165-2); *Liturgical Chant for Lent and Easter: Armenian Mekhitarist Community of Venice* (UNESCO Collection, Philips 6586 025); *Songs and Dances of Holland* (Folkways 3576); *Songs and Dances of Norway* (Folkways FE 4008); *Songs and Dances of Spain*, 5 discs, with notes by Alan Lomax (Westminster WF 12001-5); *World Collection of Recorded Music*, 6 discs, based on collections of Constantin Brăiloiu (VDE 30-425-430); *Dancing on the Edge of a Volcano: Jewish Cabaret, Popular, and Political Songs, 1900–1945* (Cedille Records CDR 90000 065); *The Rough Guide Music of the Gypsies* (The Rough Guide RGNET 1051 CD); *Unblocked: Music of Eastern Europe*, 3-CD set (Ellipsis Arts CD3570).

9

Music in Latin America

Thomas Turino

AN ANDEAN MESTIZO FIESTA IN PAUCARTAMBO, PERU

Most of the year the rural Andean town of Paucartambo seems almost empty. Many people have migrated to the nearby city of Cuzco, ancient capital of the Incas, or to larger cities on the Peruvian coast in search of employment and what they are told is a better way of life. In the weeks before the festival for the town's patron saint, the Virgen del Carmen (July 15–18), the place begins to stir in preparation. All the houses are freshly whitewashed, the streets are cleaned, and people who now live elsewhere begin returning home. The men who have accepted the roles of fiesta sponsorship visit the homes of relatives and friends who have promised financial contributions. Through tremendous expenditure, the main sponsor hopes that his lavishness will make this a fiesta that people will always remember. Meanwhile, food, liquor, beer, and fireworks arrive in truck after truck—there is never enough. The primary participants in the fiesta are mestizos (people of mixed Spanish and indigenous cultural heritage) from the town itself; the people of the surrounding Quechua-speaking indigenous communities are excluded from taking part, and come mainly to watch. In the weeks before the fiesta, the members of the various dance ensembles begin to rehearse for long hours on patios behind closed doors. They practice so that they may please the Virgin with their dancing and so that, this year, their group will be considered the finest. Meanwhile, the women sew the elaborate costumes and older men make the ceramic masks.

Twelve or more costumed dance ensembles perform during the fiesta, and each one tells part of the story that the fiesta conveys about the town and its people. The heroes of the fiesta drama are a dance group known as the Qhapac Chunchos, the "rich and powerful jungle Indians," (Paucartambo is located in a beautiful river valley on the eastern slopes of the Andes near the jungle region.) Their costume includes the feathered headdress associated with Peruvian jungle Indians, and spears indicating their role as warriors. Within the fiesta drama, the Chunchos represent heroes, the "home team"; throughout the fiesta the Chuncho king and his soldiers express the nobility of the town through dignified behavior and disciplined martial dance. The Chunchos open the festivities by dancing for the Virgin on the church steps (Fig. 9–1). During the processions of the statue of the Virgin, the Chunchos dance around her litter serving as an honor guard.

The other main protagonists of the fiesta drama are the Qollas, representing uncivilized outsiders, the traders of the high plateau of southern Peru (Fig. 9–2). These mestizo dancers act out their part as "savages from the puna" (places of extremely high altitude) in various ways. They lead their llama (loaded with the goods that actual Qolla traders would carry) in and out of stores upsetting things as they go, they whip each other in one part of their dance, and they conduct themselves in an unruly manner throughout the fiesta days. Their dramatic persona thus contrasts fundamentally with the reserved, disciplined, dignified behavior of their rivals, the Chunchos.

Figure 9–1   Chuncho Dancers—Paucartambo, Peru.

Figure 9–2   Qolla Dancers—Paucartambo, Peru.

According to one legend told in Paucartambo, the statue of the Virgen del Carmen originally belonged to the Qollas of Puno, Peru, but through battle the Chunchos won her and brought her to Paucartambo, where she remained as the provider of prosperity, health, and all good things. In another version, I was told that the Virgin originally belonged to Paucartambo. On one occasion, the Qollas tried to steal her (the statue) away but were attacked by the Chunchos, who defended her and, by winning the battle, kept her safe in Paucartambo. As a reminder of these and other legends surrounding the Chunchos, the Qollas, and their special relationship to the Virgin, a dramatic mock battle is fought during the fiesta, and each year the Chunchos win.

The Saqras (or "devils," in the native Quechua language) are also central to the meaning of the fiesta, since they serve as foils to the holy saint. The Saqras' costumes include clothing representing the colonial Spanish, blonde wigs alluding to Europeans, and ceramic animal or monster masks (Fig. 9–3). Their choreography is reminiscent of a genteel European contradance, and this fortifies the satiric portrayal of Europeans. These devil dancers thus combine imagery that expresses Peruvian attitudes about the evil that comes from beyond this world, as well as the evil that arrived in ships from beyond the Andean world beginning in the 1500s. During the two fiesta processions, the statue of the Virgin is carried through the streets accompanied by dancers, music, and the people of the town. At these times, the Saqra

Figure 9–3 Saqra (Devil)
Dancers—Paucartambo, Peru.

dancers climb on to the red-tiled roofs and, as the saint passes, shield their eyes from her brightness and slowly disappear behind the rooftops. Both in the drama and according to local beliefs, the Virgin blesses each house, ridding it of evil, as she passes during the processions.

Most of the other dance groups in the fiesta also represent and parody outsiders. The Doctores, for example, represent lawyers and government officials who are known for their exploitation of rural Peruvians. As the Doctores move through the streets, they frequently capture people of the local indigenous communities who have come to town to watch the fiesta. Once the dancers have encircled an unfortunate man, they begin beating him with the heavy law books that they carry as a part of their costume while shouting insults and abuses. The nature of the law book used as a weapon against common people is enacted by making it a concrete weapon—much to the hilarity of onlookers lucky enough not to have gotten caught.

The cast also includes: the Negros, a dance ensemble representing black slaves brought during the colonial era; the Chilenos, expressing the enmity towards the devastating Chilean army of the War of the Pacific (1879–1884); the Chuk'chus, or malaria carriers from the jungle; the Majeños, exploitative liquor traders from the city of Arequipa; and the Maqtas, or clowns, who serve as the policemen during the fiesta, among other dance ensembles. As a wonderful addition, some dancers have lately begun to dress up as young hippie tourists. They wear backpacks and floppy hats, and stick toy cameras into people's faces as they move through the streets, thereby commenting on the most recent invasion of outsiders and indicating the ongoing creativity of these fiesta dancers.

Each dance group is accompanied by its own band and a series of distinctive pieces that, through association over the years, have become as important to the characters presented by the groups as their costumes, choreography, and dramatic behavior. Some of the music is particularly pictorial, such as the staggering melody played by a brass band to fit the Majeño liquor traders' drunken dance. The Chunchos music (CD 2, #11), played on flutes and drums, is reminiscent of nearby lowland Indian styles and thus, like the dancers' feathered headdresses, adds to their portrayal of jungle Indians. Much of the music in the fiesta is based on major local genres such as the mestizo wayno, or is more European in form like the contradance music used by the Saqras and other groups. The fiesta includes indigenous-styled flute and drum bands, like the one that accompanies the Chunchos; brass bands; and a type of local dance band (orquesta) that combines indigenous flutes with European instruments such as violins, harp, and accordion. These orquestas are a microcosm of the European-indigenous mix that characterizes the fiesta and mestizo culture as a whole. Unlike the dancers, who are mestizos from Paucartambo, the bands are hired by the dance groups and usually comprise semiprofessional musicians from elsewhere.

Upon entering the town of Paucartambo during the fiesta days, one is struck by the apparent chaos and intensity of multiple bands playing simultaneously and strange costumed characters roaming the streets as if they had taken over the town. The plaza is filled to capacity with drunks, dancers, fighters, lovers, and spectators. Beneath the surface, many stories are being told, woven together, by the dance groups and their musicians who are essential to the meaning and the very existence of the festival. The townspeople say "Paucartambinos were born to dance," and for four days a year they do little else—in honor of their beloved saint and simply for the joy of it. For four days a year the plaza and cobblestone streets are transformed into a stage for a music drama that turns the normal order of daily life upside down, but that, at the same time, expresses some of the most important things that Paucartambinos have to say about themselves. These things are too old or too complicated or too deep to say directly with words, and so they dance.

SOCIOCULTURAL HERITAGES AND HISTORICAL BACKGROUND

Within the Latin American region there are many radically different lowland and highland Native American societies. There are African American cultural enclaves where African beliefs, practices, and styles are primary models for social and artistic life. There are also social groups, especially in major cities, predominantly characterized by European and cosmopolitan social and cultural style. The worldview, lifestyle, and artistic practices of a lowland Amazonian Indian in Brazil may bear little or no relation to those of a member of the cosmopolitan elite in Rio de Janeiro, or to those of the members of an Afro-Brazilian religious candomblé cult house in Bahía, northeastern Brazil. This diversity, even within a single country, makes it difficult to talk about Latin America as a single unified cultural or musical area.

At the same time, the common historical experiences of Iberian (Spanish and Portuguese) colonialism since the sixteenth century, the formation of contemporary nation-states in the nineteenth century, and North American economic and cultural domination in the twentieth, have resulted in certain widely diffused cultural and musical features. Iberian influence is the oldest and most profound common denominator in Latin America. This is exemplified by the wide diffusion of the Spanish language (Portuguese in Brazil), Catholicism, and a number of musical characteristics. Iberian cultural elements, however, have been combined with regionally specific indigenous lifeways to form local mestizo cultures in some regions, and with African heritages to form African American cultures in others. The mestizo fiesta in Paucartambo is one example of the result.

Various indigenous groups of the Amazon and other lowland forest areas have maintained the greatest distance from European and North American lifeways. Contact with missionaries, white settlers, and capitalists, however, has had a long and in many cases disastrous effect on these peoples, on the rain forests, and thus on the planet as a whole. The major pre-Columbian states of the Aztecs and Mayas were located in Mesoamerica, and the Incas in the Andes. The large native populations in these regions supplied much of the necessary labor for the Spanish colonizers. It is in these areas where highland Amerindian cultural styles, values, and practices remain vibrant in some communities, or have combined with Iberian elements to form particularly distinctive examples of Latin American mestizo musical cultures. African influences remain the strongest and have fused most prominently with the Iberian in the Caribbean and along the coasts of Venezuela, Colombia, Ecuador, the Guiana region, and northeastern Brazil, where slave labor supported the plantation economy. Other Latin American countries such as Argentina and Chile, are characterized by the predominance of European heritage and cosmopolitan cultural style, as are the middle-class and elite populations in most major Latin American cities. Because of intense rural to urban migration throughout this century, however, the capitals of Latin American nations have typically become heterogeneous social and musical microcosms of their countries as a whole.

Given this social diversity, it is best to approach the study of Latin American music through a consideration of the different types of cultural groups in specific locations—with the understanding that it is the Native American, mestizo, and African American cultures that have generally produced the most unique Latin American musical styles and practices. We will begin with some widespread characteristics of Latin American music that largely pertain to the mestizo culture.

MESTIZO MUSICAL VALUES AND MUSICAL STYLE

General Features of Mestizo Music

The term *mestizo* must be understood as a relative concept that indicates a blending of European with local Native American cultural heritages and worldviews: in some cases African elements may be included as well (e.g., the marimba in Central America). As we shall see, distinctions between indigenous and mestizo cultures are often a matter of degree rather than kind, as well as a matter of how local peoples define their own ethnic and class identities.

General features of mestizo musical culture include costumed dances very similar to those described for Paucartambo. During the colonial period, missionaries used music and costumed dances to attract indigenous peoples to Christianity. Costumed dances have been performed in Catholic festivals from Mexico to Chile since that time. Characters brought to life through dance—old men; soldiers; devils, monsters, and other supernatural beings; figures from Biblical stories; animals; Spaniards; Africans—are widely portrayed in mestizo festival dance dramas (Fig. 9–4). Nonetheless, the music used to accompany the dances and the stories told through them will vary widely from one country, region, and even community to another. Moreover, a region's repertoire of dances changes over time, as we saw with the recent addition of "hippie-tourist" dancers in Paucartambo.

In the colonial era, missionaries taught European stringed instruments, especially an old type of European diatonic harp (Fig. 9–5) and violin. Along with harps

Figure 9–4   Devil Dancers—Michoacán, Mexico.

Figure 9–5   Latin American diatonic harp played by a street musician in Cuzco, Peru.

and violins, guitars and mandolin-type instruments are central to music-making among both indigenous and mestizo musicians in many areas (Fig. 9–6). As far as we know, stringed instruments did not exist in pre-Columbian Central and South American societies, but once European models for these instruments were available they spurred tremendous creativity. The centuries following the colonial conquest gave rise to a dazzling array of local variations of stringed instruments, especially the guitar; Latin America has more unique variants of the guitar than any other region on earth.

Based on the military band tradition, brass bands became part of mestizo town and village festivals throughout Latin America beginning in the nineteenth century. Town and village bands play local dance music and song genres as well as more cosmopolitan religious, nationalistic, and popular music. In some places band instruments (e.g., saxophones, clarinets, trombones) are found in novel combinations with local indigenous flutes and percussion instruments; harps, violins, and guitars; and marimbas. In the twentieth century, diatonic button accordions as well as piano accordions have come to be widely used in many local mestizo ensembles and urban bands. More recently diffused from North America, electric guitars, electric organs, and synthesizers have attracted Latin American musicians and have been incorporated into, in some cases, very distinctive local styles.

Figure 9–6   Indigenous Quechua bandurria players accompanying a Carnival Dance in Canchis, Cuzco, Peru.

European scales and harmony were widely taught by missionaries throughout Latin America and they became commonly incorporated within local mestizo musics. The seven-note (do-re-mi) scale, minor scales, and other older European scales are commonly used, as are European-based chord progressions. An especially common trait in mestizo instrumental performance and singing is the use of parallel thirds (e.g., the interval from do to mi) or sixths (do to la). Strophic form (the music stays the same while the lyrics change from stanza to stanza) is a ubiquitous characteristic of mestizo music. Iberian verse types such as the copla (a four octosyllabic-line stanza) are widespread, six-line stanzas and many other varieties are also often found.

A common form of rhythmic-metric organization in mestizo music results from the combination of duple and triple rhythms—as if musicians were playing in both 3/4 (waltz time) and 6/8 (jig-time) meters within the same piece. Known as sesquialtera (or hemiola), duple and triple rhythmic patterns can be juxtaposed sequentially by the same instrument or are played simultaneously by different instruments within an ensemble. Thus, a bass instrument might emphasize a triple (3/4) feeling against the duple feeling played by a guitarist, with the maraca player moving back and forth between duple and triple patterns. The tension that results from juxtaposing duple and triple rhythms creates a wonderful excitement in the music. In addition to sesquialtera rhythmic organization, local variants of the waltz in 3/4 time are widespread as are variants of the European polka, marches, and other genres in 2/4 and 4/4 time.

Return to Paucartambo

The Fiesta of the Virgen del Carmen in Paucartambo clearly illustrates the nature of mestizo culture. At the most concrete level, the townspeople define who and what is mestizo by excluding the active participation of people from nearby indigenous Quechua communities. (Restricted participation distinguishes mestizo and indigenous status, rather than residence, since mestizos who have moved elsewhere can still return to dance in the fiesta.) In other ways the event reflects the complex combinations of indigenous and European heritages and worldviews that are the hallmark of mestizo culture. In regard to religious meaning, for example, the festival celebrates the Catholic saint, but for many people in the town her significance is fused with that of Pachamama (Earthmother, provider of life), a pre-Columbian divinity. The Catholic festival also combines elements of indigenous harvest rituals with local mestizo merchants' more immediate desires to attract people to their stores. Nowhere is the blending of cultural heritages and values more evident than in the bands that perform music for the event.

Three types of ensemble are heard. Several brass bands are hired—for the Majeños dancers, the processions and sometimes for other dance groups. Because of their volume and the expense of hiring brass bands, they are the most prestigious type of ensemble. The Chunchos and several other groups use side-blown flute and drum ensembles (CD 2, #11); the combination of flutes (of many different types) with drums is a tradition that hails from pre-Columbian times in the Andes, Mexico, and other regions of Latin America. The major ensemble type used to provide mestizo dance music in Paucartambo, however, combines European and pre-Hispanic Andean instruments within the same band. These groups, known simply as orquestas tipicas (typical orchestras), feature a large diatonic harp, violins, accordion, and sometimes mandolin. Indigenous vertical end-notched flutes known as kenas, however, are also included, as are drums (CD 2, #12). Along with panpipes and trumpets, kenas were one of the main wind instruments played in the Andes before the Spanish arrived.

The musical style played by orquestas in Paucartambo combines European (triadic) harmonies with Andean syncopated rhythms and styles of instrumental performance, including a dense, breathy tone quality on the flutes. Consistent with music throughout the Andean region, a variety of scales ranging from five to seven pitches are used in Paucartambo, and in this fiesta music, duple meter (as opposed to triple or "waltz time") predominates. Like most Andean musical genres, the majority of Paucartambo dance pieces consist of between two and four short sections that are repeated in forms such as AABB or AABBCC.

The Qollas' "Despedida" (farewell) song (CD 2, #12) illustrates these features. The syncopated five-note melody is carried by the violins, kenas, mandolin, and accordion to produce a densely blended timbral quality. It has a descending melody (moving from higher to lower pitches), common in both mestizo and indigenous

Andean music. The song has three short sections (AABBB' B') in which both the text and melody are repeated in the first two (AABB), each section having two short melodic phrases (A = a,b; B = c,d), and the B' section consisting of the melodic phrase with new text.

The songs sung to the Virgin by the Qollas and other dance groups are in Spanish, the indigenous Quechua language, or sometimes both, and thus clearly illustrate the blending of European and indigenous cultures that defines Andean mestizo identity generally. For example, one verse from the Qollas' "Despedida" is:

Adios, Adios   [A section, musical phrase/text line a]
Compañeros míos   [phrase/text line b]
Adios, Adios   [A section repeated]
Compañeros míos
(Spanish = Goodbye, Goodbye, my companions)
Hasta el año   [B section, phrase/text line c]
Venidero   [phrase/text line d]
Hasta el año   [B section repeated]
Venidero
(Spanish = Until the coming year)
Ah Señorallay   [B' section, phrase d, text line e]
(Spanish, Señora = lady; llay = Quechua suffix expressing emotion)
Ay Ñust'allay   [B' section, phrase d, text line f]
(Quechua, ñust'a = princess)

Other music heard during the fiesta is representative of the major mestizo genres of Peru: the wayno, the marinera, the yaraví, marches, and religious hymns. Not tied to specific contexts, the first three popular genres are performed in all types of social gatherings and private music making occasions ranging from serenades and family birthday parties to drinking bouts with friends and theater stage performances. The wayno (or huayno, see Arhoolie 3025 in the discography), the most important Peruvian mestizo genre is best recognized by its rhythm which wavers ambiguously between a duple ((♪♫)) and triple (♫♪) feel within a 2/4 or 4/4 meter (sometimes three-beat measures occur at the end of phrases). The mestizo wayno is a social couples dance involving fast foot tapping, subtle flirtatious movements, and sometimes the use of a handkerchief waved in the hand; in these general traits it resembles many other mestizo social dances of Latin America. Like much Latin American mestizo music, the wayno is strophic with usually two, three, or four text lines within short repeated melodic sections (e.g., AABB, ABAB). Texts on a variety of joking, romantic, political, or topical themes are, like the Qollas' songs, in Spanish, Quechua, or a combination of the two. My friend and teacher Julio Benavente, a mestizo musician from Cuzco, Peru, once told me that when he really wanted to speak his mind and heart through a song, he would compose a wayno because it could encompass any topic and was a genre of profound feeling. The song texts frequently use nature imagery and in this, the use of Quechua, and the rhythm, the wayno is closest to indigenous roots of all the major Peruvian mestizo genres.

The marinera is also a couples "handkerchief" dance. It is typically in the European major scale with European tonal harmony, and is characterized by sesquialtera (duple-triple hemiola) rhythm in moderate tempo. The form is typically AABBCC, and this is repeated twice with a short break in between as "La Primera" (First) and "La Segunda" (Second) parts. The song texts are almost always on light love themes, sung in Spanish. In many social situations such as at a private evening party at the fiesta sponsor's house in Paucartambo, marineras will be coupled with a faster wayno to animate the dancers. Unlike the marinera and wayno, the yaraví is not danced but is rather used to serenade a lover, or for a serious moment at social gatherings, or to express deep feelings when one is alone. It is a slow lyrical song, usually on sad themes of unrequited love, leaving family or home, or the absence of loved ones; yaravís are almost always sung in Spanish. The genre features the sesquialtera combination of 3/4 and 6/8 meters but, because of its slow tempo, the sesquialtera does not create the same excitement as when used in faster genres such as the marinera, the Venezuelan joropo, and the Mexican son. Musically and historically, the Peruvian marinera is closely related to the Chilean and Bolivian cueca and the Argentine zamba; the triste in Bolivia and Argentina is kin to the Peruvian yaraví.

Mestizo Music in Veracruz, Mexico

Regionalism is extremely important for understanding Latin American musical styles as well as the ways people conceptualize their own identities. In Mexico, mestizo musical styles are strongly identified with their regions of origin, yet because of the mass media and tourism, many of the most important regional musics can be heard presently in any major city of the nation, along with the most popular international Caribbean, Latin American, and North American styles. A visit to the city of Veracruz will introduce us to the vast array of mestizo musics of Mexico.

Like other Mexican cities, Veracruz has several locations where outdoor cafes line the street or plaza. These social centers attract a host of full-time professional "strolling" musicians who perform different Mexican regional styles at patrons' tables for a fee. At other restaurants, loudspeakers blare international popular music such as old recordings of Cuban dance music, contemporary salsa, and other Caribbean styles. As a seaport on the gulf coast, Veracruz has long-standing musical ties with the Caribbean, particularly Cuba, which has produced some of the most successful, widely diffused popular music in the world. In addition to this recorded music, during a single night in the cafes of Veracruz I heard local jarocho ensembles, a huasteco trio from the northern gulf coast region, several mariachi bands associated with the state of Jalisco, a marimba group from southern Mexico, and several norteño accordion groups.

The local mestizo Jarocho ensemble, associated with the rural southern coastal region of Veracruz state, consists of a large diatonic harp with between 32 and 36 strings, a requinto (a small four-string guitar), and one or more jaranas (a small guitar type with eight strings in five courses) for the fast, rhythmic, strummed chordal accompaniment. These groups specialize in a regional variant of Mexico's most important mestizo song-dance genre: the son. The famous 1950s rock'n'roll song by Richie Valens, "La Bamba," is, in fact, a son jarocho that has been played in Veracruz since at least the turn of the nineteenth century.

Sones in the jarocho and other Mexican regions are typically strophic songs. Sung verses are alternated with instrumental interludes which, in some regions, are variations or improvisations on the sung melody or a set instrumental melody. Individual musicians also have their own repertoire of instrumental "riffs" (melodic formulas) that they can plug into a given performance. Sones in most regions are played with duple and triple rhythmic patterns juxtaposed within a quick 6/8 (or in some regions 12/8) metric frame (sesquialtera). There are sones in both major and minor modes, and basic European chord progressions, for example, the use of I, IV, and V chords played in repetitive patterns, are common.

The song texts are frequently about women and romantic love, but may also be playful, joking songs, expressions of regional pride, or simply about music and dance occasions. A stanza from "La Bamba" includes a typical type of word play:

En mi casa me dicen
(In my house they call me)
En mi casa me dicen el inocente
(In my house they call me the innocent one)
Porque tengo muchachas (x2)
(Because I have girls)
Entre quince y viente
(Between fifteen and twenty)
Y arriba arriba,
(and upward and upward)
Y arriba arriba, arriba-ré
Yo no soy marinero (x2)
(I'm not a sailor)
Por ti seré, por ti seré
(For you I'll be, for you I'll be).

The texts of sones are often set in four or six-line stanzas although there is flexibility such that longer stanzas such as the one above are sung, and verses of unequal length may even be included in the same song. Some texts are fixed, but frequently performers have a wide repertory of different stanzas that they can choose from and order at will. New stanzas may also be improvised so that no two performances of a son will be alike; this is certainly true for the classic son jarocho, "La Bamba." Unlike the bilingual mestizos of Paucartambo, Peru who may sing waynos and fiesta songs in both Spanish and the indigenous language, Quechua, mestizo sones in Mexico are typically sung only in Spanish. As this example shows, Native American elements are less pronounced in Mexican mestizo culture as compared to mestizo culture in southern Peru and Bolivia. The stronger European orientation of Mexican mestizo culture is the more typical case for mestizos in Latin American generally.

After the jarocho ensemble moved away from my cafe table in Veracruz, I was treated to the music of a Huasteco trio, one of the hottest and most virtnosic styles Mexico has to offer. Typically, however, these professional "strolling" musicians would be heard at cafes, restaurants, parties, and festivals in their own native huasteca region of northern Veracruz and the state of Tamaulipas. Specializing in sones huastecos, the trios consist of violin as the lead instrument accompanied by two local guitar variants: the huapanguera (larger than a guitar with eight strings in five courses), and the smaller five-stringed jarana. These instruments are strummed, ambiguously mixing duple and triple (sesquialtera) rhythms within 6/8 meter (CD 2, #14). The violinist is at the center of the ensemble, his playing rich with powerful, syncopated rhythmic bowing, slides and other ornaments, double stops (bowing two strings at once) and extremely quick finger work. The lead singer of the trio frequently uses falsetto singing to create an exciting effect that distinguishes this style from jarocho and other regional son styles.

Mariachis, Mexico's most famous type of ensemble, are also heard in the cafes and on the streets of Veracruz as well as all over the country. Mariachis originated as a local string band style in the western Mexican state of Jalisco. In the early decades of the last century, rural mariachi groups were small string bands with several violins accompanied by the percussive strumming of a vihuela (small five-string guitar type with a convex back), and guitarrón (large acoustic bass guitar with a convex back); band instruments like a trumpet, trombone, or flute might have been occasionally added to the basic string quartet.

Feelings of nationalism spurred the symbolic glorification of Mexican peasants and local rural culture around the time of the Mexican Revolution (beginning in 1910). This led to a greater interest in rural music within urban higher-class circles. During this time, and through the 1920s, a few mariachis from Jalisco began to gain popularity in Mexico City playing at parties, cafes, and occasionally at theaters. It was the mass media, however, that acted as the springboard to national prominence for this type of regional ensemble; mariachis began to be featured on radio and, after 1931, in Mexican movies—just as singing cowboys were becoming popular figures in Hollywood movies around the same time.

With their entrance into mass popular culture, mariachis evolved into their current form: they grew in size, their repertories became more diverse, fancy "Mexican cowboy" costumes (trajes de charro) became standard, and the music became increasingly more arranged and polished. One, and later two, trumpets were added as standard instruments, violin sections were enlarged, and guitars were added to the vihuela and guitarrón as additional rhythm instruments. While originally specializing in sones from Jalisco, after mariachis entered the national arena, they also began to play sones from other regions as well as polkas, canciones rancheras (often slow, tearful, love songs), corridos (Mexican ballads usually on historical or topical themes using the copla text form), marches, and other genres.

In the restaurants and cafes of Veracruz one can also hear conjuntos norteños and marimba groups. As their name implies, conjuntos norteños are associated with northern Mexico and southern Texas. Currently a three-row diatonic button accordion serves as the lead melody instrument and provides extended "fills" between sung lines. The accordion is backed by a large twelve-string guitar (bajo sexto), and when playing in stationary locations such as bars and nightclubs, electric bass and drums are standard. These conjuntos perform corridos, waltzes, boleros (a relatively slow romantic song-dance genre from Cuba), but polkas and canciones rancheras often make up a large portion of their repertories. Like the norteño style itself, canciones rancheras have working-class and romanticized-rural associations. Rather than being defined by particular musical characteristics, the particularly popular ranchera genre is best defined by its sentimental aesthetic and crying-in-your-beer, truck-driving, hard-drinking, cantina imagery. In many ways ranchera songs are the Mexican equivalent of North American country and western.

Sitting in a cafe in Veracruz, it is almost comical to watch the marimba players struggle with their heavy tablelike instrument as they move about competing for patrons with the other strolling musicians. In the south of Mexico, throughout Guatemala, and in many Central American countries, the marimba is a primary musical instrument. This xylophone has wooden keys tuned to the western scale and hanging resonators that produce the marimba's characteristic buzzing sound. Various ethnomusicologists have shown that the marimba originally came to the Americas from Africa, and the marimba's buzzy timbre is similar to many African instruments (see Chapter 7). While marimbas are still played by African-American communities on the Pacific coast of Colombia and Ecuador, in southern Mexico and Central America, the instrument has been adopted both by Indian and mestizo musicians. In the mestizo traditions of southern Mexico and Guatemala, and as I saw it performed in Veracruz, several musicians play lead and accompanying parts on the same large marimba. While marimba groups in Veracruz could play a wide range of Mexican genres and international pop songs, local sones are the standard fare in its traditional home in southern Mexico. Unlike the sones from the other regions we have discussed, in southern Mexico, as in Guatemala, many sones are in a moderate 3/4 waltz time. This feature, like the many types of ensembles encountered in the city of Veracruz, illustrates the tremendous regional diversity of mestizo music in Mexico.

NATIVE AMERICAN MUSICAL VALUES AND MUSICAL STYLE

Highland Indians in Mexico, Guatemala, and in the Andean highlands of Ecuador, Peru, Bolivia, and Northern Chile have interacted with mestizos and people of European heritage for centuries. Hence, they have been involved in the same processes of musical syncretism that characterize mestizo music. Cultural differences between indigenous highland peoples and mestizos are often more a matter of degree than of kind. Yet even after centuries of contact, indigenous communities, especially in the southern Peruvian and Bolivian highlands, have maintained their own languages, a distinct social ethos, and have continued to develop their music along their own aesthetic lines to a significant degree. A closer look at the Aymara-speaking people of southern Peru will help clarify this.

The Aymara of Southern Peru

Quechua and Aymara speakers comprise the two major indigenous groups of the Andean highlands. Quechua speakers are in the majority and are located throughout the Andean region. Aymara communities are located around Lake Titicaca in Peru and Bolivia, and further to the south in Bolivia and northern Chile. Here we concentrate on Aymara musical life in Conima, a district in the Province of Huancané (like a county), on the north side of Lake Titicaca in the state of Puno, Peru.

Like indigenous highland and lowland communities in other parts of Latin America, the Aymara of Conima emphasize the importance of collective community life. As highland agriculturalists and herders of llamas, sheep, alpaca, and some cattle, Aymara peasants are tied to their land, and they depend on good relations with their neighbors for support in labor exchanges and communal work projects, as well as for social and moral support. Reciprocity, egalitarian relations, and community solidarity have come to constitute core values for ordering the Aymara social world. It is, therefore, not surprising that ways of making music emerge from these same principles of collective social life.

While there are two small village brass bands in the district of Conima (the indigenous musicians having learned these instruments during military service), Aymara musical life revolves around the performance of local indigenous wind instruments and drums. Men play siku (panpipes) and, historically, end-notched vertical cane flutes (kenas) in dry-season festivals (April–October); these instruments are of pre-Columbian origin. Aymara musicians also play cane pinkillus and wooden tarkas (vertical duct flutes with a recorderlike mouthpiece) during the rainy season. Side-blown cane flutes (pitus) are played all year round. Panpipe ensembles are typically accompanied by large double-headed drums known as wankara or bombos, pinkillus are accompanied by large indigenous snare drums known as cajas (Fig. 9–7), and tarkas are accompanied by Western snare and bass drums. The different wind instruments are not mixed in ensembles (sikus are only played with sikus, tarkas with tarkas, etc.). Different size instruments are used in siku, tarka, and pitu ensembles to create parallel harmonic lines (Fig. 9–8). Stringed instruments were not played in the Andes before the Spanish arrived, and they have not been incorporated into Aymara music making in the Province of Huancané. Stringed instruments such as the harp and violin, however, have been adopted by indigenous Quechua

Figure 9–7 Aymara Pinkillu (Flute) Ensemble—Huancané, Puno, Peru.

communities and by Indian musicians in many Latin American regions. Elsewhere in southern Peru and Bolivia, the charango (a ten-string Andean guitar variant the size of a ukulele) has a special place in both Quechua and Aymara communities. Unlike Andean Quechua culture, vocal music is relatively rare in Aymara festivals.

In the district of Conima, community and intercommunity festivals may be held as often as once a month. Many festivals are connected to the agricultural cycle and to local Aymara deities. Aymara communities also collectively celebrate life cycle events (weddings, first haircutting ceremonies for babies) and collective work projects (e.g., roof raisings) with music and dance. Some festivals may be linked with Catholic celebrations, although usually Aymara deities will be granted greater prominence than Catholic imagery. For example, in Conima, the Catholic festival called "Virgen de la Candelaria" or simply "Candelaria" (February 2) is actually an agricultural ripening festival in which prayers and rituals are offered for Pachamama (Earthmother), the ancestors, and local mountain deities. This festival is Christian primarily in name, not in substance, whereas the mestizo fiesta in Paucartambo is really dedicated to the Catholic saint (Virgen del Carmen) with only a few indigenous

Figure 9–8 Aymara Sikuri (Panpipe)
Ensemble—Huancané, Puno, Peru.

elements included. This is what I meant by differences between the two cultures
being a matter of degree not of kind.

Aymara peasants in Huancané generally only play music in large community
wind ensembles for these public communal festivals; even practicing music by one-
self is rare. During festivals any man is welcome to play with his community regardless of his musical knowledge or ability. Also, Aymara musicians do not usually
comment on or correct other players in their group so as not to offend them. In
keeping with egalitarian values, there is no formal ensemble leader who has the
power to direct others or restrict participation. Music is performed so that the community can come together in dance, music and celebration; music is judged on the
quality of the social relations and total experience that it engenders as much as on
the quality of sound produced. From this perspective, to ask a less skilled person not
to play, or to embarrass him by correcting him publicly would do more damage to
"the music" than any inappropriate sounds he might make.

In Aymara communities in Conima, individuals generally do not like to stand out or be singled out in social situations, both because the group is granted greater importance than individual identity, and perhaps for fear of arousing jealousy. Likewise, there is no place for soloists in ensemble performance. Rather, the primary aesthetic ideal expressed by Aymara musicians is that ensembles should "play as one" or sound like a single instrument, and no individual's instrument should stand out from the dense sound of these Andean wind ensembles (CD 2, #13). The preference for a dense, well-integrated sound is also reflected in Andean instrumental performance techniques and instrument construction. Flutes and panpipes are blown to create a breathy sound, which aids group blending, and instruments are tuned slightly differently so that a rich combination of overtones will result. The act of "playing as one" and creating a thick, well-blended sound with no soloists thus becomes a clear musical articulation of the central ways of being for this egalitarian, collectively oriented society.

The Aymara siku (panpipe) tradition also illustrates this cooperative style of performance. Panpipes are constructed with two separate rows, the seven-tone pitch series alternating between them. The rows are divided between two musicians who, having only half the pitches needed to make a melody, must interlock their notes (hocket) with those of their partner to perform a piece. Aymara panpipe ensembles, sometimes having up to fifty players, are actually made up of these paired musicians who must interact reciprocally and blend with the whole.

Approaching music and dance as a collective activity that fosters community participation and unity is common to many highland Indian communities in Latin America. Yet, the Aymara of Conima represent the extreme case where music is *only* performed in large community ensembles during public festivals. Native Americans in other regions also perform music solo for enjoyment or other purposes. For example, a Quechua boy in the Andes might play his kena flute for solitary entertainment while herding llamas or his charango to court a girl friend; a Quechua women might sing to her children or while working in the fields; a Purépecha Indian of Michoacán, Mexico might play his violin at home after work to entertain himself and his family (Fig. 9–9). In my experience, these types of musical activities are as rare among the Aymara of Conima as they are common elsewhere among indigenous musicians.

The equal access to musical activities among Aymara men is not shared by the women. Aymara women in Huancané, and with a few exceptions indigenous women in general, do not perform musical instruments. Rather they dance and sing in festivals. In fact, in Andean Quechua communities, women are the favorite singers because of a preference for high pitched voices. In Native South American societies, many social roles are strictly divided by gender, and in Conima there is a good deal of gender segregation in public settings. I was surprised that even at weddings an Aymara bride will spend most of her time with the women away from the groom who sits with the men. In the Aymara communities I worked in, gender segregation and

Figure 9–9   José Romero, Purépecha violinist from Michoacán, Mexico.

roles were rarely questioned. Aymara women in Conima do not seem troubled by the fact that they do not play musical instruments, just as most North American men are not concerned that it is unacceptable for them to wear dresses. Through socialization, such things often simply become unquestioned habits.

Throughout the Lake Titicaca region, large ensemble wind music is comprised of three sections which are repeated AABBCC. The music comprises shorter motives repeated within and across sections especially at section cadences (end points; CD 2, #13). Scales differ. Tarka music in Conima uses five and six tone scales while panpipe, pinkillu, and side-blown flute music feature seven-tone scales. The lion's share of music has syncopated rhythms set in a duple meter with drum parts either playing a rolling repeated pattern (pinkillu music) or following the rhythm of the melody of panpipe, tarka, and side-flute ensembles. In Conima, ensembles create new pieces each year, and musical composition takes place in collective "brainstorming" sessions at rehearsals the night before a given fiesta. In contrast to stereo-types of Indian or "folk" music being old and unchanging, Aymara musicians in Con-ima, Peru emphasize new compositions using these set forms, scales, and rhythms for the different genres they have fashioned.

A Lowland Indian Case: The Suyá of the Brazilian Amazon

Musical aesthetics and conceptions about music among lowland Amazonian Indian groups share some of the elements described for Conima but differ radically in other ways. Whereas Aymara musical culture centers around wind instruments and drums, and singing is unimportant, the music of the Suyá Indians of the Brazilian Amazon is predominantly vocal, sometimes accompanied by rattles. As with the Aymara, collec-tive participation in musical performances during Suyá festivals is a vital way to rep-resent and maintain social unity within a village, and the blending of voices in unison singing embodies an important aesthetic value. But the Suyá also have songs that are individually owned and sung, indicating that there is more room for individual expression than among the Aymara of Huancané, where solo performance is basi-cally nonexistent.

To take this one step further: while the Aymara stress "playing as one," ethno-musicologist Anthony Seeger has shown that some Suyá performances include a variety of individuals singing their own, different, akía songs simultaneously, along with shouts, laughter, and other vocal sounds. This type of Suyá performance results in what to our—or Aymara—ears would be cacophony. Yet for the Suyá all these simultaneous songs and sounds contribute to the total creation of a performance. The Suyá aesthetic often favors the dense combination of multiple, relatively inde-pendent sounds to form the whole. It reflects a different conception, relative to the Aymara, of the relationship of individuals to the community.

The Suyá believe that songs come from and are learned from animals, insects, fish, and plants of the forest. As with other Amazonian groups, important Suyá festi-vals and song types are named for and involve the representation of natural species. These have symbolic importance in relation to the ecological environment that sus-tains the Suyá through hunting, fishing, and agriculture. Many indigenous Andean festivals and song types are similarly related to the specific environment and Andeans' occupations as agriculturalists and herders. In addition to ecological-economic issues, musical styles and genres are used almost universally to distinguish and represent distinct groups within societies. For the Suyá, gender and age are cen-tral criteria for delineating important social categories and status within a village, and musical genres and singing styles are similarly differentiated according to gen-der and age.

While musical instruments are not prominent in Suyá society, they have a wealth of distinct vocal genres that range from everyday speech to more formalized genres of political, historical, and artistic oratory; chantlike performance genres; and, finally, a variety of different singing styles. The prominence of vocal music among the Suyá is typical for lowland Indian societies. However, some lowland Indian groups also play panpipes, side-blown and vertical flutes, valveless trumpets, drums, and various types of percussion instruments. As with many native lowland and highland groups, dance is a central aspect of most musical festival occasions and is a deeply integral aspect of musical life.

AFRICAN AMERICAN MUSICAL VALUES AND STYLES

After reading about African music in Chapter 7 we are in a better position to appreciate the influence of the African heritage in Latin America. The use of cyclical forms, call-and-response, interlocking melodic and percussion parts, and an appreciation of dense overlapping textures are all part of Afro-Latin American music making as is the use of African musical instruments.

For example, along the Pacific coast of Ecuador and Colombia, an area with an African American population, historically the marimba was used for the currulao, a community dance where women and men may meet and form new relationships. A currulao performance exemplifies a variety of African musical features (CD 2, #15). The marimba (twenty to twenty-eight wooden keys with bamboo resonators, played by two musicians) is accompanied by single-headed conical drums (like conga drums) of two different sizes which are classified as male and female, as is often the case for African instruments. The currulao ensemble also includes two deeper double-headed drums (bombos) and bamboo shakers which add rhythmic-timbral density much like hosho in a Shona mbira performance (see Chapter 7). Like most Sub-Saharan African music, the basis of this marimba music is an ostinato with improvised variations. The drums and shakers play separate but interlocking rhythmic parts, often in duple and triple meter simultaneously. This African-derived style of ensemble performance is used to accompany a solo singer, who interlocks his or her vocal part with a female chorus in call-and-response fashion. The vocal quality of the singers (CD 2, #15) is distinctly African and contrasts with indigenous and mestizo singing styles in Latin America. It is also striking that the women singers yodel in a style somewhat reminiscent of Shona and other African singing traditions.

Along with the marimba, African-styled drums, and the musical bow (e.g., in the Caribbean and the berimbau of Brazil) were diffused to the Americas from Africa, as were lamellaphones (e.g., the mbira, or "thumb piano"). In the Caribbean, a large box lamellaphone (marímbula) serves a bass function in a variety of ensembles. A smaller hand-held lamellaphone of Angolan character was used in Brazil in the last century, and the smaller type is still played among the Saramaka of Surinam. Runaway slave communities established in the forests of Surinam maintain their own amalgamation of African cultural practices to this day. Among these is the playing of papai benta, a lamellaphone with reed keys mounted on bridges on a flat board. Held between the knees and played with the index fingers, the instrument is used to perform pieces which are ostinatos with variations, as is the case with African mbira music. Drums are also prominent among the Saramaka of Surinam, used to accompany dancing and historical songs, and to call the gods and ancestors.

Afro-Brazilian Music

The use of African-derived musical styles, concepts, and instruments is perhaps best exemplified in Latin America by certain religious traditions in the Caribbean and Brazil. In the Candomblé religions of Bahía, northeastern Brazil, music and dance are fundamental to worshiping various orixas (deities) hailing largely from the Yoruba religion of Nigeria. The songs, often in call-and-response, are accompanied by a trio of different-sized single-headed drums (atabaques), also of Yoruba origin, and a West African styled double bell (agogó). Strikingly, the roles of the double bell and of the different drums in the trio mirror those for the same instruments in Yoruba musical performance. The bell plays an ostinato pattern that serves to orient the other musicians, the two smaller drums interlock to play the ground ostinato part, and the largest, or "mother" drum, is used by a lead drummer for improvisation and to interact with the dancers. Even West African words are retained in the songs, although their meanings are largely forgotten. African rituals such as "the baptism of drums" (drums being considered sacred instruments, and dedicated to the deities) are practiced in Bahía. Candomblé activities are organized within specific religious centers (cult houses), each of which has its own religious and musical leaders and group of religious initiates. The initiates undergo special training and rituals to become the mediums of specific deities. At ceremonies, the music is played for dancing, for invocations to the gods, and in the context of spirit possession among the initiates.

Brazil's most famous musical event is carnival in Rio de Janeiro with its long parades, floats, huge percussion ensembles, and multitude of elaborately costumed dancers and singers. Samba, Brazil's most famous musical genre, is associated with this carnival although, in fact, samba has a number of rural and urban variants and is performed in a variety of settings. For example, beginning after World War I, but especially during the 1930s and 1940s, an urban ballroom type of samba became popular in Brazil and internationally through such singing stars as Carmen Miranda. This type of samba was performed by Western-style dance orchestras or smaller string ensembles with a small Afro-Brazilian percussion section.

The special kind of urban samba heard at carnival comes from the predominantly black hillside slums of Rio that grew through urban migration from northeastern Brazil and elsewhere during this century. In keeping with its Afro-Brazilian roots, this type of samba is accompanied by massive percussion ensembles in which the different instruments—for example, surdos (large bass drums), agogós (double bells), pandeiros (tambourines), tamborím (small hand-held drum played with a single stick), reco-recos (metal spring scrapers), and cuícas (friction drums), and cavaquinhos (small four-string guitar variant)—all play their own syncopated inter-locking parts. The samba songs accompanied by the percussion ensemble are sung in Portuguese in call-and-response fashion, also illustrating an Afro-Brazilian source.

Since the 1920s, carnival performance in Rio—percussion music, song, chore-ographed dance, and parading—has been organized by the escolas de samba (Samba schools). Samba schools are not formal educational institutions. Rather, they emerged as grassroots Afro-Brazilian neighborhood institutions largely from the poorer black areas of the city. They were primarily carnival performance ensembles that represented their neighborhoods during the celebration. Over the years the samba schools have grown tremendously. Nowadays they have bureaucratic leader-ship structures and are divided into separate specialized "wings," including wings for samba composers, for dancers, and for percussionists. During carnival, the different samba schools compete against each other, and they spend much of the year prepar-ing for the event. Numerous songs are composed and the best selected, costumes and floats have to be designed and made, and as carnival approaches, the different wings rehearse intensively.

Rio's carnival has grown to become the country's largest musical spectacle, and it has become big business. The costs for samba schools to launch a competitive per-formance are enormous and require major sponsorship; the stakes for doing well in the competition are also high. Critics claim that as carnival has become increasingly commercialized and controlled by outside economic and media interests, it has lost much of its original grass-roots basis. Yet Afro-Brazilians from the neighborhoods still join in the dance and percussion ensembles with a pride in this tradition, and simply for the exhausting joy of participating in one of the world's largest parties.

Cuba

The Caribbean, and particularly Cuba, has produced some of the most internation-ally influential urban-popular music to come out of Latin America. This music is heavily indebted to the strong African presence in the region and to the interaction of African and European musicians. (The indigenous populations of Caribbean islands were wiped out early in the colonial period and African slaves were brought to support the European plantation economy.)

Various important Cuban genres evolved during the nineteenth and early twentieth centuries, including the danzón, derived from the European contradanza. A distinctive recurrent rhythmic pattern in 2/4 called the *habanera rhythm* (2/4 ♫♪♪ or ♫♫ ♪♪) is related to this complex of dances and is also a basic feature of the Argentine tango. A fundamental component of the danzón is the cinquillo rhythm (4/4 ♩ ♫♫♪♪ ♩), which some writers suggest is of Afro-Haitian origin. In Cuba, the danzón was in a form resembling the European rondo. It was performed by large orchestras comprised of European wind and stringed instruments and per-cussion, or with European salon instrumentation (flute, piano, bass, violins) accompanied by Cuban percussion (e.g., güiro or gourd scraper, and drums). By the end of the nineteenth century, however, Afro-Cuban and European musical elements had been combined in the danzón. Black danzón bands added greater syncopation into the more restrained European style, and often concluded danzónes with a rhythmically animated section comprising improvised solos. In effect, this last section resembles the second more animated section of one of Cuba's most influential genres, the son.

The Cuban son is an Afro-Hispanic genre with two major sections. The first section, like so much Latin American mestizo music, is in strophic form with verses or verses and refrains sung with music repeated from verse to verse. The second part, known as the montuno section, exhibits African musical principles more clearly. The montuno involves call-and-response singing over a short harmonic ostinato. The performance becomes more animated rhythmically, and instrumental improvisation comes to the fore.

Hence, in the very form of the son, Hispanic and African features are juxtaposed in the two sections. The instruments used to play sones earlier in this century similarly, combined European or mestizo stringed instruments such as the tres (a small Cuban guitar variant with three courses of two or three strings each) with Afro-Cuban percussion (bongos and claves). The rhythmic underpinning of both sections was a 3 + 3 + 2 pattern (in the string bass) and some variation of what has become known as the *clave pattern* (4/4 𝄽 ♩ ♩ 𝄽 | ♩.♩.♩). By the 1930s, the son had become the most popular dance genre in Havana, and it was soon to have a major impact internationally. In the 1940s and 1950s, Arsenio Rodríguez led a large ensemble consisting of tres, piano, bass, trumpets and other winds, and Cuban percussion instruments such as timbales (tuned, high pitched drums played with sticks), conga drums, bongos, bell, and güiro. The son, as played by dance orchestras like that of Rodríguez (who worked for a time in New York), provided fundamental ingredients for contemporary salsa music.

Another important source for Cuban popular music was the Afro-Cuban rumba guaguancó, which shares features with and parallels the development of the son and yet sounds more distinctly African because of the instrumentation. By the late nineteenth century, rumba guaguancó was performed by a lead singer and chorus accompanied only by drums and rhythm sticks. Like the son, however, the rumba guaguancó has two main sections. Typically, after a brief vocal introduction, the main verses and chorus refrains are sung in the first part followed by the second call-and-response section in which the chorus repeats a single melodic phrase in alternation with the lead singer's improvisations (like a montuno). Also like the son, the lower drum of a guaguancó ensemble plays a 3 + 3 + 2 pattern, and the sticks play variants of the "clave pattern."

From core styles such as these, Cuba has given birth to a whole range of genres that have had a profound effect internationally including the mambo, the chachacha, the bolero, and the rumba. The 3 + 3 + 2 bass and "clave pattern" can be heard in locally produced popular music as far away as China. After the 1950s in the Congo region of Africa, and later throughout southern and East Africa, "rumba" music became the rage, although African rumba was more closely based on the Cuban son than on guaguancó or other more strictly Afro-Cuban rumba genres. Also from the lineage of the son, salsa music has currently become one of the most widely diffused urban popular styles in Latin America. Originally developing in New York-Caribbean diaspora communities, salsa has spread to cities throughout North and Latin America with centers of activity in Miami, Los Angeles, Caracas, Venezuela, and Cali, Colombia. Popular artists like Ruben Blades have helped salsa cross over to non-Hispanic audiences in North America. But more important, salsa remains a key musical emblem for Latin American identity, and, in North America at least, it is a strong draw for bringing people of Latin American heritage together in dance and in celebration of that identity.

The use of music to construct and express social identity is a universal phenomenon. Different styles of rock music serve as identity emblems for North American teenagers, enabling them to join together with others of like mind. The Suyá of the Brazilian Amazon consider a particular type of song, akía, to be basic to what it means to be Suyá, since they consider akía to be unique to themselves. Aymara communities in Huancané compete with other local communities and express social solidarity and uniqueness primarily through the performing style and original repertory of their village musical ensembles. Brazilians from Rio say that "everything ends in samba." Finally, a fundamental aspect of what it means to be from Paucartambo is the ability to dance in the fiesta for their patron saint. "Paucartambinos were born to dance," the Suyá to sing, the Aymara to play panpipes (Fig. 9–8). There is tremendous cultural variation in the different regions and societies of Latin America, and this variation is expressed musically as well as in other ways. There are also shared historical experiences and processes that have led to widespread features of Latin American music. What remains particularly constant is that people represent and recognize themselves through the music that they create and enjoy.

LATIN AMERICA BIBLIOGRAPHY

General   Gerard Béhague, "Folk and Traditional Music of Latin America: General Prospect and Research Problems," *The World of Music* 25/2 (1982); Dale A. Olsen, "Folk Music of South America—a Musical Mosaic," in Elizabeth May, ed., *Musics of Many Cultures: An Introduction* (Berkeley: University of California Press, 1980); Dale A. Olsen and Daniel E. Sheehy, eds., *The Garland Encyclopedia of World Music, Vol. 2: South America, Mexico, Central America, and the Caribbean* (New York: Garland Publishing, 1998); John M. Schechter, ed., *Music in Latin American Culture: Regional Traditions* (New York: Schirmer Books, 1999).

Highland Indigenous and Mestizo Music   Max Peter Baumann, "Music of the Indios in Bolivia's Andean Highlands (survey)," *World of Music* 25/2 (1982); Robert Garfias, "The Marimba of Mexico and Central America," *Latin American Music Review* 4/2 (1983); Karl Gustav Izikowitz, *Musical and Other Sound Instruments of the South American Indians* (Göteborg, Sweden: Elanders Boktrycheri Aktiebolag, 1934); Manuel Peña, *The Texas-Mexican Conjunto: History of a Working-Class Music* (Austin: University of Texas Press, 1985); John Schechter, *The Indispensable Harp: Historical Development, Modern Roles, Configurations, and Performance Practices in Ecuador and Latin America*, (Kent, Oh: Kent State Press, 1991); Thomas Stanford, "The Mexican Son," *Yearbook of the IFMC* (1972); Robert Stevenson, *In Aztec and Inca Territory* (Berkeley: University of California Press, 1968); David Stigberg, "Jarocho, Tropical, and 'Pop': Aspects of Musical Life in Veracruz, 1971–1972," in Bruno Nettl, ed., *Eight Urban Musical Cultures* (Urbana: University of Illinois Press, 1978); Thomas Turino, *Moving Away From Silence: Music of the Peruvian Altiplano and the Experience of Urban Migration* (Chicago: University of Chicago Press, 1993); Raul Romero, *Debating the Past: Music, Memory, and Identity in the Andes* (New York: Oxford University Press, 2001); Helena Simonett, *Banda: Mexican Musical Life Across Borders* (Middletown, Conn.: Wesleyan University Press, 2001); Zoila Mendoza, *Shaping Society Through Dance: Mestizo Ritual Performance in the Peruvian Andes* (Chicago: University of Chicago Press, 2000).

Amazonian Cultures   Anthony Seeger, *Why Suyá Sing: A Musical Anthropology of an Amazonian People* (Cambridge: Cambridge University Press, 1987); Anthony Seeger, "What Can We Learn When They Sing? Vocal Genres of the Suyá Indians of Central Brazil," *Ethnomusicology* 23/3 (1979): 373–94.

African American Traditions   Gerard Béhague, "Patterns of Candomblé Music Performance: An Afro-Brazilian Religious Setting," in Gerard Béhague, ed., *Performance Practice: Ethnomusicological Perspectives* (Westport, Conn.: Greenwood, 1984); Harold Courlander, "Musical Instruments of Cuba," *Musical Quarterly* 28 (1942); Luis Heitor Correa de Azevedo, "Music and Musicians of African Origin in Brazil," *World of Music* 25/2 (1982); Larry Crook, "A Musical Analysis of the Cuban Rumba," *Latin American Music Review* 3/1 (1982); Alma Guillermoprieto, *Samba* (New York: Vintage Press, 1990); Peter Manuel, *Popular Musics of the Non-Western World* (New York: Oxford University Press, 1988); Peter Manuel, ed., *Essays on Cuban Music: North American and Cuban Perspectives* (Lanham, Md.: University Press of America, 1991); Charles A. Perrone, *Masters of Contemporary Brazilian Song: MPB 1965–1985* (Austin: University of Texas Press, 1989); Alison Raphael, "From Popular Culture to Microenterprise: The History of Brazilian Samba

Schools," *Latin American Music Review* 11(1), 1990; Norman E. Whitten, Jr. and C. Aurelio Fuentes, *Black Frontiersmen: A South American Case* (New York: Schenkman, 1974); Katherine J. Hagedorn, *Divine Utterances: The Performance of Afro-Cuban Santeria* (Washington, D.C.: Smithsonian Institution Press, 2001); Robin D. Moore, *Nationalizing Blackness: Afrocubanismo and Artistic Revolution in Havana, 1920–1940* (Pittsburgh, Pa.: University of Pittsburgh Press, 1997).

LATIN AMERICA DISCOGRAPHY

Highland Indigenous and Mestizo   *Mountain Music of Peru*, Vol. 2 (Smithsonian Folkways CD 40406); *Musik im Andenhochland/Bolivien* (Museum Collection Berlin [West] MC 14); *Huayno Music of Peru*, Vol. 1 (Arhoolie CD 320); *The Inca Harp: Laments and Dances of the Tawantinsuyu, the Inca Empire* (Lyrichord LLST 7359); *Your Struggle Is Your Glory: Songs of Struggle, Huayno and Other Peruvian Music* (Arhoolie 3025); *Kingdom of the Sun: Peru's Inca Heritage* (Nonesuch H-72029); *Music of Peru* (Folkways FE 4415); *Mexico: Fiestas of Chiapas and Oaxaca* (Nonesuch H-72070); *Texas-Mexican Border Music* [Vol 24]: *The Texas-Mexican Conjunto* (Folklyric 9049); *Marimba Music of Tehuantepec* (University of Washington Press UWP 1002); *Music of the Tarascan Indians of Mexico: Music of Michoacán and Nearby Mestizo Country* (Asch Mankind Series AHM 4217); *Music of Mexico: Sones Jarochos* (Arhoolie 3008); *Music of Mexico* [Vol 2]: *Sones Huastecos* (Arhoolie 3009); *Amerindian Ceremonial Music from Chile* (Philips 6586026).

Amazonian Cultures   *Why Suyá Sing* (cassette, Cambridge University Press); *Indian Music of the Upper Amazon* (Folkways FE 4458).

African American   *La História de Son Cubano, Sexteto Boloña* (Folkyric 9053); *In Praise of Oxalá and Other Gods: Black Music of South America* (Nonesuch H-72036); *Afro-Hispanic Music from Western Colombia and Ecuador* (Folkways FE 4376); *Afro-Brazilian Religious Songs: Cantigas de Candomblé* (Lyrichord LLST 7315); *An Island Carnival: Music of the West Indies* (Nonesuch 72091); *The Sound of the Sun: The Westland Steel Band* (Nonesuch H-72016); *Meringues and Folk Ballads of Haiti* (Lyrichord LLST 7340); *Cult Music of Cuba* (Folkways FE 4410); *Music from Saramaka: A Dynamic Afro-American Tradition* (Folkways FE 4225).

10

Native American Music

Bruno Nettl

"NORTH AMERICAN INDIAN DAYS"

A Modern Ceremony

The scene is the town of Browning, Montana, in the middle of the Blackfeet Native American Reservation. To the west are the rugged mountains of Glacier National Park, and in all other directions one sees the yellowish look and the curved contours of the high plains in late afternoon. We are on the edge of the small town with its handful of stores, boarded-up businesses, and streets with potholes, and have gone to the center of a large circle of tents, some the kind you can buy at any camping store, but others are canvas versions of the grand tepees of the Plains tribes with their ceremonial painted decorations. We are entering a kind of miniature stadium with entrances on four sides and an expanse of grass in the middle (Fig. 10–1).

Some three hundred people are sitting on benches or folding chairs; about half of them seem to be Native Americans, the rest whites, many with cameras and cassette recorders. There is a podium on one side, and a master of ceremonies is speaking over a loudspeaker, asking dancers (who are not visible just yet) to prepare for the grand entry. Around the edge of the grassy center several bass drums are spaced, each representing a singing group of a half-dozen men that seems to be setting up amplification equipment. Eventually, eighteen singing groups take their places; a few of them include one or two women, but one of them is entirely made up of

Figure 10–1   North American Indian Days in Browning, Montana, in the early afternoon. *Photo: Bruno Nettl.*

women. The MC proceeds to call the roll, naming and locating each group and giving it a number; each responds with a stroke on the drum. It turns out that the groups (called Drums) come from various locations on the reservation or from the Blackfoot reserves in neighboring Alberta; and about half of them are from other tribes, from Eastern Montana, the Dakotas, Arizona, and Washington. Their names indicate locations or family names, and it becomes clear that the members of a "drum" are often members of an extended family.

Grand Entry

The MC, who happens to be the chief of the tribal council and a well-known politician in the Native American world of the 1970s, engages in a bit of lighthearted banter and then calls on one of the "drums" to sing the song for the "grand entry." The singers (Fig. 10–2 shows them in the middle of a song) set up a steady rhythm by beating on the edge of their bass drum. The drum's leader sings a phrase in a falsetto voice, very tense, harsh, loud, and ornamented; the phrase is repeated by a second singer, and the whole group enters, singing a stately melody moving down the scale until it flattens out an octave below the beginning, then rising again, coming to the end of the song, and going on to repeat the whole form several times, illustrates this kind of performance (CD 2, #16). Note that the first two stanzas are sung and drummed softly, and then tempo, intensity, and loudness all increase rapidly. Throughout the song, and, indeed, throughout most of the powwow, the members of the singing group sit in a circle, facing each other but essentially looking at their drums or the ground, bent forward, singing with great concentration, ignoring the audience and also the dancers when they finally enter the enclosure. The song obvi-

Figure 10–2   Blackfoot singing group at North American Indian Days. *Photo: Bruno Nettl.*

ously has no words, only vocables or meaningless syllables, but all of the singers sing these in unison.

Then, rather suddenly, we see dancers in flamboyant costumes entering from all four sides of the enclosure, each group in single file, moving to the right and steadily clockwise around the center of the circle, eventually making a wide stream of bodies, perhaps 150, moving rhythmically to the drumming. The men wear brightly colored cloth-and-feather outfits, each unique; the women wear long dresses decorated in various ways with beads and colored cloth, simpler and more modest than the men's costumes. Each dancer, however, has a costume in some sense of the word, while the singers wear blue jeans, T-shirts, and farmers' caps. From one entrance emerges a line of male dancers moving very athletically, with large steps and jumps; on the opposite side, men with more restrained movements (called, we find, fancy and traditional dancers, respectively); and the women, though with very much more restrained motions, divide themselves along the same lines in the other two entrances. All dancing is "solo"; couples do not dance, but while the men move singly and idiosyncratically, some of the women dance slowly, grouping themselves two or three abreast.

The song ends after seven or eight repetitions; the MC indicates that the next one will be sung by Drum no. 7 from Heart Butte (a small town thirty miles south of Browning) and that it will be (as most turn out to be) a type of song called intertribal; and the singing and dancing begins again. It goes on like this for several hours, each drum or singing group taking its turn. The series of songs are frequently interrupted by related events such as a song and brief procession to mourn a recently deceased member of the community, different dances such as circle and owl dances (the latter danced by couples), dance contests, and brief ceremonies. The style of the music is very much the same throughout, and the singing groups from all locations sound similar and share a repertory. Members of the audience talk, walk in and out, speak with dancers and singers, take photos, and record the singing on cassettes. The scene is similar to that of a small-town sports event.

Ancillary Events

While the main events of North American Indian Days take place in the dance enclosure, there are other activities with music that are worthy of attention. In a small hut, a traditional gambling game, played by two teams facing each other and hiding a bullet or stick, is in progress. The team hiding the object sings constantly, songs with a small melodic range consisting of the alternation of only two brief musical phrases, all the while beating rhythmically and rapidly on a plank. But the high, intense, pulsating singing of the dance songs is here replaced with a lower, more relaxed style. A couple of blocks away, there is a kind of barn dance taking place in a parking lot, with a country-and-western band composed of members of the Blackfoot tribe singing old Nashville favorites. A half-mile further, south of the town, a small rodeo is in progress. It is billed as an "Indian rodeo"; its content is like that of other small-town rodeos in Montana, but the participants are all Native Americans. Before and between the events there is recorded music, played over a loud speaker and attracting little attention; it is patriotic music, such as the national anthem, and "America, the Beautiful," and also Sousa marches. The next morning there is a parade with many dozens of floats representing businesses and institutions of the area—some Native American, others white; this is a central event in North American Native American Days. Some of the floats have music, live or recorded, and for once one hears traditional Native American music—the modern intertribal songs—along with rock, jazz, and Christian hymns.

North American Indian Days is a spectacle that characterizes Native American culture in North America in several ways. First, it is a successor of the midsummer religious ceremonies that were held traditionally by many Native American societies. Furthermore, as an intertribal event, it symbolizes to both Native Americans and whites the broad Native American identity that is important to them. The fact that the same songs are known to singing groups from all over, that the same style (with some regional diversity) is used by many tribes, and that linguistic differences are submerged as the songs have no words (or occasionally English words) all of this underscores that function of the powwow. The coexistence of several events, each with different music—gambling games from an ancient tradition, dancing from a modern Native American one, other events with Western music performed by Native Americans—symbolizes the present life of Native Americans as a separate population which nevertheless participates in the mainstream culture. The comparison of traditional and fancy dancers reflects the dual role of the event—traditional ceremony and modern entertainment. What is important for us to note is the way in which traditional Native American music is used to exhibit the old tradition but also to tie the various strands of the culture, old and modernized, to each other.

SOME OLDER CEREMONIAL TRADITIONS

The concept of "song" in most Native American cultures is a relatively short unit, rather like our nursery rhyme or hymn. Songs are ordinarily presented, however, in large groups and sequences as parts of elaborate ceremonies and rituals. Most religious ceremonies are elaborate affairs, lasting many hours or even several days. In many ceremonies, the songs to be sung and their order are specifically prescribed. In others they are not; in the Peyote ceremonies of Plains tribes each singer must sing four songs at a time, but they may be any songs from the Peyote repertory, and only at four points in the ceremony must particular songs be sung.

Thus, the "Night Chant" (Yeibechai) of the Navajo, a curing ceremony, requires nine days and nights, and includes hundreds of songs and their poetic texts. The Hako, a Pawnee ceremony of general religious significance, required several days and included about one hundred songs. The medicine-bundle ceremonies of the Northern Plains peoples might consist of several parts: narration of the myth explaining the origin of the bundle; opening the bundle and performing with each of the objects in it; a required activity—dancing, smoking, eating, praying; and the singing of one or several songs (usually by the celebrant, sometimes by him and others present) for each object. The Blackfoot Sun Dance, the largest and most central of the older tribal ceremonies of this culture, required four preparatory days followed by four days of dancing. The Peyote ceremony, which became a major religious ritual in many tribes of the United States in the course of the late nineteenth and twentieth centuries, consists of a night of singing. Each participant—there may be from ten to thirty sitting in a circle—sings four songs at a time, playing the rattle while his neighbor accompanies him on a special drum.

Secular events, too, are structured so that songs appear in large groups. The performance of a Stomp Dance, a social dance of southeastern origin performed by a line of dancers moving in snakelike fashion with responsorial singing, leader and group alternating, includes a dozen or so songs. And the North American Native American Days powwow, described earlier, takes four days.

THE WORLD OF NATIVE AMERICAN CULTURES AND MUSIC

Native American Societies Past and Present

American Indian life today may be rather a mixed bag. There are some tribal societies that maintain their special identity, and there are also groups of tribes that were, through happenstance or force, obliged to share a reservation and have somehow fashioned a unified culture. There are activities and ceremonies, such as the powwow we have described, of an essentially intertribal nature. Native Americans from various tribes find themselves in large cities and join together to establish for themselves a common Native American identity. In most respects, of course, they share the culture of their non–Native American compatriots, speaking English or Spanish. It is largely in music and dance that their Native American background is exhibited to themselves and to others.

Most of what is known about Native American music comes from the last hundred years, when recording techniques and ethnography were developed, and in this period Native Americans had already come into much negative and positive contact with whites. In the early part of that period, however, one could still get a picture of what Native American music and musical culture may have been like before contact. It is clear, first of all, that each tribe had its own musical culture, its own repertory, musical style, uses of, and ideas about music. There were between one thousand and two thousand tribal groups in North America, almost all speaking distinct languages. The average population of a tribe was around a thousand, but some were much larger and others had only one hundred to two hundred persons. Each tribe, however, had a large number of songs and used them in many ceremonies, for curing, to accompany dances, and to draw boundaries between subdivisions of society such as age groups, clans, and genders.

Anthropologists have classified these cultures into six to eight groups called culture areas, each with characteristic types of housing, ways of acquiring and preparing food, clothing, religion, and economic and political structure. Thus, for example, the peoples of the North Pacific Coast fished, built wooden houses, had a rigid class structure including slaves, had complex ceremonial sculpture such as totem poles and masks, and had special "potlatch" ceremonies to exhibit personal and family wealth and status. The Native American people of the Plains specialized in hunting buffalo as the prime source of food, housing, and clothes, doing this first on foot with the help of dogs and later on horseback. They were nomadic, lived in tepees, and had a rather informal and egalitarian political structure. Their religion was based on guardian spirits that were acquired by men in dreams, and their ceremonial life included many kinds of acts that showed personal courage. The Pueblo Native Americans of the Southwest, on the other hand, lived in towns of cliff dwellings, grew corn and other plants, and had an extremely complex ceremonial life. In California, there were a great many very small tribes who lived seminomadically, with complex ceremonial life but subsistence based on hunting small animals, including insects, and gathering plants.

Unity and Diversity in Native American Music

Comparing the sound of Native American music of North America with that of Africa or Japan shows that Native American music is relatively homogeneous. It is almost always monophonic, and with few exceptions it is vocal. While there are a number of distinct singing styles, they have in common a tense sound and the use of pulsations on longer notes. Two or three types of forms predominate. There are strophic songs, rather like folk songs or hymns in that a stanza of several lines is repeated several or many times; there are very short songs that consist of one or a pair of lines repeated many times; and there are forms in which two contrastive sections of music, one usually higher than the other, alternate. Almost all of the singing is accompanied by percussion, usually drums or rattles. Thus, the many Native American musical cultures have a good deal in common.

But if one goes into great detail, analyzing hundreds of songs and making a statistical study of their characteristics for each tribe, one sees that each group has a unique musical repertory and style. There are differences even between neighboring tribes. The picture is not totally confusing, however, as there are units, which we might call music areas, that coincide roughly, though not always precisely, with the culture areas. It is worth mentioning that they do not coincide well at all with language areas; that is, societies speaking related languages often do not share either cultural or musical characteristics. There are about seven music areas.

Musical Areas

The Plains area coincides well with a culture area. It has the singing style most distant from standard Western singing, emphasizing high pitch, rhythmic pulsations on the long tones, tension, and harshness. Its characteristic form consists of stanzas internally arranged as follows: A short phrase is presented and repeated; there follows a descending line of three or four phrases ending with a low, flat cadence that is sometimes a version of the initial motif an octave lower; this long second section is repeated, so that the total may have the following scheme: A A BCD BCD. The Blackfoot song already discussed in connection with the great powwow (CD 2, #16) is a typical Plains song.

The Eastern part of the continent has a greater variety of forms, which usually consist of several short phrases in different arrangements; a rounder and more relaxed vocal sound; some singing in which a leader and a group alternate brief bits of music, the so-called call-and-response pattern; and resulting from this, occasional bits of polyphony (CD 2, #19).

A group of cultures representing the Yuman-speaking peoples of the southwestern United States and some cultures in southern and central California specialize in a form in which one section, a phrase or short group of phrases, is repeated several times but is interrupted occasionally by another, slightly higher and definitely contrastive section, called by some Yuman peoples and also by ethnomusicologists the rise. Here also we have a very relaxed kind of vocal style. CD 2, #23 is a song from the Walapai, a Yuman culture, with some of these characteristics.

Also in the southwestern United States we have the Athabascan style of the Navajo and Apache peoples. Its typical traits are a large vocal range, a rather nasal-sounding voice, and even rhythms that can almost always be written by using only quarter- and eighth-notes (CD 2, #19).

The style of the Pueblo Native Americans shares features with those of both the Athabascan and the Plains peoples but has a low, harsh, pulsating vocal style and long, complex forms. Related to both Plains and Pueblo songs are those of the Papago people (CD 2, #20). The Great Basin style, found in Nevada and Utah as well as northern California, and also in the Ghost Dance songs of the Plains people, has songs with small vocal range, and with a characteristic form in which each of a group of phrases is repeated once, for example, AABBCC. It is illustrated in the Ghost Dance recording of CD 2, #22.

The Northwest Coast peoples and some of the Eskimo or Inuit peoples share a typical singing style and complex rhythms often pitting patterns in voice and drum against each other. The Northwest Coast is also the area richest in wind instruments and has a well-documented, if not prominent, polyphonic tradition. However, CD 2, #21, while from a Northwest Coast culture, does not illustrate that area's general song style but belongs, rather, to the special style of game songs which is distributed widely throughout the continent.

IDEAS ABOUT MUSIC

What It Is and What It Does

If one asks how it was that Native American peoples, for all their interest in music and their large repertories, did not develop longer, more complex forms with greater interactions, the answer would have to be threefold. First, it is true that oral tradition places some limitations on the complexity of materials to be remembered. Second, there is really quite a lot more complexity, at a microscopic level, than the listener may at first perceive. But, most important, the idea of technical complexity has never been a criterion of musical quality to Native American peoples. Rather, music is measured by such things as its ability to integrate society and to represent it to the outside, its ability to integrate ceremonial and social events, and its supernatural power. The rather athletic view of music taken in Western culture, where star performances by individual composers and performers and their ability to do very difficult things is measured, is replaced in Native American cultures by quite different values.

Music has supernatural power. In Blackfoot culture, it is the songs that, as it were, hold the power. Thus, each act must have its appropriate song. In a ceremony in which a medicine man is trying to influence the weather, he will have a bundle of objects which he opens and displays, but their supernatural power is not activated until the appropriate song is sung. In many Native American cultures, songs are thought to come into existence principally in dreams or visions.

Composition and Creativity

In the Plains, a man has visions in which powerful guardian spirits appear to him, and these are validated by the songs they sing to him. As many songs have no words, it is clearly not simply the texts but the act of singing—producing a kind of sound that has no other function in life—that embodies spiritual power. The strong association with religion, unusual even when we consider that religious music is a cultural universal, is characteristic of Native American music.

Beyond the composition of songs in visions by Plains people, the creation of songs is viewed differently in Native American traditions than in most European and Asian cultures. It may be that songs are thought to exist in the cosmos and need to be brought into human existence through dreams. In some tribes songs are extant in the supernatural world but need to be "unraveled" by humans in dreams in order to be realized. In an Eskimo culture, there is a finite quantity of songs, and new ones can be made up only by combining elements of extant ones. In some tribes, making up songs is associated with emotional or mental disturbance. Except in modernized musical contexts, one rarely finds a situation in which humans are given credit for creating music. If there are specialists in making up songs they are ordinarily also specialists in religious matters, and their technical competence or aesthetic creativity seems not to be an issue.

Music, a Reflection of Culture

In Native American cultures even more than others, the musical system is a kind of reflection of the rest of culture. A Blackfoot singer said, "The right way to do something is to sing the right song with it"; and indeed, in theory at least, the Blackfeet have particular songs for all activities, and the more an activity is technically subdivided—as, for example, a ceremony—the more specific the association of songs with its various parts. In the Beaver Ceremony, the ceremonialist has a bundle of 168 objects, mostly dressed skins of many birds and animals of the environment but also some handmade objects, rocks, and sticks. For each he must sing the appropriate song. Traditionally, the men of the tribe divided themselves into seven societies by age, and a man was initiated successively into them roughly every four years. Each society had its ceremonies and certain duties in social life and warfare, and each had its separate group of songs. There were special songs for warfare, riding, walking. The most important social division, between men and women, was also reflected musically. Women had, so it seems, a separate and much smaller repertory, although they might join in singing certain men's songs; but more important, their singing style was different, with smoother and more nasal tone than the men's, and with the pulsations being not rhythmic stresses but melodic ornaments. In many Native American cultures, the major divisions in society are represented by major divisions in musical repertory and style.

MUSICAL INSTRUMENTS

Types of Instruments

In North America, the Native American music is prevailingly vocal. Almost all instruments are percussive, and their function is to provide rhythmic accompaniment to singing. Solo drumming is actually rare. But there is a great variety of drum and rattle types. Large drums with two heads or skins, small hand-drums with a single skin (Figs. 10–3 and 10–4), kettle-drums filled with water for tuning, pieces of rawhide simply suspended from stakes—these are examples of drum types widely distributed. There are container rattles made of gourds, hide pieces sewn together (Fig. 10–5), or a turtle shell; others fashioned of strings of deer hooves; and more. Although the musical function of these instruments is essentially the same, a culture may have many types, distinguished in the details of decoration with beads, feathers, animal skins, carving, and painting, each type associated with a particular ceremony. There are other idiophones as well such as notched stick scrapers, clappers, beaten planks, stamping tubes, and jingles. Small metal bells, introduced centuries ago by Europeans, have become established and incorporated in some of the cultures.

Among the melody-producing instruments, the most widespread type is the flute. Various kinds of flutes are found, including true, end-blown flutes in which the player's pursed lips direct a ribbon-shaped column of air against an edge of the blowhole, as well as duct flutes rather like European recorders. In some tribes, the repertory of flute music consists simply of songs which may also be sung. Elsewhere, particularly in the southwestern United States, flute music is separate in content

Figure 10–3   Plains Indian hand drum with drumstick covered with rawhide. *Photo: Wanda Nettl.*

Figure 10–4   Northwest Coast Indian drum. *Photo: Wanda Nettl.*

though its style is not markedly different from that of the songs. Among the instruments found in small numbers among a few tribes, we should mention the use of simple reeds and trumpets for recreational and ceremonial occasions on the North Pacific Coast. The musical bow, similar to or identical with a hunting bow, appears to

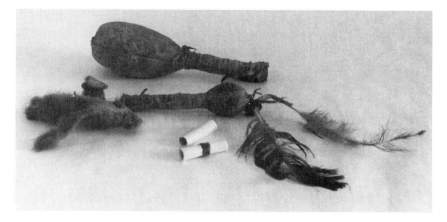

Figure 10–5   Blackfoot ceremonial objects: Two medicine bundle rattles, pair of gambling bones, *Photo: Wanda Nettl.*

Figure 10–6 "Apache fiddle" or Navajo violin. *Photo: Wanda Nettl.*

have been used as an instrument in the southwestern United States, and has been succeeded by the "Apache fiddle" or Navajo violin (Fig. 10–6), a bowed instrument with one horsehair string and a cylindrical body about twelve inches in length, probably created as a combination of the bow and the Western violin.

Instruments, Singing, and Words

Most important, however, the instruments of Native Americans are largely non-melodic percussion instruments, and melody-producing instruments have special and restricted functions. In this respect they are similar to other cultures with small populations such as the tribes of Australian aboriginals whose main instruments are percussion sticks of eucalyptus, struck against each other, and the didgeridoo, a long trumpet used mainly to play a single-tone drone. It is important to know, however, that the didgeridoo requires complex playing techniques such as circular breathing and changes in the shape of the mouth cavity for varying the tone color. In Polynesia instruments are used mainly to accompany singing, and in Melanesia and Micronesia the principal instruments are panpipes.

If the relative dearth of melody-producing instruments is noteworthy in Native American cultures of North America, it is important to keep in mind that, in many of them, songs may not be primarily a vehicle for words. While some Native American song texts, like those of the Navajo and Pueblo peoples, are often highly elaborate poems, in Plains people culture songs may have no words at all but only vocables. Where there are words, they are usually brief and occupy only a short portion of the melody. Here are the texts of two Blackfoot songs: "Sun says to sing" (song of the Sun Dance ceremony); and "It is spring; let others see you" (sung at the beginning of a medicine-bundle ceremony, before the bundle is opened). In a sense, we could conclude that songs without words substitute for the absent instrumental music.

ASPECTS OF THE HISTORY OF AMERICAN NATIVE AMERICAN MUSIC

Reconstructing Prehistory

There is little direct or written information about the history of American Native American music, yet various kinds of circumstantial evidence permit reasonable guesses toward a rough reconstruction. Native Americans have been in the Americas for at least fifty thousand years, but they originally came, probably in waves, from Asia; thus, if there is musical material that they share with Asian cultures, it may be very ancient. The only thing to which one can reasonably point is the existence, in many Indian cultures, of a stratum of short, simple songs consisting of one or two repeated lines and built on a scale of three or four tones, associated with children, games, and love charms. Among these, it is game songs, usually called gambling songs, that remain most widespread today. CD 2, #21 is a song sung to a game in which a team hides sticks, singing while the other team tries to locate them. Figure 10–7 shows a group of Blackfoot men singing while playing such a hiding game.

This type of music, consisting of short tunes with few pitches repeated or varied many times, is found in many parts of the world and may possibly be a remnant of a highly archaic stratum of human music. Comparison of North and South American Native American music may be indicative. There are musical styles shared by

Figure 10–7   Singing and beating percussion plank at a Blackfoot gambling game. *Photo: Wanda Nettl.*

the two regions; peoples of the Gran Chaco have forms and a singing style not too different from that of the North American Plains. Ideas about music—the reflection of cultural categories in modes of performance, music's central role in myths about the origin of culture, music as a way of communicating within and with the supernatural world—often seem similar in the two regions. On the other hand, South American Native American music is, in most respects, very different from North American; there are more instances of major participation by women, and there is much more instrumental music. This suggests that the musical styles of North America developed independently and perhaps later. As cultures tend to hold on to their languages more tenaciously than to other things, and as language groupings do not often coincide with musical areas, the music of one society may have changed rapidly and frequently. If so, the picture of Native American music history must have been quite variegated, tribes changing their music as they changed important aspects of their culture.

Archeological evidence is not very plentiful for the area north of Mexico. It is assumed that large ceremonies and massed populations generally give rise to complex musical structures, and thus Aztec and Mayan societies had choral music and probably polyphonic structures. But this kind of correlation is not found in East Asia, and as few instruments were either extant or preserved in archeological sites, little can be known about the music of the classical Mexican cultures. Similarly, archeological sites in the United States and Canada give us little information about musical life.

Modern Music History

Since the Coming of White People   Native American history since the coming of white people is better documented, and aspects of it have been widely studied. The unhappy social and political history is accompanied by a great reduction in the content of musical culture. Clearly, as entire tribes were wiped out and virtually all Native American peoples were relocated, suffering cultural disintegration through devastating famines and epidemics, knowledge of ceremonies and rituals as well as social repertory decreased and much was simply forgotten. As Native Americans were motivated to take up Western lifestyles and religion, they also began to participate in Western music, and sometimes to adopt Western conceptions of music for their own musical culture. So in the Plains, for example, the notion that all songs have a supernatural origin has been replaced by the acceptance of human composition. And to the emphasis on music as a carrier of supernatural power has been added the concept of music as entertainment.

But the tragic history of the Native Americans also brought with it, as a happier kind of by-product, interesting new developments in music, as Native American people came to use music as a weapon to fight back against total absorption and for the preservation of their cultural identity.

The Ghost Dance   The modern music history of Native Americans may be said to begin after the great tragedy of the massacre at Wounded Knee in 1890, which resulted in part because Sioux and Arapaho people had taken up the practice of the Ghost Dance religion. This messianic cult began in the Great Basin area (Utah and Nevada) and was taken up by the Plains tribes, who hoped that it would help them in combating and defeating the white people, bringing back the dead, and restoring the buffalo—in other words, bring back the good old days. As these Plains people learned the Ghost Dance ceremony, they learned its songs, which were composed in a simple style that also made them think of a simpler, better time. But these songs and their style also enriched Plains music. CD 2, #22 is a Ghost Dance song in the style of Great Basin music, but sung by a Plains Pawnee singer. Its form, typical of Ghost Dance songs, consists of a few short phrases, each of them repeated once: AABBCC. This style of music, taken up by many tribes—thus, an intertribal style— was superimposed on the older song traditions.

Peyote Music   The songs of the Peyote religion (mentioned in our discussion of ceremonies, above), like the Ghost Dance songs, an intertribal overlay upon the individual tribal and area styles. While Ghost Dance songs are hardly ever sung any more, Peyote songs are a major element in the contemporary Native American music scene. Based on the hallucinogenic buttons of a cactus native to Mexico, the Peyote religion spread through much of the North Native American world between 1700 and 1940. Peyote religionists developed a distinct song repertory; you can easily recognize a Peyote song regardless of the singer's tribal identity. Their singing style is probably derived from that of the Navajo, the rhythmic structure uses elements of Apache rhythm, the "incomplete repetition" type of form and the descending melodic contour come from the musical practices of the Plains (and heard in CD 2, #16), and the percussion accompaniment is a kettle-drum filled with water that possibly originated in the southeastern United States. You can identify a Peyote song by its words—or rather, "meaningless" vocables or syllables sequences, as they are quite unique; examples are "heyowitsinayo," "heneyowitsine," and "heyowanene," and each song ends with an amenlike "heneyowe." The origin of these vocable patterns is not known, but conceivably they came from the Comanche language of the southern Plains. This is a religion that tries to tie Native American peoples together and takes a conciliatory position toward Christianity, and thus Christian texts in English are occasionally used. Here, too, we see the forced culture change resulting in the new musical style and the broadening of Native American musical culture.

CD 2, #17 and 18 illustrate the intertribal Peyote style, but both are sung by a Kiowa singer. Number 17, using the syllables he-ne-ne-ne-ha-yo-wi-tsi-na-yo, has a structure in which a line is repeated, then replaced by another, and finally a last one followed by the closing formula he-ne-yo-we. Number 18 uses a different and more common composition technique; a line of syllables (and an associated rhythmic pattern) is repeated, but each time with a slightly different set of pitches, moving down the scale: he-yo-wa-ne-ne, ka-ya-ti-ni-ka-ya-ti-na-yo. These are songs that must be sung at certain points in the night-long ceremony, at the beginning and at sunrise; most songs can be selected by the singers at their discretion, as long as they are Peyote songs. The Peyote religion has some Christian overtones; the name of Jesus appears occasionally among the vocables, some religionists claim that "Indians know Jesus better than do white people," and the Peyote organization is known generally as a "church." Quite apart from Peyote music, there is also a body of Christian hymnody based on traditional Native American music, with hymnals which include traditional Anglo-American hymn tunes and monophonic songs in traditional style with Christian words.

The Powwow Culture   In the second half of the twentieth century, the most significant trends have been the development of the powwow culture as perhaps the most visible strategy for building an intertribal Native American culture and the consciousness of ethnic identity that goes with it, and the establishment of a Native American popular music whose sound is clearly in the mainstream of American popular music styles, but which is still recognizably native. In a related development, Native American artists have made significant contributions to the world of concert music and dance.

The establishment of an intertribal style based on Plains music, and of a common song repertory for the powwow culture as observed in the Blackfoot North American Native American Days. Powwows take place throughout the United States and Canada, in places of concentrated Native American population, where they serve to celebrate ethnic identity and intertribal unity, and also where there are few Indians, where they are used to make non-Natives aware of Native American culture. Native Americans have used the powwow as a powerful wedge for making themselves—but also, it's important to note, others—aware that they are no longer the "vanishing American."

A celebration on the campus of the University of Illinois in Urbana illustrated the use of the powwow for education and empowerment dramatically. Presented by a small number of Native Americans, largely visitors from out of town, with the main purpose of instructing local people in the structure, content, and functions of intertribal powwows. The visitors received pamphlets on "Powwow Etiquette" with instructions that included certain ritual actions—certain times to stand, to sit, to remove hats, to dance or not to dance, times to take pictures and to refrain, but above all, to follow the directions of the master of ceremonies. All this was justified by reference to unspecified older sacred Indian traditions, but the main purpose of the rules was to create a situation in which a distinction between whites and natives was drawn, the distinction defined by the natives; but also that there were certain respects in which the distinction was ignored. Music and dance were used to negotiate and symbolize, to establish times in which whites were to stay out of the native business, and other times in which they were to participate. As in the powwow at

Browning, discussed at the beginning of this chapter, here too music and dance were used to cope with the nonnative "other" in a number of ways.

A part of the powwow repertory is the body of so-called 49-songs or forty-niner songs, which ordinarily have mildly romantic, or amusing (and sometimes considered by powwow dancers as uproariously funny) words in English, such as "I don't care if you're married sixteen times, I will get you," or "When the Dance is over, sweetheart, I will take you home in my one-eyed Ford" (both illustrated in CD 2, #24), or "My sweetheart, she got mad at me because I said hello to my old-timer, but it's just OK with me."

A Native American record industry marketing native music—but mainly the intertribal powwow repertory—mainly to Native Americans began to be established in the 1950s (with the label North American Soundchief) and flourishes in the late 1990s. Clearly, many young Native Americans spend much of their music listening time with these CDs and tapes. The concept of music as mainly ritual and communication with the supernatural has given way to one of music as entertainment and an expression of ethnic identity. There are now virtually countless singing groups, or "Drums," some known only on their own reservation, others traveling widely, following the powwow circuit, entering contests which provide substantial monetary prizes.

Women in Earlier and Modern Music   It is widely stated, and perhaps it is even true, women's role in Native American musical activity before about 1900 was restricted and, at any rate, quite different from that of men. But surely the many tribes differed greatly in this regard; in some California tribes and among the Navajo, women played important ceremonial roles. In Plains cultures, they were restricted to private events while musical performances in public or for addressing the supernatural were men's activity. In modern Native American culture, women have played increasingly prominent roles. For one thing, it turns out that they have often held on to older traditions better than men. Judith Vander found that Shoshone women knew and could sing old songs, including those of the Ghost Dance, better than men. My male informants among the Blackfoot sometimes turned to their wives for jogging their musical memories.

The matter of gender sometimes played a special rule in musical life. In some Plains cultures, Berdaches—men who dressed as women and did women's work, and might be homosexual, were sometimes extolled as great singers. And among the Blackfoot, women identified as "manly-hearted," often daughters of influential men, associated themselves culturally with men, could be heterosexually promiscuous, and carried out the male roles in ceremonies, singing men's songs in men's singing styles.

As observed at North American Indian Days in Montana, women have increasingly become active as members of Drums, or powwow singing groups. In the powwow tradition of 1960, a Drum was usually based on the men of an extended family—father, sons, nephews, sons-in-law—along with some close friends. Occasionally a woman of the family might sit in. Gradually, however, the participation of women increased, to the extent that many Drums have several female members, and a number of Drums traveling the powwow circuit consist entirely of women. And some Drums consisting largely of men have female leaders.

Popular Music   Of particular interest is the entry of Native American music in the mainstream of American popular music. There is a genre known simply as "Indian rock music," which combines the use of some traditional tunes, the percussive sound of Native American songs, and texts derived from or referring to Native American culture. Among the famous exponents of this music in the 1960s and 1970s was the jazz/rock musician Jim Pepper, a Native American musician performing with a multiracial ensemble. His popular "Newly-Wed Song" uses material from the two forty-nine songs quoted above (CD 2, #24). In the 1980s, rock groups devoting themselves more explicitly to protest, such as XIT, came to the fore, along with Native American singers, such as Buffy Saint-Marie and Peter LaFarge, who performed Western-style popular music with words about Native American issues.

In the 1990s, the Navajo flutist Carlos Nakai has developed a variety of styles based on, or referring to, Native American culture, composing for traditional, popular, and classical music contexts, performing solo and with Western instruments. The ensemble Ulali, led by a female singer, music syncretizing Western and Native style, singing Plains-like tunes but in vocal harmony and backed by chords on synthesizers and guitar. Flutes, which played a modest role in many Native cultural traditions, have increased in importance, to the extent that flute music accounts for perhaps half of the Native music recordings produced for the mass market. This shift in emphasis probably results from the importance of instruments in Euro-American culture.

These recent developments in musical sound and in ideas about music as well as contexts for performance, show that American Native American music is very much alive. Native American peoples use it, and dance, more than anything else to show to each other and other Americans that they are a distinct ethnic group. To them, music functions both as a way of maintaining their cultural integrity and as a form of mediating between themselves and other culture groups. In this sense it continues a tradition, for in earlier times, too, its function had been that of mediation, but between humans and the forces of the supernatural.

In historic times, Native American tribes were probably concerned about their natural environment, as is evident to the attention to wildlife as natural phenomena in their traditional ceremonies. No doubt, however, they sometimes also violated the environment, taking occasion, for example, to slaughter more buffalo than needed for survival. In the second half of the twentieth century, they became increasingly involved in preservation and protection, as their areas of residence were impacted by large-scale industry, mining, fishing, and agriculture. Much of the modern popular music produced by Native American musicians speaks to environmental issues, and Euro-Americans have increasingly interpreted Native American culture as symbolic of environmental and spiritual concerns, and made it part of the "New Age" cultural movement. Native American musicians have sometimes accepted these attitudes, seeing the New Age movement as an ideological ally as well as a market for Native art and music. Thus, for example, one can find numerous CDs of Native American flute music labeled as appropriate for meditation.

Much of the Native American popular music does not differ in its musical style and sound from mainstream rock, blues, and pop, but its words deal with social, economic, and political issues faced by American Indians. Traditional sounding music such as the powwow repertory but also including other non-ceremonial genres continues to be hugely popular in Native American communities as indicated by the thriving CD and prerecorded cassette market. Recent surveys uncovered twenty-three different tapes and CDs of Blackfoot music in a shop frequented by Blackfoot customers in Montana, and thirty-three CDs of older traditional, modernized, New Age, and popular Native American music in a large bookstore in a Midwestern college town.

NORTH NATIVE AMERICAN BIBLIOGRAPHY

North America as a Whole   Marcia Herndon, *Native American Music* (Hatboro, Pa.: Norwood, 1980); Bruno Nettl, *North American Indian Musical Styles* (Philadelphia: American Folklore Society, 1952); Helen H. Roberts, *Musical Areas in Aboriginal North America* (New Haven, Conn.: Yale University Press, 1936); Bryan Burton, *Moving Within the Circle: Contemporary Native American Music and Dance* (Danbury, Conn.: World Music Press, 1993); Richard Keeling, ed., *Women in North American Indian Music: Six Essays* (Bloomington, Ind.: Society for Ethnomusicology, 1989); Victoria Lindsay Levine, *Writing American Indian Music: Historic Transcriptions, Notations, and Arrangements* (Middleton, Wisc.: A-R Editions for the American Musicological Society, 2002); Tara Browner, *Heartbeat of a People: Music and Dance of the Northern Pow-wow* (Urbana: University of Illinois Press, 2002); Luke Eric Lassiter, Clyde Ellis, and Ralph Kotay, *The Jesus Road: Kiowas, Christianity, and Indian Hymns* (Lincoln: University of Nebraska Press, 2002).

Plains Cultures   Bruno Nettl, *Blackfoot Musical Thought: Comparative Perspectives* (Kent, Oh.: Kent State University Press, 1989); Frances Densmore, *Teton Sioux Music* (Washington, D.C.: Bureau of American Ethnology, 1918); Robert Witmer, *The Musical Life of the Blood Indians* (Ottawa: National Museum of Man, 1982); Alan P. Merriam, *Ethnomusicology of the Flathead Indians* (Chicago: Aldine, 1967); William K. Powers, *War Dance: Plains Indian Musical Performance* (Tucson: University of Arizona Press, 1990); James Howard and Victoria Levine, *Choctaw*

Music and Dance (Norman: University of Oklahoma Press, 1990); Luke E. Lassiter, *The Power of Kiowa Song* (Tucson: University of Arizona Press, 1998).

Other North Native American Peoples   Charlotte Frisbie, ed., *Southwestern Native American Ritual Drama* (Tucson: University of Arizona Press, 1980); David P. McAllester, *Peyote Music* (New York: Viking Fund Publications in Anthropology, 1949); David P. McAllester, *Enemy Way Music* (Cambridge, Mass.: Peabody Museum of American Archeology and Ethnology, 1954); Judith Vander, *Songprints* (Urbana: University of Illinois Press, 1988); Judith Vander, *Shoshone Ghost Dance Religion: Poetry, Songs, and Great Basin Context* (Urbana: University of Illinois Press, 1997); Frank Mitchell, *Navajo Blessingway Singer*, ed. Charlotte J. Frisbie and David P. McAllester (Tucson: University of Arizona Press, 1978); Thomas Johnston, *Eskimo Music by Region: A Comparative Circumpolar Study* (Ottawa: National Museum of Man, 1976); Beverley Cavanagh, *Music of the Netsilik Eskimo: A Study of Stability and Change* (Ottawa: National Museum of Man, 1982); Ruth Murray Underhill, *Singing for Power: The Magic of the Papago Indians of Southern Arizona* (Berkeley: University of California Press, 1938); Richard Keeling, *Cry for Luck: Sacred Song and Speech Among Yurok, Hupa, and Karok Indians of Northwestern California* (Berkeley: University of California Press, 1992).

Instruments   K. G. Izikowitz, *Musical and Other Sound Instruments of the South American Indians* (Götesborg, Sweden: Kungl, Vetenskap-och Vitterhets-Samhälles andlingar, 1935); Thomas Vennum, Jr., *The Ojibwa Dance Drum* (Washington, D.C.: Smithsonian Institution Press, 1982); Beverley Cavanagh Diamond and others, *Visions of Sound* (Chicago: University of Chicago Press, 1995).

NATIVE AMERICAN DISCOGRAPHY

Anthologies   *A Cry from the Earth: Music of the North American Indians* (Folkways FC 7777; 1979); *An Anthology of North American Indian and Eskimo Music* (Ethnic Folkways FE 4541; 1973).

Blackfoot   *An Historical Album of Blackfoot Indian Music* (Ethnic Folkways FE 4001; 1979); *Blackfeet* (Indian IR 220; ca. 1980); *Blackfeet Pow-Wow Songs* (Canyon C-6119; 1974).

Other North American Peoples   *American Indians of the Southwest* (Ethnic Folkways P420; 1951); *Music of the Sioux and Navajo* (Ethnic Folkways P 401; 1949); *Kiowa Peyote Ritual Songs* (American Indian Soundchief Kiowa-590; ca. 1970); *The Great Plains* (Canyon ARP 6052; 1966); *Indian Music of the Canadian Plains* (Ethnic Folkways FE 4464; 1966); *Papago Dance Songs* (Canyon 6098; 1973); *Popular Dance Music of the Indians of Southern Arizona* (Canyon C-6085; 1972); *Inuit Games and Songs* (UNESCO Collection Musical Sources, Philips 6586 036;

1978); *Indian Songs of Today* (Library of Congress AFS L36; ca. 1960); *Omaha Indian Music* (American Folklife Center, Library of Congress AFC L71; 1984); *Inuit Games and Songs* (Auvidis Unesco AD 090); *Native American Traditions: Music of New Mexico* (Smithsonian/Folkways SF 40408); *Creation's Journey: Native American Music* (Smithsonian/Folkways SF 40410); *Heartbeat: Voices of First Nations Women* (Smithsonian/Folkways SF 40415); *Dancing Buffalo: Cornel Peewardy and the Alliance West Singers*; Dances and Flute Songs from the Southern Plains (Music of the World CDT-130); *Talking Spirits: Native American Music from the Hopi, Zuni, and San Juan Pueblos* (Music of the World CDT-126).

Recent Developments   *Spirit Horses: The Music of James Demars [Concerto for Native American Flute and Chamber Orchestra]* (Canyon CR 7014); *Solo Flights: Various Native American Artists* (Soar 1245-CD); *Ulali: Mahk Jchi* (Thrush Records CD 0605287581); *Walela: Unbearable Love* (Triloka 7930185209-2); *Northern Wind: Jingle Dress Songs* (Arbor Records AR-11282).

11

Ethnic North America

Philip V. Bohlman

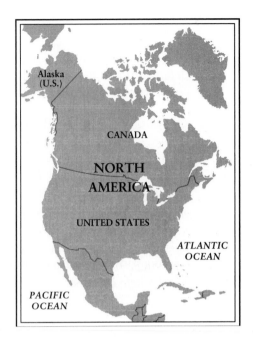

MUSIC AT THE URBAN FOLK FESTIVAL

Performing Ethnicity in Pittsburgh

The Lithuanian folk dancers from Toronto have just concluded their program to the enormous, yet slightly reserved, applause of the audience assembled at the annual Pittsburgh Folk Festival. For the Polish folk musicians and dancers, a young Pittsburgh troupe from the community surrounding a Catholic church on the west side, there will be only twenty more minutes before their performance. It's a time for nerves, and very understandably so. The Lithuanians always manage to give a very polished and professional performance. They are, after all, imported for the festival by the Lithuanian community in Pittsburgh, itself too small to form a sufficient folk-music ensemble, yet too proud of its presence in this city of countless ethnic communities not to display its culture with music and dance at the festival. For the festival organizers, this issue of fair representation is of utmost importance; the larger the number of ethnic communities displaying their culture, the greater the justification for the festival. The politics of ethnic festival organization don't help to relax the Polish troupe as the allotted time for their performance draws closer.

For several years, the Polish troupe had been attempting to reshape their repertory into a purer, more authentically Polish sound. Getting back to their roots meant finding specific pieces, dance forms, and ensemble combinations that were just like those their ancestors of a few generations ago would have known in Poland (CD 2, #8). The easiest way to determine a more Polish ethnic music is to identify rural forms—not just the rural polka and its more syncopated duple-meter relative, the krakowiak, but also a healthy portion of virtually forgotten mazurkas along with the now ubiquitous oberek, which by the 1980s had succeeded in winning a place for Polish dance forms in North America, albeit only at the cost of pushing out several other traditional dance forms. Also characteristic of the new sound the Polish troupe was searching for was a generally more asymmetrical phrasing structure and a more syncopated violin and concertina style. The musicians had worked hard over the past few years attempting to refine their sound, much to the chagrin of their parents and community sponsors, who had long found the urban Polish American polka sound of Chicago effective as their banner of ethnic music distinction. Nobody—neither performers nor community members—was quite comfortable with the revived old-country sound that the Polish troupe was about to perform for the folk-festival audience.

Underlying the Polish troupe's nervousness was yet another area of tension, namely between the notion of ethnicity that the festival organizers wished the troupe to display and a notion that the troupe itself had formed through its understanding of the history of the Polish community of Pittsburgh. The festival had long relied on a philosophy that each group should present itself in the same way: food booths were to be the same size, displays of crafts should concentrate on similar items, and the music and dance performances should obey the same rules. No group should stick out.

The Polish troupe was uncomfortable being like every other performing group. First of all, in their performances in the community itself they were accustomed to relatively long suites, in which complex forms could unfold according to tradition; here at the festival they had only twenty minutes, and if at all possible their performance should reflect variety, the key to holding the audience's attention, act after act. Second, this was again the year during which the festival planners requested that each group employ line dances, the preferred form of presentation because it filled the stage and brought the audience face-to-face with the performers. Line dances were particularly problematic for the Polish troupe, for the rural aesthetic and the dance forms they were attempting to revive stressed couple dances, many of which—for example, the oberek—relied on ring formations as well. Third, the Pittsburgh Civic Center required a big instrumental sound to fill the auditorium, with several musicians playing each part when possible and with traditional and nontraditional sounds mixed together, thereby symbolizing the health of ethnic music and the ethnic mixture of the city.

The bigger-is-better aesthetic of the festival organizers was fine for the professional ensembles like the Duquesne University Tamburitzans, which represented Balkan communities in Pittsburgh and had long played an indispensable role with the festival organizers in putting the festival together. The big-band sound encouraged by the festival, however, was precisely what the Polish troupe wanted to avoid. Their small ensemble of strings—violins, viola, and double bass—preferred a more relined and subdued style, one that could back up but not dominate the vocal parts, which the singers had practiced so hard to sing in reasonably correct Polish, a language none of them knew fluently.

In the end, the festival was to symbolize Pittsburgh's ethnicity, not the ethnicity of individual communities. Even though the Polish troupe was uncomfortable with the festival philosophy, it took to the stage and conformed as well as it could to the festival's twenty-minute frame. The Polish American musicians and dancers were not as professional as the Lithuanians from Toronto, and they did not employ the slick acrobatics of the Tamburitzans. They managed to compromise, however, in ways that satisfied just about everybody's requirements. Between couple and ring dances, they managed to stick in a few line dances. By careful miking of their small ensemble, they avoided the need to enlist the heavy "dyno" sound that many polka bands used to give the feeling of mainstream popular styles. Their songs were unobtrusive because they decided to forgo extra verses. During their performance ethnic music had become not just a symbol of Pittsburgh's west-side Polish community, but of a large and pervasive ethnic presence in Pittsburgh and North America. Music had demonstrated the essential unity of cultural diversity.

Festivals and Ethnic Musics Today

Though folk festivals assume many forms and serve many different communities, they provide one of the most powerful metaphors for the music of ethnic North America. In fact, folk festivals have proliferated and grown in popularity at a time of sweeping transformation in most ethnic communities. During this period, largely since World War II, older ethnic groups, especially European, have formed a type of mainstream, while newer ethnic groups, particularly those from Asia, Latin America, and Africa, have established themselves as distinctive communities on the larger North American cultural landscape. The folk festival frames many of the changes and patterns of interaction that characterize this period of new ethnicity. The festival increasingly establishes a central position for the celebration of diversity in American and Canadian society.

The processes of ethnic transformation are acutely present in the music that we encounter at a folk festival. Music must change to fit the conditions of the festival in the same way that immigrant traditions change to adapt to the conditions of a new nation. This makes the festival itself a context for the making and remaking of traditional musics. Musicians must shape and change their traditional performances to suit the purposes of the festival. Music takes its place with other community activities, with organizations in any community working together and strengthening their communal ties in order to make Filipino or Vietnamese ethnicity more palpable. Music undergoes modernization at the festival because of the need to amplify a

Croatian tamburitza orchestra for a large auditorium or to make a place for a Latvian rock band in Chicago that embeds its Latvianness in a heavy-metal sound.

The music that we hear at the folk festival belongs specifically to the festival but also to the experiences of modern North America. By the time the Polish troupe took the stage, it was performing repertories that were totally different from anything in the old country. The instruments and social function had changed and the sound would probably seem stranger to Poles in Warsaw than to Polish Americans in Pittsburgh. The prerequisites of the festival probably meant that the sound of the Polish performance was in some ways less foreign to the German and Lebanese Americans in the audience than it would be to those from the rural villages of Poland whose music the young Pittsburghers were reviving. The different components of the music have a symbolic importance derived from the festival, not from original social function. The festival becomes a cultural event that forces the musicians and the community to make decisions. This provides the imperative and guidelines for expressing Polish American ethnicity in Pittsburgh.

By choosing to perform at the festival, musicians juxtapose two seemingly contradictory tendencies. On one hand, the musicians accommodate the festival requirement that they perform in a way that resembles every other group. On the other hand, at the moment they succumb to the requirement of similarity, they must also affirm that their community is unique and culturally distinct from all others. The festival turns ethnic culture on its head, confusing similarity and difference. It builds a larger culture with a reformulated vitality from many smaller subcultures. It crystallizes the forces at work in the many domains of cultural activity in ethnic North America.

THE MULTIPLICITY OF MUSICS IN NORTH AMERICA

The Meaning of Ethnicity for Music in North America

In this chapter we examine the music of North America as a whole with many parts. The predominance of these parts, and the fact that we create the larger picture of music in North America only by first looking at the parts and then determining how they fit together, distinguishes this chapter in some ways from the other chapters. The musics of the culture area we are calling ethnic North America have historical origins elsewhere. They accompanied the influx of population groups from somewhere else in the world. The relation of these musics to concepts like "traditional music" or "folk music" is necessarily problematic in ways unlike those the reader has witnessed in other chapters. In the continental music culture most comparable, Latin America, the interaction between imported and indigenous musics is quite different, as Thomas Turino has shown in his examination of the aesthetic and political undertow evident in the persistence of Andean Indian musical styles, instruments, and meanings. In North America the contacts among ethnic groups and between these and Native North Americans have been less likely to create hybrid styles than to stimulate change within the music, in effect reaffirming identity at all costs. Even musical styles that several ethnic groups share (for example, the polka), retain ethnic markers that continue to identify substyles (for example, Slovenian or Dutchman-German—polka). It will be one of our tasks to discover how the music of ethnic North America has remained a whole with many parts.

Ethnicity itself is a concept and set of cultural practices spread over many parts of society. Understood from the perspectives of ethnomusicology, ethnicity links music to culture in a multivalent fashion. Music that is ethnic, therefore, reflects patterns of organization within the group and reveals the ways in which the group understands and maintains its identity. Because the overriding concerns for organization and identity are products of the New World, ethnic music itself becomes connected ever more to the group after it has immigrated to the New World. Ethnic music is, therefore, not simply music that clearly sounds French, Korean, or Ewe at a festival in Ottawa or in the clubs of Miami, but rather the music that particular groups of people have created to express their identity and experiences in North America.

Venues of Musical Practice in a Multiethnic Culture

Where does one go to experience music in a multiethnic culture? In what kinds of places does one hear ethnic music? Is ethnic music really folk music that has been relocated to another setting? These straightforward questions have rather complex answers that reveal important differences between the music of ethnic North America as we shall understand it and the usual concepts of folk music associated with a particular community and place. We might effectively understand how place and musical practice are linked by constructing a continuum and locating certain musical venues along it. This continuum exhibits extremes that, at one end, reflect musical practices removed from direct contact outside the community and, at the other, describe conditions of considerable contact with other ethnic traditions. The place of musical practice has a direct relationship to the different paths and speeds of change that accompany the transformation from immigrant to ethnic musical traditions.

At one extreme of our continuum, musical practice centers largely in the home and accompanies the activities of family life. In the home there is little pressure on traditions to change, and preservation occurs without conscious effort, at least in the initial generation or two after immigration. The venues for family musical practice frequently encompass several generations, hence making the family a place where old-country, immigrant, and ethnic musical traditions coexist. As contact outside the home develops, musical practice also takes place at a level occupied by religious, social, or even cultural organizations. Again, the retention of tradition is a priority, and we can observe that many organizations form explicitly to provide a venue for ethnic (including musical) traditions. The choruses of German and Scandinavian American communities in the Midwest, for example, maintain musical traditions that distinguish shared ethnicities, but that would probably disappear without the organization itself. It is a quality of these organizations that they overlap, undergirding ethnic culture. Religious organizations might maintain musical ensembles while relying on financial assistance from an ethnic fraternal lodge with connections to insurance and financial services.

Juxtaposition of musical practices is considerably more extensive at the level of the community than in the home or social organization. Whereas the organization is the product of individuals who come together because of similarities, the community depends on reconciling patterns of difference. The German American community of Cincinnati, for example, can count among its members those with Catholic and Protestant Christian, Conservative and Reformed Jewish religious heritages. The German community of Cincinnati would be incomplete without any one of these distinct parts. The German American musical activity of the city, in turn, has historically depended on these different groups and their willingness to support particular musical practices and the institutions that supported them. Strengthening the community might mean such forms of negotiation as the combination of musical activities by former residents from both sides of the common Polish-Ukrainian border, whose linguistic and musical differences are considerably fewer than those related by political and religious organizations. The ethnic community's musical identity, therefore, results from working out the differences the community's residents bring with them in their search for commonality.

Ethnic communities often bolster their sense of identity by engaging in activities with communities elsewhere in a city, region, or nation. German choral activities in North America, to take one example of extensive intercommunity organization, form around leagues or unions at each of these levels. Several dozen German choruses in Chicago share a common home, namely the DANK Haus (Deutsch-Amerikanischer National-Kongress) in a once predominantly Central European neighborhood on the city's North Side. These many choruses represent different regions and cultural areas of German-speaking Europe (e.g., Rhineland Germans or Burgenländer Austrians). The choruses maintain a variety of relations with other societies in the Midwest, and many are members of national organizations that periodically sponsor competitions and conventions.

Intercommunity contact has benefited considerably from the presence of the mass media as a stimulus to ethnic cultural activity. During the early centuries of settlement in North America, the print medium was the most powerful means of providing music to those at a great distance from a critical mass of fellow immigrants. The proliferation of ethnic hymnody throughout the nineteenth century and the ready availability of hymnbooks in Swedish, Danish, or Czech, for example, made it possible for those who were parishioners of ethnic churches to couple linguistic and musical literacy, and to do so through musical practices in the home (CD2, #25). Ethnic sound recordings in the twentieth century reached an extraordinary number of North American homes, keeping the sounds of Spanish, Arabic, and Ukrainian music alive and doing so affordably. Ethnic records continue to provide one of the most vivid means of documenting the musical styles and repertories shared by immigrants. At the beginning of the twenty-first century, ethnic radio and television have become significant media for broadcasting music and establishing a place for it in the ethnic community. In large cities many ethnic groups regard it as extremely important to their identity to support at least periodic programming in the mass media, thereby increasing the access of all to the sounds of ethnic music.

We now reach the other extreme of the continuum, at which ethnic musical activities stretch beyond the home, the organization, or the community, in fact to other ethnic communities. At this extreme we witness the ways in which diverse ethnic communities and musics reinforce the desire to retain and strengthen patterns of diversity. The folk festival, for example, offers a prime example of a multiethnic setting in which communities confront each other and emphasize their differences. It is important for us to realize that the growing importance of cultural activities that bring many communities together actually encumbers any tendency toward a melting pot. In order to participate in a folk festival or to contribute a performance to the series of ethnic Christmas shows at a civic museum, ethnic communities more commonly expand their musical repertories, engaging in both research and the reorganization of musical ensembles to create a performance convincing to those both inside and outside the ethnic community. The multiethnic cultural environment of North America, therefore, stimulates rather than stems the diversity of musical activity.

IDEAS ABOUT MUSIC

Preservation

Preservation, survival, isolation—all are concepts that have surrounded North American ideas about folk music. These are concepts that are laden with notions of what North Americans want their folk music to be. Preservation allows the best of the past to survive; it establishes links between the generations; it isolates the differences between one group and another. Preservation stems from the tendency to idealize the past and to valorize differences. Preservation has driven folk-music scholars to collect only those pieces that survive and prove that isolation has been good for a community. If a group preserves its music, it can also withstand the melting pot, the inevitable tendency to give in and capitulate to a different culture and homogeneous value system.

Preservation is an idea about music that we can find in every ethnic group in North America. It provides one of the ways for an ethnic group to define its cultural core and articulate those values it wants to survive. Preservation may, however, be more a reality in some groups than in others. The classic case of musical preservation in North America is the culture of the Amish. The Amish form a religious community that preserves not only language (dialects of German from western Germany and Switzerland) and folkways (e.g., shunning modern technology), but also musical practices that are unique to their areas of settlement, which are found largely in Pennsylvania and the states of the central Midwest.

Amish music, though largely in German, is only remotely comparable to other German American genres of traditional music. Preservation results because the Amish themselves have deemed it of special value. Particular settings, usually religious and communal, prescribe musical practice, hence associating the preservation of music with religious identity. Amish hymnody may well preserve a musical style and even repertory characteristic of German pietistic Protestantism in the sixteenth and seventeenth centuries, although there is no way of proving this, for the long, lugubrious chorale tunes performed by the Amish are not in written tradition, rather only in the oral traditions that form an important part of Sunday services in the home, where hymns from the Amish hymnbook, the *Ausbund*, are sung (see Fig. 11–1 and listen to CD 2, #25). Borrowing also takes place, but German folk and religious songs adapted by the Amish for more "secular" occasions also move toward a core of preservation, entering the so-called *Gesangbuch* ("Songbook").

Preservation takes a different form when embedded in ideas about African music in North America. With the Amish it was the totality of their special religious subculture that survived. With African Americans, musical elements have survived to give music a fundamental link to community. Preservation is inseparable from a system of values that music symbolizes and embodies. It is not surprising that the growing awareness of African musical elements in the music of African Americans accompanied an historical period in the mid-twentieth century when African Americans successfully resisted the hegemony of white cultural values and their political justification.

Remarkable as it may seem today, many scholars formerly insisted that the music and culture of African Americans derived from the European-dominated mainstream. Black spirituals, as some theories argued, derived from white hymn traditions; jazz depended on a store of white popular tunes and the harmonic structure that these provided as a basis for improvisation. The most forceful rebuttal of such aesthetic hegemony recognized and identified the ways in which African American music preserved musical elements that are essential to the structure of African musics, for example, call-and-response structures. As musicians and scholars recognized more and more genres that had maintained such elements from African music, it became possible to redress the cultural politics that privileged European musical and cultural transformation. Scholars increasingly understood African American musical styles as a receptacle that could preserve distinctive musical qualities while enabling these to transform other musics in North America and elsewhere in the world.

Ausbund,

Das ist :

Etliche schöne

Christliche

Lieder,

Wie sie in dem Ge-
fängnüß zu Passau in dem
Schloß von den Schweitzer=Brüdern,
und von anderen rechtgläubi-
gen Christen hin, und her
gedichtet worden.

Allen und jeden Christen
welcher Religion sie seyen, un-
partheyisch fast nützlich.

───────────────

Germantown:
Gedruckt bey **Christoph Saur** / 1742.

Figure 11–1   Title page of the first Amish songbook/hymnal (*Ausbund*) published in North America. *Publisher: Christopher Saur; published in Germantown, Pennsylvania, 1742.*

Maintaining the Generations: Oral Tradition and Ethnic History

If music can preserve and be preserved, it might also provide a link to the past. One of the most common ideas about music in ethnic North America is that it functions to recall another time and place: the old country in the age of our ancestors. Clearly, an earlier use of hyphens to separate one geographic location from another—Chinese-American, Ukrainian-Canadian—symbolized that link. Ethnicity is unquestionably a construct that endeavors to maintain the generations and that undergirds the history of an ethnic community. Many ideas about music depend on the importance placed on maintaining culture across the generations. Songs passed from generation to generation are valued not only because they reflect the integrity of the family but because they establish a claim for the tenacity of oral tradition. Even as groups revive ethnic musical traditions, they establish a place for these expressions of continuity, preferring to restore a truncated oral tradition rather than to perform what otherwise would seem like a frozen tradition of the past with no link to the present (Figs. 11–2 and 11–3).

Identity has been one of the unifying themes throughout this chapter. The many musics in the multiethnic panorama of North America almost inevitably become banners of ethnicity, ways of telling others that difference is a significant way of achieving identity. Music often exists as a practice that has unique forms within the group, whether it is because of the use of a language, or whether music functions in ways that would be relatively meaningless in other contexts. Music assumes a salient position along the boundaries separating us from them (Fig. 11–4).

Figure 11–2 Norwegian Emigrant Song, "The Emigrant to Ottawa." *Reproduced in:* Sven Schroder Amundsen and Reimund Kvideland, *Emigrant viser:* Oslo: Universitetsforlaget, 1975. Page 187.

O Susanne,

græd dog ej for mig!

Jeg gaar til Kalifornien og graver Guld til dig.

Ny Vise om den søde Susannes Lykke.

Figure 11–3   Title page for Danish emigrant song for America, "O Susanne," which has the California Gold rush as its topic. *Published by the Strandberg Press, the largest Danish broadside publisher, 1980–81.* (This song sold 50,000 copies in 1881. Reproduced in: Lisbeth Steenstrup Jensen and Søren Koustrup. *Udvandrersange*. Munksgaard: n.p., 1976.)

Different musical styles may function as boundaries to varying degrees. Even within related ethnic groups it is possible to observe rather different ways of maintaining boundaries. Among French ethnic groups in North America, for example, two distinct forms of musical boundary maintenance have developed. The boundaries that are most firmly entrenched are those of the Québecois, the French of Canada. Here, the distinctiveness of identity has assumed political proportions. The musical culture of the Québecois exhibits considerable centrality, resulting from the ways French Canadian music differs completely from that of other Canadians. Social dance, especially that which employs clogging, has great importance, thus allowing

Figure 11–4   Boro Roganović, player of the single-string, bowed fiddle gusle. A Montenegran American from Chicago, Roganović performs Serbian epics in ethnic communities of the Upper Midwest. *Photography by Randy Tunnell, used with permission of the photographer.*

folk music to exhibit a form of public communality. Preservation is extreme, and the instrumentarium of ensemble music has solidified around a core of fiddles, accordions, and harmonica, with special ethnic accent provided by spoons and jew's-harp.

In contrast, the music of the Cajuns—French-speaking residents of the American Gulf Coast, particularly the Bayou country of southern Lonisiana—have created distinctive musical boundaries by allowing them to admit change, by recognizing that musical style can filter influences from the outside and reformulate them as Cajun. Cajun music is no less distinctive than Québecois, but it has incorporated elements of musical style from surrounding non-French communities. The accordion of Cajun music, therefore, bears witness to German influences and lends itself to a style of social dance that is less refined than French Canadian social dance, taking place instead in public halls and being shared by the entire community. Cajun music absorbs the music of the cultures outside the community's boundaries, whereas the performers of Québecois music use it to differentiate with an inviolable uniqueness (CD 2, #29).

Regionalism

Regionalism has long shaped North American ideas about music. People living within a region or those outside often speak with assurance of the musical styles and repertories that belong to the Canadian Maritime Provinces or the American South. Even within regions distinctions develop and persist, for example, in the Midwest, where the Upper Midwest has its own musical traditions. Musical regionalism grows for a number of different reasons which often interact. Shaping each region are the patterns of immigration and settlement specific to it. The American Midwest, settled largely from the mid- to late-nineteenth century, has a significantly larger number of the Central and Northern European ethnic groups than the Southwest, where Hispanic communities predominate in many areas. The music of the Midwest reflects the influences of German and Scandinavian traditions, whereas the Southwest has a wide range of Mexican traditions.

Regionalism is not an idea about music that depends on isolation or preservation. Regional music styles form after musical contact between the different groups. The repertories that we recognize as characterizing the American South, for example, show that European communities have long interacted with African Americans, and the coexistence of African American and European American musical traits is evident in a wide range of genres. It is probably impossible to find any form of Southern music in which the centuries-long presence of African Americans does not assert itself in identifiable musical traits.

There are regional styles that develop largely from contact between ethnic groups settling in the region. The American polka, for example, developed in regions where large communities of Central European and Eastern European immigrants settled, forming what is often referred to as the "polka belt," which stretches from New Ulm, Minnesota, to Buffalo, New York. CD 2, #31 illustrates the polka sound, called conjunto, along the Texas-Mexico border. The polka itself is an amalgam of Germanic and Slavic folk-music elements, and contact across boundaries in Europe is often easy to identify—for example, in German-Czech and Austrian-Slovenian styles. Interethnic contact became more prevalent in the American Midwest, especially in large industrial cities like Cleveland and Chicago. Polka was, therefore, ideally suited to the contact between ethnic groups that the Midwest and its economic and settlement patterns occasioned.

Ethnic Music and "Truly American" Music

Although ethnic music would seem to resist association with ideas about music that lay claim to "truly American" music, there have been attempts to associate ethnic music with more sweeping Americanness. At one level, this results from a belief in representativeness. During the folk-music revival of the 1950s and 1960s, many enthusiasts believed that a common lode of American folk music was located in the Southern mountains. This music was rural and presumably had its origins in the British Isles before being relocated to the isolated areas of the South. Certain types of ballads received privileged treatment, and the revivalists often plumbed the Southern repertories for evidence of protest and class conflict (CD 2, #30). The musical instruments associated with Southern folk music, especially the guitar and the banjo, received most-favored status, and these, too, quickly became symbolic of an American folk-music instrumentarium. What is interesting for our examination of music in ethnic North America is not whether the revivalists were right or wrong about the representativeness of Appalachian folk music. From our ethnomusicological viewpoint, we recognize that there is a certain motivation at work, that is, the urge to find a musical voice for the entire nation.

The contributions of African American music to more comprehensive American ideas about music are especially notable. Not only do we hear African American musical traits in many styles and genres no longer specific to African American culture—the best-known example being rock and roll—but an aura of Americanness surrounds certain musical styles that have remained rooted in African American music culture. The notion that jazz is the "true classical music" of North America is another—and perhaps the most widespread—reflection of the way in which ideas about music establish links between the particular and the general, between the music of one group and that of the entire continent. The classicization of jazz is even more remarkable, for it suggests that music in the intensely ethnic matrix of North America can subvert some cultural values. Jazz has, therefore, succeeded in forging a position for African Americans in the larger society that centuries of social struggle could not completely bring about, Ethnicity, with its problematic questions of difference and identity, nonetheless plays an indispensable role in determining the most far-reaching yet culturally central ideas about music.

Figure 11–5   Scott Joplin. *New York Public Library at Lincoln Center.*

MUSICAL INSTRUMENTS

North America's Store of Musical Instruments

A secondhand store just about anywhere in North America provides a fine place to introduce the musical instruments of the continent. Not that we shall find every kind of musical instrument here, but we can observe the care with which instruments are preserved, passed on to another generation, and transformed into artifacts and icons. The secondhand store reveals something of the way North Americans think about musical instruments, that is, the way they classify instruments according to function and social value and the way they willingly jumble instruments together to create new ensembles and new sound mixes. Not every secondhand store yields the same instruments. More guitars are found in the Southwest, concertinas in the Upper Midwest, and Ukrainian banduras in Manitoba. It is because the secondhand store's collection reflects the ethnicity and musical styles of its region that we can turn to it to learn about the musical instruments of ethnic North America. For our purposes, let's visit a store in central Kansas, seeing what it can tell us about the musical instruments from the center of the United States.

The section devoted to musical instruments in the secondhand store quickly makes it clear that instruments are regarded with pride and that they acquire a value that makes it important to pass them from generation to generation. As we look at the instruments, we notice that just about every conceivable type is found. A baby grand piano painted a smeary white stands in one corner; a sign on its lid proclaims that it was the house instrument of a local "ballroom," at which jazz and polka bands played five nights a week for forty years. Some brass and woodwind instruments sprawl across a big table, and the clerk tells us that these have accumulated over the years. They have been traded to the store by several generations of musicians from the high-school band, the fireman's marching ensemble, and the band of the Swedish Lutheran Church. For someone who wants a cheap saxophone and can repair the pads and joints, this is the place to get a deal.

The clerk, knowing that we are in the area to learn about ethnic music, pulls us over to a wall of violins. "You might be interested to know that this area was well known for its Swedish fiddlers," the clerk tells us. "These fiddles belonged to a family group that toured throughout central and eastern Kansas." There are other fiddles, too, most without the fine, laminated maple work of the Swedish fiddles, some obviously homemade. "The Russian-Germans used fiddles a lot," offers the clerk, "but never with the virtuosity of the Swedes. You'll see that their violins aren't as fancy. Still, did you know that they all came from Austria, where they really know how to make violins? If you want German instruments, let me suggest that you look at the accordions and buttonboxes on that table over there!" On "that table over there" we encounter a completely different concept of musical ensemble: accordions of every shape, tuning, and extent of mother-of-pearl inlay. Accordion heaven! Were there so many accordion players here in central Kansas? Anticipating our query, the clerk notes, "There used to be a German music store in town, and the owner was nuts about accordions. Always said the accordion was one of Germany's gifts to the world. Once, a German company sent one of its touring groups over, the sort that stopped with demo records and a trunk full of instruments at every little town. Well, this storeowner, he bought one of those trunks, and you're looking at about half of it right now."

Pride of place goes to the wall whose occupants are identified with a sign announcing "jazz instruments." This part of central Kansas was on a circuit for bands coming from Kansas City and other cities of the old "Southwest," a cauldron for the development of swing during the 1930s and 1940s. The Bennie Moten band and the Count Basie Orchestra played fairly often in this part of Kansas, pulling into town in big touring cars and leaving before the night was over. A little note taped to one tenor saxophone says "played by Lester Young," and the store clerk is very proud. Whether or not Lester Young, one of the greatest of all Kansas City tenor-sax players from the Swing Era, ever did play this horn seems less relevant than the aura now surrounding these instruments. They establish a musical link to another time and place, a musical culture that is difficult to imagine today. They may seem out of place, witnessing the vitality and social conditions of an ethnic group not likely to have much to do with the Swedish Lutheran band or the German accordion fanatic. And yet all of these instruments do belong to this store and its particular place in North America (Fig. 11–6).

Musical Instruments in a Multiethnic Culture

The secondhand store is a metaphor for concepts of musical instruments in North America. At first glance it seems like a hodgepodge, instruments discarded and assembled only in random fashion. The more time we spent with the instruments, however, the more that hodgepodge exhibits patterns that are themselves the products of the regional, socioeconomic, and ethnic history of the town in which the store was located. Juxtaposition has occurred, but it nonetheless belongs to the multiethnic community in which the store is located. It is, moreover, the juxtaposition itself that is such a persuasive metaphor for the multiethnic culture of North America.

Instruments in many ensembles result from conditions not unlike those we found in the secondhand store. The old and the new mix, establishing links with both tradition and modernity. Instruments have many functions, depending on how they are used and who uses them. A fiddle may be Swedish, Cajun, German, or Appalachian. An accordion might have specific ethnic associations, or it might belong to a popular mainstream in which ethnic distinctions have disappeared. Function plays a fundamental role in determining just what music can be adapted to particular instruments and ensembles (Fig. 11–4). The instruments in the secondhand store show that exchange is common, if not normative, in the multiethnic culture. An

Figure 11–6 Broadside of a popular emigrant's song from the fin-de-siècle Vienna stage, "Mondlied," from Bruno Zappert's *A Bohemian in America. Graphic collection, Deutsches Volksliedarchiv, Freiburg i. Br., Germany.*

instrument may begin its life in North America as an artifact from the old country, only to cross ethnic boundaries to perform an entirely new repertory. Repertories and styles similarly participate in exchange. Instruments may themselves undergo transformation. Musicians who attempt to authenticate Norwegian musical traditions in North America use the hardingfele as a symbol of Norwegianness. The "Hardanger fiddle," actually a relatively new addition to the Norwegian folk music, is a violin to which special resonating strings have been added.

The store suggests ways in which ensembles form in ethnic North America. On one hand, the distinctiveness of an ensemble remains, perhaps because of the Swedish Lutheran church band or the big-band jazz collection. On the other hand, the store blurs the boundaries. The accordions might seem to belong to a tradition of

Dutchman polka bands, but there is no reason that they cannot cross the boundary to Slovenian or Polish groups. Musicians are likely to base their purchasing decision on the sound, the construction, or the reputation of the manufacturer. Assembled in the store, the instruments are but stages in the history of ethnic ensembles. Their past is linked to their future by the transformation that their sojourn in the second-hand store symbolizes.

The Fiddle and the Banjo

Few instruments are as ubiquitous in North American ethnic communities as the fiddle. Wide distribution notwithstanding, the fiddle is one of the most malleable instruments in ethnic music. Not only can it be a part of broadly different ensembles, but it can adopt the sound of just about any ensemble, whether it be a small group playing in a Lebanese club in Montreal or the fiddle-and-guitar duo accompanying folk dance in rural New Mexico. We might wonder whether this extreme adaptability is a possible explanation for the currency of the term "fiddle," as if to distinguish its many ethnic varieties from the stalwart violin of Western art music. Its

Figure 11–7   Louis Armstrong's Hot Five, Chicago, 1925 (**from left to right**): Armstrong, Johnny St. Cyr, Johnny Dodds, Kid Ory, Lil Hardin *Archive Photos, Frank Driggo collection.*

name and its functions underscore its familiarity; the fiddle is never a foreigner in ethnic musical styles.

Although the fiddle is adaptable, the ways in which it enters ethnic musical traditions and comes to function in them are quite distinctive. For some groups ethnicity seems almost to coalesce around the fiddle. The hardingfele is the most pronounced symbol of Norwegian American music, much as painted wood handicrafts occupy a position of extreme Norwegianness in the material culture of American folklore. In the revival of klezmer bands in Jewish American culture, the fiddle also becomes the most Jewish of all the instruments. This is because of a long tradition of associating the violin with musical specialists in Eastern European Jewish society. In Cajun music, too, it is the fiddle that verifies the link with French Canadian music, whereas other instruments bespeak the influences from outside the French-speaking community in Louisiana.

From its twentieth-century contexts one would hardly suspect that the banjo came to North America with the Africans brought as slaves. The banjo now has almost no place among African American musical traditions. It is an instrument that has largely been abandoned by one ethnic group to be adopted by others. During its peregrinations it has become an entirely new instrument, with new styles, repertories, and functions. It has crossed back and forth between genres, and it has enjoyed popularity in every sector of North America's musical life. Its ethnic qualities derive from its remarkable adaptability, but also from its ability to ascribe a range of ethnic meanings to specific musical styles (Pete Seeger's use of the banjo in CD 2, #30).

An instrument characterized generally by the tight skin or plastic stretched over the circular frame of a long-necked lute, the North American banjo probably had its origins in West Africa. Accounts of slave musicians from the seventeenth century describe instruments that are likely ancestors of the banjo. A variety of early names existed—banjar, bandore, banza—enabling historians to document the banjo as an instrument accompanying African American dance. In African American slave society and in the South after the Civil War, the banjo largely served rural forms of music; to the extent that it has survived in African American communities into the twentieth century, it has retained its association with folk music.

Ironically, it was because the banjo was such a powerful icon of African American music that it crossed ethnic boundaries into white musical genres. During the 1840s and 1850s the banjo rapidly achieved enormous popularity in the urban North, largely because minstrels—white musicians smearing their faces with blackened cork and performing a repertory of popular songs that used parodies of black musical styles—incorporated the banjo into their ensembles, where it became the stereotypic minstrel instrument. In white society, the banjo first enjoyed success in urban areas, entering parlor music in the years following the Civil War. It became an instrument of the rural South again, this time a favored instrument of rural whites. By the 1920s the banjo was crossing yet another boundary into the urbanized styles of Dixieland jazz and early country music. Jazz largely dropped the banjo when new styles developed in Chicago and New York. As country music and bluegrass proliferated, the banjo again moved toward the core of an almost entirely white music. Pete Seeger exploited rural connections again, touting the banjo during the folk-song revival of the 1950s and 1960s.

The banjo is an instrument that has demonstrated an ability to belong to many ethnic groups and many styles of ethnic music. We might conclude, then, that the banjo played a role in ascribing ethnicity, in serving as a conscious symbol of some sort of association with another group's differences. We might also conclude that the banjo came to fulfill the need of musicians to represent difference and ethnic diversity. In so doing, the banjo also responded to a fundamental quality of the music of ethnic North America.

SOCIAL STRUCTURE/MUSICAL STRUCTURE

In what ways is the music of an ethnic community a reflection of the distinctiveness of that community? Does Filipino American music sound Filipino American? There is no question that it sounds different from Korean American music, but what distinguishes it as characteristic of the Filipino community in North America? How extensively do social structure and musical structure in ethnic North America reflect each other?

This section investigates a number of ways that social structure determines aspects of musical structure. It will be apparent that there are rarely simple correspondences between these aspects of structure. Far more often, we encounter mediating structures. For example, religion determines institutions and practices that, in turn, play a role in creating distinctive musical styles and repertories. The confrontation with modernity, clearly necessitating change in social structure, also produces change in musical structure, rendering some forms more powerful and sweeping in their negotiation between past and present. By no means are social and musical structures really parallel. They do, however, influence each other in ways that help us distinguish how music expresses the multiethnic culture of North America.

Music and Religious Community

Religious communities have consistently fostered ethnically distinct musics. North American religious history is largely a chronicle of differences sanctioned both by political policies that made religion a matter of individual preference and by the relation between ethnic and religious ideals. New immigrants frequently seek out coreligionists in order to move into a community where others already share their beliefs. The music of an ethnic religious community is highly codified. The church, synagogue, or mosque already provides both texts and contexts for music making that clearly delineates the community. Music accompanies the performance of standard religious texts and rituals. Liturgies embody both music and the language of

Figure 11–8   New Orleans funeral procession. *Sydney Byrd.*

religion, wedding them in a metalanguage that the community not only shares but performs. Religion also determines a distinctive musical repertory. Ethnic religious repertories are necessary for celebrating rites of passage, holidays, and normal social gatherings. Religion reinforces ethnicity while becoming itself the beneficiary of the particularizing force of music.

In many communities religious ethnic music predominates, replacing secular forms. This has been the case in many rural Midwestern communities with Protestant German and Scandinavian ethnic groups. The particularity of religious denomination was so extreme in the nineteenth and early twentieth centuries (and, in some cases, at the beginning of the twenty-first century) that Norwegians, Swedes, Danes, and Germans formed separate denominations of Lutheranism. Each group formulated its own religious and musical languages, which articulated its own doctrines and then began to function within local organizations.

Larger religions may also subsume a great number of diverse ethnic communities. Muslims in a large North American city may come from musical backgrounds ranging from North Africa to southeastern Europe to the Middle East to India and Indonesia. Black Muslims, too, exert an important presence in urban North America, contributing yet another musical language to the larger Islamic community. At one level, the musical life of each Muslim ethnic group remains distinctive. However, at another, each group reckons with the central musical influence of the Koran and the recitation of prayers. Widely divergent communities share certain paraliturgical genres and forms of popular song. Where do we find the musical life of a Bosnian American community or of Rajasthanis in Toronto? How do we interpret the nasal quality of Nigerian American popular genres, which distinguishes immigrants as Hausa, therefore more likely Muslim? Which is the more important distinction— Hausa, Muslim, Nigerian, or African American? Religion plays a direct if extremely complicated role in the creation and perpetuation of musical style. Unraveling that role is not always easy, but investigating ethnic musical style without also examining the impact of religion is impossible.

Mass-Mediated Ethnicity

Polka has become big business. A successful polka musician can earn fame and fortune, even a Grammy Award, for a record that has topped the polka charts for a long period. Polka clubs go on European tours and enjoy videos of their idols. Polka is not far from earshot during the commercial breaks of ethnic radio and TV shows. Polka has become an ethnic music for all North Americans. Just why has polka come to occupy this central position among ethnic musics? Polka has a long history of remarkable musical and social adaptability. In many ways, these two forms of adaptability have enjoyed a reflexive relation, making it possible for polka to expand stylistically just as it expands into new ethnic and regional marketplaces.

Polka in North America has largely developed in the industrialized North, especially in those regions of the Midwest and Middle Atlantic states in which large numbers of immigrants from Central and Eastern Europe settled. It is also a popular instrumental and dance form in smaller pockets where settlers from these areas established communities, for example, among the Czech and German towns of Texas's hill country. Polka's adaptability and malleability have even enabled it to cross unexpected ethnic borders, for example, from the folk-dance styles of Austrian settlers in Mexico to the "chicken scratch" music of Native Americans of the American Southwest (e.g., the conjunto style in CD 2, #31 is a Tex-Mex polka relative). Polka has a long history in North America, occupying a place with other forms of genteel social dance by the mid-nineteenth century. The polka came to be widespread in North America, as it had found its way into the repertories of national folk musics at some distance from its presumed nation of origin, the Czech Republic.

With mass immigration from Europe during the period from about 1880 until World War I, polka's European forms flooded the North American scene. Although polka was widespread among these rapidly growing ethnic communities, it nonetheless took forms related to the specific music of each group, for example its instruments. Czech Americans employed a rather full brass component, and German American (or Dutchman) bands settled heavily on the bass line with a blatty tuba. The Polish American ensemble used piano accordions, while the button box variety dominated the Slovenian American sound. The polka as genre remained intact, while more and more individual forms of expression proliferated within the genre. An example is Frankie Yankovich's introduction of the banjo into Cleveland's Slovenian style (cf. the two bands in Figs. 11–9 and 11–10).

Figure 11–9 Photograph of the "Kurtz Orchestra," an ensemble performing salon music in the Burgenland American communities of eastern Pennsylvania in the 1920s and 1930s. The "first-generation" Austrian American orchestra was the predecessor of the polka band of the early twenty-first century. *Photograph courtesy of Rudolf Pietsch, Vienna.*

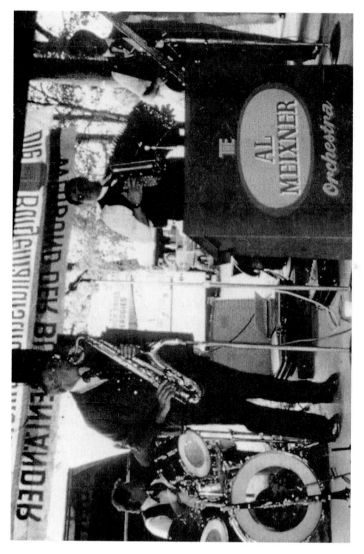

Figure 11–10   The Al Meixner Orchestra plays at a picnic of the Lehigh County, Pennsylvania, Burgenländische Gemeinschaft, an Austrian American social club, in 1986. Trained in the traditions of the Duquesne University of Tamburitzans, the band leader, Al Meixner (buttonbox), plays ethnic music professionally at EPCOT Center in Orlando, Florida. *Photograph courtesy of Rudolf Pietsch, Vienna.*

The polka illustrates a number of processes of change that musical style can engender. It tends toward popularity, transforming local traits in folk music to a broader appeal of music that thrives because of the mass media. Polka juxtaposes aspects of both unity and diversity in ethnic music. It lends itself to the commodification of style, yielding a product that all North Americans can enjoy. Polka has long been a component of ethnic social gatherings, providing an opportunity to assert ethnicity. Musical structure and social structure enjoy an unusually close relation in the polka. Both remain resilient against the challenges to ethnicity, yet they combine to reflect the changing needs of ethnic North America.

THE MUSIC OF AN AFRICAN AMERICAN COMMUNITY

With this section we make a special excursion into the music of a single, extraordinarily complex community: the African American, particularly in the city of Chicago. In many ways, this section deserves to be a chapter of its own, indeed an entire book. By treating it as a case study within the framework of a chapter on ethnic North America, I do not mean to detract from the larger importance of the music of African Americans. Quite the contrary, I intend to underscore that importance by claiming on one hand, that African American musical traditions have a remarkable history and coherence that derives from the integrity and strength of an ethnic community during three-and-a-half centuries of extraordinarily difficult, often abhorrent social conditions. On the other, the importance of African American musical traditions is not separable from the enormous influence they have had on the musics of ethnic North America as a whole. It would be impossible to write a chapter on the music of this cultural area without emphasizing the music of African Americans—without, in fact, recognizing that African Americans have contributed to the diversity of musics in North America far more extensively and profoundly than any other group.

I shall not pretend in this section to do justice to the enormousness of the special role of African Americans in the music of ethnic North America. Rather I wish to turn our attention to African American music in a single city, Chicago, whose complex ethnic makeup and vital African American musical life are broadly paradigmatic for this chapter. We can understand Chicago as a microcosm for many of the ideas and musics that we find throughout North America. Chicago has earned the reputation of being a very "ethnic" city, whose cultural geography refuses to yield to a melting pot. The city is a complex of neighborhoods, each with a name and an identifiable ethnic history. Neighborhoods were originally the product of vast city planning in the wake of the Chicago Fire of 1871, which devastated much of the city. The rebuilt, gridlike neighborhoods at the end of the nineteenth century quickly became home to the massive influx of immigrants in the period of rapid industrialization prior to World War I. Each neighborhood has its own ethnic history—for instance, Andersonville, once Swedish, is now Korean, Chinese, and Assyrian. The ethnic complexion of each neighborhood is a commonly understood fact of cultural life in Chicago.

The history of Chicago's African American community has been one of neighborhoods and interaction with other ethnic groups. The influx of African Americans from the South accompanied the rapid industrialization of the city, especially before and after World War I. The rural poor of the South saw in the expanding city a land of occupational opportunity, and they flooded into the city in search of jobs. The first major African American settlement of Chicago was comparable in many ways to that of the European-Americans, that is, as the goal of immigration. African Americans recognized in the grid of urban neighborhoods the chance of building a community that was distinctive, yet no more or less exceptional in the urban landscape than that of other immigrant groups. There is no need here to review the many reasons that the egalitarian grid of neighborhoods was often more exclusive than inclusive for African Americans; the long history of racial prejudice in the United States made Chicago's ethnicity as much an enemy as a friend for African Americans.

The history of settlement in Chicago also channeled some extraordinary streams into the larger music history of African Americans. Rural migrants brought with them rural musical styles: spirituals, Mississippi Delta blues, and folk-music repertories. Those who came from southern cities also brought distinctive musical styles with them: Dixieland jazz, ragtime, and gospel traditions from Nashville or Birmingham. The city was a catalyst and a cauldron, a center for the juxtaposition of styles, the mixing of repertories, and the transformation of musical life. The changes that African American musics underwent in Chicago are therefore similar in many ways to those we have observed throughout the multiethnic culture of North America. During the first half of the twentieth century the music of African Americans in Chicago thrived because of its adaptability to new social conditions and musical influences. The several musical styles at which we look in this section, then, are no less African American because of these changes, but they owe much of their distinctiveness to the community's history in Chicago.

Religious Music

The boulevards and avenues of Chicago's South and West Sides are lined with storefront churches. Some of these are indeed converted stores; others are conversions of a different type, that is, from a church that was formerly mainstream (e.g., Methodist) to a religious center that more directly speaks to the African American religious experience by adopting the name of a religious figure like St. Charles Lwanga. Each structure, large or small, immediately bears witness to an extraordinary exuberance of religious expression that is personal, yet rooted in public performance. The exuberance is evident in the many ways the building itself has been refashioned. Signs full of information about worship services, Sunday school, and choir rehearsals quickly reveal that there is almost no time in the week when the church is not the site of some kind of religious and musical activity. The signs prose-lytize, they aim to attract anyone into the community of performance and belief, yet they clearly reflect the depth of belief that binds the community together. Each church among the thousands in these African American neighborhoods has been a venue for religious musical practice.

It would be impossible to identify a single style or core repertory in this musi-cal practice. That English Protestant hymnody has long contributed a store of musi-cal texts is obvious; that African musical performance practice has molded these in distinctive ways is even more obvious. Rather than strict performances from a hym-nal, those in the storefront church are spontaneous and improvisatory. The structure of the new version of each hymn—obviously indebted to the spiritual tradition—has taken a Biblical verse and rendered it with the flexibility that call-and-response encourages. Rather than a sedate organ or piano accompaniment, the ensemble backing up congregational singing in the storefront church looks more like a small jazz band: guitar, drums, bass, and trumpet. It also sounds more like a small jazz band.

A fixed liturgy seems completely absent. The choir and, for that matter, individu-als in the congregation have full license to sing when they wish, when the spirit moves them to sing. Certain individuals do exhibit authority, thereby assuming the role of leaders. The minister or the choir director, for example, may spontaneously break into song. Even the band members can seize the moment when they feel the spirit moving. The music is also performed in ways that obviously have special meaning to the con-gregation. Each individual has the right to feel the presence of God so deeply that she or he can move from singing and dancing into trance; the rest of the congregation sup-ports this by suspending musical performance so that the feeling of spirit from the trance can engulf the community as much as possible. In all respects, the music moves through the personal acts of performance toward the core of the community, express-ing the African Americanness of its ideas about both music and Christianity.

The Chicago Blues

The migration of the blues from the Mississippi Delta to Chicago was one of the most powerful metaphors for the African American experience in the twentieth cen-tury. The blues is a music of resistance—against racism and the degradation of poverty. Scholars such as Houston A. Baker, Jr., have argued that the blues has coa-lesced as a canon—a core of ideas and forms of expression—for African American culture and the aesthetic representation of that culture. There are many theories about how the blues has come to exert such a powerful presence in African Ameri-can culture, most of which recognize the importance of the poetic and musical form and its adaptability. This combination of adaptability and particularity has appeared as a common theme in this chapter, and perhaps there is no better example of this theme than the blues. Take a moment to familiarize yourself with these in CD 2, #32, "Blind Lemon's Penitentiary Blues."

The structure of the blues depends on aspects of both text and musical form. The text consists usually of three lines that assume an AAB structure. The first and second lines generally create a sort of question or establish a situation in need of solution, which the third line then revolves, hence always giving the three-line verse a dynamic quality. The following verses, the first and last two from a classic early Chicago blues piece, Blind Lemon Jefferson's "Long Lonesome Blues," show these aspects of poetic construction:

> I walked from Dallas, I walked from Wichita Falls,
> I walked from Dallas, I walked from Wichita Falls,
> After I lost my sugar, that was no walk at all.
>
> Woman see you comin' man, go get the rocker chair,
> Woman see you comin', go get the rocker chair,
> I want to fool this man and make out he's welcome here.
>
> Tell me what's the matter that I can't get no mail,
> Won't you tell me what's the matter, papa Lemon can't get no mail,
> I was sad last night 'cause a black cat crossed your trail.
>
> I got up this mornin', these blues all 'round my bed,
> I got up this mornin', these blues all 'round my bed,
> Couldn't eat my breakfast and there's blues all in my bread.
>
> **Blind Lemon Jefferson: "Long Lonesome Blues."**
> **Transcribed in Jeff Todd Titon,**
> *Early Downhome Blues* **(Urbana: University of Illinois Press, 1977).**

Musically, the blues also takes advantage of the tension between the first and last lines, which the second line mediates. The most common harmonic pattern of the blues

(A)   I—I—I—I
(A)   IV—IV—I—I
(B)   V—IV—I—I

shows a first line with harmonic stasis, followed by a second line, in which the stable feeling of the first line is disturbed by movement in the harmony. The harmony of the third line destabilizes the verse further by beginning with the tension of new harmonic relationships, which, however, the final part of the line then resolves. These points of tension and stability are often—but not always—stretched over the three lines in twelve measures, or "bars," hence the name "twelve-bar blues." Structure of any kind in the blues, however, is only the basis for variation and improvisation during performance, and again we witness the importance of individuality and performance context in expressing the essential African Americanness of the genre. Listen again to "Blind Lemon's Penitentiary Blues" and find the points of tension and stability.

The blues in present-day Chicago also embodies a number of tensions in the African American experience. We can go to two parts of the city to visit blues clubs: the traditional, urban blues bars on the poor, black South Side and the affluent, upscale clubs on the largely white North Side. The blues experiences in these two parts of the city are worlds apart. On the South Side, the blues seem more at home. The musicians and the audiences identify directly with the meaning of the music; social structure and musical structure are reflexive. On the North Side, audiences are largely white, even though most of the blues bands are still black. But here the gulf between the African American experience and the audience is vast. The music is different here: more polished, conceived for entertainment rather than listening. We see in both settings for the blues that the central themes and the basic forms retain their intimate association with the African American community. The blues continues to embrace both the tragedy and the integrity of the community's history in ethnic North America.

The Art Music of African Americans

African American composers of art music have engaged in a long struggle to achieve appropriate recognition. There are many reasons to explain why recognition has not been forthcoming. First, the composers of art music have been no less the victims of prejudice and oppression than other African Americans. Second, these composers have by and large written with a very distinctive voice, which, however grounded in American art music, too often remains foreign to the institutions and audiences of that music. Third, even scholars and critics trying to write favorably about music in the lives of African Americans have frequently tended to ghettoize when making claims for the many ways in which distinctive black musical voices arise from the blues, gospel, and other vernacular traditions. We must ask ourselves, then, why should the art music of African Americans be any different from that of any other community?

Asking just this question and providing increasingly convincing answers is the Center for Black Music Research, based at Columbia College on Chicago's most fashionable street, Michigan Avenue. It is a fundamental tenet of the Center and its director emeritus, Samuel A. Floyd, Jr., that African American music must be viewed in relation to a historical mainstream, whose traditions it participated in forming. This tenet radically redresses many prevailing ways of understanding black music in North America, certainly also the notion of ethnicity that underlies this chapter. There is probably no stronger body of evidence supporting this attempt to relocate the music of African American composers than the music they created. Accordingly, it is of central importance to the Center for Black Music Research to bring as much of this music to performance as possible and to expand the canon even further by recording it.

Just what type of musical voice did African American composers in Chicago really seek? If we ask this question of the distinguished female composer Florence Price (1888-1953), we find considerable support for the form of redress advanced by the Center for Black Music Research, Born in Arkansas, Florence Price studied at the New England Conservatory and moved to Chicago after several years of teaching in both Arkansas and the East. She composed in many different forms and for numerous ensembles, winning prizes and performances with major orchestras. Her compositions that were best known during her lifetime were those that either set spirituals for voice or drew upon African American literature such as works by Langston Hughes. It was uncharacteristic of her writing simply to incorporate spiritual or folk melodies into her compositions. She sought to find ways that her personal idiom might combine numerous aspects of the American musical heritage. Florence Price's voice did fall silent after her death, but it has been discovered again. In its discovery we also recognize that there were many other African American composers who deserve our attention, for example, William Grant Still and William Dawson.

Chicago Jazz

Chicago jazz is really many different styles, repertories, and moments in the history of jazz. More than anything, it is perhaps cultural geography that has defined jazz in the city. Chicago became important in the history of jazz, first, because it was a momentary mecca for migrating musicians and, second, because the city itself provided the backdrop for the clubs and neighborhoods necessary for the support of jazz. Chicago jazz, perhaps more than the other musics I have discussed in this section, has formed from complex ethnic interaction, with white musicians apprenticing with and learning from African American musicians.

Jazz lives today in Chicago with an aura of history surrounding it. It is in fact not the case today that jazz is a vital part of the African American community. True, its influences are heard in other African American styles, and some of the city's preeminent ensembles—for example, the Art Ensemble of Chicago—are important symbols of the presence of jazz in the African American history of the city. Moreover, one can hear outstanding jazz at clubs and bars, not to mention colleges and universities. There is a summer Chicago Jazz Festival, and there is no shortage of jazz airtime on the radio.

What one does not find is that jazz lives in the neighborhoods. Active jazz clubs are found downtown or on the Near North Side, intermingled with the blues clubs. Jazz is harder to find on the South Side or in the Austin neighborhood on the West

Side, once home to the so-called "Austin High Gang," whose members formed several of the most important jazz bands of the 1920s and 1930s, such as the Wolverines. Chicago jazz has historically provided non-African Americans the opportunity to participate in the vital vernacular traditions of African American music, thus giving it an important cultural function in an urban environment marked by ethnic differences. It is hardly surprising that history has transformed Chicago jazz into so many different things (Fig. 11–11).

Music Festivals in Chicago

Summer is a season of festivals in Chicago. The neighborhoods stage countless festivals in their parks and common squares. The city supports a series of festivals, beginning in May and concluding by early October. In one way or another, virtually all of these festivals are ethnic. There is no more common way to highlight the role of ethnicity in a festival than to use music. The city's major festivals are also explicitly music festivals, and each of these bears witness to some aspect of Chicago's African

Figure 11–11   Jazz singer Betty Carter performing in Carnegie Hall. *Jack Vartoogian.*

American music history. The festival season begins with the Blues Festival, moving on to the Gospel Festival and, on Labor Day weekend, the Jazz Festival. The festivals became immensely successful in the 1980s, each one drawing hundreds of thousands of listeners. The neighborhood festivals, too, are successful, although measuring success has less to do with adding up the spectators in a crowd than with assessing the relation between the festival and the community.

The large festivals are not so very different in general organization from the Pittsburgh Folk Festival. Each group has a specific time allotment for its performance. Music continues almost nonstop during the festival, and thus it behooves a performing group to make its show as interesting as possible. To do otherwise is to risk losing an invitation to next year's festival. Although the music and musicians of the major festivals are largely African American, the crowds are not. There is no single profile for the crowds, but it is clear that they are at best distantly related to the blues fans or storefront parishioners on the South Side of Chicago. And why should they be? This music—a professional gospel quartet from Philadelphia or a zydeco band from Louisiana (considered blues for the festival)—is very different from that which they hear in their neighborhoods or from that which serves to move them in their quest for God. The festivals try to include Chicago musicians whenever possible, but that means that they have to fit in, one way or another.

The neighborhood festival provides a stage for a different African American musical experience in Chicago. The festival is fluid, utilizing the cultural geography of the neighborhood as much as possible. Whoever takes the responsibility for organizing the festival also has a responsibility to ensure that it includes as many people as possible. As far as the music is concerned, this means recognizing the fundamental performance nature of many African American musics. The "performers" are not just those on a stage, but the community members who might want to dance or play a blues harp (harmonica) with a band playing at the end of a blocked-off street. No musician is much concerned about her or his "show," for there is not much to be gained financially and invitations for next year are as forthcoming as one's willingness to play for the community.

Chicago's festivals remind us of the complex presence of boundaries in the musics of African American culture. Some boundaries exist within the community; some form between the community and other ethnic groups. As always, these boundaries bear witness to the omnipresence of change. We cannot facilely say that the music at the annual Chicago Blues Festival is any less African American than that of an ad-hoc block party on the South Side. Nor can we say that one is more or less the product of Chicago and the ways African American musicians have fundamentally shaped and reshaped their musical life for over a century. African American music is intimately tied to each of these festivals and the experiences they represent. African American music is no loss intimately tied to the whole of musical experiences in ethnic North America.

ETHNIC MUSIC AND THE GLOBALIZATION OF AMERICAN POPULAR MUSIC

The World Music Festival

At the turn of the twenty-first century, ethnic music in North America was in the midst of another one of the sea changes that have repeatedly characterized its history: Ethnic music has joined forces with other world musics to produce a new global popular music. Throughout this chapter we have been watching the sea change take shape. Polka spread across North America, picking up new sounds, instruments, and generations of dancers. Irish folk music came to attract universal attention by joining forces with other European ethnic musics and igniting an explosion of Celtic musics. Jewish klezmer music developed its characteristic sound in post–World War II North America, and then it was exported to the world as a nostalgic ethnic music capable of rescuing elements of a lost and destroyed world. Claims that jazz is America's classical music fuel further claims that jazz can be exported to just about any country in the world wanting to mold its own jazz tradition. If ethnic music expressed much about the local, regional, and national culture of North America in the twentieth century, it has already become inseparable from global culture in the twenty-first. Popular world music in its various guises—world beat, "world music," global pop—would be unthinkable without American music at its core.

We do not have to go far to watch the transformation of ethnic music to global pop. Take the world music festival, for example, which during only the past decade has become a ubiquitous phenomenon of the American festival scene. The world music festival both is and is not like the Pittsburgh Folk Festival that we visited at the beginning of this chapter. The high degree of regulation and the complex marketing of identities are all present, indeed, in superabundance. The audience at the world music festival is, if anything, notably diverse. Multiculturalism, a code word for world music, is writ large wherever we look.

There are, however, ways in which the folk festival differs from the world music festival, and these, too, are notable. First of all, we see little evidence to suggest the forms of ownership and direct identity that were crucial in the folk festival. The bands on the stage play music that may or may not live in the communities and neighborhoods of the city where the festival is taking place. Local ethnic ensembles are noticeably absent from the roster of acts. The music, too, does not allow us to pin it down very easily. Emcees and announcers make a big deal about authenticity, but authenticity itself survives at best in traces, perhaps in the very few acoustic instruments or in the very few songs that still have traditional texts. The many sounds of multiculturalism are mixed together, emphasizing the potential for hybridity and global appeal. The ways in which American popular music enters the mix, too, have blurred and left us wondering just where ethnic and national borders fall in the music.

World music festivals encourage us to interpret the musical landscapes of North America in distinctively new ways. Rather than a single auditorium, park, or street as its stage, the world music festival spreads across the entire city. Rather than providing an ethnic community the opportunity to coalesce around communal musical and cultural events, the world music festival aggressively decentralizes the deployment of stages. There is no pretense of maintaining the old traditions; quite the contrary, the common currency of the world music festivals is the invention of new traditions. The paradox could not be clearer, but that, too, is the point. At the Chicago World Music Festival, first staged in 1999 as a two-week event closing the summer festival season, ethnic music fueled the invention of tradition. Musicians from many communities, for example, joined forces to give performances as the "Chicago Immigrant Orchestra," an ensemble that began to thrive after its conception for and birth at the World Music Festival. Musically, the Chicago Immigrant Orchestra weaves together whatever its players bring with them, forging an improvisatory and hybrid style that most regard as experimental rather than traditional. Individual talents are at least as critical to the musical success as the symbolic cohesion of immigrant traditions.

Critics of the world music festival like to point fingers at the overt presence of the music media and mediation. Performances move from the street to clubs and small auditoriums, on one hand, but to record stores and bookshops, and even to the lobbies of sponsoring corporate headquarters, on the other. Neighborhoods with intimate spaces to offer compete with concert halls that can seat thousands. The big-ticket acts at most world music festivals command big-ticket prices at the door. Again, we find ourselves reckoning with paradox: The festival may draw the world and its diversity closer to home, but access to that world is too often limited to those who can afford it.

Music of the Celtic World

At the beginning of the twenty-first century, Celtic music was a world music phenomenon that knew no borders. There was hardly a city around the world that did not boast a fair share of Irish pubs with regular sessions, evenings when Celtic musicians jam. Nor was there a festival that remained untouched by the successes of Riverdance, the stage show that itself took the audience on stops around the musical world, only to assure everyone that world musics bind all the world's people together. The proliferation of the sessions and Riverdance may symbolize the local and the global in a world of Celtic music, but they also reveal the ways in which the differences between the two increasingly blur. No less blurred are the differences between folk music and popular music, or for that matter between Irish and Irish-American music, Scottish and Welsh music, or the musics from French Brittany and Spanish Galicia. As Celtic music, they circulate as common currency in world music today.

Is the globalization of Celtic music, however, really all that new? Some of the most important answers to that question are to be found in the history of ethnic music in North America. Take the case of Frances O'Neill, a captain in the Chicago Police Department in the early decades of the twentieth century. An immigrant from Ireland, O'Neill worried that the traditions of the home country would disappear in urban America, so he set about to record, transcribe, and publish as many old tunes in Chicago as he could. Soon after his volumes of Irish music appeared in the United States, they found their ways into Irish imprints and from there into the repertories of Irish traditional musicians. In the course of the twentieth century, O'Neill's tunes increasingly circulated back and forth between Ireland and North America, mapping a diaspora that itself had more to do with criss-crossing the Atlantic and emigration patterns that spread across the world to Asia, Africa, and Latin America.

Chicago would again play a crucial role as a home-abroad to one of the most sensational forms of Celtic world music at the end of the twentieth century, this time in the person of step-dancing Michael Flatley, the star of Riverdance but also a hometown Irish-American from Chicago's Southwest Side. From the outset Riverdance successfully tapped and exploited every popular music venue and medium. Its breakthrough took place on the stage of the Eurovision Song Contest, when the troupe performed at intermission for the international broadcasting networks at the Eurovision (see Chapter 8). The Riverdance troupe overtly displayed its Irishness and did so by modernizing and amplifying dance styles and instruments alike. They also made calculated decisions about the forms their hybridity would take. In the mid-1990s, the African American components were more restrained, especially in the reverent presentation of gospel music by robe-bedecked choirs, but by the turn of the century, hip hop and breakdancing were going head-to-head with frenetic fiddling and acrobatic stepdancing at Riverdance stage performances. All this complemented the Africanization of Celtic music in Europe, notably in the late-1990s experiments of the band calling itself the Afro-Celt Sound System. The paradox was clear: The Americanness of Riverdance at once erased and enhanced its Irishness.

As we encounter the transformation of ethnic Irish music to world Celtic music, we find paradox almost unavoidable. The same is no less true when we encounter the popularization of American klezmer or the infusion of techno into polka. The search for the popular has many of the same motivations as the search for the authentic: Tradition is preserved as space opens for innovation; the search for diverse expressions of identity become more rather than less complex; the past is reimagined as the future in an American society that insists on its multicultural character.

The Modernity and Postmodernity of Traditional Music

Festivals have populated this chapter in a variety of ways, serving as a unifying metaphor. The festivals we have visited have been of many types—neighborhood events, citywide ethnic performances, world's fairs, world music extravaganzas—but their similarities have been striking. Also striking is that festivals are growing in popularity in North America. Visiting Toronto on most weekends during the year, one needs but to pick up the entertainment section of a newspaper to find abundant opportunities to visit an ethnic community's celebration of its culture. The festival season in most cities has become so popular that it is often necessary to book rooms a year in advance.

Festivals have proliferated, and so, too, has the music essential to their local and global character. Local groups are wont to stage pageants, and display booths for traditional arts rarely lack tables given over to CD bins. Some ethnic communities continue to record on their own labels, but the number of labels dedicated to genre—from polka to powwow, from reissues of old 78s to remixes of the folk and rock grooves—grows each year. Festivals were always sites for reviving the local; in the twenty-first century they have become stages for forging the global.

The musical performances at the festival belong more to the world reframed by the event itself than to the Old World. Performers, organizers, and audiences may employ symbols proclaiming that "this is the way it was," but the really important concern is making ethnic music part of "the way it is today." Ethnic music has become modern music, and it resonates publicly with the sounds of a contemporary world. For North Americans of European ancestry, music increasingly needs to represent the sweeping changes that have transformed a Europe struggling for unification in the twenty-first century. The Eastern European troupes at the Pittsburgh Folk Festival endeavor more to recapture the spirit of nationalism and reform from the turn of our own century than the imaginary pristine countryside of another century. Asian and Hispanic Americans, as well as the many "new immigrants," are no less concerned that their music be integrated into the festival and into the multiethnic culture of North America. African Americans, too, turn to festivals to underscore the diversity of their musics, not just jazz and blues but reggae and hip hop, which together reinforce public consciousness of the virtual omnipresence of African influences in American music.

In the twenty-first century, the music of ethnic North America is world music. As world music, however, it is no less distinctive of the continent where its history unfolded and whose diversity and unity it embodies. The music of ethnic North America also has a modern sound to it, which perhaps ironically makes it traditional in a world where cultural and musical boundaries are easily traversed. Modernity is one of the most distinctive markers of all the music we encountered in this chapter, so it is hardly surprising that modernity is one of North America's contributions to world music. The music of ethnic North American is a grand mixture, but the mixture does not eliminate the differences between musics and people, as in a melting pot. Difference and diversity, instead, are more and more important, and they rise to the very surface of the mixture. The characteristic juxtaposition of musics has effectively sharpened the awareness that each community, old or new, has of its own music, making that music far more than just a means of remembering the past. Ethnic music in the twenty-first century is the music of a modern world with a multiethnic culture that will connect North America to the world well into the future.

ETHNIC NORTH AMERICA BIBLIOGRAPHY

North America as a Whole   Gilbert Chase, *America's Music: From the Pilgrims to the Present*, rev. 3rd ed. (Urbana: University of Illinois Press, 1987); Richard Crawford, *The American Musical Landscape* (Berkeley: University of California Press, 1993); Charles Hamm, *Music in the New World* (New York: W. W. Norton, 1983); H. Wiley Hitchcock and Stanley Sadie, eds., *The New Grove Dictionary of American Music*, 4 vols. (London: Macmillan, 1986); Donald W. Krummel, *Bibliographical Handbook of American Music* (Urbana: University of Illinois Press, 1987); Terry E. Miller, *Folk Music in America: A Reference Guide* (New York: Garland, 1986); Bruno Nettl, *Folk Music in the United States: An Introduction*, 3rd ed., rev. and ed. Helen Myers (Detroit: Wayne State University Press, 1976); David Nicholls, ed., *The Cambridge History of American Music* (Cambridge, U.K.: Cambridge University Press, 1998); Nicholas Tawa, *The Sound of Strangers: Musical Culture, Acculturation, and the Post-Civil War Ethnic American* (Metuchen, N.J.: Scarecrow, 1982); Kip Lornell and Anne K. Rasmussen, eds., *Musics of Multicultural America: A Study of Twelve Musical Communities* (New York: Schirmer Books, 1997).

Music of Asian Ethnic Communities   Nazir A. Jairazbhoy and Sue Carole DeVale, eds., "Asian Music in North America," Special Edition, *Selected Reports in Ethnomusicology* 6 (1985); Ronald Riddle, *Flying Dragons, Flowing Streams: Music in the Life of San Francisco's Chinese* (Westport, Conn.: Greenwood, 1983).

Music of European Ethnic Communities   Roger D. Abrahams and George Foss, *Anglo-American Folksong Style* (Englewood Cliffs, N.J.: Prentice Hall, 1968); Philip V. Bohlman and Otto Holzapfel, eds., *Land without Nightingales: Music in the Making of German-America* (Madison: Max Kade Institute for German-American Studies, University of Wisconsin-Madison, 2002); Alan Lomax, *The Folk Songs of North America in the English Language* (Garden City, N.Y.: Doubleday, 1960); James Porter, ed., *Selected Reports in Ethnomusicology* 3/1 (1978) (Special edition devoted to the traditional music of Europeans in America); Mark Slobin, *Tenement Songs: The Popular Music of the Jewish Immigrants* (Urbana: University of Illinois Press, 1982); Robert L. Wright, *Swedish Emigrant Ballads* (Lincoln: University of Nebraska Press, 1965); Rochelle Wright and Robert L. Wright, *Danish Emigrant Ballads and Songs* (Carbondale: Southern Illinois University Press, 1983); Mark Slobin, ed., *American Klezmer: Its Roots and Offshoots* (Berkeley: University of California Press, 2002).

Music of Hispanic American Communities   Ruth Glaser, *My Music Is My Flag: Puerto Rican Musicians and Their New York Communities, 1917–1940* (Berkeley: University of California Press, 1995); Steven Loza, *Barrio Rhythm: Mexican American Music in Los Angeles* (Urbana: University of Illinois Press, 1992); Américo Paredes, *A Texas-Mexican Cancionero: Folksongs of the Lower Border* (Urbana: University of Illinois Press, 1976): Américo Paredes, *With His Pistol in His Hand: A Border Ballad and Its Hero* (Austin: University of Texas Press, 1958); Manuel Peña, *The Texas-Mexican Conjunto: History of a Working-Class Music* (Austin: University of Texas Press, 1985); J. D. Robb, *Hispanic Folk Songs of New Mexico* (Albuquerque: University of New Mexico Press, 1954).

Ethnicity and Ethnic History of North America   Larry Danielson, ed., "Studies in Folklore and Ethnicity," Special Edition, *Western Folklore* 36/1 (1977); Robert A. Georges and Stephen Stern, *American and Canadian Immigrant and Ethnic Folklore: An Annotated Bibliography* (New York: Garland, 1982); Milton M. Gordon, *Assimilation in American Life* (New York: Oxford University Press, 1964); Neil V. Rosenberg, ed., *Transforming Tradition: Folk Music Revivals Examined* (Urbana: University of Illinois Press, 1993); Anya Peterson Royce, *Ethnic Identity: Strategies for Diversity* (Bloomington: Indiana University Press, 1982); Stephan Thernstrom, Ann Orlov, and Oscar Handlin, eds., *Harvard Encyclopedia of American Ethnic Groups* (Cambridge, Mass.: Harvard University Press, 1980).

Regional Studies   H. M. Belden, ed., *Ballads and Songs Collected by the Missouri Folk-Lore Society* (Columbia: University of Missouri Press, 1973); Robert Cantwell, *Bluegrass Breakdown: The Making of the Old Southern Sound* (Urbana: University of Illinois Press, 1984); Helen Creighton and Calum MacLeod, *Gaelic Songs in Nova Scotia* (Ottawa: National Museums of Canada, 1979); Helmut Kallmann, Gilles Potvin, and Kenneth Winters, eds., *Encyclopedia of Music in Canada* (Toronto: University of Toronto Press, 1981); George Korson, ed., *Pennsylvania Songs and Legends* (Baltimore: Johns Hopkins University Press, 1960); Timothy J. McGee, *The Music of Canada* (New York: W. W. Norton, 1985); Bill C. Malone, *Southern Music/American Music* (Lexington: The University Press of Kentucky, 1979); Vance Randolph, ed., *Ozark Folksongs*, 4 vols. (Columbia: University of Missouri Press, 1980); Howard N. Thorp, *Songs of the Cowboys* (New York: Clarkson N. Potter, 1966); David E. Whisnant, *All That Is Native and Fine: The Politics of Culture in an American Region* (Chapel Hill: University of North Carolina Press, 1983).

Music and North American Religious Communities   Michael Hicks, *Mormonism and Music: A History* (Urbana: University of Illinois Press, 1989); Donald B. Hinks, *Brethren Hymn Books and Hymnals, 1720–1884* (Gettysburg, Pa.: Brethren Heritage Press, 1986); Doreen Helen Klassen, *Singing Mennonite: Low*

German Songs of the Mennonites (Winnipeg: University of Manitoba Press, 1980); Jeff Todd Titon, *Powerhouse for God: Speech, Chant, and Song in an Appalachian Baptist Church* (Austin: University of Texas Press, 1988).

Contemporary and Popular Traditions of Ethnic Music   Robert Cantwell, *When We Were Good: The Folk Revival* (Cambridge, Mass.: Harvard University Press, 1996); R. Serge Denisoff, *Great Day Coming: Folk Music and the American Left* (Baltimore: Penguin, 1973); William Ferris and Mary L. Hunt, eds., *Folk Music and Modern Sound* (Jackson: University Press of Mississippi, 1985); Henry Glassie et al., *Folksongs and Their Makers* (Bowling Green, Oh.: Bowling Green University Popular Press, 1970); Victor Greene, *A Passion for Polka: Old-Time Ethnic Music in America* (Berkeley: University of California Press, 1993); John Greenway, *American Folksongs of Protest* (Philadelphia: University of Pennsylvania Press, 1953); Judith McCulloh, ed., *Ethnic Recordings in America: A Neglected Heritage* (Washington, D.C.: Library of Congress, 1982); Neil V. Rosenberg, *Bluegrass: A History* (Urbana: University of Illinois Press, 1985); Richie Unterberger, *Music USA: The Rough Guide* (London: The Rough Guides, 1999); Mark Slobin, *Fiddler on the Move* (New York: Oxford University Press, 2003).

Musical Instruments   James M. Borders, *European and American Wind and Percussion Instruments: Catalogue of the Stearns Collection of Musical Instruments* (Ann Arbor: University of Michigan Press, 1988); Philip F. Gura and James F. Bollman, *America's Instrument: The Banjo in the Nineteenth Century* (Chapel Hill: The University of North Carolina Press, 1999); Miles Krassen, *Clawhammer Banjo* (New York: Oak Publications, 1974); E. Annie Proulx, *Accordion Crimes* (New York: Scribner, 1996); L. Allen Smith, *A Catalogue of Pre-Revival Appalachian Dulcimers* (Columbia: University of Missouri Press, 1983).

African American Music   Houston A. Baker, Jr., *Blues, Ideology, and Afro-American Literature: A Vernacular Theory* (Chicago: University of Chicago Press, 1984); Paul Berliner, *Thinking in Jazz: The Infinite Art of Improvisation* (Chicago: University of Chicago Press, 1994); Harold Courlander, *Negro Folk Music, U.S.A.* (New York: Columbia University Press, 1963); Dena J. Epstein, *Sinful Tunes and Spirituals: Black Folk Music to the Civil War* (Urbana: University of Illinois Press, 1977); Samuel A. Floyd, Jr., *The Power of Black Music* (New York: Oxford University Press, 1995); Charles Keil, *Urban Blues*, 2nd ed. (Chicago: University of Chicago Press, 1994); Paul Oliver, *Songsters and Saints: Vocal Traditions on Race Records* (Cambridge: Cambridge University Press, 1984); Eileen Southern, *The Music of Black Americans: A History*, 2nd ed. (New York: W. W. Norton, 1983); Eileen Southern, *Readings in Black American Music*, 2nd ed. (New York: W. W. Norton, 1983); Jeff Todd Titon, *Early Downhome Blues: A Musical and Cultural Analysis* (Urbana: University of Illinois Press, 1977); Richard A. Waterman, "African Influence on the Music of the Americas," in Sol Tax, ed., *Acculturation in the Americas* (Chicago: University of Chicago Press, 1952).

ETHNIC NORTH AMERICA DISCOGRAPHY

Discographical Note

Because of the enormous number of recordings that document the music of ethnic North America, this discography will note some of the most important and comprehensive series of recordings rather than individual discs. Students interested in specific suggestions for recordings of the music of an ethnic group or in a particular genre can find these in discographies and special musical studies, for example, of jazz or the blues. A further source, in which new releases of ethnic and folk music are reviewed in brief, is the discography section of the quarterly *Journal of American Folklore*. A remarkably rich and detailed discographical source for American ethnic music is Richard K. Spottswood, *Ethnic Music on Records: A Discography of Ethnic Recordings Produced in the United States, 1893–1942*, 7 vols. (Urbana: University of Illinois Press, 1990.)

During the 1970s and 1980s, a comprehensive collection of American music recordings appeared on the New World Records label. Funded by the Rockefeller Foundation and conceived to celebrate the American Bicentennial in 1976, the first one hundred releases were distributed without cost to most college and university libraries, where students using this book will often find them. Although New World Records intentionally included all American traditions, folk and ethnic traditions are well represented, and the connections among diverse musical traditions are evident. Students will find it very helpful to compare these different traditions, their histories, and their cultural contexts. Comprehensive critical notes accompany each recording.

The Library of Congress has also produced excellent recordings of folk and ethnic music. Some of these document local and regional traditions, others specific genres. Students wishing to hear Child ballads recorded in the United States will find the Library of Congress recording *Child Ballads Traditional in the U.S.* (AAFS L57-58) very valuable. The fifteen-volume series *Folk Music in America* (LBC 1-15), edited by Richard K. Spottswood, is an excellent survey, particularly of early recordings and otherwise hard-to-find styles such as folk music of rural southern African Americans.

The Folkways label has recorded diverse traditions of American folk music, although ethnic music is not particularly well represented, with the exception of Anglo-American and some African American traditions. Still, because many of the recordings released by Folkways were made in New York City by immigrants and exiles in the decade following World War II, students have an interesting opportunity to study the repertories maintained by first-generation musicians. The Smithsonian Institution is rereleasing many Folkways recordings, often with new and thorough notes. Harry Smith's three-LP *Anthology of American Folk Music* (Folkways FA 2951 and FP 252–253; rereleased by Smithsonian-Folkways on CD in 1997) remains one of the richest and most diverse collections of songs from recordings made in the first half of the twentieth century.

The Smithsonian Institution has also produced several sets of "classic" American musical genres, namely jazz, country-and-western, and labor and protest songs. These multirecord collections are of the highest quality, and the explanatory notes that accompany the sets are at once scholarly and accessible. These recordings further help the student understand the ways in which different musical traditions interact and ethnic music has historically influenced those traditions we might not immediately consider as ethnic.

Glossary

ABHINAYA: (India). Gestural interpretation of text in dance.

AEROPHONE: Scientific term for all types of wind instruments, including trumpets, flutes, and the organ.

AGENG: (Indonesia). Large, as in gong ageng (Jv.).

AGEUTA: (Japan). A type of song in higher vocal range used in Noh plays.

AGOGÓ: (Africa). Double bell of West African origin, also used in Brazil.

AKADINDA: (Africa). Large twenty-two key xylophone of the Ganda.

AKAN: (Africa). A major ethnic group in Ghana.

AKÍA: (Latin America). An individually owned and sung song of the Suyá Indians of Brazil.

ALAP(ANAM): (India). Raga improvisation in free rhythm.

ANGKLUNG: (Indonesia). A kind of pitched bamboo rattle.

ANUPALLAVI: (India). Second section of kriti or other Karnatak song form.

APACHE FIDDLE: (North American Indian). Bowed instrument with one string, probably made in imitation of the Western violin, used in the culture of the Navajo and Apache peoples.

ARAGOTO: (Japan). Rough-style acting in the kabuki theater.

ARJA: (Indonesia). A type of Balinese opera.

ASHEQ: (Middle East). Middle Eastern singer of romantic narratives.

ATABAQUES: (Latin America). Drums of West African origin, used in Brazilian candomblé music.

ATOUTA: (Japan). The last song in the jiuta cycle.

ATSIMEVU: (Africa). Large Ewe (Ghana) lead drum.

ATUMPAN: (Africa). Paired drums central to the Akan people of Ghana.

AUSBUND: (North America). The hymnbook of the Amish, with texts only, but melodies transmitted orally.

AVAZ: (Middle East). In Persian classical music, the improvised, nonmetric section, rendered vocally or instrumentally, that is central in the performance.

AXATSE: (Africa). Ewe shaker with beads on a net on the outside of the gourd.

AYMARA: (Latin America). Indigenous Andean language, second largest indigenous ethnic group in the Andean region.

BAJO SEXTO: (Latin America). A twelve-string guitar used in Mexican norteño music.

BAKHSHI: (Middle East). Iranian folk singer of narratives about war and romance.

BALO: (Africa). A Mande xylophone.

BALUNGAN: (Indonesia). Skeletal melody in Javanese music.

BAN: (China). Generic term for Chinese clappers.

BANDURA: (Europe). Ukrainian plucked lute of different sizes and ranges, often played in ensembles.

BANDÚRRIA: (Latin America). A mandolin-shaped instrument with four courses of strings.

BANSURI: (India). Hindustani flute.

BANTU: (Africa). A major group of African languages.

BARONG: (Indonesia). A mythical lionlike creature in Balinese sacred dramas.

BARUNG: (Indonesia). Specifying the middle range of some types of Javanese gamelan instruments.

BAYA: (India). Small, bass kettle drum of tabla pair.

BECAR: (Europe). Instrumentalist and musical specialist in southeastern Europe, often distinguished by great mobility.

BEDHAYA: (Indonesia). Sacred court dance of Java.

BESHRAV: (Middle East). Introductory metric ensemble piece in Turkish classical music.

BHAJAN: (India). Hindu devotional song.

BHANGRA: (India). Folk dance of the Punjab in northwest India and in Pakistan, recently adapted for pop music by Indian emigrants.

BHARATA NATYAM: (India). Major dance style of South India.

BIN: (India). Hindustani plucked lute associated with dhrupad style.

BIRA: (Africa). A Shona religious ceremony involving spirit possession.

BIRIMINTINGO: (Africa). An instrumental interlude or "break" during which a Mande jali departs from the basic ostinato.

BIWA: (Japan.) A type of lute.

BOL: (India). Rhythmic syllable in Hindustani music.

BONANG: (Indonesia). Multioctave bronze instrument responsible for elaboration in Javanese gamelan.

BONSAN: (Japan). Japanese Buddhist chants in Sanskrit.

BROADSIDE BALLAD: (North America). Composed narrative folk song, printed on large sheets and sold inexpensively.

BUBARAN: (Indonesia). A small-scale Javanese gendhing having sixteen beats.

BUDDHISM: Religion of compassion and salvation based on the teaching of the Indian prince Siddharta ("the Buddha," 563–483 B.C.E.). Influential in Chinese, Japanese, and Korean societies.

BUGAKU: (Japan). Japanese court dance with instrumental accompaniment.

BUKA: (Indonesia). Introduction to a Javanese gendhing.

BUNRAKU: (Japan). The main form of puppet theater in Japan.

CADENCE: A pause or ending in music.

CAI YUANPEI (1868–1948): (China). Chancellor of Peking University (Beida) from 1916 to 1926. Important supporter of the May Fourth Movement.

CAJUN: (North America). French-speaking culture of Louisiana, with historical links to French-speaking Canada.

CANDOMBLÉ: (Latin America). An Afro-Brazilian religion heavily involving West African religious beliefs and musical practices.

CANTO POP: (China). Popular song genre sung in the Cantonese dialect produced in Hong Kong since the 1970s.

CARANAM: (India). Last of three sections in Karnatak kriti or other song form.

CARNATIC: *see* Karnatak.

CELEMPUNG: (Indonesia). The plucked zither of Javanese gamelans.

CHAHAR MEZRAB: (Middle East). Virtuosic composed metric solo piece in Persian classical music.

CHAHARGAH: (Middle East). One of the twelve dastgahs, or modes of Persian classical music.

CHARANGO: (Latin America). An Andean ten-string guitar variant, the size of a ukulele.

CHEN GEXIN: (China). Composer of popular songs active in Shanghai between the 1930s and 1940s.

CHILENOS: (Latin America). Dance drama group of Paucartambo, Peru representing Chilean soldiers from the War of the Pacific.

CHOBO: (Japan). The Gidayu duo on the kabuki stage.

CHORD: A group of at least three tones sounded simultaneously in combination.

CHORDOPHONE: Scientific term for all types of string instruments, including violins, guitars, and pianos.

CHOU: (China). Generic name for a clown role in Chinese theater.

CHUNCHOS: (Latin America). Dance drama group of Paucartambo, Peru representing jungle Indians.

CHURCH MODES: (Europe). Seven-note scales, thought by many to characterize more recent styles of folk music.

COLOTOMY: (Indonesia). The structure of a Javanese gendhing determined by the total number of beats it contains and which of those beats are sounded on particular instruments.

CONCERTINA: (North America). The button-box accordion favored in polka bands of the Midwest.

CONFUCIANISM: System of ethics based on the teachings of Kongfuzi (Confucius, 551–479 B.C.E.). Confucianism formed the dominant ethic of Chinese social units from the imperial government to the peasant family. It is also influential in Korean and Japanese societies.

CONJUNTO: (Latin America). Popular dance music along the Texas-Mexico border.

COPLA: (Latin America). An Iberian-derived verse form with four octosyllabic lines per stanza.

CRIOLLO: (Latin America). In some regions criollo refers to American-born Spaniards, or largely European-derived ethnicity in Latin America, "white."

CULTURAL REVOLUTION: (China). Complex social and political upheaval that began as a struggle between Mao Zedong and other top Communist Party leaders for domination of the Party and went on to affect all China with its calls for "continuing revolution" and "class struggle." Dates for the movement are usually given as 1966 to 1976.

CURRULAO: (Latin America). Afro-Colombian, Afro-Ecuadorian dance context in the Pacific Coast region in which marimba is featured.

DA-DAIKO: (Japan). The largest of gagaku drums.

DAHINA: (India). Treble drum of tabla pair, having a tunable head.

DALUO: (China). Big Chinese gong.

DAN: (China). Generic name for a female role in Chinese theater.

DAN: (Japan). A musical section in Japanese music of various forms.

DANGDUT: (Indonesia). A type of popular Indonesian song often having morally edifying lyrics with an Islamic orientation and revealing strong musical influence from Hindi film songs.

DANMONO: (Japan). Sectional form.

DANPIGU: (China). A single-headed drum used in Chinese theater.

DARBUCCA: (Middle East). (also Darrabuka). A single-headed drum ordinarily made of fired clay, used mainly in Arabic popular and classical music and in popular music throughout the Middle East.

DARVISH: (Middle East). Leader of a community of Sufis and, in rural Iran, street singer of religious narratives.

DASTGAH: (Middle East). Generic name of the twelve modes of Persian classical music.

DATONGGU: (China). A big Chinese barrel drum.

DEBAYASHI: (Japan). The on-stage musicians of the kabuki theater.

DEMUNG: (Indonesia). The low-range saron.

DEVADASI: (India). A Karnatak dancing girl whose art was dedicated to temple deities.

DHALANG: (Indonesia). Puppeteer of wayang kulit.

DHRUPAD: (India). A severe classical song and instrumental form of Hindustani music.

DHUN: (India). A regional song of North India sometimes borrowed for Hindustani performance.

DIATONIC: Refers to the European, seven-note (do-re-mi) scale.

DIDGERIDOO: Long trumpet, made of a hollowed eucalyptus branch, used in Australian aboriginal cultures as a drone accompanying singing, and more recently, a general symbol of Australian musical identity.

DISIKE (Disco): (China). A recent Chinese popular song style.

DIZI: (China). A Chinese transverse bamboo flute with six finger-holes.

DOCTORES: (Latin America). Dance drama group of Paucartambo, Peru representing lawyers and government officials.

DOMBAK: (Middle East). Term used for various single-skin drums in the Middle East, but principally for the goblet-shaped drum used in Persian classical music. In Indonesia, a Middle-Eastern, hourglass drum, used in gambus.

DONDON: (Africa). Ewe hourglass-shaped "talking drum."

DONKILO: (Africa). The basic sung melody of Mande jali songs.

DOTAR: (Middle East). Large lute with long neck, frets, and two or three strings, used in folk music in Iran, and in folk and classical music of Afghanistan and Central Asia.

DRUT: (India). Fast.

DUNDUN: (Africa). Hourglass-shaped "talking drum" of the Yoruba of Nigeria.

EDUPPU: (India). The beginning of a phrase in Karnatak music used as a cadence for improvisations.

ENNANGA: (Africa). Ganda bow-harp.

ENTENGA: (Africa). Royal Ganda tuned drum ensemble.

ERHU: (China). A two-stringed Chinese spike fiddle with hollow wooden cylindrical sound box.

ERHUANG: (China). Basic aria-rhythmic patterns used in the Peking Opera.

FEI SHI: (China). The pseudonym of an early twentieth-century Chinese reformer.

FILMIGIT: (India). Film songs.

FLAT: Pitch lowered by a half tone.

FRET: A device of metal or string which divides the finger board of plucked instruments and against which the player presses the playing strings to get different tones.

FUJIAN NANQU: (China). A genre of song suite with instrumental accompaniment popular in Fujian province in southern China, and in Taiwan as well.

FUSHI: (Japan). A term for melody in general.

GAGAKU: (Japan). Japanese court orchestral music.

GAKU-SO: (Japan). The gagaku zither.

GAMBANG: (Indonesia). A xylophone instrument in the Javanese gamelan; an archaic instrument, g. gangsa, is related to the saron.

GAMBUH: (Indonesia). An archaic type of Balinese court opera and its accompanying orchestra.

GAMBUS: (Indonesia). A type of Islamic song having Arabic influence; the name of the plucked lute used to accompany this song.

GAMELAN: (Indonesia). An ensemble of instruments such as those found in the central Javanese courts. Other specific types are: g. gong gede, archaic Balinese gamelan with large gongs; g. gambuh, archaic Balinese orchestra of large flutes, rebab, and light percussion used for dramas; g. Semar pegulingan, archaic Balinese bronze ensemble for court entertainment; g. gong kebyar, large modern replacement of g. g. gede used for many kinds of music making and for dance accompaniment; g. angklung, small Balinese metallophone ensemble, often having only four pitches and sometimes using the angklung instrument.

GANKOGUI: (Africa). Ewe double bell.

GATRA: (Indonesia). A four-beat phrase in Javanese music.

GAT-TORA: (India). The section of Hindustani instrumental performance, accompanied by tabla, in which a tune, the gat, is alternated with improvisational passages, tora.

GBOBA: (Africa). Large Ewe (Ghana) lead drum.

GEDE: (Indonesia). Large, as in gamelan gong gede.

GENDER: (Indonesia). An instrument having thin bronze slab keys individually suspended over tube resonators.

GENDHING: (Indonesia). A piece of Javanese music for gamelan.

GERONGAN: (Indonesia). A male chorus that sings with Javanese gamelan.

GESANGBUCH: (North America). Meaning "songbook," a printed collection of Amish religious songs, many entering from outside the community.

GESELLSCHAFT FÜR MUSIKFREUNDE: (Europe). "Society for the Friends of Music": center for musical performance in Vienna, Austria, with extensive music libraries and archives.

GEZA: (Japan). The off-stage music of the kabuki theater.

GHARANA: (India). A school of professional musicians who originally traced their heritage to a family tradition but which now includes nonbiological descendants as well.

GHAZAL: (India). A form of poetry associated with Perso-Arabic Muslim culture enthusiastically taken up by Urdu speakers in North India and Pakistan where it is often sung.

GHOST DANCE: (North American Indian). Native American (principally Plains) religious movement of protest against U.S. government excesses, of the 1880s.

GIDAYUBUSHI: (Japan). A major Japanese musical narrative style accompanied by the Shamisen created by Takemoto Gidayu.

GONG: (Indonesia). Gong.

GONGAN: (Indonesia). A phrase concluded with a stroke on gong ageng or siyem.

GOTTUVADYAM: (India). A Karnatak plucked string instrument whose strings are stopped with a sliding ball of glass, like the Hawaiian guitar.

GU: (China). Generic name for Chinese drum.

GUANGDONG YINYUE: (China). A genre of Chinese instrumental ensemble music originating in Guangdong province which became popular not only in other parts of China but also Chinese ethnic enclaves in the west known as "China Town."

GUITARRÓN: (Latin America). In Mexico, a large acoustic bass guitar with a convex back.

GURU: (India). A Hindu teacher.

GUSHEH: (Middle East). Subdivision of a dastgah, and smallest constituent part of the radif, in Persian classical music.

GUSLE: (Europe). Bowed stringed instrument of the Balkans, used to accompany epic singing. Also used in North American ethnic communities from the Balkans to accompany epics.

HAJI: (Indonesia). A male Muslim who has made a pilgrimage to Mecca.

HAKO: (North American Indian). A complex ceremony of the Pawnee, carried out for the general welfare of the tribe and the world, requiring four days of singing, dancing, and ritual.

HALAM: (Africa). A West African banjo-like lute with a neck, gourd sound box, and skin stretched over the face of the sound box.

HANAMICHI: (Japan). A ramp used in the Kabuki theater which connects the back of the theater to the stage.

HARDANGER FIDDLE/HARDINGFELE: (Europe and North America). Elaborate Norwegian folk fiddle, with elaborate woodwork and extra resonating strings.

HARMONIUM: (India). A small organ whose bellows are pumped with one hand while the other fingers the keyboard. Used in both North and South Indian music since missionaries introduced it in the mid-nineteenth century.

HAYASHI: (Japan). Drum and flute ensembles.

HETEROPHONY: Music in which two or more versions or variations of the same melody are performed simultaneously. Found in various East and Southeast Asian musical cultures.

HEURIGER: (Europe). Austrian wine garden, which is often a site for traditional music.

HEXATONIC: A scale of six tones.

HICHIRIKI: (Japan). A double-reed gagaku instrument.

HIGHLIFE: (Africa). A form of urban-popular dance-band music of Ghana; also played in Nigeria and elsewhere in West Africa.

HINDUSTANI: (India). In music, referring to North Indian musical style.

HOCKET: Interlocking pitches between two or more sound sources to create a single melody or part.

HOGAKU: (Japan). Native Japanese music.

HOGOROMO: (Japan). A noh play.

HUAPANGUERA: (Latin America). A Mexican guitar variant from the huasteca region, larger and deeper than a normal guitar with eight strings in five courses.

HUA SAN LIU: (China). A Chinese instrumental piece belonging to the Jiangnan sizhu repertory.

HUASTECA: (Latin America). A Mexican region including northern Veracruz State and Tamaulipas, and the musical style from that region.

HUI: (China). Position markers on the qin.

HUMMEL: (Europe). Swedish dulcimer.

IBERIAN: Referring to Iberian Peninsula, Spain and Portugal.

IDIOPHONE: Scientific term for all instruments whose bodies vibrate as the principal method of sound-production, including rattles and many other percussion instruments.

IMPROVISATION: Performance that is spontaneous rather than predetermined.

INTERLOCKING: The practice of fitting one's pitches and beats into the spaces of other parts, or alternating the pitches or phrases of one part with those of others to create the whole; hocket.

INTERVAL: The distance between two tones.

IQ'A: (Middle East). Generic name of rhythmic modes, or type of musical meter, in Arabic classical music. Called usul in Turkish.

JAIPONGAN: (Indonesia). A type of Sundanese popular music that has gained popularity in other parts of Indonesia.

JALATARANGAM: (India). A set of small bowls partially filled with water to tune their pitches and struck with thin sticks.

JALI. pl. jalolu: (Africa). Professional Mande musician and verbal artist.

JARANA: (Latin America). In the jarocho region of Mexico, a small guitar type with eight strings in five courses; in the huasteca region, a small five-stringed guitar variant.

JAROCHO: (Latin America). A Mexican region on the Gulf Coast in the state of Veracruz, and the musical style of that region.

JAVALI: (India). A lyrical song form of Karnatak music.

JENGLONG: (Indonesia). An archaic Javanese instrument.

JHALA: (India). The concluding section of instrumental improvisation following jor in Hindustani music during which the performer makes lively and fast rhythmic patterns on the drone strings of an instrument.

JIANGNAN SIZHU: (China). A type of Chinese chamber instrumental ensemble made up of strings and winds popular in the areas around Shanghai.

JIANZIPU (Abbreviated characters tablature): (China). Tablature for the Chinese seven-stringed zither, the qin; it is made up of clusters of abbreviated Chinese characters.

JING: (China). Generic name for a painted-face role in Chinese theater.

JINGGE: (Energy Song): (China). A recent Chinese popular song style.

JINGHU: (China). The leading melodic instrument in the Peking Opera theater. It is a two-stringed bamboo spike fiddle with a very high and piercing range and timbre.

JIT, also jiti: (China). Informal Shona village dance, song, and drumming. Also a genre played by electric guitar bands in Zimbabwe.

JIUTA: (Japan). A major koto genre.

JO-HA-KYU: (Japan). A basic aesthetic concept in Japanese music. Jo denotes "introduction"; ha denotes "development"; kyu denotes the final section of a composition.

JOR: (India). The section of Hindustani instrumental performance which follows alap and introduces a pulse.

JÙJÚ: (Africa). A form of Nigerian popular music associated with the Yoruba that combines electric instruments with indigenous drums and percussion.

KABAKA: (Africa). King of Buganda.

KABUKI: (Japan). The main form of Japanese popular musical theater.

KAGANU: (Africa). Small Ewe (Ghana) accompanying drum.

KAGURA: (Japan). A generic term for Shinto music.

KAGURA-BUE: (Japan). A flute used in Shinto music and court music.

KAKKO: (Japan). A small horizontal drum used in court music.

KAMANCHEH: (Middle East). Spiked fiddle, with three or four strings, bowed with horsehair bow, used throughout the Middle East.

KANG YOUWEI (1858–1927): (China). Confucian scholar, influential in late Qing reform movements.

KANSAN: (Japan). Japanese Buddhist chant in Chinese.

KARAWITAN: (Indonesia). Learned music in the Javanese tradition.

KARNATAK: (India). In music, referring to South Indian music style.

KATHAK: (India). Major style of Hindustani dance.

KEBYAR: (Indonesia). A modern type of Balinese music and the dance it accompanies.

KECAK: (Indonesia). A type of dance drama accompanied by a large male chorus that chants rhythmically.

KEMPUL: (Indonesia). A type of small suspended gong in the Javanese gamelan having a colotomic function.

KENA: (Latin America). An indigenous Andean end-notched flute with six top finger-holes and one back hole, of pre-Columbian origin.

KENDANG: (Indonesia). Javanese double-headed drum.

KENONG: (Indonesia). A relatively large horizontal gong in the Javanese gamelan having a colotomic function.

KENONGAN: (Indonesia). A colotomic phrase in Javanese music marked by a kenong stroke.

KETAWANG: (Indonesia). A type of Javanese gendhing having thirty-two beats.

KETHUK: (Indonesia). A small, horizontal gong in Javanese music having a colotomic function.

KEY: The pitch at which the major or minor scale begins.

KHORASAN: (Middle East). District of Iran located in the northeast corner of the nation.

KHURDAK: (India). Small kettle drums used to accompany shehnai.

KHYAL: (India). The major vocal style of Hindustani music.

KIDI: (Africa). Middle-sized Ewe accompanying drum.

KLEZMER MUSICIANS: (Europe). Jewish instrumental ensembles that performed, often professionally, for both Jewish and non-Jewish social functions.

KOMA-BUE: (Japan). A flute used in court music.

KOMA-GAKU: (Japan). Japanese court music of Korean origin.

KONTINGO: (Africa). A five-stringed plucked lute played by Mande jalolu with a skin head stretched over a gourd sound box.

KORA: (Africa). A twenty-one-string bridge harp played by Mande jalolu.

KORAN: Sacred book of Islam.

KOTO: (Japan). A thirteen-stringed zither with movable bridges. It is Japan's main zither.

KOTOBE: (Japan). A heightened speech style used in the noh theater.

KO-TSUZUMI: (Japan). A small hourglass-shaped drum.

KRAKOWIAK: (Europe and North America). Duple meter folk dance, associated with the region near Cracow.

KRATON: (Indonesia). Javanese royal court.

KRITI: (India). The major song type of Karnatak music.

KRONCONG: (Indonesia). A type of popular Indonesian music originating from Portuguese derived sources.

KUMBENGO: (Africa). The basic instrumental ostinato which serves as the foundation for Mande jali performance.

KUMIUTA: (Japan). A suite of songs accompanied either by the koto or the shamisen, or by both.

KUNJU: (China). Classical Chinese musical drama.

Kuse: (Japan). The dance section of the first act of a noh play.

Kushaura: (Africa). "To lead the piece"; the first part, or lead part played by one Shona mbira player.

Kutsinhira: (Africa). "To accompany"; the second accompanying part played by a second Shona mbira player.

Kyogen: (Japan). Literally, "mad words"; it is a comic play inserted between noh plays.

Kyogenkata: (Japan). The clapper player in the kabuki theater.

Lamellaphone: A general class of musical instruments of African origin in which tuned metal or reed tongues are set on a bridge on a soundboard or box; it is played by striking the tongues (or keys); "thumb piano."

Laras: (Indonesia). Tuning system in Javanese music.

Lay(a): (India). Tempo.

Li Jinhui (1891–1967): (China). Modern Chinese composer and innovator of the first modern Chinese popular song genre, the liuxing gequ of Shanghai.

Li Shutong (1880–1942): (China). Poet, educator, and pioneer of the modern Chinese School Song. He later became a Buddhist monk.

Liang Qizhou (1873–1929): (China). Student of Kang Youwei and also an influential reformer. He used his writings to raise support for the reform movement.

Liu Jinguang: (China). Famous composer of Shanghai liuxing gequ, and younger brother of Li Jinhui.

Liuxing gequ: (China). Popular song produced in Shanghai since the late 1920s that is a hybrid of various Western and Chinese musical genres. Its lyrics are sung in the Chinese national tongue, the so-called Mandarin.

Lute: a stringed instrument with a sound box and a distinct finger board, the strings stretching over both.

Mahour: (Middle East). One of the twelve dastgahs, or modes, of Persian music, using a scale like Western major.

Majeños: (Latin America). Dance drama group of Paucartambo, Peru representing drunken liquor traders.

Majles: (Middle East). In Persian classical music, a small, informal gathering of men assembled to hear a concert.

Major: Referring to the quality of a scale having its pitches arranged as follows: tone, tone, semitone, tone, tone, tone, semitone.

Makam: (Middle East). Turkish spelling of maqam.

Mao Zedong (1893–1976): (China). An early member of the Chinese Communist Party who rose to party leadership in the 1930s. Led the Party on the Long March and then to establish the People's Republic of China in 1949. Until his death in 1976 he was the paramount political leader and theorist of Chinese communism.

MAQAM: (Middle East). Generic term for mode, or system of composing melody, in Arabic classical music. The term is used throughout the Middle East, and the concept occasionally appears with different names such as dastgah and gusheh in Persian, or mugam in Azerbaijan.

MARIACHI: (Latin America). Ensemble type originally from Jalisco, Mexico consisting of two or more violins, vihuela, guitarrón, two trumpets, and various guitars.

MARINERA: (Latin America). Mestizo song-dance genre of Peru in sesquialtera rhythm.

MAY FOURTH MOVEMENT: (China). Term used to describe student demonstration that took place in Tiananmen Square on May 4, 1919, in protest against unfair terms of the Treaty of Versailles. Also refers to the period of iconoclastic intellectual ferment that followed the protest.

MAZURKA: (Europe). Polish and Polish American folk dance, often stylized in art-music compositions.

MBAQ'ANGA: (Africa). A South African urban-popular music featuring electric instruments and horns, with the bass often particularly prominent.

MBIRA: (Africa). A twenty-two-key Shona lamellaphone, originally associated with the Zezuru Shona of central Zimbabwe.

MBUBE: (Africa). "Lion," one name for Zulu migrant choral music.

MEVLEVI: (Middle East). Order of Sufis (members of the mystical movement of Islam) in Turkey, in which the preservation of classical music plays an important role.

MEMBRANOPHONES: Scientific term for all instruments using a stretched membrane for sound production, that is, all true drums.

MENTALITÉ: A collective way of thinking, expressed in the cultural activities of a group or community.

MESTIZO: (Latin America). A relative concept referring to the blending of European and Native American cultural heritages, also used as a term of ethnic identity.

METALLOPHONE: An instrument classification term for idiophonic instruments made of metal.

METER: A measure of musical time that organizes beats into larger units also called *measures* or *bars*.

MINNESINGER: (Europe). Medieval singer, who often accompanied himself on the lute and was one of the first musical professionals.

MINOR: Referring to the quality of a scale having its pitches arranged as follows: tone, semitone, tone, tone, semitone, (tone, tone) or (tone and a half, semitone).

MODE: Generic term for a concept indicating tendencies or rules for composing melody. Examples of modes include Indian ragas, Persian dastgahs, and Arabic maqams.

MOLIMO: (Africa). A Pygmy ceremony for the forest; a straight valveless trumpet used in the ceremony.

MONAQEB-KHAN: (Middle East). Singer of narratives about the virtues of Imam Ali, in small-town Iranian musical culture.

MONOPHONIC: Referring to music comprising a single melody; without chords or other melodic or harmonic parts.

MORSHED: (Middle East). Reciter of heroic verse such as *Shahnameh* to accompany exercises in the Zurkhaneh, traditional Persian gymnasium.

MOTREB: (Middle East). Generic name for musician in various Middle Eastern cultures; performer of vocal and instrumental music at teahouses in Khorasan.

MRIDANGAM: (India). Double-headed, barrel-shaped drum of Karnatak music.

MUGAM: (Middle East). Term for maqam in Azerbaijan (Caucasus).

MUKHRA: (India). Initial phrase of a khyal or gat used as a cadence for improvisational passages in Hindustani music.

MUSICA HUMANA, MUSICA MUNDANA, and MUSICA INSTRUMENTALIS: (Europe). Medieval distinction of different domains of music making: humanly made music, music of the spheres, and music played by instruments.

MUSICAL BOW: (Africa). A bent stick with a single string which is struck with another stick or plucked; a gourd resonator is attached to the bow or, on a second type, the mouth cavity serves as resonator.

MUYU (WOODEN FISH): (China). A carved, hollow, wooden Chinese instrument struck with a pair of wooden sticks.

NAGASVARAM: (India). Karnatak double reed instrument.

NAGAUTA: (Japan). A lyric genre of shamisen music.

NAOBA: (China). A small pair of Chinese cymbals.

NAQQAL: (Middle East). Reciter of the *Shahnameh*, Iranian national epic, in teahouses in small-town Iran.

NARODNIK MOVEMENT: (Europe). A Russian agrarian socialist movement of the late nineteenth century.

NATURAL: A pitch that is neither raised (sharped) nor lowered (flatted).

NAUTCH: (India). An English colonial name for various kinds of Indian dance, derived from a word in Indian languages for "dance."

NAY: (Middle East). End-blown flute (ordinarily with five finger-holes) used throughout the Middle East; sometimes spelled Nei or Nai.

NETORI: (Japan). Introductory section of gagaku music.

NIRAVAL: (India). A type of improvisation in Karnatak music that retains the text and its rhythmic articulation but alters the pitches of the melody.

NOH: (Japan). Japanese classical drama.

NOHKAN: (Japan). The flute used in noh.

NOTATION: Graphic representation of music.

NRITTA: (India). Pure dance.

NYAMALO: (Africa). Craft specialists in Mande societies, a category including professional musicians.

O-tsuzumi: (Japan). A larger hourglass-shaped drum.

Oberek: (North America). Polish and Polish American folk dance in triple meter.

Old Style and New Style: (Europe). The major stylistic categories of Hungarian folk music.

Organology: The study of musical instruments.

Orquesta: (Latin America). Orchestra.

Ostinato: A repeated or cyclical melody or rhythmic pattern.

Oud (or ud): (Middle East). Principal lute of the Middle East, and most characteristic instrument of Arabic cultures, with eight strings, no frets, used mainly in classical music. The European lute is derived from it, as is the word "lute" (from al-Ud).

Pachamama: (Latin America). Earthmother, an Andean concept of the living, spiritual earth.

Padam: (India). A lyrical type of Karnatak song that may accompany dance.

Pakhavaj: (India). A double-headed, barrel-shaped drum of Hindustani music associated with dhrupad.

Pallavi: (India). The opening section of a Karnatak song form.

Panerus: (Indonesia). The types of saron or bonang having the highest ranges.

Parallel harmony: Refers to two or more melodic lines moving in parallel motion, or consistently remaining the same harmonic interval apart, for example, parallel thirds, a common trait in Latin American music.

Pathet: (Indonesia). A particular way of using a scale or laras in Javanese music.

Peking: (Indonesia). The saron with the highest range.

Peking Opera: (China). The main type of Chinese popular musical theater that first emerged in the Chinese capital Beijing (Peking) in the later eighteenth century.

Pelog: (Indonesia). The heptatonic tuning system of Javanese music.

Pentatonic: Having five pitches.

Peshrev: (Middle East). Alternative spelling of beshrav.

Pesindhen: (Indonesia). Javanese female vocal soloist.

Peyote music: (North American Indian). Songs, in a characteristic style, accompanying a ceremony surrounding use of Peyote, a drug derived from a cactus. The Peyote religion is a major component of twentieth-century Native American culture of the Plains and Southwest.

Pinkillu (Aymara, pinkullu, Quechua): (Latin America). Andean vertical duct flute usually made of cane, but also of wood in some regions.

Pipa: (China). A pear-shaped, four-stringed plucked lute with a short bent neck and many frets.

Pishdaramad: (Middle East). Literally "before the introduction." Introductory piece, composed, metric, and usually played by an ensemble, in a performance of Persian classical music.

PITU: (Latin America). Andean cane side-blown flute.

POLKA: (Europe and North America). Dance in duple meter, originally Czech but disseminated throughout European and North American regions and ethnic groups.

POLYPHONIC: Generic term referring to all music in which one hears more than one pitch at a time, for example, songs accompanied by guitar, choral music, orchestral music, or two people singing a round together.

PONGZHONG: (China). A pair of small Chinese hand-bells.

POWWOW: (North American Indian). Tribal or intertribal gathering in twentieth-century Native American culture, a principal venue for performance of traditional and modernized music and dance.

PUSAKA: (Indonesia). Javanese royal heirloom.

QANUN: (Middle East). A type of Middle-Eastern plucked dulcimer.

QIN: (China). A Chinese seven-stringed zither. It is the most revered instrument and was patronized by members of the educated class.

QINQIN: (China). A two- or three-stringed plucked lute with a long, fretted neck.

QIUGE (JAIL SONGS): (China). Popular Chinese songs of the 1980s and 1990s. Their lyrics deal with convicts' lives in labor reform camps.

QOLLAS: (Latin America). Dance drama group of Paucartambo, Peru representing high altiplano traders.

QUÉBECOIS: (North America). French-speaking residents of the Canadian province of Québec.

QUECHUA: (Latin America). The most widespread indigenous Andean language, the state language of the Inca, largest indigenous ethnic group in the Andes.

RADIF: (Middle East). In Persian classical music, the body of music, consisting of 250–300 short pieces, memorized by students and then used as the basis or point of departure for improvised performance.

RAG(A)(M): (India). A scale and its associated musical characteristics such as the number of pitches it contains, its manner of ascending and descending, its predominant pitch, and so forth.

RANCHERA: (Latin America). A Mexican song genre with rural and working-class associations.

RASA: (India). The affect or emotional state associated with a raga or other artistic expression.

REBAB: (Indonesia). A type of Javanese bowed lute.

RENG: (Middle East). In Persian classical music, the final piece of a performance, based on the musical traditions of folk dance.

REQUINTO: (Latin America). A small four-string guitar variant in the jarocho region, more generally simply a slightly smaller six-string Spanish guitar.

RITSU: (Japan). A basic Japanese scale.

Roma and Sinti: (Europe). The two largest groups of Gypsy communities in Europe.

Rouzeh-khan: (Middle East). Singer of narratives about the martyrdom of the Imam Hossein, in small-town Iranian musical culture.

Ryo: (Japan). A basic Japanese scale.

Ryuteki: (Japan). A flute used for Togaku music in the gagaku repertory.

Saami: (Europe). Circumpolar peoples, living in northern Norway, Sweden, Finland, and Russia.

Sageuta: (Japan). A type of song in noh plays.

Saibara: (Japan). Folk song arrangements in the gagaku repertory.

Sam(am): (India). The first beat in a tala.

Samba: (Latin America). The most important Brazilian musical genre often associated with carnival in Rio but performed in other rural and urban contexts.

Samurai: (Japan). Warrior.

Sanghyang: (Indonesia). A heavenly spirit who may possess certain performers in Javanese and Balinese trance dances.

Sangita: (India). Music and associated performing arts.

Sankyoku: (Japan). Jiuta music played by a trio.

San-no-tsuzumi: (Japan). An hourglass-shaped drum used in court music.

Santour: (Middle East). Trapezoid-shaped hammered dulcimer, played with two balsa wood mallets, used throughout the Middle East but particularly in Iran and Turkey.

Santur: (India). A Kashmiri hammered dulcimer now used in Hindustani music.

Sanxian: (China). A three-stringed plucked lute with a long, fretless neck and an oval-shaped sound-box.

Saqras: (Latin America). Dance drama group of Paucartambo, Peru representing devils.

Sarod: (India). A fretless, plucked string instrument of Hindustani music originally coming from Afghanistan.

Saron: (Indonesia). A type of Indonesian instrument having thick bronze slab keys lying over a trough resonator.

Sataro: (Africa). A speechlike vocal style performed by Mande jalolu.

Satokagura: (Japan). Folk Shinto music.

Sawal-jawab: (India). "Question-answer," rhythmic challenges between soloist and accompanist in Hindustani music.

Scale: A set of pitches arranged in ascending or descending order.

Schrammelmusik: (Europe). "Schrammel-Music": urban folklike music of Vienna, named after a family of musicians.

Sesquialtera: (Latin America). The combination/juxtaposition of duple and triple rhythmic patterns, both simultaneously in different instrumental parts, or sequentially in the same part, hemiola.

SESSION: A traditional gathering of musicians at an Irish pub to play together in an intimate jam session.

SETAR: (Middle East). Small, long-necked, fretted lute with four or (sometimes) three strings, plucked with the nail of the right index finger, used in Persian classical music.

SHAGIRD: (India). Pupil of Muslim master.

SHAHNAMEH: (Middle East). National epic of Iran, dealing with mythology and pre-Islamic history, written by Ferdowsi in the tenth century C.E., and ordinarily performed by singing in tea-houses.

SHAKUBYOSHI: (Japan). Clappers used in court singing.

SHAKUHACHI: (Japan). An end-blown flute.

SHAMISEN: (Japan). A three-stringed plucked chordophone.

SHARP: A pitch raised by a half tone.

SHASHMAKOM: (Middle East). Body of composed music of Uzbekistan (literally, "six makams"), the Central Asian counterpart of the Persian radif and of the Middle Eastern maqam system generally.

SHENAI: (India). A Hindustani double-reed instrument.

SHENG: (China). A Chinese free-reed mouth organ.

SHENG: (China). Generic name for a male actor in Chinese theater.

SHEN XINGONG (1870–1947): (China). Educator and pioneer of modern Chinese School Song.

SHINNAI-BUSHI: (Japan). A musical narrative form accompanied by the shamisen, found in Shinnai Tsuruga.

SHINTO: (Japan). Native religion of Japan literally meaning "the way of the gods."

SHISHYA: (India). Pupil of a Hindu master.

SHITE: (Japan). Principal actor in noh.

SHO: (Japan). A mouth organ.

SHOKO: (Japan). A suspended bronze drum used in gagaku.

SHOMYO: (Japan). Japanese Buddhist chanting.

SHUR: (Middle East). The most important of the twelve dastgahs, or modes, of Persian classical music.

SIKU: (Latin America). Double-row Andean panpipe, sikuri refers to the ensemble and to a siku player.

SITAR: (India). Primary plucked string instrument of Hindustani music.

SIYEM: (Indonesia). The smaller of the two large gongs in the Javanese gamelan.

SLENDRO: (Indonesia). The pentatonic tuning system of Javanese music.

SOGO: (Africa). Middle-size Ewe (Ghana) accompanying drum.

SOKYOKU: (Japan). A generic term for koto music.

SON: (Latin America). A specific song or song-dance type in Cuba and Mexico, the same term refers to different musical types in these two countries.

Songs for the Masses: (China). Chinese communist political songs.

Sruti: (India). A microtone; an ornamented pitch.

Staatsoper: (Europe). National, or "State," Opera of Austria.

Strophic form: Song form in which the verses change but the music used to accompany each verse remains the same.

Sufism: (Middle East). The principal mystical movement of Islam, in which the activity of music is regarded as "another way to know God"; found throughout the Middle East and elsewhere in the Islamic world, but as a force in musical life, sufism is particularly important in Turkey, Iran, and Pakistan.

Sula: (Africa). Social category in Mande societies, referring to "ordinary people" in contrast to craft specialists.

Suling: (Indonesia). Indonesian vertical flute.

Suona: (China). A Chinese conical double-reed oboe.

Suyá: (Latin America). Amazonian Indian group of Brazil.

Suzu: (Japan). A small bell tree used in some Shinto dances.

Svarakalpana: (India). Improvised singing of pitches using their names in Karnatak music.

Syncopation: Accenting rhythms where they would not normally be accented.

Tabla: (India). A pair of drums used in Hindustani music.

Taiko: (Japan). A generic term for drum; also a drum struck by a pair of sticks used in the noh theater.

Takht: (Middle East). Literally "platform." An ensemble of musicians, often including violin, santour, flute, and two drums, used to accompany singing and sometimes dancing in performances of Arabic popular music.

Tal(a)(m): (India). Meter.

Tambura: (India). A stringed drone instrument.

Tamburitza: (Europe and North America). Folk-music ensemble in the Balkan countries of southeastern Europe.

Tamburitza orchestra: (North America). Folk-music ensemble in ethnic communities with southeastern European heritage, consisting largely of string instruments.

Tan: (India). A rapid and florid kind of improvised melodic passage in Hindustani music.

Tanam: (India). The improvised instrumental or vocal performance that follows Karnatak alapanam and which introduces a pulse.

Taqsim: (Middle East). Nonmetric improvised instrumental piece consisting of several short sections, in Arabic and Turkish classical music; spelled Taksim in Turkish.

Tar: (Middle East). Lute with long neck, frets, six strings, and heavy, waisted body, plucked with a pick, used in various parts of the Middle East but principally in Iran, in classical but also popular and folk musics.

Tarka: (Latin America). An Andean wooden duct flute.

TASNIF: (Middle East). Type of composed, metric song in Persian music, with words (though sometimes performed instrumentally), and a part of a full classical performance though also found in popular music.

TAVIL: (India). A double-headed barrel drum played with a stick and thimble covered fingers to accompany nagasvaram.

TEGOTO: (Japan). Instrumental interludes in koto music.

TEGOTOMONO: (Japan). A generic term for instrumental koto music; it is also used as another term for jiuta.

THUMRI: (India). A lyrical type of Hindustani song and a style of instrumental performance modeled on it.

TOGAKU: (Japan). Court music of Chinese and Indian origin in the gagaku repertory.

TONGSU YINYUE (LIGHT POPULAR MUSIC): (China). Chinese popular music of the 1980s and 1990s.

TORIMONO: (Japan). Shinto songs in praise of the gods.

TRAJES DE CHARRO: (Latin America). Fancy western Mexican "cowboy" costume worn by mariachis.

TRIADIC HARMONY: A European style of harmony with three pitches sounding simultaneously, each a third apart.

TRIKALA: (India). A type of Karnatak improvisation in which the durational values of the notes in a phrase or piece are systematically augmented or diminished.

TRITONE: The interval, or distance between two pitches, whose dissonant character caused it to be associated with the devil.

TSURI-DAIKO: (Japan). Suspended drum used in gagaku.

TSUYOGIN: (Japan). A strong-style noh music.

TWENTY-ONE DEMANDS: (Japan). Issued by Japan in 1915, in which Japan demanded various economic and political concessions from the Chinese government touching off popular Chinese protests.

UD: *see* Oud

USTAD: (India). A Muslim teacher.

USUL: (Middle East). Turkish term for the Arabic iq'a.

VARNAM: (India). A type of song with which Karnatak recitals generally begin; also a type of song that constitutes the chief item in a Bharata Natyam recital and requires both gesture and abstract dance.

VEDIC CHANT: (India). Intoned verses for ancient religious ceremonies performed by Brahman priests.

VENU: (India). Karnatak flute.

VICHITRA VINA: (India). A Hindustani plucked string instrument whose strings are stopped with a ball of glass; *see* Gottuvadyam.

Vihuela: (Latin America). In Mexico, a small five-string guitar variant with a convex back, used for percussive strumming.

Vilambit: (India). Slow.

Vina: (India). Primary plucked string instrument of Karnatak music.

Vocables: Nonsemantic syllables that are sung; "nonsense syllables."

Volkslied: (Europe). German term for "folk song," coined by the philosopher Johann Gottfried Herder at the end of the eighteenth century.

Volkstümlich: (Europe). "Folklike" music, often referring to ethnic popular music in ethnic communities from Central Europe.

Wagon: (Japan). A six-stringed zither.

Waki: (Japan). The supporting actor in noh.

Wasan: (Japan). Buddhist hymns in Japanese.

Wayang kulit: (Indonesia). Indonesian shadow play accompanied with gamelan music.

Wayno, or huayno: (Latin America). The most widespread Andean mestizo genre, also performed by some indigenous musicians.

Wenchang: (China). The instrumental ensemble in Peking Opera made up of melody instruments.

Wenzipu (Prose tablature): (China). Archaic Chinese tablature for the qin written in prose.

Wuchang: (China). The instrumental ensemble in Peking Opera made up of percussion.

Xiao Youmei (1884–1940): (China). Chinese composer, music educator, and reformer. He established the first modern Chinese music department at Peking University in 1920, and in 1927 he established the first modern Chinese music conservatory in Shanghai, the Shanghai Conservatory of Music, which is still in existence today. Xiao served as its Director until his death in 1940.

Xiao: (China). A Chinese end-blown flute with six finger-holes.

Xiaoluo: (China). Small Chinese gong.

Xiaotangu: (China). A small Chinese barrel drum.

Xibei feng (Northwestern Wind): (China). Popular Chinese song genre of the 1980s and 1990s. It combines a disco beat with Chinese folk music and its lyrics are deliberately artless and simple.

Xipi: (China). Basic melody-rhythmic patterns used for arias in the Peking Opera.

Xylophone: An instrument with keys made from wooden slabs.

Yangqin: (China). A Chinese dulcimer struck with a pair of bamboo sticks.

Yaraví: (Latin America). A slow, sad, lyrical mestizo song genre from Peru.

Yayue: (China). Literally meaning "elegant music," it was Chinese court music of imperial China.

YEIBECHAI: (North American Indian). A major curing ceremony, lasting nine days, of the Navajo; also known as "Night Chant."

YOIKING: Traditional vocal repertory of the Saami people of circumpolar Europe, reflective of the Saami interaction with the nature of the Arctic, for example, reindeer herding.

YOKYOKU: (Japan). Choral singing in noh.

YOULAN (ORCHIDS IN A SECLUDED VALLEY): (China). The earliest extant qin piece; it was notated in "prose tablature" in a manuscript dating from six century C.E.

YOWAGIN: (Japan). Soft-style noh music.

YUAN SHIKAI (1859–1916): (China). Leader of the powerful North China army who was instrumental in arranging the abdication of the Qing emperor in 1912. Because of Yuan's strength, Sun Yat-sen, the founder of the Chinese republic in 1912, offered Yuan the presidency of the new republic. Yuan abused the office and proclaimed himself emperor in 1915, but he died six months later.

YUEQIN: (China). A four-stringed Chinese plucked lute with a round sound box.

YUNLUO: (China). A Chinese suspended gong set.

ZARB: (Middle East). Literally "drum." In Persian music, alternate name for Dombak.

ZENG ZHIMIN (1879–1929): (China). Modern Chinese music educator and a pioneer in writing modern School Song.

ZHAO YUANREN (Y.R. CHAO) (1892–1982): (China). Influential modern Chinese composer of songs, choral works, and piano compositions, Zhao was also an internationally known linguist. He received his education first from Cornell University and then from Harvard University; he later joined the faculty of the University of California at Berkeley.

ZITHER: An instrument with strings that stretch along the whole length of the sound board.

ZURKHANEH: (Middle East). Literally "house of strength." Traditional gymnasium in Iran, used by men to exercise accompanied by a morshed reciting heroic verse with percussion.

ZYDECO: (North America). African American popular music from Louisiana, also including Caribbean and Cajun elements.

Index